IMMIGRANT DREAMS

A Memoir

Barbara Goldowsky

TBR Books
New York

TBR Books is a program of the Center for the Advancement of Languages, Education, and Communities. We publish researchers and practitioners who seek to engage diverse communities on topics related to education, languages, cultural history, and social initiatives.

CALEC - TBR Books
750 Lexington Avenue, 9th floor
New York, NY 10022
www.calec.org | contact@calec.org

Front Cover Illustration: Barbara Goldowsky,1959. Family Archives.

Cover Design: Nathalie Charles

ISBN 978-1-63607-004-9 (hardback)

ISBN 978-1-63607-003-2 (paperback)

ISBN 978-1-63607-005-6 (eBook)

Library of Congress Control Number: 2020943260

Dedication

In memory of my mother, Wilfriede Moll, who gave me courage, and of my brother, Roland Pitschel, who lived a life committed to leaving the world a better place. We shared dreams.

Also by Barbara Goldowsky

Ferry to Nirvana - 1983 National Writers' Press, Boulder, CO
Poems

Ferry to Nirvana and New Poems - 1991 Amereon, Mattituck, NY
Poems

Restless Spirits - Four Stories - 1992 - Amereon., Mattituck, NY
Fiction - Short Stories

The Tuesday Night Ballroom - 2007 - Southampton, NY
Poems.
With Photographs by Richard Mizdal

Peace of the Hamptons - 2007 - iUniverse, Lincoln, NE
Fiction - Short Stories

Praises

Immigrant Dreams is vital, memorable, and wise. An accomplished stylist, Barbara Goldowsky explores, in lively and luminous prose, a personal journey that reaches across languages and cultures. Rendering the delightful, sobering, and always compelling particulars of one immigrant's passage, Goldowsky accesses the deeper core not only of the immigrant experience but also of the human dream: In this account, the realization of immigrant dreams celebrates resolve, and talent, and inspiration; it also celebrates love.

—Becky Kennedy, Ph.D.

What first strikes the reader of Immigrant Dreams is its complexity of perspective -- age-appropriate, phase by phase, yet subtly focalized through the memory, understanding, emotions, and values of the author-narrator. History is pervasive, of course, but backgrounded to emphasize key personal experiences and their impact, both immediate and life-long. The result is exceptionally engaging and enlightening. Highly recommended.

—David Lee Rubin, Guggenheim Fellow
Professor Emeritus of French
University of Virginia

Barbara Goldowsky's exquisite, poetic prose is both daring and satisfying. This vibrant, evocative immigrant tale offers poignant insights into love, loss, and remembrance, revealed with a sharp eye for detail. With its deep resonance of the past, Immigrant Dreams is a book of substance.

—Victoria Hartman,
Southampton, New York

Acknowledgments

Sincere thanks are extended to my family, whose love, support, and encouragement bring joy to every day of my life. Endless thanks to Becky Kennedy, who has been my mentor, steadfast guide, painstaking editor, and friend throughout the years it took to produce this book. Grateful thanks to David Lee Rubin, who provided thoughtful, enlightening insight as the manuscript developed. I thank Philip Shabecoff, who made helpful comments on the early chapters and I am immensely grateful to my fellow residents, the management, and the staff of Lasell Village for maintaining an environment that nurtures lifelong learning and creativity. Sincere thanks to Jane Ross for her friendship and timely advice.

Table of Contents

Acknowledgments _____ 9
Introduction _____ 13
Wise Child _____ 15
My Mother and the Nazi Judge _____ 21
The Stork Brings My Brother _____ 27
Good Morning and Heil Hitler _____ 35
Turning Point _____ 39
Liberation _____ 45
Peace _____ 53
Confronting the Past, Imagining the Future _____ 59
Hope _____ 65
Departure _____ 79
America! _____ 85
The Dream: Education _____ 95
The Dream: Independence _____ 101
Love Children _____ 109
Flying _____ 123
My Mother's Dream _____ 129
Gaining Altitude _____ 135
Hullabaloo _____ 149
Flight Plan _____ 169
Commencement_____ 183
The Lies of Summer _____ 199
Horizons _____ 217
Beat Poets and Zen Buddhists_____ 229
Adventures _____ 237
A Degree and a Revolution_____ 255
Another World_____ 269
High Hopes_____ 287
Crash_____ 303
A Different Course_____ 317
Into the Sixties _____ 327
Dreams Come of Age _____ 347
New Life_____ 359
House and Home _____ 371
Changes _____ 381

Endings and Beginnings _____ 401

Chamber Music _____ 419

A Child from Dachau _____ 429

About the Author _____ 443

About TBR Books _____ 445

About CALEC_____ 447

Introduction

I am an immigrant, born in Germany under a dictatorship. As I write this memoir, I hope not to die under another one. When I began writing this book, in 2018, my worst fear was that the United States would let itself slide into autocracy. Sadly, in 2020, this fear still haunts me. But I also hope. I place my hope in the country that made many of my immigrant dreams come true: The United States that allowed me to become a citizen of a free, religiously, and ethnically diverse country. I love and admire the United States that gave me the opportunity to acquire education as the first step toward making a living; a chance to meet people of different ancestry and culture; and, most of all, the joy of knowing my children and grandchildren would never have to live under an evil regime like Adolf Hitler's.

I place my hope in the strength of the United States Constitution and in the honest civil servants and public officials who have sworn to uphold and defend it. I place my hope in the continued courage of the members of the free press who brave personal danger to report the facts -- the real facts, not the "alternative" ones -- and to expose abuses, hate speech, and complaisance. On a personal level, I place my hopes in my children and grandchildren. To the best of my ability, I want to give them an understanding of what the American Dream means to me and how to carry on as informed citizens who care about ideals: freedom, inclusion, compassion, and government that serves the people instead of trying to dominate and subdue them.

The story of every life is both fairy tale and mystery. "Facts" provided by parents may or may not be verifiable. Even birth certificates can lie; mine did, ascribing "pure Aryan" parentage to a bastard child whose true father remained unnamed. My stories honor the memory of my loving, courageous, often unconventional mother and the memory of my beloved brother who lived a life committed to leaving the world better than he found it.

Some of the anecdotes in these narratives were told to me by my mother in great detail, others in outline. For some, I have invented

13

dialogue consistent with her voice and favorite idioms. The names of a few persons have been altered to protect privacy.

Acknowledgment: Parts of chapters 23, 24, and 25 appeared, in slightly different form, in *Chicago Review's* web feature of December 2019 as the memoir *Beat Poets and Zen Buddhists on the Midway*.

CHAPTER 1

Wise Child

My mother had four husbands. None of them was my father. I did not learn this intriguing fact until I was a teenager, living in Chicago with Mother and my brother -- my half-brother, another fact of life I hadn't known.

"It's a wise child that knows its own father," says the proverb. Tell me who is endowed with such wisdom.

Born in 1902 in a village near Karlsruhe, Germany, my mother had a conventional, middle-class upbringing. Her father was the *Bäckermeister* (master baker), whose shop supplied bread to almost every household in town. My mother was the third of four children, two boys and two girls, close together in age and all baptized in the Lutheran faith. When the children got to be six or seven years old, they were required to help with the business, delivering fresh rolls to customers before breakfast. Getting up at dawn in all kinds of weather, climbing dark flights of stairs, with no tips or thanks, convinced all four siblings not to learn the family business. All four kept their resolve. When my mother, decades later, married a man who happened to be a retired baker, she said, "My mother is sitting up there in heaven and laughing her head off. Now I finally married a baker -- like she always wanted us girls to do!"

My mother's stories about her youth described a contented family, in which the children completed daily chores and did their homework before going out to play and everyone went to church on Sunday. This tranquil unit was drastically disrupted when my mother was in her early teens. She and her siblings did not understand why the family's routines suddenly changed. Instead of attending the Lutheran church, parents and children now went to services held by the New Apostolic Christians, a stern, fundamentalist sect that emphasized serious prayer and forbade "frivolous" pursuits. At home, there was no more singing of traditional German ballads after supper. Dance lessons for the older children were canceled.

Under my grandmother's new discipline, work and chores continued as usual. Evenings were either gloomy with silence or loud with terrifying visits from grim-faced brethren who preached about the wages of sin, sometimes ranting in incomprehensible tongues.

Mother, who loved laughter and gaiety, hated this new lifestyle. While her siblings meekly, if glumly, accepted the stark dogma, she rebelled. By the time she was sixteen and was under pressure to study for her already overdue confirmation, her courageous spirit woke up. It stretched and swung into a dance step. In spite of her mother's shock and censure, my mother refused to be confirmed. The church elders threatened her with hellfire. Mother stood her ground. She was formally excommunicated. Her mother wept.

It would be many years before my mother learned what had caused her mother to embrace the grim rituals of the New Apostolic Christians.

"It had to do with a love child," my mother related. "There was a young housemaid; my father got her pregnant. It was hushed up. But my mother turned bitter; I don't think she ever got over the pain."

My mother was a talented seamstress; she had dreamed of studying dress design in Paris. Her parents would not allow it, insisting on a secretarial school instead. "And after that, you'll find yourself a proper job for a young woman," her mother decreed.

My mother enrolled in the business college, but after graduating, she left home and moved to the nearby city of Darmstadt on her own to study vegetarian cooking, *Rohkost* (raw food), and the teachings of Rudolf Steiner and anthroposophy--the philosophy that strives to combine science and mysticism. Her openness and sense of adventure led her to other young people, Christian and Jewish, who explored Eastern religions, liberal politics, and pacifism. She became a vegetarian.

"Think of it," my mother said. "By the time I was twenty, I'd lived through the First World War, a major inflation, and the influenza pandemic of 1918. My brother Karl came back from the war with terrible injuries; he lost his right eye.

"I was not alone," she reminded us. "Many families suffered. It made people pay attention to books like *Die Waffen Nieder!* by Bertha von Suttner. I joined the peace movement in Germany. We wanted a better world -- a more spiritual world. We all read Tagore." The Indian poet and guru, Rabindranath Tagore, had received the Nobel Prize in literature in 1913, the first Asian to do so.

Photos from the 1920s show my mother as a perfect flapper: small and gracefully built, with a mischievous face. She looked good in hats. If color photography had been available then, pictures would have shown eyes that were exactly the color of her aquamarine ring. She had chosen that stone because her astrological sign was Aquarius. Those eyes were admired throughout her life. Men fell at her feet.

Sometime during that turbulent decade, my mother married husband number one. He remains a mystery. Mother never told me how they met or whether she had loved him. She did say that she had found herself in an alien world after the marriage. Her husband had money and spent it lavishly. There were vacations in Paris, Switzerland, and Luxembourg. My mother was given a pricey red sports car, an *Adler*. She was driving alone on a Swiss mountain road when a collision with a bus wrecked the car but fortunately did not injure her. For the rest of her life, she did not want to drive a car. I do not know if she had ever had a driving lesson.

Why did my Mother marry this playboy who died young and left her to care for a demented mother-in-law? My best guess is that Mother had longed for a child. The marriage did not produce one.

Mother had a cousin in Munich who was married to a businessman. In 1934, after the death of her husband, Mother wrote to her cousin and asked if the family firm could offer her a job in the office. For once she was glad of her business training. Cousin Rosa agreed. The young widow escaped to Bavaria.

How did she meet my father? Who was he? How could she *not* know he was married to another woman when she became pregnant with me?

In November 1936, my mother bore a love child.

"We wanted you -- you were longed for and welcome," my mother said when she told me the story years later. "Your father and I were overjoyed. We promised to love you and each other always and forever."

Mother remained true to her vow. Hans (the only name she ever gave -- who knows if it was his real one?) remained the love of her life.

 On her deathbed, at almost ninety, happily married to husband number four, Mother told me in a moment we had alone together, "I will see your father now. He's just beyond that door." The smile on her face was that of a young woman head over heels in love for the first time.

Who was my birth father? He loved walking in the country, Mother said. He was educated and witty; he wanted a child to complete their love. Was he Christian? Jewish? Why had he concealed his marriage? Who was his legal wife? Why was there no divorce? I do not know.

When my mother learned from a mutual friend that Hans was married, she sent her lover away. He disappeared -- not only from her life but from that of his friends. After 1936, no one heard from him. Because of that disappearance, I now believe my father was a Jew. My mother refused to confirm or deny it. To the very end of her life, she revealed no personal details about Hans. She never stopped guarding the secret that, in Nazi Germany, could have killed us.

I was born on November 11, 1936, in the picturesque medieval town of Dachau, Bavaria, not in the infamous concentration camp. Since the nineteenth century, Dachau had been an artists' and writers' colony. By order of Heinrich Himmler, the Nazi chief of police, the camp took over the grounds of a dismantled gunpowder and munitions factory, on a lonely stretch of moorland a few kilometers from the town center.

When she came to work for her cousin's business, Mother rented rooms in the home of a well-known landscape painter. (A contemporary guidebook lists a street named after him.) The painter's wife befriended the young woman "in trouble" and attended my birth along with the midwife.

Ironically, Bavaria was not an early stronghold of the Nazi Party. In fact, for a brief time, a Communist-led state government declared itself a Soviet republic. The first prisoners incarcerated in the Dachau camp were Communists. In 1936, Adolf Hitler had been in power for three years and had turned Germany into a monolithic police state. Jewish artists, scientists, and intellectuals fled or were expelled, beginning in 1933, when Hitler came to power.

The Nuremberg Laws defined who was a German Aryan with a right to live, and who was a Jew (or had Jewish blood) and was no longer a citizen. Illegitimate children without provable lineage for generations past were at high risk. My mother's pedigree was no problem. But unless a father with proper credentials was named, my mother was warned, she would be a criminal, in violation of the 1935 law "for the protection of German blood and German honor."

Mother never named my birth father. Not then, not ever.

CHAPTER 2

My Mother and the Nazi Judge

When I was two or three months old, my mother was shocked to receive an official summons to appear before the local magistrate. "*Gott im Himmel,*" she cried, "I haven't done anything wrong." The official at the door did not explain. "Tomorrow, nine o'clock, before the judge."

"But I have to be at work..."

"You think I care? Be there!"

Mother worked as a bookkeeper in her cousin's textile business. The artist's wife looked after me during the day. This kindly soul comforted my mother and proposed a clever solution. "Take the child," she said. "That sweet little doll can melt a heart of stone."

Mother and baby presented themselves, as ordered, before a horrified judge. "What is the child doing here? How dare you?"

"There's no one else to look after her; she's still nursing," Mother explained sweetly. (At this point in the story she always giggled, remembering the sudden hot pink in the judge's cheeks. He looked as if he'd just been soundly slapped as punishment for his dirty thoughts.)

"Unheard of," the judge muttered as he seated himself behind his oaken desk and motioned for Mother to sit in the chair in front of it. She moved the baby carriage close.

"May I know what the charges are?" she asked. The judge opened a massive binder and read off a list of dates. On those occasions, he said, Mother had been observed "consorting with members of the banned DFG." The DFG was the *Deutsche Friedensgesellschaft* -- the *German* Peace League. Didn't she know that organization was subversive and its "traitorous ringleaders" incarcerated?

Mother could not deny that many of her friends were opposed to

21

the government in power. The judge's dossier proved he already knew, and they were all under surveillance. She was certain the judge was a Nazi, so she tried a conciliatory answer. "We were listening to lectures about anthroposophy," she said. "Nothing to do with politics."

"What about your husband? He isn't listed here."   It was an accusation, not a question.

"I am not married…"

"What? And this… this…" He pointed to the pram. "Who is responsible for this? Is this a Jew brat? What is his name? Is he a Jew?"

My mother, frightened but now in a fury, refused to answer.

The loud, angry voice of the judge was answered instead by a soft whine from the pram. Mother picked up the baby. "Shh," she soothed, but she turned a scorching blue stare on the judge. He stared back, taking in my mother's pretty face and her trim figure.

"Oh, it's a girl? Eyes just like mother's," he said, his voice softening. My mother let the moment pass. She was not unaware of her effect on men.

"Well, who is he? Are you protecting a Jew? You know such relations are forbidden!" The judge recovered his officious manner.

My mother's voice was firm as she said, "Her name is Barbara. I will not name her father."

The judge must have glimpsed the steel spine inside the slender, five-foot-two figure. He chose a reasonable tone. He explained the rules known as the Nuremberg Laws. He explained "racial purity" and the duty of all German mothers to produce worthy new, untainted future citizens for the Reich.

"You'd better marry the father -- unless he's Jewish of course -- or somebody with a name to give the girl," the judge warned.

My mother did not explain why marrying my father was impossible.

"If I didn't have a wife, I would volunteer to do the honors," the judge said in an intimate whisper, so the secretary in the outer office couldn't hear.

My mother did not acknowledge that she had heard the suggestion and waited for the judge's next question.

"Personally, I would like to dismiss this case. However, my superiors expect me to teach you a lesson," the judge said. "You are sentenced to one night in the city jail. Take it as a warning not to engage in anti-Reich activities in the future!

"Go home, find someone to take care of your child, and be sure to report back to this office."

My mother, who well understood the grim fate she had been allowed to skirt, thanked him sincerely. She knew what lay on the outskirts of town. She would remember the judge with gratitude. "I felt I had one leg in the striped pants already," she said whenever she told this story. The prisoners in the camps wore blue and grey striped uniforms.

This is not the end of the judge. He will reappear in my mother's life some forty years after her night in jail.

Did my mother deliberately choose a Nazi, though he claimed he was disaffected, as husband number two? The Nazi judge's ultimatum must have weighed on her mind.

And so, in August 1937, Mother married August, husband number two, who became my little brother's father five years later. After Mother and August married, my birth certificate, bound into a book embossed with swastikas and eagles, gave me his surname, and listed, as required, ancestors who were all impeccably Aryan. I was now a legal German citizen. A year later, I was baptized in the Lutheran Church. If I had a Jewish parent, he was now effectively concealed. Did my mother tell her new husband who my real father was? I doubt it. For all his claims of not liking the Nazis anymore, he went to Party congresses every November and did as his local *Gauleiter* (regional leader) told him.

With this marriage of convenience -- necessity really -- I got a big brother. August had a son by a previous marriage. Ernst was eleven or twelve in 1937. When I puzzled later over Mother's choice of a marriage partner, I realized this boy must have played a role. His father expected silent obedience and disciplined him for even slight faults. I am sure that my mother, feeling sorry for this boy who had no mother to comfort him, was determined to make a difference. She did what she could to calm August's volatile temper. He yelled at me -- he yelled at everybody -- but he refrained from hitting me. Ernst was not so lucky, nor was my brother Roland, later. August insisted he was doing what was necessary to raise manly sons. When Mother was not around to physically intervene, he administered "correction," as he termed punishment.

Mother began to understand, she related later, that August had lied about his Nazi sympathies before she agreed to marry him. She said they had agreed on *Gedanken Freiheit* (freedom of thought, or conscience). Each would not try to convert the other to his or her particular worldview. But it soon became clear that Mother's "freedom" consisted of staying silent while August went off to Party meetings and enrolled his son in *Deutsches Jungvolk*, the Nazi youth organization, and once he was old enough, in the *Hitler Jugend*.

I did not know the man I called *Vati* (Father) was not my birth father. I was an infant when he came into my life. I did not love him. I do not remember any tenderness from him, no hugs, no words of endearment. He was contemptuous of me, calling me "the princess."

August was tall, dark haired, loud voiced and chronically angry. I was afraid of him and stuck close to Mother and my great-aunt Luise, whom I called *Oma* (Grandma). Big brother Ernst showed no interest in me. He and his buddies spent little time in the house, preferring pistol-shooting practice in the garden. When I was a bit older, I was sometimes allowed to watch.

I had few playmates. Children my age did not come to visit. Occasionally I played in the courtyard between our house and the neighbors', but I was never invited into their home. When I started school, I would walk home with one girl or another, never boys, but we did not discuss our parents. If I thought about it at all, I just assumed all mothers were gentle and all fathers violent. I was not unhappy, thanks to my mother's love and protection. She was tender but fierce: a dove with the razor-talons of a hawk.

Tante Luise, a devout Christian, also enveloped me with love. She was a childless widow, always clad in a long, black, high-necked dress, who had helped Mother take care of me since I was born. She did her best to make a Christian out of me. I did not know there were other religions in the world. Every night we prayed: *Lieber Gott, mach mich fromm, dass ich in den Himmel komm.* (Dear Lord, make me pious so I may go to Heaven.)

Dear Tante was scandalized when I ad-libbed a last line: "And I want to come down again too." She was even more offended when she reported this, and Mother, instead of lecturing me, burst out laughing and said, "We have a little heathen here!" My secularism started early and persists to this day. I am not a Christian. Tante, who knew about my out-of-wedlock birth and who did not judge Mother or me, was the true Christian.

I was many years older and lived in another country when I learned about my real father, and about what a strange tangle of relationships and fabrications my family was. And it was in the new country, the United States, that I married my first husband, a Russian Jew.

CHAPTER 3

The Stork Brings My Brother

The early 1940s found the family in Alsace-Lorraine, renamed *Westmark* by Hitler's government. At age four, I had no idea why we had moved from Dachau to this new place called Saarburg (now Sarrebourg). I remember meeting the shy little boy who lived next door. When he was coaxed to say hello, I didn't understand a word he was saying. His name was Jeannot and Mother explained that he was speaking French. "He will have to learn German," she added. "Then you can talk." It was all very mysterious, but no further explanation followed. Adults expected you to accept situations as they were and not pester them with questions.

What understanding I have of the complex history of Alsace and Lorraine, as the territory endured multiple wars between France and Germany in the past hundred years, came much later. When Hitler started his war of conquest, the provinces west of the Rhine were French. After the fall of France in 1940, Nazi troops marched in and occupied them. In 1942, the inhabitants were declared German citizens so they could be drafted into Hitler's army, where these conscripted soldiers called themselves the malgré-*nous* (against our will). The Alsatian and French languages were forbidden; learning German was mandatory.

Our family was there because August had been ordered by his Nazi superiors to set up a blue-printing shop. He was not in the army. His experience as a draftsman in the Dachau Department of Buildings -- or perhaps it was called Public Works -- was considered essential to the war effort, so he was told to move. I did not understand any of this then, of course. As time went on, I pieced together snippets of family history from Mother.

We lived on the main business street of Saarburg. The shop was in the back of the house. In the front rooms, which had large picture windows, Mother set up a gallery and sold paintings and drawings created by her artist friends in Munich and Dachau. Though my mother was part of the occupation, her outgoing personality made her business quite successful. She had some tourist French, acquired during her previous, cosmopolitan life, and there were families that spoke German -- a result of intermarriages in the past as the Alsatian territories were passed from France to Germany and back again. Mother was good at making friends in any language. If she had met the Grinch, she would have invited him to Christmas dinner, fed him *Glühwein*, and charmed him out of stealing the holiday.

Jeannot learned a few words of German and I learned a few words of French. We chased each other around the courtyard. Soldiers in formation marched down the street regularly, their eyes fixed strictly forward, following the red, white, and black swastika banners. They were marching to "the front," we were told. We could not visualize this faraway destination. We did not know why they were marching. How could we possibly comprehend that their leader was a madman, a murderer who would destroy millions of lives during his bloody reign of terror? We waved at the soldiers; they did not wave back.

"War" was a word we heard every day but, fortunately for us, the actual shooting and bombing were far away. Although foodstuffs were rationed, we had enough to eat. Imported goods like coffee and sugar became increasingly rare. Housewives became adept at substitutes. I remember the delicious, nutty aroma of roasted chicory, the ersatz coffee. We had milk for the children, bread from a bakery, and even fresh eggs from a flock of chickens Mother kept in a walled section of the garden. I did not like the chickens. Every time I was asked to feed them, the rooster flew at me, his sharp claws outstretched at my eye level. Much as I hated him, I still refused to eat when he was served for dinner. Fruit trees grew in the garden -- apples, pears, and small yellow plums, called mirabelles. These intensely sweet plums are the major agricultural product of the Alsace-Moselle region, used to make jelly and liqueurs. I filched as many as I could reach or shake down.

Since there was no refrigeration, meat, when available, came fresh from the butcher. It appeared rarely, and the largest portions were given to the men -- Vati and Ernst, whose teenage appetite would have taken care of the entire roast if it had been allowed. Alsace is a wine-growing region. The neighbor ladies encouraged my mother to drink a liter of red wine every day while she was pregnant with my brother-- for iron." A moderate drinker, Mother laughed heartily whenever she told this story. "Maybe they wanted to get rid of me in a nice way," she joked.

The war that was raging through Europe dominated the news but, amazingly enough, it had caused only minimal hardship to the family as yet.

News of the war came over the radio, via the official government-controlled channel. Listening to foreign stations was *verboten*. I did not understand much of what I was hearing. Hitler's harsh, barking voice sounded just like Vati's and frightened me as badly. I heard the words "Poland," "Russia," without understanding the atrocities occurring in those places. When the grownups wanted to discuss politics, I was sent to my room. Because I heard it so often, I remember the main message of every newscast: German forces were winning every battle, on every front. The *Führer* was invincible. The radio announcers would repeat this, right to the end.

Growing up in the midst of this Nazi country, I must have heard the word *Jude* -- Jew -- but at the time it meant nothing to me, shielded as I was by Mother. The children I knew were either Catholic or Protestant. There were no Jewish children for me to meet; the Jewish population of Alsace-Lorraine had been expelled by Hitler's regime. The Bible stories Tante read to me mentioned Jews, but to me, they were historical Old Testament figures, far in the past. I did not understand that, in a peaceful world, I would have had Jewish contemporaries.

I was not to meet a Jewish person until we emigrated. Mother had Jewish friends before the war. She never told me their stories, if she knew them, and she did not talk about the tragedies that she knew were happening and that she was powerless now to prevent. She was trapped. The price for security was silence.

I am sure August was as anti-Semitic as the rest of his cronies, but he did not rant in front of me. I know now that Mother restrained him, undaunted by his evil temper. It was a brave stance; he had the power to denounce her. He could have gone to his Nazi bosses and said, "My wife tricked me. She has a bastard Jew child and made me think it was mine." They would have believed the Party member. Perhaps having his own little son with her gave him a bit more patience. Perhaps he even loved her.

Sometimes Mother talked about how things used to be *im Frieden* -- before the war. I could not imagine peace; Mother's stories sounded like tall tales. For instance, who could believe in city streets so bright with electric lights that you could read a newspaper? I knew that the streets were dark and that our house and all the others in the neighborhood were blacked out with heavy drapes as soon as the sun set. Going out at night was unthinkable as well as forbidden. Mother was inventing fantasies, I thought. But I didn't mind; I liked stories.

In 1942, I was still young enough to believe in fairy tales. Hansel and Gretel were smart, resourceful children who kicked the witch into the fire. Sleeping Beauty's Prince kissed her, and she awoke to live happily ever after. Max and Moritz were wicked boys who ended up ground to bonemeal between millstones. The stork brought babies.

It was easy to believe in the stork. I saw the storks every day, right across the street, from our upstairs living room window. On the roof of the bakery, snug against the chimney, their stick nest housed eggs, hatchlings, and the adults in their elegant black and white plumage. They stood taller than I was at five and a half. One parent remained on guard while the other went fishing in a nearby weir. Nobody bothered them. They brought good luck.

That summer, Mother asked me which I would like better, a little sister or a brother. Oh, I wanted a brother-- a *little* brother, someone my size who would play with me, not some near-adult like Ernst who talked about motorcycles and race cars but was never home. I'd teach the little guy to become a racing driver like me, cornering without flipping over, as I practiced daily with my doll carriage.

"You know about the stork?" Mother asked.

"I do, I do, but how do we get him to come?" Mother said he would stop by if he saw some sugar on the windowsill. Aha! That was something I could do all by myself. Left alone to play, I sneaked into the pantry, took the bag of sugar up to my room, and set it on the narrow brick ledge outside the window, in full view of the stork's flightpath.

In the afternoon, I heard Helene, our housemaid, wheezing loudly as she came running upstairs. I was surprised because she normally walked so slowly that Mother often admonished her to get a move on. Now Helen and my mother burst into the room where I had just bashed my doll carriage into the wall, angry at having missed a tricky curve.

"Der Zucker, der Zucker!" Helene whimpered. "Don't beat me, it's not my fault…"

My mother, who never would raise a hand to anyone, shushed her. "Be still!"

I must have glanced at the window. Mother moved towards it.

"Leave it there, leave it, it's for the stork!" I wailed.

"Gott im Himmel, the whole month!" Helene lamented as my mother retrieved the strictly rationed treasure.

"The stork needs only one sugar cube," my mother explained to me. "But you may have two. The rest goes back to the kitchen."

My brother Roland was delivered on August 15, 1942. A week later, the baker's wife had a baby boy. It worked; you see. Two sugars, two babies.

After all the excitement, this brother, too, proved disappointing. He was little, all right, but incompetent. He couldn't walk or talk, never mind play race car. He slept all swaddled up in blankets like a giant larva -- even in the daytime! And when he woke up, he cried, and mother would nurse him. I was so upset I asked for some of the milk, too. Mother let me taste. "He'll grow bigger, you know," she comforted me. "Soon…"

"Soon" took a long time but it finally happened. Roland could crawl, pull himself up by grabbing on to the sofa, wave a rattle, or fling it on the floor, where Fritz, the dachshund, gleefully retrieved it and delivered it back, slimy with drool. Fritz and Roland were about the same size, one horizontal, one (sometimes) vertical. Mother dubbed them Max and Moritz as they became a wicked duo bent on mischief. If Fritz wanted a piece of *Zwieback, Roland* would snatch it from the crib for him. If a rubber ball rolled under the bureau, Fritz would torque his sausage body underneath it and fetch. As the big sister, I was supposed to keep order, but it was much more fun to join in. While Mother was busy in her gallery and Tante napped, I contributed my ragdoll, Schlumpi, to the game. She was dragged around and chewed on, but she didn't mind. She had been banged around plenty in the race car, which sat idle now that I had playmates.

If August was excited by this new child, I did not notice it. I never saw him hold or cuddle the baby. He did take many family photos with his Leica. I am not sure if this showed he was proud of us, or if he was simply indulging his hobby. August was strict, even harsh, with Ernst. But he clearly favored his older son, who was growing up in the Nazi ideology. With the approval of his father, Ernst was going to a training camp where he would learn to fly gliders for the *Luftwaffe*. What Mother thought of it, she did not say in front of us younger children.

Being ignored by August did not bother me. Both Roland and I felt more comfortable when Vati paid no attention to us.

CHAPTER 4

Good Morning and Heil Hitler

I started first grade in the fall of 1942; I would turn six in November. I had not gone to kindergarten. Government-run, school was a brainwashing center for the young. All instruction was in German. No concessions were made to local children like Jeannot. For them, it was sink or swim. Before we entered the classroom in the morning, we assembled outside around a tall flagpole flying a huge swastika banner. We raised our right arms and shouted *Heil Hitler*. We had to keep our arms up while singing *"Deutschland Über Alles"* and the *"Horst Wessel"* song. A teacher then harangued us with instructions to obey our parents, our teachers, and the *Führer*, and so become worthy of the *Vaterland*. This ceremony took place in all weathers. No one even thought of whining, which we knew would only get us punished.

We marched to our desks, girls on one side of the room, boys on the other. Before receiving permission to sit we greeted our teacher, in unison, with "Good Morning, Mr...." and another *Heil Hitler*.

On slates the size of an iPad, we wrote the letters of the alphabet- - lines of *aaa, bbb, ccc,* and so forth, in cursive. I knew a few letters already, mostly capitals. At home, I copied the signs of the shops on the other side of the street: BANK, BÄCKEREI. I was also fond of a heavy volume called the *Duden*, a dictionary kept on a high shelf. All those words! When I was a big girl, I would read them all and they would be as delicious as the contents of a magic, everlasting box of candy.

"Isn't it sweet? She loves the *Duden* so much that she climbs up the back of the sofa to get at it," Mother remarked.

"What -- the lexicon? Don't let her do that again!" Vati shouted. "That's not a book for children -- far too many unsuitable words!"

I heard the exchange because I was just coming into the sitting room. I slunk away quietly and from then on, I made sure Vati was out of sight whenever I wanted to sneak a look at the dictionary.

For writing, I liked the slate and stylus. If you made a mistake you could rub it out and start over. Later, we would use paper, pen, and ink -- a steel nib in a wooden holder. Homework became nerve-wracking: dip the pen in the ink, hold your breath while you try not to make a blot, form each letter lightly so as not to gouge through the paper....

"Paper is scarce. If you ruin this sheet there won't be any more," Mother would remind me when I labored over my homework. But I knew the page had better be perfect because the teacher would punish you for mistakes. He would snap, "*Tatzen,*" using the word for *paws*. And then he would hit your open palms with his stick.

I learned to read without effort. The words were the best part of school; I loved them. I hated the stockings. The girls wore dresses, never pants of any sort. We had knee socks for warm weather, long woolen stockings (usually turd-brown) for cold. The wool itched; when it got wet, it smelled like a sheep pen.

If wet wool was disgusting, frozen wool was actually dangerous, as I learned on one winter's day on the way home from school. I can't remember whether it was my first or second year of school. As usual, I walked with a classmate who lived near us. A bridge over the river Saar was about halfway home. It was a bitter winter and the Saar, not a fast-moving river at that point, was frozen over. My friend and I stopped on the bridge, looking down on what looked like solid ice.

"It looks like the ice goes right to the bottom of the river," I said to my companion.

"How do you know? You haven't tried it, have you?" she asked.

"Well, no -- but look -- we don't weigh very much. And it looks so solid. If we throw a heavy stone down on it and it holds -- don't you think it'll hold us?"

I pointed to a paving stone lying at the edge of the sidewalk. "Let's try that one. It's huge; let's throw it down," I urged.

The stone was so heavy my friend and I barely managed to heave it over the bridge railing. It fell with a thud -- then rested quietly on top of the ice. No crack developed. We crossed the bridge and made our way down the bank. My friend hesitated. "Should we really...?"

"Come on, I'm going," I said and walked -- no more than two steps before the ice gave way and I fell in.

"*Hilfe!*" I cried for help.

I expected my friend to reach for my hand, or to scream as she ran to find help. She did not move towards me. She did run -- in the opposite direction, away from the bridge -- but she did not come back. I looked around. Not a single human being was in sight. I stopped yelling and thrashed around in the icy muck until I could get hold of a shrub on the bank. Its branches were rather flimsy, but the ground was frozen stiff enough to keep the roots from coming loose. I pulled myself out and walked home. I was more angry than scared.

"What happened to you?" Mother looked me over. I was soaked. My clothes were stiff with cold, stockings frozen to the skin of my legs. My fingers, white and numb, were unable to unlace my leather shoes.

"I fell in a puddle," I whispered.

"Really? Some puddle!" Mother sounded concerned but she did not scold. She made me warm milk, put me to bed with a copper hot-water bottle, wrapped me in blankets, and told Tante not to leave my side. She never uttered a word of blame while I took a month and more to suffer through pneumonia and frostbite. I drank chamomile or linden-blossom tea fragrant with honey. I was not allowed outside, which was fine with me because it seemed winter had lasted my entire lifetime and was not about to end, ever.

One day much later, when I was well again, mother said, casually, "That was no puddle, was it? That was the Saar."

I started to cry, ashamed of having lied.

"It was your second time in deep water," she said, gathering me into her lap. And she told me a story.

"You were tiny, not even a year old," she said. "I went to the river -- the *Amper* in Dachau-- to swim. You couldn't crawl, and I thought you couldn't turn over, so I laid you down on the bank and went in. I looked back -- I was about up to my chest in the water -- and you *were not there!*" Mother's voice was shaking. "I looked; you were not there, not on the grass -- then, down in the water by my feet, I saw this little pale face...thank God you I got you to breathe; I thought I'd lost you." Mother held me close, breathing hard. "So, watch out from now on; watch out for deep water!"

Surprisingly, I did not develop a fear of water. I love to swim. But I never again walked on a frozen pond or river. When I learned to skate, it was at the Wollman Rink in Central Park, in New York.

CHAPTER 5

Turning Point

While my brother was learning to crawl, I was in my first year of school, learning to read and write, and drilling the multiplication tables through the twelves. Every day began with the mandatory assembly, during which we stood with our arms thrust upward, shouted *Heil Hitler,* and sang *"Deutschland, Deutschland Über Alles."* Every day our teacher reminded us to stand up straight and proud like our *Führer,* who was leading the great German nation to victory. Every day we were assured that the magnificent German armies were winning against all enemies; ultimate victory would be ours in a few months.

No one at home told me that the course of the war was changing because Hitler's mad attempt to conquer Russia was about to fail. When the grownups, including Ernst, talked after dinner, I was sent to the nursery to play. Tante did not speak of the war, but she included a prayer for peace in our bedtime devotions. She never asked the Lord to bless Hitler and to let Germany win; she prayed for an end to the slaughter. Only after the war would I understand that the leader we were supposed to honor and love was mad. I did not love Adolf Hitler; he was too much like Vati.

One day in the late fall of 1942, Mother sat me down at the table with her.

"You may help me write to Wolfgang," she said. "He's in the army, poor soul because all the young men have to serve in the army -- it's something he'd never volunteer for; he's a painter, you know; he should be with his father, studying art."

Wolfgang had visited us several times in Saarburg. He was the son of artists who lived in Munich and were old friends of Mother's.

"You're doing so nicely with your ink pen," my mother said to me. "I'll let you write the beginning. He'll like that; now make the letters nice and neat."

"But what are we going to write?" I asked, daunted by the unfamiliar task.

"I'll tell you; don't worry," Mother reassured me and moved the inkwell close to my hand.

Dear Wolfgang," she dictated slowly. "You are so far from us now, at the front..."

Painstakingly, careful not to tear the paper, I wrote the first two words in my very best script.

"Where is Wolfgang?" I asked.

"He's been sent to the Russian front -- I found that out from his mother -- he may be as far away as Stalingrad, God help him," Mother answered.

I had heard the word *Stalingrad* on the radio. I knew it was a place in Russia; it was very cold there.

"Do the soldiers get letters? Does the mailman go all the way there?"

"Not the same mailman who comes here," Mother said. "The army has its own people for bringing things to the soldiers -- at least I hope so."

Joseph Goebbels, in daily radio broadcasts, assured the nation that trainloads of provisions were dispatched to the troops regularly. When my mother spoke about the war in later years, she said that she had feared that the propaganda minister was spreading false hope. Hitler's army had been ordered to march into the teeth of the fierce Russian winter and the troops faced the same tragic fate that had befallen Napoleon in 1812. She had wondered how many of those wagonloads of medical supplies and food would actually get through.

While we were writing our letter to Wolfgang, Mother did not share her true feelings with me. Instead, she said, "*Grün ist die Hoffnung.*" It was a phrase she used often, meaning that hope springs eternal.

By the end of January 1943, the news from the Russian front was so terrible that even the strictest censorship could not keep it from being reported in Germany. Hitler's Sixth Army, encircled and decimated at Stalingrad, had surrendered. Four days of national mourning were declared in Germany. In school, the teachers made speeches extolling the bravery of the troops, who had followed their orders to fight to the last man and who had died as heroes of the *Vaterland.*

My mother did not comment openly on the news or the speeches.

In 1944, I was seven years old; I would turn eight in November. Roland would be two, in August. We did not know it, but our stay in Saarburg would soon be over. Our mother protected us from frightening news as best as she could, but it was difficult because Vati wanted the radio to be on.

When I asked about the bombs that were falling on German cities, Tante would quickly shush me.

"Be thankful to the Lord that your home has been spared," she would say. "Pray for the innocents who died."

One day in early April of 1945, my mother said, "Take your brother's hand and go downstairs -- now! Get in the back seat of the car with Tante. No questions; I'll tell you later -- it will be a long ride."

I did not have to look for my brother. He was right at my side, having heard the word *car*. Neither one of us had ever ridden in August's black Opel. We hurried down the stairs and saw that it was parked in front of the house. A wooden crate full of squawking chickens was strapped to the rear luggage carrier. I recognized our Leghorns. I wondered why they were going with us, but Mother's tone had been forbidding so I did not dare to ask.

I squeezed into the seat next to Tante and settled Roland in my lap. An assortment of bundles was piled around our feet.

August was in the driver's seat. Before Mother got into the car to sit next to him, she muttered, "*Gottverdammte Nazi!*"

Her voice was so low that I was not sure I had actually heard the curse word; she never used profanity, unlike August, who swore constantly. I did not know why she was so angry and many days would pass before I learned that our hasty exit from Saarburg was due to the advance of the American and Allied armies who had liberated Paris and had pushed Hitler's occupation forces out of Alsace Lorraine. General Eisenhower had reached the Rhine. What had made her so upset, Mother would explain later -- and out of August's hearing -- was that the Nazi bosses in Saarburg had sneaked out of the city without telling the German civilians that the Americans were about to march in. The bigwigs had commandeered most of the available gasoline as well.

Roland and I and Tante sat in the back seat of the Opel, and Mother and Vati were in the front seat of the car. Ernst was not with us. I knew that was because he was in basic training, or perhaps he was already on active duty, flying gliders. But where was Fritz, the dog? I whispered my question to Tante.

"He can't come along; he had to stay," she said very quietly, but Roland heard her answer and began to whimper.

"Don't fret, baby," Tante soothed him. "Helene will take good care of him. You know she loves him; she's always feeding him treats when he's fat enough already."

"Can't we go back and pick him up? Where are we going to anyway?" I asked.

"We're not going back. We're on our way to Dachau, God willing," Tante said into my ear. On the back of the car, the chickens screeched loud enough to drown out Roland's crying.

I did not know on what road we were traveling. Our car joined a long column of motor vehicles, bicycles, and pedestrians, some pulling wooden handcarts piled high with possessions. Because so many people were walking, the caravan moved slowly. A short time after getting on the road, we heard machine-gun fire in the distance, and shortly after that, fighter planes roared overhead, flying low. They may have been British or American; there was no time to look up and identify their insignia.

Tante prayed, *"O Lieber Gott."* August took the Lord's name in vain. Mother opened her car door and turned around in one swift movement. Roland was napping on my lap. She pulled both of us out of the back seat and yelled, "Run! Into the ditch!"

I ran, hugging Roland to my body, and dumped both of us into the shallow drainage gully that ran alongside the highway. Fortunately, it was dry. August stayed at the wheel, cursing in his thick Bavarian dialect. Mother was slow to join us because she had tried to persuade Tante to leave the car, and Tante had refused, saying she was too old and too slow. Her fate was in God's hands, she said.

After a few minutes, the planes were gone and all was silent, except for the chickens, who screeched more hysterically than ever. As we scrambled back to the car, we saw no injuries. Other people who had run for cover made their way back as well. The caravan moved on, at its snail's pace. The airplanes buzzed us again several times that day and each time we repeated our dash into the ditch or the woods. Tante resolutely stayed in the car, and Mother carried Roland; he could walk, but not fast enough. Mother also feared that if she did not hold onto him, he might take the opportunity to explore the woods rather than hide. We did hear guns in the distance, but all the travelers we could see remained unharmed. The fighter pilots may have realized that the crowd on the road consisted of unarmed civilians who could not return their fire.

The distance between Saarburg (now Sarrebourg) and Munich is approximately 425 kilometers --264 miles -- and can be driven, on today's modern highways, in four or five hours. It took us much longer. Our route was eastwards, first to Strasbourg and the Rhine crossing there; then, once back in Germany, southeast towards Munich and Dachau. Mother and August talked to each other about *die Brücke* -- the bridge; I could tell it was an important milestone. I could feel their anxiety.

By late afternoon, the airplanes had disappeared and the caravan on the road moved on without further excitement. The chickens had quieted down, exhausted. Tante dug into one of the satchels and conjured up a baby bottle of milk for Roland and some dried apple slices for me. Roland drank his bottle and fell asleep as soon as he had finished it. I looked out the window, waiting for the bridge that had become a grand, fairytale structure in my imagination.

We reached the bridge at twilight. It was undamaged, as far as we could see. Vehicles were moving across it. A railroad track crossed the river on a parallel span. Though the bridge was larger and taller than the ones over the Saar, to me it looked ordinary. No knights in armor guarded it. In fact, there were no soldiers at all.

"*Gott sei Dank,*" said Tante.

"*Amen,*" said Mother.

We did not reach Dachau that night. We stayed -- I do not know in what town or village -- with relatives of Mother's. Some of the chickens were bartered for food and lodging. August managed to wangle a few coupons for gasoline. We may have stayed a second night; my recollection of the rest of the trip is hazy.

Once back in Dachau, we moved into a different house from where we had lived before, not that I remembered much about that one.

It was April 1945. Hitler and his henchmen would soon immolate themselves in flames and blood. And World War II, for Europe, was about to be over.

CHAPTER 6

Liberation

The family returned to Dachau only weeks before the April 29, 1945 liberation of the concentration camp.

We moved into a country villa called the *Moosschwaige* (Moss Cottage) that had been owned by artists since early in the century. Now it was shared by several families that had been displaced, in one way or another, by the war. I do not know what happened to the prewar owners, who were not in residence.

Instead of the spacious house we had inhabited in Saarburg, our family of five now lived in three rooms on the ground floor. We shared a bathroom and the kitchen with the other tenants. The kitchen, in a half-basement, was huge and cold. It had a tile floor, two coal-fired cook stoves, two stone sinks, a massive butcher-block table in the middle of the room, and cupboards on all the walls for storing food. There was an icebox, but no ice was ever delivered to it. Below the kitchen, down another six or seven steps, was the cellar that also served as the air raid shelter.

I had not experienced any air-raid warnings in Saarburg. In Dachau, the alarms sounded at unpredictable times. The city of Munich, about eleven miles away, and its environs were bombed as the air war over Germany intensified in 1944. Dachau town records show there had been ninety-seven air- raid alarms in 1944. Raids continued until the very end; bombs fell in Dachau, but once again, luck was with us. The Moosschwaige was not hit. The prisoners in the concentration camp were spared by careful planning. British and American pilots were concerned for them and marked out the exact location of the camp so they could avoid it.

When the sirens howled, everyone in the house hurried down to the cellar, which had been outfitted with straw mattresses and a kerosene lamp. I had been instructed by Mother to grab Roland,

45

awake or asleep, and take him to the cellar with me.

"Always take him with you. Don't wait for me or anybody-- just go," Mother said. I shared a bed with Roland, and many of the warnings came at night, so it was not too difficult to do my job. During the raids, the cellar was crowded with adults and children of various ages. It was stuffy and boring. It was impossible to nap on the scratchy mattresses; each time we waited impatiently for the "all clear" to sound. One night, the action outside seemed to last an unbearably long time. I fidgeted while the grownups dozed or stared at nothing with dull eyes. I poked Roland and made a sign to be quiet. Slowly and carefully, I led him up the cellar stairs, up through the kitchen, and out the front door.

The sky was ablaze with lights! Brighter than stars, flares dropped by the planes looked like some unearthly magic. "Christmas trees," I said, for lack of a better way to describe the brilliant, sparkling triangles hung all over the night sky. We heard airplanes, and far-off anti-aircraft fire. After watching the spectacle for as long as possible, we made it back to the cellar just as the "all clear" sounded. The raid was over; we were safe. And no one had noticed our sneaky exit and equally stealthy return.

At the time, I thought the purpose of the flares was to illuminate targets on the ground so the bombers could hit them. Later, I learned that it was the opposite -- the signal rockets marked the area of the concentration camp, warning the planes to go around it.

At least a dozen children, from babies to preteens, belonged to the families who shared the Moosschwaige. Those of school age, myself included, walked to the local *Volksschule* (grammar school) where the daily program went on much as it had in Saarburg. We sang and chanted and heard the teachers declare that Germany was a glorious, victorious nation. One day, when Mother asked me what I had learned, I said, "Teacher says we are winning."

"What? Don't you believe it," Mother snapped, startling me. She rarely lost her patience. "But don't dare say that out loud," she added quickly, taking my hand. "Don't tell anybody." I hated seeing my mother upset; I obeyed her without argument.

After school, all the children roamed freely through the villa's gardens, inventing games, and breaking off bits of old wooden fencing that we brought back to the kitchen. This was actually stealing -- we did not own the villa -- but the grownups welcomed the extra kindling. Firewood and coal, like many other necessities, were scarce. Instead of reprimanding us, the adults came up with a phrase that let everyone off the hook -- "Oh, you *found* that? Good."

The grounds must have been magnificent in better times, when they were cared for by dedicated gardeners. Now they were neglected, but 1 saw beauty. Yellow primroses and small white daisies popped up alongside the paths; dandelions, like flecks of sunshine you could pick up, bloomed in abundance. I was fascinated by the *espaliered* fruit trees -- I had never seen anything like them. With branches trained on horizontal wires, they looked as if they had opened their arms to offer me their just-budding flowers.

Roland, not yet three years old, was giddy with joy. Liberated from the rule of an older sister and two even older females, he suddenly had male allies -- big boys who let him join the madcap gang they led. The boys not only accepted him, but made the curly-haired, frisky child a sort of mascot. They made sure he didn't hurt himself with sharp sticks, and shared their treats -- pieces of brown bread smeared with lard -- with him. Girls were tolerated as members but were mocked when they urged caution. There were no complaints, as I recall. I certainly enjoyed trying new adventures, like playing Red Indians, fashioning whistles out of willow twigs with pocketknives, chasing tadpoles in the small brook that ran through the property. I missed Fritz, our dog. He too would have loved the noise, the unsupervised fun.

Mother went back to work, part time, in her cousin's business, which was slow. There was a shortage of textiles, and imports were at a standstill. I do not know where August went in the daytime. Perhaps his old job had been held for him. When he was home, he was angrier than ever. His temper was made worse by the lack of tobacco -- another imported product that had disappeared from the market. He chewed the stem of his empty pipe. When he tried a mixture of herbs other desperate smokers had recommended, it made him ill. He seethed and frequently erupted -- a volcano deprived of smoke. Surely, he knew the end was near. Did he understand his *Führer* was mad? Did he fear the future? Did he fear for his son Ernst? Did he even know where Ernst was? August shared nothing with small children. We kept out of his way. We went to bed at nightfall, glad to be snug under the covers. I whispered tales of my own invention to Roland -- stories about cowboys and Indians. They were modeled on books by Karl May, retold by the older boys. May was a prolific, wildly popular author of adventure stories. HIs fictional heroes were Apache chiefs who lived in the American Wild West -- which their creator had never visited. I knew I would never be allowed to read such "trash." Once, when August had caught Ernst with a May book, he had torn it up and thrown it in the kitchen fire. I wonder if August knew that young Adolf Hitler had adored these tales.

Though we remained unhurt by the war, daily life was difficult. Food, fuel, and clothing were in short supply. Mother spent her free hours standing in line for milk, vegetables, flour, bread. She missed our chickens. Without them, eggs were seen only once a week, if that. Root vegetables that had survived the winter, like potatoes, turnips, and beets, could be bought or bartered from the local farmers. Some housewives claimed the peasants now owned Persian carpets and silver teapots, taken in trade for a chicken or a pork chop.

Unlike many children, I liked vegetables, so I did not miss meat. But the low-protein diet made me look, according to Tante, much too thin and pale. Mother was persuaded to feed me a spoonful of iron tonic every evening. The foul-smelling liquid tasted horrible and stained my teeth. Within weeks, I looked like an underage nicotine addict. Roland and I also had to swallow cod-liver oil. Mother told me to smile and pat my tummy to show Roland how good it was. If I made a face, she said, he would never take it. I grimaced, hoping it looked like a grin, and said, "Yummy." Sure enough, Mother was right. Roland loved the stuff!

At the end of April, the children's grapevine buzzed with exciting but confusing news. The older boys told me and the rest of the gang. It was not clear where their intelligence came from. The gist of the message was that *der Feind* -- the enemy we had been told, over and over again, could never win -- was marching towards Munich...no, towards Dachau... no, they were almost here now; any day now we'd see them!

"The Russians?"

"No, it's the *Ammis* (Americans)."

"Oh no, they're going to shoot us!"

"Or stick us with their bayonets."

"Some of them have black skin, like coal!"

Seeing the anxious faces of the younger kids, the older ones couldn't resist escalating the fear. "They might be cannibals...hide if you spot any!"

Roland's vocabulary did not yet include words like "cannibal" and "bayonet," but he sensed the tension. He stared at me with wide blue eyes. I made a skeptical face copied from Mother when she was told whoppers. I said what I thought she would say: "We'll see about that."

At first, I wanted to run to Mother as soon as possible and ask her if she knew about all this. But then I decided not to share the rumors, in case she ordered us to stay inside, hide under the bed, and not come out for a week. I wanted to *see* these Americans, bayonets and all. I didn't believe the cannibal part; those boys were always trying to spook us. There were good hiding places outdoors -- drainage ditches from which we could spy on the main road. We used them often in our Wild West games. That's where we would go if they actually marched in. I told Roland not to worry. I would take him with me, naturally; I always did.

The ditch was where the children of the Moosschwaige crouched when the Americans came. They came in tanks, camouflage-painted trucks, and Jeeps. I did not know the calendar date. I do not remember how we got word that the American army was on its way. I do remember the dash we made to our hiding place, too excited to be afraid. The ditch was overgrown with grass and stinging nettles, but the thrilling rumble of the tanks on the pavement made us oblivious to discomfort. Since no one paid any attention to the shoulder of the road, the children, by ones and twos, crept up to the top of the gully and, ever so carefully, stuck their heads up far enough to see the giant caterpillar tracks of the tanks. By craning your neck really hard, you could see the Jeeps, and the soldiers holding machine guns. They did not jump out to hunt us down. If they had bayonets, they kept them sheathed.

It was Sunday, April 29, 1945, the day troops belonging to the US Seventh Army liberated the town of Dachau and, later on the same day, the concentration camp.

None of us children, of course, witnessed the unfathomable horror the Americans confronted that day at the camp. After watching the tanks for a long time, relief and excitement made us sleepy so we went back to the house. In the months to come, we would learn more than we wanted to know -- more than anyone should ever have to know.

The Americans encountered no resistance in the town. The mayor and the Party bigwigs had fled, leaving a lone deputy mayor in charge. The citizens had hung white towels and bed sheets from their windows and waited silently behind closed doors. The deputy mayor surrendered to the senior American officer and watched as the police were stripped of their weapons and locked into a meeting room. Later, he helped distribute the orders of the military command to the civilians.

At the concentration camp, prisoners could actually see American soldiers advancing cautiously, machine guns at the ready. The SS men in the watchtowers fired at them but were soon overpowered. Shortly after 5:00 PM, the great wrought-iron entrance gate to the camp opened, and the first American soldier stepped through. The nightmare -- the heaps of dead bodies, the multitude of starving prisoners too sick to rise from the ground, the skeletal figures of those still able to walk -- made the American soldiers so furious that they grabbed a number of the SS guards and executed them on the spot. The rest were locked up to await trial for war crimes.

In Berlin, in his bunker, Adolf Hitler was preparing for his suicide and fiery funeral the next day, April 30. His regime -- an age of darkness -- would survive him by only a week.

In Dachau, August was not seen in the house for several days. He may have been in hiding with friends or relatives in the area. Tante prayed for the souls of the slain. Mother was calm. She knew her own liberation had come. Soon she would begin to work out the details.

CHAPTER 7

Peace

In the months after Germany's capitulation in the first week of May 1945, so many events happened that I can no longer remember the exact sequence. Some things happened almost at the same time. The American army took charge of the town of Dachau and of the liberated concentration camp. They deliberately made the camp the prison for the remaining SS guards and other high-ranking Nazis, and they set up military courts. A group of elite Nazi Party members who lived in town and boys who had been in the Hitler Jugend were brought to look at the camp, the crematoria, and the train full of corpses that had been abandoned on the railroad siding in front of the camp. Civilians had to help bury the dead.

American soldiers patrolled the streets and searched houses for Nazis in hiding and for weapons. The townspeople were questioned about their Party affiliation and about political activities during Hitler's reign, in order to determine the extent of their complicity.

At the same time, the soldiers driving through the neighborhood were friendly and kind to children. One day, I was idling in the front yard with some members of our gang, when a Jeep came driving up and slowly rolled to a stop. The driver was a large man with black skin and very white teeth bared in a huge smile. He was the first person of another color any of us had ever seen. He waved and called out a greeting. We did not understand the words, but the meaning was clear. We stared, not knowing how to respond. We did not have a white flag. Should we raise our hands in surrender? Or was it not necessary now that the war was over?

The soldier reached down for something to his right. Was he drawing his gun? No--the hand came up filled with small, colorful objects that looked like-- could it be--candy? His large black hand flung the -- yes, it was -- candy at us. Still we stood frozen. This was a problem. All through the war, we had been warned never to accept any treats from strangers, and never to pick anything up from the street. It might be an enemy trick. If it was food, it would be poisoned. If it was a toy, it would blow your head off. The soldier kept smiling, making eating motions, and saying a word we would soon learn: *"Okeh,"* it sounded like. His grin was so warm. We were so hungry. We started picking up the treasure; then, remembering our manners, we said, *"Danke!"*

"Okeh," he replied, visibly pleased, and threw another handful of sweets. We recognized the bonbons and could smell the chocolate wrapped in silver foil and shiny, dark brown paper with silver lettering. I remembered chocolate from Saarburg. Mother, who always had admirers, had often received fancy gift boxes and she had always shared them. Other candies puzzled us. There was a small rectangular box that contained five flat, hard ribbons, each in a separate envelope. The stiff ribbons broke into little pieces that tasted sweet. The label said "GUM."

We pronounced it *goom*. *Goom?* What was *goom*? And why had they bothered with all that extra wrapping? What strange tastes American kids had. The soldier in the Jeep sat and smiled at us as we stuffed our mouths and pockets. There was so much loot -- it was more than we had ever got at one time, even on Christmas. I told Roland we would save some for later.

The soldier patted his stomach and asked, "Good?" This word sounded enough like the German *Gut* that we understood.

"Jah, jah, gut, sehr gut!" we yelled, jumping up and down now that our fear had gone. *"Sehr gut! Prima!"* The superlative meant "excellent, first-class."

"Prima?" The soldier repeated.

"Jah, prima. Prima!"

He pointed to his broad chest with both thumbs. "Me Prima-Prima!"

And so, we called him every time we saw him again -- quite a few times that summer.

At home, I told Mother about Prima-Prima, our new hero, and showed her the candy treasure. Tante accepted a tiny nibble of chocolate; Mother, Roland and I shared our first taste of America: a Hershey bar. We would consume many packs of *goom* before some clever scout informed us that the ribbon candy was rubber and we were to chew it but not swallow it. Rubber candy! Wacky Ammis.

Another fascinating novelty appeared around that time -- this one was quickly confiscated by grumpy adults who gave no good reason (in our opinion) for their disapproval. This was a toy, not candy. It came in a small foil packet. Inside the envelope was a limp, whitish tube that could be blown up into a balloon. None of us had ever had a toy balloon; we were thrilled. The older boys who were lucky enough to possess one were pursued by the rest of us, asking for a turn to touch it and toss it up into the air.

Alas, our fun did not last long. Horrified grownups grabbed the toys as soon as they saw them, saying only, "Not for kids!"

When interrogated about where and how they had stolen the balloons, the boys stoutly maintained they had not *stolen* -- they had *found* them. Later, it became known that some local citizens had raided the SS storehouse at the concentration camp, taking uniforms and foodstuffs and whatever else they could carry. So, it was the adults, after all, who had found the things. I did not learn the name or the purpose of this not-for-kids item for many years.

The friendly soldier Prima-Prima was our sunshine in those days. On the dark side, there were the lice and the fear of typhus. When the concentration camp was liberated, a typhus epidemic was raging. Despite prompt attention by army doctors, many prisoners were already too weak to survive; more died in the following months. Lice, fleas, and mites transmit the bacteria for this disease. In the horrific sanitary conditions of the camp, these pests had thrived. Inevitably, they had spread to the town.

The Americans acted quickly, setting up a field hospital at the camp and a medical aid station in the town square. All the citizens, old and young, were urged -- or possibly ordered -- to come for typhus vaccinations and delousing treatments. We stood in line and got our shots. Then our heads were sprayed with a white powder. I had long, brown, wavy hair. Mother said she was sorry; she would probably have to cut it short in order to get all the nits out. I asked if we could wait and see, and she agreed. We walked home, looking like refugees from the eighteenth-century court of Versailles. For the next several days, Mother and Tante took turns using a fine-tooth comb on Roland's and my hair. It was tedious; Roland squirmed. Mother assured us it had to be done thoroughly so we would not re-infest each other and the whole household. One morning -- success! Our heads were clean. Tante was impressed by the American louse powder. "It is really strong stuff," she said. "Look how well it worked!" We did not know it then, but it was indeed powerful. It was DDT.

The military government continued to search for Nazis and civilian sympathizers, and for concealed weapons. One afternoon, Roland and I were home with Mother when a loud knock on the front door startled us. She got up to look, Roland and I close beside her. Before she could reach it, the door was poked open by the tip of a gun barrel. A tall soldier in a white helmet stood in the opening. He was not smiling or relaxed like Prima-Prima.

"Nazi? Man? Here?" he demanded. While he was still speaking, Mother reached out and swatted at the gun.

"Put that down, "she said in German. "Don't you see there are little children here?"

It may have been that he understood the word *Kinder*. Or maybe it was Mother's authoritative tone that made the soldier lower his weapon. But that was his only concession. Gun pointed at the floor, he strode into the room and made it clear he had come to search. Sternly, he repeated, "Nazi? Here?"

August was not in the house. I did not know where he was. We had seen him only once after the Americans came, when he had collected some of his photographic gear. I don't know if Mother knew his whereabouts. She answered, truthfully, *"Nicht hier."*

The soldier motioned Mother to walk in front of him while he searched our rooms. She complied calmly as he opened doors and cupboards, finding nothing. Mother went with him as he searched the kitchen and cellar. She even showed him a hidden closet under the stairs that he had missed in the dark hallway. It contained broken furniture. The soldier said, "Okeh," and then he left. That was one American word we knew. It meant the same as *gut*. The letters MP on his helmet stood for military police, Mother guessed. The initials would be the same in German.

Later, Mother said she was glad the search had missed the pieces of our flag. In Saarburg, every householder had been required to own and display one. Mother had cut the black swastika from the center and destroyed it, but she had saved the sturdy red cloth because you could not buy textiles. As soon as she had time, she said, she would make us all underpants. "And then," she said, "I can do what I've always wanted to do with this stupid flag--wipe my ass!"

About a week after the MP's search, Mother had news of both Ernst and August. Ernst had returned, unharmed, and had found lodging with friends; he would not be moving back in with us. August had been arrested by the Americans and sent to a detention camp -- one of the Dachau work camps -- outside of town. Mother did not know how long he would be detained, or what punishment he would receive. Interrogation and, eventually, denazification, were steps in a slow process. I felt neither sorrow nor joy at the news. Roland never asked about his father; I don't know how much of the situation he understood. Tante -- whom August had regularly called "Old Dragon" to her face -- wondered if August would get enough to eat. This had not occurred to me. Mother said she would try to put aside a few potatoes and find out when she could bring them to the camp. I did not ask to go along; I did not care if he got potatoes or not.

What did worry me was Mother's further news that she too had to show up at the military command post for questioning. As the wife of a known Nazi, she would have to fill out a lengthy questionnaire to account for her actions during the last twelve years. Mother said her interview might take a long time; she might have to stay overnight in the town jail; there were many people to be processed. I did not want to alarm Roland, so I said nothing, but Mother knew that I was frightened. She made a joke of it: "First the Nazis put me in jail, and now the Americans want their turn, too."

When the day of her appointment came, Mother collected her knitting and told us not to worry. "Can you finish my sweater?" I asked innocently. I was looking forward to this garment. It was made entirely of remnants of wool Mother had unraveled from old, worn socks and pullovers. Every piece of yarn was a different length. Mother spliced them together expertly to create what she called confetti.

She was not entirely amused by my question. "Oh," she said, "My daughter wants me to stay in jail long enough to finish her sweater?"

I was crushed. That night, Roland and I decided to sleep in Mother's bed, cuddling her nightgown between us.

All three of us cried the next day, when Mother returned about noontime and happily reported that all was well. She had been able to prove that she was never a Party member and had provided character witnesses, including her cousin, who knew of her affiliation with the German Peace League. I imagine her past arrest by the Nazis counted towards her exoneration as well. Mother said this was all good news, wasn't it?

We had been sitting on the bed. Now Mother got up and headed for the kitchen to make a pot of chicory and prepare the midday meal. We followed, staying close, relieved to have her back. When she had filled the water kettle, she turned to us and repeated, "It's good news for now, and for the future too, you understand? Now it will be possible to get permission to emigrate and go to live in America. Can you imagine America?"

CHAPTER 8

Confronting the Past, Imagining the Future

Going to America sounded like another fairytale. This story, instead of beginning, "Once upon a time," would start, "Once, at a time in the future..."

America. Chicago. Aunt Mary. Mother had mentioned all of these names over the years and had even shown me a letter from her older sister, Mary. Chicago, where Aunt Mary had lived since long before the war, was a city larger than Saarburg, larger than Munich, much larger than Dachau. Aunt Mary had a husband and a son a few years my senior; they lived in a house they did not share with any other families. America was so far away, you had to cross the ocean. To do that, you had to stay on a ship for more than a week. I had never seen the ocean; I had never been on a ship; not even a rowboat. When Mother revealed her plan to emigrate, I was both fascinated and puzzled.

"Are we all going?" I asked.

"No, only you and Roland and I. Aunt Mary has room in her house, until we get settled."

"Is Tante going?" She was my most important concern. August and Ernst had not been included in Mother's list; I was content to leave it that way.

Mother said, "Tante feels she is too old to leave her homeland. She wants to go back to Ettlingen, our hometown, and go to the church she went to as a little girl." I could not bear that thought, and was about to protest when Mother continued, "But don't cry. It will take a long time to get the papers. Thousands of people want to go to America, and only so many can go at one time. That's called a *quota*. We have to get in line. Probably you'll have to finish another whole year of school before we can get started."

The thought of leaving Tante was too sad, so I decided to put it aside. Maybe, by magic, the story would turn out differently; that happened all the time in fairytales.

Mother was not finished. "Besides," she said, "We don't have time to worry about the future now. Tomorrow or the next day, we have two new people moving into our front room. They were prisoners in the camp and have no home anymore. I just hope I can get something besides dried-out turnips for dinner."

It certainly was a big day for news.

Mother's taking in survivors was not an unusual act in Dachau after the liberation of the camp. More than thirty thousand prisoners had been released from the main camp and many thousands more from the smaller ones on the outskirts of town. The American army saw to it that these homeless people were cared for. Survivor accounts confirm that many townspeople had tried to help prisoners, slipping a piece of bread or a radish to the men on work details when they encountered them in town. They had to act quickly, to evade punishment by the SS guards who wielded whips and guns. Now, after the liberation, shelter was offered by families who could make room, even if lodgings were cramped. Citizens who were reluctant to volunteer had to be prodded to help by the military government.

Mother got ready for our new housemates by rigging up a clothesline and a pair of old curtains to partition the room we used as a family and dining room. Somewhere she found two cots and spare blankets.

Two thin men, one taller and more broad-shouldered than the other, arrived a day or two after Mother's announcement. They were dressed in slacks and sweaters and shapeless jackets too large for their emaciated frames -- donated clothing, probably from the International Red Cross. Mother introduced them formally, as Mr. Stefan and Mr. Casimir -- she had memorized their last names, but they were hard to pronounce, so it was agreed then and there to use the familiar form. Mother explained to Roland and me and Tante that the gentlemen had been in the Polish army and been captured by the Nazis. The men kissed Mother's hand, bowed respectfully to Tante, and shook hands with us children. The one called Stefan -- the shorter, thinner one who stood up as straight as an oak tree -- thanked Mother in perfect, only slightly accented German. We learned later that he had been a major in the Polish army. Casimir, a corporal, had only two or three words of German, but his large, dark eyes shone with emotion.

Dinner, the main meal of the day, was customarily served around noon. I do not remember what Mother had found to cook that day. A typical menu might have been *Mehlsuppe* --flour soup-- made by toasting a bit of flour in a cast iron pot, then dousing it with water and salt. The main course would be cabbage and potatoes or turnips. If we had a few slices of dried apple they were served for dessert. When the simple meal was over, Stefan and Casimir rose from their chairs and bowed to Mother and Tante. Stefan, again in graceful German, expressed their thanks. This ceremony was to be repeated at every dinner.

I had never heard August say one word of appreciation or thanks for Mother's efforts to serve a complete meal, even if the soup was mostly water. Nor had I seen August carry a bucket of coal up from the cellar for Mother, as Casimir did the next day, and from then on, whenever it was needed. With her usual dry humor, Mother later remarked that it was kind of him, but there was never enough coal to make a heavy load.

Stefan and Casimir were not Jewish but Roman Catholic -- this was the largest ethnic group in the Dachau camp at the time of liberation. They must have talked with Mother about their experiences, but at first, they did not speak of them with us children. I knew the abbreviation KZ stood for concentration camp. All I knew then was that it was a jail -- a bad place you wanted to avoid. People would say, "You don't want to put on a striped jacket; you'll never get out of it."

The two ex-prisoners now living with us had survived. The experiences they chose to share as time went on provided a window into a barely imaginable inferno. Stefan spoke of men so desperate that they deliberately threw themselves at the electric fence in order to die quickly. He spoke of others so exhausted by the daily hard labor that they could not get up for the roll call. They were taken away and shot by the guards.

One evening, I saw Stefan at the table, drawing what looked like a row of tiny skeletons -- stick figures with skull-shaped heads. He saw me watching and called me over to explain. He was making a chart, he said, of prisoners from different nations who had died in the camp. There were Czechoslovakians, Poles, Hungarians, Romany, and Jews, including a few Jews who had lived in the town of Dachau. There were Catholic and Protestant clergymen who had spoken out about Hitler, and communists, pacifists, and other political dissenters. Each stick figure, Stefan said, stood for one hundred persons killed. There were rows and rows of the tiny icons.

Mother put down her knitting and joined us. She explained to me that Stefan and Casimir were working as guides for groups of American soldiers and locals who came to see the camp. The site had been cleaned up and disinfected after the typhus epidemic had been brought to an end. Mother said the two of us should go with Stefan one day.

"You are eight years old, soon to be nine," she said, "and I know that is very young. But you need to see that the *Führer* was an evil man and that his kind can never again be allowed to lead a country."

When we went, Mother and I were part of a small group of townspeople -- nobody we knew. Roland had been left with Tante. Stefan's presentation was effective and calm. He took the group to see the nine-foot-high electrified fence topped with barbed wire and overlooked by guard towers, the barracks where the prisoners had lived, and the square where daily roll calls had taken place. He showed us the whipping block and the gas chamber that looked like a shower room. He related how prisoners were tricked into thinking they were going in for delousing. Finally, he showed us the crematorium with the huge ovens. The visitors were silent, hardly taking a breath. Stefan recited some of the statistics he was charting. He was working from lists kept by the Nazi administrators of the camp -- a bureaucracy of death. The records listed many thousands of victims, whose only crimes had been their religious or political convictions, or their ethnic origin. Hundreds of thousands had passed through this hell; few came out alive. The population of the town of Dachau at the time was less than twenty thousand. My eight-year-old brain could compare, but not comprehend, these numbers.

I remember the utter silence of that tour. Indeed, what could one say? When citizens of Dachau were interviewed by reporters later, they expressed a sense of grief and helplessness. "What could we have done? The camp was sealed off by the SS. You could not make contact with the prisoners. We knew they were suffering, but if you tried to help them when they were driven out on work detail, you risked getting shot. We tried as much as we could."

Dachau was only one camp. Over the next months and years, I learned more about the others. I learned about the horrific medical experiments, and about Hitler's "final solution" -- his goal of deporting and killing every Jew in Germany and the occupied territories. For this, there had been the extermination camps further east -- Auschwitz, Buchenwald, Terezin. The crimes were so enormous that I sensed there would never be an answer to the question, Why? How could this happen?

To this day, scholars, historians, survivors, their children, and their children's children still seek answers. The Dachau Memorial Site is known as "the place where birds never sing."

At home, life became a bit easier when we started to receive food assistance from the United Nation Refugee and Rehabilitation Agency (UNRRA). Interesting new foodstuffs were delivered: square slices of snow-white bread that tasted like air, powdered eggs that could be mixed with water to make omelets, small cans of super-sweet condensed milk, dried beans, sugar. Once only, there was a dark brown, curved fruit with a thick skin and a creamy inside. Mother was the only one who knew it was a banana. She said they grew in the *Urwald* -- the primeval jungle. I guessed that this forest must be even further away than America. No wonder only one fruit ever made it our house. Roland traded his pieces of white bread for the rye he was more accustomed to; the boys in the gang were happy with that deal.

Later in the year, amid great excitement, a package arrived from America. Mother cried when she saw her sister's return address. It was not Christmas yet, but Aunt Mary's generosity outshone that of

Saint Nicholas. There were basic foods as well as items not seen in Germany for many years. Among the luxuries were coffee beans -- real coffee-- and tea in small bags Tante wondered at. Why did they keep their tea leaves in such hard-to-open containers? The staples included milk powder, tinned meat, and a can labeled "Del Monte Small Green Peas."

"Green peas?" Mother asked, looking at the picture on the label. "It must be very expensive to send packages. Why spend postage on something that's possible to get here?" When Tante and Mother together had managed to open the can, they found that the green peas had been transformed into white sticks with a familiar aroma.

"Cigarettes?"

"Really?"

Yes, really. There was no doubt about it. My respect for Aunt Mary shot up a thousand percent. Rumpelstiltskin had helped the miller's daughter spin straw into gold; my aunt had turned peas into tobacco.

A letter in the package, on the thinnest paper I had ever seen, casually mentioned that Aunt Mary owned a home-canning machine. Mother understood at once. It was illegal to ship cigarettes because they were the most desirable currency in postwar Germany. On the black market, American cigarettes were better than gold.

CHAPTER 9

Hope

When my mother had first mentioned going to America to live, she had said, "You will probably finish another school year before we can leave." She had no way of knowing then that it would be nearly five years until we finally took ship in November 1950.

Those years were filled with changes, reunions, and separations, as our family and the country readjusted to peacetime. At the Moosschwaige, life in our unconventional, multinational, multigenerational household was not luxurious. We were six people in three rooms, and we all shared a bathroom with other tenants, but despite the makeshift arrangement there was a feeling of harmony and a sense of hope. We were all grateful the war was over, and we could sleep through the night. Thanks to the UNRRA food assistance, and help from Mother's sister in the United States, our diet became more varied and nutritious.

Mother carefully rationed her precious coffee beans. For the morning pot of her favorite beverage, she counted out seven beans, ground them in the mill with its doll-sized wooden drawer, and mixed them with the usual chicory. Generous as always, she shared with the other adults.

Stefan and Casimir continued to be polite and undemanding housemates. They always had a smile or friendly wave for us children; their manner was so different from August's constant agitation.

Casimir was as fond of the garden as I was. I knew he had a favorite place-- an old beech tree with wide-ranging roots that embraced the earth like arms. I thought of it as his church because one morning I had seen him kneeling at the base of this tree, a small, creased holy picture of the Virgin Mary propped up in front of him. I did not disturb him; I knew he was giving thanks. That he had managed to preserve this flimsy piece of cardboard through all the years of his imprisonment was a miracle in itself.

Stefan consulted refugee agencies in order to locate his wife and to send for her. He had no wish to return to Poland now that the Russians were in control. I didn't know if Casimir had a family, but I was sure that Stefan, with his better language skills, would give him whatever help he needed to find relatives and a place in the postwar world.

Mother never discussed her private life with me, but she did talk with Tante. In our crowded apartment, conversations were not always private, and I had "long ears," as the Germans say. I had a nagging fear that August would turn up and demand to go to America with us. So, when I heard the words "divorce" and "lawyer," I was reassured that she was taking steps to free herself of him forever.

I did not fully realize it at the time, but my mother's freedom came at a price. With August interned, and later to be divorced, Mother was the only breadwinner, responsible for two young children and an elderly aunt. The Polish survivors received subsidies from the government. Mother still worked for her cousin whose business was slow to recover from wartime shortages. Mother was a relative, so she remained employed. I never knew what her salary amounted to, but it could not have been substantial. None of this was discussed in my hearing. What I did notice, though, was that Mother started to make "buying trips" and came home with all sorts of goods -- fresh eggs, cuts of meat, a bag of cherries, a pair of shoes for Roland.

Only the black market could have accounted for such extras. I knew about the black market; everyone knew. Though I did not understand all the reasons for this alternative economy of barter, I knew that paper currency was practically valueless. People who had commodities to sell preferred payment in gold, or in coffee, tea, or cigarettes. I understood that thanks to Aunt Mary's magic cigarettes, Mother had trading goods. I never doubted that she would provide for us, as she had done, by herself, since the war ended.

The black market was illegal, as Mother knew for sure and I vaguely deduced. If this ever worried her, she never spoke of it. She relied on luck and on her charm to manage without getting in trouble. And she never stumbled.

Mother's most spectacular purchase was a parachute-- we thought it was American because the strong, white, smooth material was unfamiliar. It was called nylon, Mother said; she was not sure if the *Luftwaffe* had used it.

Roland and I were thrilled. Tante was puzzled: "Why a parachute, of all things?"

"The children need shirts, don't they? And couldn't you use a new nightgown?" Mother's inventive mind was at work.

The thing was enormous. It filled the room like a giant thunderhead dropped through the ceiling. It slid and slithered from the table to the chairs, to the floor. It had countless cords and ropes, all smooth as glass. Dismantling the leviathan took many days. We cut and coiled up all the different cords, separated the metal parts, and unraveled yards and yards of the thread that was impossible to tear with your hands. What luck, Mother kept saying -- all her thread spools were empty, or nearly so. Because the canopy of the chute seemed intact, we hoped the paratrooper--whoever he was -- had made it safely to earth. The cloth was strong and pliable, but Mother had a hard time hemming it; the slippery nylon did not hold a crease. I don't remember exactly how she discovered heat sealing; perhaps she accidentally scorched the material with a hot iron. Noticing that the burnt edge no longer unraveled, she set up a candle and passed the edges of the cut cloth through it, fusing it to form a selvage. This made fashioning garments much easier and proved to be a great advantage when Mother used her extra stock of material to trade for other goods.

At the end of June 1946, I had completed four years of grammar school, starting in Saarburg and ending in Dachau, and was issued a transfer diploma that entitled me to move to a *Gymnasium* (high school) or to a vocational or specialized trade school. Under the German system, the academic track consists of eight years of literature, mathematics, history, geography, and languages including

Latin, Greek, and, as of 1945, English. After successful completion of this curriculum, a student is qualified to apply to a university.

Mother valued higher education. She hoped both Roland and I would choose the academic option. Roland's choice, of course, was far in the future; he had not even started first grade. I was enthusiastic and willing; I loved school and had done well. My grades were good -- with an "excellent" in math. Each report card had noted that "the pupil works very diligently and shows faultless deportment."

The girls' high school I would attend was in Munich (it is still there, in a slightly different incarnation) and required an interview and an entrance exam. It would also require a half-hour trip on the commuter train between Dachau and Munich. I was not yet ten years old but none of this worried me. Mother warned that the trains would be terribly crowded because so many carriages had been diverted to wartime use and had not made it back into civilian railways. I asked Mother to go with me to the interview and show me how to walk from the train station to the *Luisenschule* at *Luisenstraße 7*. I was already looking forward to studying ancient Greek; I have forgotten why that seemed the most attractive subject.

When we went for the interview, I saw Mother had been right about the train. It looked so impossibly full I wondered if we should wait for the next one. Mother explained there was no "next one" this morning; the schedule was unreliable. "Squeeze in," she ordered; she gave me a push and hopped onto the step close behind me.

Mother said that she had taken me to Munich many times when I was little, before we had moved to Saarburg, but I did not remember those visits. The city I saw when we left the train station was in ruins. Heaps of broken bricks covered long stretches of the sidewalks. On every street we walked along, houses with only one or two walls left standing outnumbered the buildings that had been spared by the bombs.

"Remember how often we had to run down to the cellar?" Mother asked. "This is what was happening. And it happened because Hitler was a madman who wanted to rule the world and started a war. In war, innocent people suffer with the guilty. Maybe in your lifetime good leaders can learn to live without war. But I wonder--"

As we walked through another city square, Mother pointed out one of Munich's most famous landmarks, the *Frauenkirche* (Our Lady's Church).

"This church has stood here since the Fifteenth Century. Look at the towers now! They had domed roofs. Look how much has been destroyed. We will be living in America and I'll be old and grey before this is rebuilt."

I did not want to imagine my mother as an old woman who always dressed in black, like Tante. I squeezed Mother's hand.

When we arrived at the school, we saw that its building had been damaged as well. At least a third of the large, ornate facade was missing from the building at Luisenstrasse 7.

The city-run *Gymnasium* had been established in 1822 as a high school for "young ladies of the upper class." In 1901, the pupils had moved to the present building designed by the famous architect Theodor Fischer. Now, in 1946, the historic building was only partly habitable.

"Please follow me -- this way, to the left," the teacher who met us at the entrance said. "To the right is our atrium, but it is unsafe -- there is a great deal of structural damage. Classes are being held in the rooms that are safe for the girls and teachers. We must do the best we can."

Later in the year, I would find that even the usable rooms had problems, such as heating systems that did not work. Our teachers allowed us to wear gloves which we removed when doing a written exercise.

At my interview, Mother explained our circumstances and promised she would do her best to get me to school on time despite the unpredictable schedule of the commuter train. I was given a date for the written entrance exam, a week, or ten days away. When that date came, Mother was busy with an appointment that could not be put off, so I took the train by myself. I was the only girl who had come unaccompanied by a parent. I have no memory of what was on the test, but I remember writing my answers very, very neatly, in ink. I passed.

Except for half a year in 1949, I attended the *Luisenschule* until we left Germany. My report cards continued to note my industriousness and good behavior; my grades stayed high. The only subject marked "unsatisfactory" was needlework, which consisted of knitting socks -- a task Mother could do in the dark, but a hopeless enterprise in my hands. I had three years of English, and two of Latin, but never got to Greek. I regret that. How special it would have been to read the *Iliad* in the original!

Outside of school, I learned to swim -- in the Amper, the river I had almost drowned in as a baby -- and I learned to ride a bicycle, using an old wreck that had been abandoned at the Moosschwaige. One of the older kids had a bicycle pump and put air in the tires. He could not fix the brakes, which worked only sporadically. It was good enough; after a number of tumbles, I managed to stay upright and cruised around the gravel paths, coasting to a stop when the brake refused to grip.

Pursuing her divorce from August, Mother had appointments with a lawyer in Munich. She said the attorney was confident the case was proceeding well. To Tante, but within my hearing, she said, "He is in his fifties, but he lives with his mother. I wonder why; he's not bad looking--you'd think he'd have a wife, at his age."

Stefan's wife had been found, and there was great excitement and a tearful reunion when she arrived from Poland. Mother had bought a chicken that she killed and cooked in honor of the occasion. I refused to eat any of it. Roland was fascinated by the ax Mother had left on the chopping block outside, and he tried to split a piece of wood with it. He cut into his thumb instead. Fortunately, the wound was not serious, and thanks to Stefan's quick emergency attention, it was bandaged and caused no further harm. Stefan promised he would teach Roland the proper way to handle an axe so that he would never hurt himself again.

Mother now started looking for different lodgings for our family, to give everyone more privacy. In town, she found a widow who owned a two-storey house and was willing to rent out the ground floor, while she herself would use the second floor.

We moved to the small house, where we shared the kitchen with the landlady, but we got a bathroom of our own, as well as two bedrooms and a living room. The landlady gave me and Roland permission to use a small plot in her backyard as a garden bed. She gave us radish seeds to plant for our first crop. Mother offered to pay something extra if she could get an egg or two from the widow's chickens.

One sunny Saturday, while Roland and I were weeding our vegetable patch -- we had planted pole beans along with the radish seeds -- a car horn sounded. This was rare because the street was not a busy one. What we saw when we ran out to the front of the house was even rarer: a gleaming, sky-blue car that was almost as large as an army truck but was much more elegant. Its sleek design was not of German manufacture; I had never seen anything like it in Dachau or Munich, or Karlsruhe. The driver, a well-dressed, smiling man, got out and waved hello.

"*Guten Tag*," he said in German. "Is your mother here?"

She was -- actually she was already on the doorstep, having heard the unfamiliar sounds. Our visitor walked forward to meet her, hand outstretched. "*Guten Tag*," he repeated. "I am the milkman from Chicago."

His German was clear, and we understood "Chicago," but the rest was still puzzling. "Milkman" was not a profession I had heard of. I was familiar with fetching milk from a small store in town. Perhaps he owned one of those? Or was he a farmer and owned the cows?

Mother shook hands and said she was pleased to meet him. He replied, "I know your sister, Mary, in Chicago. I bring her milk every day."

The mention of Aunt Mary helped. Understanding dawned. Mother asked questions and our visitor explained that he was touring Germany, where his parents had been born, and that Aunt Mary had asked him to be sure and stop by to see us. He said his parents' native city was not far away; he was on his way there.

While we were greeting our visitor, other children who had been playing outdoors drifted over to gawp at the exotic vehicle. A few reached out tentative hands towards the shiny finish, but none of us quite dared to touch it. The milkman saw this and gave an encouraging laugh. "Okay, it's okay," he said, using our favorite English expression. "You can touch. Nice, isn't it? It's a nice car, a Cadillac."

"Cad...," we tried this strange word.

"Cad-ee-lack," he coached, breaking it down into pronounceable syllables.

"Cad-ee--lack," we repeated. "Cadillac."

"Want a ride?" the man asked, as he picked up Roland, set him on the hood of the car, and motioned for me to hop up too. The other kids looked longingly at us. So, the wonderful man helped another two of them up. He promised the remaining children they would get a turn.

And there was more to the treat! The man got into the driver's seat, started the car, and slowly backed it around so he could drive a few yards down the street. The motor was so quiet we felt it more than we heard it. True to his word, the milkman gave rides to seven or eight young admirers before Mother stepped in and said we must not take advantage of his good nature any longer. Surely, he was ready for a cup of coffee by now?

I thought Chicago must be a very glamorous city, if people drove around in cars as big as railway carriages.

Mother served coffee, having made sure it contained more coffee beans than chicory. I enjoyed this pleasant and instructive visit. The milkman explained that in Chicago, he delivered milk to the doorsteps of customers like Aunt Mary. And no, he did not use the Cadillac to do it-- that was his personal car. A truck carried the milk. He had brought the Cadillac to Germany on the ship. I could not imagine this, but Mother simply smiled without comment. The man praised Aunt Mary. "Such a nice, friendly lady," he said. "She can't wait to see you."

"Is Germany the way you imagined it? Do you see things your parents described?" Mother asked.

"My parents left long before the war -- before so much was destroyed. I see there is some rebuilding, but it is very sad -- there was so much suffering."

"Politicians talk about winning wars -- that's not possible," Mother said. "Nobody wins!"

"My parents want pictures of their hometown. I'll try to find the lovely old trees in the woods they told me about. But another reason I had for coming is that I wanted to visit the concentration camp and say a prayer for the dead prisoners."

"Thank you, and thank you for this visit," Mother said. "Let us hope for better times, now that we have peace. And I know you will find many beautiful sights on the way to your parents' house."

When our visitor left, the neighbor kids popped out of their yards again and ran after the Cadillac, yelling and waving. He blew the horn. He was the Pied Piper on wheels.

I continued at the *Luisenschule* for the 1947 to 1948 academic year. We still had not heard anything specific about our emigration visas. Roland and I made a few new friends in the new neighborhood. We still played at being Indians. Roland found a broken umbrella and thought the ribs would make excellent arrows. We tried it and he was right-- the steel shafts flew straight and true. I said we should shoot them up into the air only, not at people. Years later, I felt guilty; a really good big sister would have stopped this dangerous game entirely. Roland acquired a pocketknife; I have no idea how. For the rest of his life, he was never without one, whittling increasingly ornate, intricate whistles, bird calls, and walking sticks.

Our friends were mostly boys. I seemed to have no luck with girlfriends. In Saarburg, my classmate had deserted me when I fell into the river. In Dachau, a girl I liked -- the daughter of a physician -- was suddenly forbidden to speak to me. "Because my father found out your mother deals in the black market," she said when I asked. I never reported this to Mother. Dorothea could go to hell; I didn't like her anymore.

Given the importance of possessing the correct documents in Nazi Germany-- the right birth certificate was literally a matter of life or death -- it is no wonder my mother was a meticulous collector and preserver of records. She saved and dated papers, and she assembled scrapbooks and photo albums that I prize to this day. It is thanks to her that I have my report cards going back to 1942. It is thanks to them that I now can reconstruct my school years so fully.

In 1949, our family underwent a big change, one that brought home the reality of our leaving Germany. For the first time, I realized that Mother's long-held dream of a new life in a distant country was something that would actually happen; it was not wishful fantasy. I thought about leaving Dachau, wondering if I would miss it. No sad feelings surfaced. I had no close friendships; I was still leery of an unwanted return by August. I sensed that Dachau would always be associated in my memory with what I had seen at the concentration camp, and with Stefan's skeletons.

Mother knew I liked school, so she reassured me that my studies would continue in America. She said American cities had not been bombed. Whatever school I went to there would be comfortable. It would have a roof covering the entire building. Imagine-- my toes would not go numb with cold!

I was excited by our impending adventures but saddened when I recalled that leaving Germany would mean separation from Tante. I had pushed this reality into a dark corner of my mind; now I had to face it. Tante had never wanted to emigrate. She said now that the children were growing up -- I was in high school and Roland had started first grade--life would be easier for Mother, and she herself was getting old. She needed to return to Ettlingen, where she had cousins who would welcome her back. My mother's side of the family all came from this small town a few miles from Karlsruhe, at the edge of the Black Forest. Tante was a relative by marriage, not blood, but she had been born there too.

Mother understood; I tried to, but this family decision made me terribly sad. Mother said that since her own mother lived in Ettlingen as well, we would all go and visit. Our first task would be to make sure Tante was properly settled. Mother's older brother Karl and his family lived in the area; we would take our time and say our goodbyes to everyone. I liked Uncle Karl. He had come several times to Saarburg, where he alternately fascinated and frightened the housemaid and us children with his glass eye -- a legacy of his service in World War I. I could not remember meeting my grandmother. Perhaps she had seen me as a baby, but she had never been to Saarburg. Roland had never met her at all.

Ettlingen, a small town in the upper Rhine valley, about five miles from Karlsruhe, was an important crossroads village in Roman time when it belonged to the province of *Germania Superior.* Mother showed us a Roman fountain in the center of town, and the *Neptunstein* -- a stone with a Latin inscription that commemorates a flood of the Rhine. She sang us a funny old drinking song that is a sly commentary on the history of conquest and the fate of nations:

Die alten Germanen sie lagen

zu beiden Uferns des Rheins.

Sie lagen auf Bärenhäuten

Und soffen immer noch eins.

Da kam aus fernem Süden

Ein Römer mit biderem Sinn--

"Grüss Gott, Ihr alten Germanen,

Wisst dass Ich Tacitus bin…"

(The Ancient Germanic tribesmen lived on both banks of the Rhine. They lay about on bearskins and drank too much mead and wine. There came, from the distant Southland, a Roman with manner quite courteous -- "God's Greetings to ye, ancient Germans! My name is Tacitus…")

For our extended visit, we stayed with Tante and her relatives in one of Ettlingen's oldest neighborhoods. The half-timbered house was on a cobblestone street no wider than an alley. No cars were in sight. When the weather was warm enough, children jumped rope right in the street -- there were no sidewalks. One day, with Tante, we visited a field the family had owned for generations. It was on a hill at the edge of town, overlooking farms and orchards. Apple and pear trees, mature and tidily pruned, grew there. The air smelled of sun-warmed grass. Sheep belonging to a neighboring farmer moved lazily beneath the trees.

"The farmer pays us for the grazing rights," Tante explained. "The sheep keep the grass short. It saves us money because we don't have to mow the field."

Tante pointed out the crater where a stray bomb had fallen and damaged several trees. She said we should remember to thank God that it had happened here, and not in town, where children went out to play. Roland was intrigued by the sheep. He ran up to one, attempting to pet it, but the ewe panicked, bolted, and ran right over him. Tante cried out, *"Gott im Himmel,"* but Roland bounced up laughing. He remembered the encounter for years and enjoyed recounting the experience.

Mother planned to stay in Ettlingen as long as it took to make sure that Tante's situation was comfortable for her, and that her old-age pension would be sent to her new address. Mother also looked forward to unhurried visits with the rest of her family. At the same time, she did not want me to fall behind in school, so she enrolled me in a *Gymnasium* in Karlsruhe. I would never have remembered the dates but, thanks once again to Mother's archives, I know I attended the *Fichte Schule* for girls from February until July 1949. My certificate on leaving shows satisfactory grades but many absences. These must have been due to the round of family visits we were making.

The meeting with Mother's mother was not a success, in my opinion. Grandmother lived in an old, narrow, brick house near the town's market square. This was where the bakery had been when my mother was my age. Grandfather, the master baker, had died long before. Grandmother, small and upright, dressed in widow's black, met us at the door, unsmiling. I made the obligatory curtsy, and Roland bowed, as Mother had instructed. In return we got a curt hello but no hugs, no welcoming chat, no questions. Grandmother took us up a flight of steep wooden stairs to a sitting room.

"Sit there and be quiet," she said to Roland and me as she pointed to two low stools. She and Mother sat at a round table and talked -- I don't remember if they had a cup of coffee or not. After a while,

Grandmother said, "You two may go over to the window and look out at the square."

We did as we were told. Mother brought over one of the stools for Roland to stand on so he could see past the high sill. It was not a market day; the square was tranquil -- boring, to tell the truth. We could see the clock on the nearby church tower; the hands were stuck, asleep like the beautiful princess within her walls of thorn. Then, after what seemed like an hour, the minute hand came to life and jerked forward. I gave up watching. It was too painful. We were obedient, well-behaved children, but we practically ran out the door as soon as goodbyes were said, again without any loving words or touches. This grandmother was nothing like Tante! Perhaps she was a changeling.

Our visit with Mother's brother Karl and his family was much more enjoyable. We took a short train ride to the village where he lived with his wife and daughter. It was the first time I had met this cousin, a tall, pretty eighteen-year-old who immediately asked if we could stay over the weekend so she could take me dancing. *Dancing!* I had no idea how to do that.

Uncle Karl and Aunt Elvira were warm and kind and hospitable. Roland, shy at first, laughed out loud when Karl took off his jacket and pretended to hang it on a nonexistent hook on the wall. "What is it with this coat? It just won't stay on the hook!"

Roland loved this silliness; he could have watched the jacket fall down a dozen times. We stayed for a whole week. My cousin gave me a diary that matched hers. We promised to write down our thoughts, and to exchange letters from then on. She wanted to know all about America and my new life there. When she was older and married to a rich husband, they would come to visit us, she said. I could imagine my cousin as a wife--she had rounded hips and womanly breasts. I had nothing like that, but I was not envious; nor did I desire a husband. The word made me think of my mother and August, and the end of their difficult marriage. I did not confide this to my cousin Trudy, but I decided being only thirteen and immature was a good thing; a husband was far in the future.

We did write to each other, at least for the first two years I was in America. I think a husband for my cousin came along in time, but we never met.

Back in Ettlingen, Mother visited many old friends and relatives; I went to school. For the first time, I fell behind in several subjects. I should have been in the third year of the curriculum but for some reason, I had been placed in the fourth. I could not keep up with the Latin homework. My struggles made me so unhappy that Mother found me a tutor, a Catholic priest who was helping other pupils as well. I went for lessons after school. A boy about my age came to the parish house at the same hours. The priest was helpful and friendly. After a few weeks, he invited the boy and me to sit in the garden with him after the lesson. He brought out a camera and said he wanted to take our picture.

"Stand here, close together. Hold hands," he said. I felt awkward but I was used to obeying adults, especially teachers. I took the boy's sweaty hand.

"Nice picture," the priest chuckled. "And now, you are engaged! You know that's what hand-holding means, don't you?"

He did not move to touch either one of us. But his suggestions about what we might do now as an engaged couple were so horribly embarrassing that both of us turned bright red, snatched up our homework, and fled.

I told Mother. She said only one word: "*Schwein!*" She had called him a pig.

I never went back to the priest. The school gave me no grade in Latin because I had not "advanced to the class standard." Mother said not to worry; it was not my fault. Next term, I would be back in the *Luisenschule* and it would all work out.

And then we would go to America.

CHAPTER 10

Departure

Mother, Roland, and I returned to Dachau, to the house we rented from the widow. Stefan, his wife, and Casimir had remained at the Moosschwaige.

My family -- only three of us -- felt small. It had been heartbreaking to say goodbye to Tante, but she had gently reassured us that God would watch over us no matter what country we were in. She had encouraged me to think about the bright future and had emphasized how lucky I was that I would still be living with family in America. Aunt Mary, she said, was a kind and generous woman.

"Keep watching out for your little brother," she said, as she had admonished countless times before.

Gradually, excitement overtook melancholy. Mother was busier than ever, going to Munich often to see her lawyer and to visit the consulate about our visas. Without Tante to confide in, she talked to me on a more adult level. She told me that the divorce was final, that August would not live with us again. He could stay with relatives or with his son Ernst. I still believed that August was my father; I had no reason to think otherwise; I was not to learn the truth for several more years. But I felt no warmth for him, no sadness. I felt relief and, with it, pride that Mother trusted me with these personal matters. I was growing up.

Mother had high hopes that this would be our last year of waiting, although she knew of no definite departure date yet. By 1950, she said, a place in the quota would open up; it was time. *Quota* was a Latin word. I understood that it meant a certain number -- how many Germans were allowed to enter the United States per year. What that number was, and who determined which Germans were chosen out of all the thousands waiting, I had no idea.

Letters arrived from Aunt Mary, with instructions: "Bring winter clothing; Chicago is very cold. Sell the sewing machine; we have good ones here."

Aunt Mary also relayed greetings from Gus, their younger brother, who had left Germany in the twenties and now lived in New Jersey. Mother's relationship with him was not as close as that with her sister. It was Mary who had stayed in touch and passed on the family news. Gus planned to meet us when we got off the ship, Aunt Mary wrote; he was excited and looking forward to our arrival.

Nineteen-fifty. Winter turned into spring. Mother knitted woolen hats for future winters in Chicago. Before selling the sewing machine, she made herself a dress, patterned after Christian Dior's New Look- - a fitted bodice, a low neckline, and a full skirt that fell to mid-calf. The material was cotton, black with large white polka dots. Mother said it hadn't been easy to get enough cloth; her cousin had leaned on some of his business connections.

"Dior...," Mother said dreamily. "Paris. When I was young, I loved going to Paris. I wonder if I will ever see it again."

Mother was forty-eight years old; she looked as young and chic as a fashion model. Was this bold dress responsible for what happened next?

My heart almost stopped when Mother said, one day, "Dr. L. has asked to marry me."

Dr. L. was her divorce attorney. In Germany, judges and lawyers are addressed by their academic title. If I had not been struck dumb by that revelation, I would have screamed, "No, no, no!"

Suppose she said yes! We would never see America. It was a terrible thought. It could not happen! From what I knew of Dr. L., he had a respected profession, a splendid income, and no need whatsoever to emigrate. Before I could collect myself, Mother continued, a twinkle in her eye.

"I said no," she smiled. "He is an old bachelor, not used to children, and he lives with his mother. I couldn't live like that -- I could not do that to you and Roland -- we would have no freedom."

Mother had just regained her independence after twelve difficult years. She was not about to trade it for a comfortable but restrictive lifestyle. She was ready for the New World.

It was not inspired by Dior, but I got a new dress too. This dress was special, for a special occasion, Mother explained. I was to wear it when I sat for my portrait. When we thought about Dachau in the future, Mother said, we would remember the artists who had always been her friends. Hadn't I first seen the light in the home of a painter? Now another one would produce a memento for our departure. Mother had made a deal with one of the town's most famous painters, the Swiss-born Henry Niestlé.

Mother had chosen the fabric for my dress -- lightweight white cotton sprigged with small blue flowers, which she said were "summery" and would bring out the color of my eyes. She was not sewing the dress herself. It would be made by the young women in the Catholic Home for Unwed Mothers, who were required to earn money for their keep. They specialized in fancy embroidery, Mother said, including smocking -- rows of tiny pleats gathered and stitched together in a pattern. I was more than a little daunted by all this attention. Mother was a wonderful seamstress; I would have been happy to wear anything she created; smocking sounded like a lot of fuss.

When we went to the Home for a fitting, I noticed that some of the young women were not much older than I was. They moved about quietly in silent rooms. I thought perhaps the babies were napping and kept my voice low. On the way home, Mother said that there had been no need to whisper.

"But the babies…," I said. Mother took my hand. No babies lived in the Home, she explained. They were all at the orphanage, waiting to be adopted.

The dress was lovely, more luxurious than any garment I had ever owned. Its square neckline and shirred bodice were feminine and flattering. The artist smiled approvingly when we arrived for the first sitting. Mr. Niestlé, a tall, white-haired gentleman, put me at ease by saying I wouldn't have to sit for hours on end. He would take photographs and work from them, with only a few short visits to get the colors right. He sat me in a chair and gave me a long-stemmed, pale pink rose to hold. He positioned my left forearm and hand, so they lay gracefully in my lap. He stepped away from me and focused the camera.

"Don't look straight at me," he directed. "Look to my right, up at the wall behind me. Think about something pleasant. Think of America."

I tried. I had no mental picture of America. The gaze in the finished portrait was clear and open, waiting.

Henry Niestlé had numerous commissions. The oil painting was not finished until we had been in Chicago for several months. It was eventually shipped to us, framed. How in the world had Mother paid for all of this? I did not think to ask. I do not know. It may have been a gift; I would not be surprised.

We waited to hear from the consulate. And waited. And then, all of a sudden, everything happened in a rush. It was fall. We did not have a telephone in the house, but Mother's cousin, the businessman, did. The message came while Mother was working in the office. Our documents were ready-- passports, visas, a note confirming a date in November when the ship, the SS *Washington,* was to sail from Hamburg. A cabin had been booked. Aunt Mary had advanced the money for our passage.

Mother may have informed August, and perhaps she said goodbye. Roland and I did not. There were only weeks to get ready. This was no problem because we had little to pack, and little to sell. Our furniture had been left in Saarburg; the house we lived in was rented furnished. We did not own a car.

Mother traded the second-hand bicycle she and I had shared for two suitcases, also second-hand. We packed summer and winter clothing, Mother's photo albums, and books she could not part with, including some by Ludwig Thoma, one of Dachau's renowned writers. I was allowed to add my favorites as well -- a handbook for plant identification, and a children's book Roland and I both loved. It was *Doktor Kleinermacher's Fantastic Adventures.* Dr. Kleinermacher is a scientist who has invented a magic potion that shrinks him to the size of an ant. In his miniature form, he explores ponds and streams in a tiny submarine, meeting microscopic life forms that appear to him as giant monsters.

Mother insisted on packing the hot-water bottle. She did not know yet that Aunt Mary's house had central heating.

In Karlsruhe the previous year, Mother had visited friends who were jewelry designers, and she had provided herself with gifts to bring to Aunt Mary and her husband. Appropriately, they were enameled, gold-plated cigarette cases. She had also bought, or traded for, several music boxes in the shape of birdcages, the size of mantel clocks. A feathered, mechanical bird sat on a perch in the cage and chirped when wound up. I hoped one of these lovely treasures was for us to keep. Mother warned me not to count on it; they were trading goods. We were sure to need some money on the ship--who knew what gratuities would be expected? We had little cash and no American dollars. To comfort me, Mother said she would definitely hold back one of the cages for Aunt Mary -- we could admire it every day in her house because we would be living there.

On November 11, 1950, I celebrated my fourteenth birthday. That entire month is a blur in my memory; I can't recall if our departure was before or after my birthday. I do remember taking the train from Dachau to Munich, and from Munich to Hamburg, where I think we stayed overnight; and then I remember walking through a cold, misty morning to the harbor and the ship. And soon we sailed, bound for America, our new life. Our new home.

CHAPTER 11

America!

T he SS *Washington,* built as a transatlantic luxury liner, had served as a troop transport during World War II; as of 1946, she was a passenger ship again. Our voyage was a new experience for all three of us, and it remained the only ocean crossing we would make by ship. Future transatlantic trips would be made by plane.

The ship carried more than a thousand passengers, most of them emigrants. That was more people than my brother and I had ever seen in one place, and the ship was larger and busier than any building we knew. By the second day, the view from the deck was all water-- greenish-grey waves and swells with frothy white crests, under a sky that was a darker grey. A faint blue line marked the horizon. I knew the powerful engines were moving us forward, but I was not prepared for all the other motions--up, down, sideways -- as the vessel pitched and rolled in the choppy sea. I had enjoyed supper on our first evening on board, and breakfast the next morning. I was impressed by the huge dining room, the white-jacketed stewards, the table settings and service, the foods I didn't recognize. Hesitantly using my school English, I had asked the name of the giant fruit (if it was fruit) on my appetizer plate. "Grapefruit," I was told. I said, "Thank you," but the answer did not help much. "Fruit" made sense; "grape" did not. I stored the new English vocabulary word in my mental dictionary.

Walking around the deck now, on this frigid November morning, my stomach began to feel uncomfortable. The queasiness got worse by the minute. I asked Mother and Roland to come back to the cabin with me so I could run into the bathroom. We got there just in time, using ropes strung in the corridors to help us stay upright as the ship lurched and tossed. Mother said it was only a little bit of seasickness and would pass; it wasn't a real illness like the measles. The cabin was warm but stuffy, and after I vomited, we went back up. Mother said fresh air was the cure. Breathing in the sharp, salty smell did help -- but its invigorating effect lasted for only a short time.

Unfortunately, this "bit of seasickness" haunted me for the entire voyage. I was miserable. Luckily, Mother and Roland fared better and ate their meals while I hung over the rail, feeding the fishes. Mother made friends with a group of merry Bavarians -- half a dozen adventuresome young men and women striking out to seek their fortunes in the New World. Prevention and cure for nausea was beer, they claimed. They began drinking at lunch and kept refilling their beakers for hours afterward while they strolled around the deck.

"Have a sip. It'll settle your stomach, poor little thing," they offered when they came by. Mother did not forbid it. She was willing to try anything that might help. Sadly, the sure-fire Bavarian miracle did not cure me. I took walks with the jolly band but frequently had to be escorted back to the cabin so I would not disgrace myself in public. It was a no-win situation. The warmth indoors was a relief from the cold of the deck, but nausea increased. Fresh air was definitely better, but it was also freezing. The North Atlantic in winter is a hostile environment. I wanted to die.

After seven days -- including a hurricane-force storm on the last night of the voyage -- we finally sailed into New York Harbor. Passengers crowded onto the upper deck to look at the Statue of Liberty and cheered when the Lady came into view. There she stood, rock-solid on a massive stone pedestal! More than anything in the world just then, I wanted a piece of firm ground under my own feet. Later, when I learned the poem inscribed at the base of the statue, I added "wretched" and "tempest-tossed" to my vocabulary list. I knew exactly what they meant.

Mother's younger brother, Gus, met us when we left the *Washington*, helped with the luggage, and drove us to his home in Hoboken, New Jersey. I missed all the joy of the reunion; I missed dinner and most of the train trip to Chicago. I was dazed, weak-kneed, and asleep within minutes of setting foot on American soil. When we reached Chicago the next day and were greeted by Aunt Mary and her husband, I had revived enough to hear Mother say, "I was afraid I would arrive with only one living child. Thank God she's better now."

Aunt Mary and Uncle Anton welcomed us warmly. Aunt Mary looked like Mother, but she was taller and plumper. Her husband was tall and wiry and wore glasses. He spoke in a calm voice. Both were immigrants who had worked hard to realize their own American dream. They had served as janitors in the house they now owned, saving their wages to pay off the mortgage. In addition to the house, which was in a tidy, middle-class neighborhood on the North Side, they owned a small factory that made components for major manufacturers such as Bell and Howell, makers of camera equipment and office machines.

They assured us we could stay with them until we learned English and became financially independent. We were taken to two comfortable bedrooms on the second floor. One of them had belonged to their son, who had married the year before. He and his wife now lived in an apartment nearby. There was a bathroom just for us. Roland and I had never seen a bathtub with a shower in it. Hot water ran instantly! At the Moosschwaige, we had heated bathwater on the kitchen stove and poured it into a metal washtub, where it stayed scalding hot for the first few minutes and went cold in the next few. Here you could mix water to the desired temperature -- what luxury!

We spent a few days settling in and catching up on family news. My aunt and uncle spoke German with each other and with us, but Roland and I were instructed to say "Aunt" and "Uncle." It was important to get used to English.

Aunt Mary invited some American neighbors to meet us. She served an ample meal as we sat at her beautifully appointed dining room table. The main course featured large portions of meat called steak. In Germany, each adult helping would have kept us for a week. Chicago was famous for beef, we were told. It had huge stockyards that supplied meat to the rest of the country.

I did my best to answer questions in English, but I was stumped when one of the guests asked if I was a "southpaw." I stared, bewildered.

"Left-handed," the visitor added, not helping me much.

"No," I replied, holding up my right hand, "This hand."

Another guest understood the situation and explained it. I was eating as I had been taught in Germany -- holding the fork in the left hand and the knife in the right, using both without putting them down. In America, this guest said, we ate differently. He demonstrated and I did my best to follow: hold fork in right hand, put down the fork, switch it to the left hand, pick up the knife in the right hand, cut meat, put knife on edge of plate... It seemed clumsy, but I practiced until I got it. Roland, who had trouble telling his left hand from his right, watched, completely baffled. Mother took pity on him and cut up his meat.

Uncle Anton went to his factory, in the industrial section of town, every day. Aunt Mary took us for walks to familiarize us with the neighborhood. Her house was three stories high, built of red brick. It looked very similar to all the neighboring homes on Magnolia Avenue, as the street was called. Aunt Mary said magnolia was a flowering tree that grew in the American South. I asked if the trees along the curbs were magnolias, but I was told they were not; Chicago winters were too harsh. Unlike the streets I knew in Dachau and Ettlingen, this avenue ran very straight, as did the others that met it at exact right angles a short distance away. I learned that each square enclosed by four streets was called a block.

Each block we walked along was lined with sidewalks and, at intervals, tall poles bearing lamps at their tops. When we returned from our walk in the early winter dusk, all the lights were shining brightly. Years ago, Mother had said peacetime meant lighted streets. Now she said how easy it would be to find our way home. "And it's safe," Aunt Mary added, "The children will be fine, going to school."

Another day, Aunt Mary showed us the nearest main street, lined with a variety of shops. Some, like the bakery and the butcher, were similar to stores I was accustomed to, only larger. Other establishments were new to me. Aunt Mary pointed out a Jewish delicatessen, mentioning that the neighborhood had many Jewish residents. The most puzzling business was a storefront that advertised Tailoring and Dry Cleaning. I knew the definitions of "tailor" and "dry," but how could you clean clothing without the use of water and soap?

As we walked, Aunt Mary showed us several streets that led to Lake Michigan. In the summer, she said, we could swim there at one of the many public beaches. But now it was winter, and bitter cold, so Aunt Mary took us to a grocery store which she said was called a supermarket. When we entered the brightly lit, enormous space, I decided it was not a store but fairyland-- bigger and better than the witch's gingerbread house in the story. The wide aisles full of colorful boxes on tall shelves, the refrigerated cases of meats, chickens all cleaned and plucked, the stacks of canned goods, the bins of out-of-season fruits -- all that abundance! It made the three of us stop and stare. Aunt Mary smiled patiently and said to Mother, "I guess you don't have so much in Germany, even five years later? Well, now that we're here, we might as well do the shopping."

"But how?" Mother wondered. In all this vast hall, she had not yet seen a clerk to wait on us.

Aunt Mary explained that it was self-service and walked us over to get a basket on wheels. She headed for the far aisle, towards the enticing pyramids of oranges and apples. I remembered the dark brown banana that had made its way to us from the jungle, but I felt too shy to ask if by any chance....

We were indeed in a magic land because, as if she had read my thoughts, Aunt Mary stopped in front of a heap of greenish-yellow fruit and said, "Here, put a bunch of bananas in the cart; they're good for breakfast."

The things she pointed to were shaped like the banana in my memory, but they were much longer and thicker, and the skins were not the same color. They were attached to each other in clumps. "Banana?" I asked.

"Yes, bananas," Aunt Mary answered. "Get five or six, but don't take those spotted ones; they're overripe, not good." I did as she instructed. Later I found that I had a different opinion about very ripe bananas. Of course, I never argued with Aunt Mary. But to me, squishy, brown bananas would always taste sweeter. I prefer them, to this day.

Although our relatives were kind and helpful, they made it clear that we were not "on vacation," as they put it. We were expected to acquire skills, and to become contributing members of the household. The children would be enrolled in school as soon as possible. There was work Mother could be trained for at the factory. She would be taught to operate a drill press and other machinery. Roland and I could use our time after school to do piecework -- assembling small components that fit into larger machines. Mother agreed without question. She was ready to start any time, she said. Heaven forbid we should become a burden.

In private, Mother explained to me that in Germany, none of us would ever have worked in a factory. In America, we were "greenhorns" and we would take what was offered. We must keep our eyes on the future and have *Guten Mut. Mut* means courage. Uncle Anton was giving us a fair deal, Mother said. He would pay her, albeit at a reduced salary, in order to compensate for our room and board. If we were very careful about personal expenses, she could save most of the money. In a year or so, it would be enough for an apartment of our own. My job, Mother emphasized, was to keep on with my schooling, and to qualify for a university. People with higher education, professionals with a degree, would rise far above greenhorn status.

As for Roland, Mother asked me to be especially watchful-- to make sure he learned proper English so that he could catch up with the subjects being taught in our new school. In time, he too should go to university. In the meantime, if Uncle Anton brought us work to do at home, that was an added bonus. Piecework meant you got paid for each item you finished instead of earning an hourly wage. Learn to do the task quickly -- but correctly -- and earn more money.

Mother put her arms around me and asked if I missed home--that is, Dachau or Germany. The question was unexpected and so it startled me into feeling vaguely guilty. Should I be homesick? I wasn't, in the least. I was excited and full of new impressions, and I looked forward to school and I had always watched over Roland; that was second nature. Most of all, I was proud that Mother was speaking to me as if I were a grown up. "I have plenty of *Mut,*" I said.

And then I cried anyway because I had thought of Tante and wished she were here.

We had arrived in November. After the Christmas and New Year's holidays, Roland and I started to attend the Stephen Hayt Grammar School, an easy walk from Aunt Mary's house. It was the middle of the academic year. I was old enough for high school, but it was decided that I should finish eighth grade and enter high school as a freshman in the fall. Roland, aged eight, was enrolled in the third grade.

The school was a spacious building of pale-yellow brick, with tall windows and a wide flight of steps leading up to the front door. At the side was a fenced playground that adjoined the sports field at the back.

Inside, the halls and classrooms were comfortably warm. Mother had been right again-- in this school you could take off your coat and gloves. Boys and girls sat together, each grade in a home room. Desks were assigned by last name, in alphabetical order.

At the start of each day, we stood up and recited the pledge of allegiance and sang the national anthem. The flag had thirteen stripes and forty-eight stars. After the morning ceremony, there was less formality in the classroom. Students were not required to stand up when called on by the teacher. A wrong answer did not result in corporal punishment; unlike our Nazi instructors, American teachers did not hit children.

Roland went willingly to school and sat quietly in class, but he was struggling. He had barely learned to read in German; now he was expected to read in a language he couldn't speak. No tutoring was offered; there were no instructors for English as a second language. Thanks to the English lessons at the *Luisenschule*, I fared better as far as academics were concerned, but not socially. I turned in my homework, written in ink, on clean sheets of lined notebook paper. It was always a fair copy, as I had been taught, without blotches or scratchings out. One day my teacher held a page up for the class to see, side by side with a smudgy-penciled piece of paper a classmate had submitted.

"Here's a girl from a foreign country..." the teacher began, and she went on to praise my efforts. I became a pariah on the spot. I added "teacher's pet" to my vocabulary list and became invisible to my classmates. The teacher had cast a hex on me; I'm sure she had not meant to. Good thing I had a brother. He had always been my best friend.

When we came home to Aunt Mary's after school, she gave us glasses of cold milk from the icebox. Mother would have warmed the milk because she believed that cold substances injured children's stomachs, but we happily drank what we were offered and suffered no ill effects. We did our homework. I helped Roland with English words he couldn't pronounce. He was quick at math, but I had to translate the word problems. We both learned to use dots, not commas, as decimal points. When our schoolwork was completed, we assembled parts for Uncle Anton's factory.

One of our first tasks was to put together small rollers that advanced paper checks through a printing machine. We found it was actually fun to stack up the pieces of felt and metal and to secure them with posts, top and bottom plates, screws, and washers. We challenged each other to get everything in the correct order, each trying to work faster than the other. We were paid twenty-five cents per piece. Because of our competition, we became very productive. If we were in violation of child labor laws, we didn't know it and would not have cared; we loved earning American dollars, paid to us in cash.

Another American novelty we enjoyed was television. We were allowed to watch *The Lone Ranger* and were thrilled to learn that Tonto, the Lone Ranger's faithful companion, was a real Native American named Jay Silverheels. *Captain Video* was another favorite. For us, watching these shows was an entertaining way to learn English; the adults agreed. The news broadcasts, however, were troubling.

It was 1951. American soldiers and United Nations troops were fighting in Korea. The North of the country, aided by China, had invaded the South. Seoul, the capital of South Korea, had changed hands several times.

"More war," Mother sighed. "Will there never be an end to it?"

Aunt Mary and Uncle Anton admired General Douglas MacArthur and thought President Truman had been wrong to relieve him of his command. He would have "straightened out those Commies," Uncle said. I barely knew where Korea was and did not understand the policy dispute. In April, the general visited Chicago and was hailed as a hero by millions of citizens. Uncle Anton took Roland and me to a spot on the long, winding parade route where we could join the excited crowd that cheered and waved at the passing motorcade. Uncle said we should remember the day we got a look at a truly great American.

In June, I graduated from the eighth grade at Hayt Grammar School. The ceremony required a white dress. I thought about the sad young mothers who had worked so hard on my other special outfit. Mother asked Aunt Mary how to buy fabric and a pattern. Aunt Mary said no, it was easier to buy a dress that was right for the occasion and would match what the other girls were wearing. And so, I got my first store-bought dress, a full-skirted, white cotton creation with lace trim and short, puffed sleeves. I was happy. I wanted to look like an American girl.

I looked forward to summer when we would swim in Lake Michigan, and to fall when I would enter high school.

As spring turned into summer, Aunt Mary told me she would find me babysitting jobs in the neighborhood; I could earn extra money. For Roland, whose limited English had not enabled him to make friends at school, Aunt Mary had an inspired idea: The Boy Scouts. She knew that the nearby Lutheran church sponsored youth activities, including scout troops, and offered to introduce Roland. Was that like the Hitler Jugend, Mother asked, worried. Aunt Mary reassured her that American scouts were not political even though they wore uniforms. The scouts learned crafts and took nature hikes; Roland would be with American boys his own age and would pick up English rapidly. "In a jiffy," she said in English. I added this amusing phrase to my vocabulary list.

Mother agreed. Roland loved his new activity. He adored the troop leader, a friendly, clean-cut young man who became the caring older brother Roland had never had. Through the years, Roland earned all the merit badges up through Eagle Scout. He later said the Boy Scouts had saved his life.

CHAPTER 12

The Dream: Education

For as long as I could remember, my mother had shared with me her belief that education was as indispensable to life as bread. Schooling was a necessity, not an optional frill. Sacrifices might be necessary, Mother said. For instance, going to university meant spending years without earning money. This in turn might be hard on the family budget. But, she emphasized, if we had to make such choices in the coming years, we would face them with a courageous spirit. In America even an immigrant could attain higher education by keeping his or her eyes firmly fixed on the goal and by persevering. The goal was not to merely survive. The goal was to live, fully and creatively. My mother's idealism and my love for her inspired me to believe we were on the right path. America was the land of opportunity.

The public schools I attended in Chicago reflected the ethnic and economic composition of the neighborhoods surrounding them. School desegregation was still more than a decade in the future. I don't remember any African-American students at Hayt Grammar School or Senn High School. There may have been a few, but I did not happen to meet them. The Edgewater neighborhood where we lived with our relatives was home to comfortably middle-class, white families. Some were European immigrants -- German, Swedish, Norwegian. There was a sizable Jewish population as well. The local schools ranked high in academic achievement and provided cultural enrichments like courses in art and music, along with sports and physical education.

Aunt Mary assured Mother that her own son had done well in the local schools and that Roland and I would be in good hands. I looked forward to entering high school and spent the summer of 1951 in a state of high anticipation.

Mother went to work every day; I had a number of part-time jobs. I worked as a mother's helper and did babysitting, shopping, and other errands for neighbors. I cleaned the apartment of a lady who was allergic to house dust. When Uncle's factory needed an extra hand, I went with Mother and sat on an assembly line, soldering wires onto terminals. The older, experienced employees were kind enough to show me the proper technique and made sure I didn't burn my fingers too often.

Still, there was plenty of time for all of us to enjoy our first summer in the United States. Only a few blocks from Aunt Mary's house, Lake Michigan, clean and unpolluted at the time, offered public beaches at the ends of many east-west streets. Roland and I were allowed to go swimming by ourselves; on weekends, Mother accompanied us, frequently reminding us not to stay in the frigid water too long. She would look at the American teenagers rubbing baby oil on their bodies and lying flat on their towels to cultivate a perfect tan.

"Don't do that," she commanded. "Your skin will get burnt and ugly! Put a shirt on and drape a towel over your head!" Her good advice came long before sunblock was universally recommended. Fortunately, I listened and saved my skin. I was not rebellious -- yet.

Roland and I explored the city, using some of our piecework earnings to buy tickets for the elevated trains that went downtown, to the Loop, where the cars made a dizzying, rattling circle at rooftop height, stopping at streets named after American presidents: Washington, Adams, Jefferson. We admired the giant department stores-- Marshall Field's and Carson Pirie Scott -- with their elaborate window displays. We did not venture inside but we felt comfortable roaming about Woolworth's, where an astonishing number of items could be purchased for five or ten cents.

Chicago, with its easily navigated grid layout and unmistakable landmarks like Lake Michigan at the eastern edge of the city, was not confusing for us, despite its size. We had memorized our home address and telephone number. Aunt Mary had impressed on us the need to have a dime always in our pockets in case we got lost and had to call for rescue. Like a good Boy Scout, Roland now owned a compass. We looked at it, but we did not need it to find our way.

The Boy Scout troop went on excursions to various forest preserves on the outskirts of the city. My brother's anxiety lifted as he made more friends and learned to joke around with them in English.

Nicholas Senn High School, which I entered in September, was larger and grander than the *Luisenschule*. It was within walking distance of Aunt Mary's house. I did not have to get up at six in the morning in order to take a crowded, noisy train.

The school building was impressive. I marveled at the tall Corinthian columns at the entrance, at the long hallways lined with metal lockers, and at the bustle of students going from class to class in the ten minutes between lessons. It took me several days to find my way around the spacious building in order to arrive before the bell rang for each class. I soon found that it did not help to ask for directions, because the older students gleefully sent me on wild goose chases. I thought it was because they noticed my accented English and wanted to torture the hapless immigrant, but I was wrong. They did this to all the freshmen. It was the custom; I felt better when I understood that.

I found that my German high school had prepared me well. I was up to grade level--even a little beyond -- in math. In English, I still lacked vocabulary, but my spelling and grammar were good. I wanted to keep up my German, so I took that as an elective. Latin was not a requirement, but it was available. When I learned that I could study it in summer school, I signed up. My teachers approved my choices. My classmates were scornful. Why would I willingly go to school in summer? That was for dummies who had failed in the regular term!

My favorite courses were in social studies. I loved American history and a course called civics, which explained the workings of the democratic system of government. The civics teacher encouraged us to read a daily newspaper and to discuss current events. I chose to read the *Chicago Tribune* because Aunt Mary and Uncle Anton subscribed to it. Until an armistice was signed in Korea in 1953, I followed the war news, with its grim photos of injured American soldiers in muddy uniforms being loaded into helicopters en route to the nearest field hospital.

I read the syndicated columns of the renowned Walter Lippmann, whose international reporting later won him a Pulitzer Prize. Each of his essays was a lesson in history and philosophy. His explanation of the Cold War-- a phrase he coined -- put in perspective events I had lived through but had been too young to analyze and understand.

Once a semester, a field trip to the *Chicago Tribune* was offered as part of the civics class. The *Tribune* building downtown housed the complete operation, from newsroom to printing presses. When we went on the tour, I was entranced from start to finish. I wished I could enter this magical universe -- the purposeful chaos of the newsroom, where copyboys tore yellow sheets of Western Union dispatches off the teletype machines and ran to deliver them to the appropriate destination -- city or international desk, or the features section. I wished I could sit among the reporters who were typing furiously, sometimes cradling black telephone receivers between ear and shoulder. I admired the linotype machines that were fed with molten metal and spat out perfect "slugs" of type exactly one column wide; the composing room where all these pieces of type were dropped into forms, supplied with headlines in larger type, and locked into wooden frames the size of one newspaper page. Best of all was the thunderous roar of the presses when the foreman yelled, "Start!"

Gigantic sheets of paper, rivers of words in black type that smelled of pungent ink, folding machines, stacks of newspapers on dollies being hustled out to waiting delivery trucks -- it was all stunningly impressive. It was an enchanted world and I determined that my future would be knitted into it. As I stood on the observation platform at the *Chicago Tribune,* a plan began to form in my mind. If I couldn't start as a reporter, I would learn to operate a linotype machine.

Back in day-to-day reality, I became acquainted with my classmates. It was the first time in my life that I had met anyone Jewish. At Senn, I met no recent immigrants my age, but many of the students had parents or more distant ancestors who had fled persecution in Europe. My classmates were suspicious of my accent, and, when they asked if I was Jewish and I answered no, they became distant and ended the conversation. Only a few took the trouble to listen to my halting protestations that I was not a Nazi, that my mother had never been a Nazi, that we were immigrants who wished to become American citizens. One girl invited me to her home after school and showed me the mezuzah on her front door, explaining that it held a piece of sacred text.

One boy invited me to go to a movie. I did not tell him it was my first movie as well as my first date -- in America or anywhere; I did not want to reveal what a total greenhorn I was. We went to what looked like the palace of Cinderella's prince. It was furnished with acres of crimson plush and adorned with as much gold as one of Munich's baroque churches. The whole place smelled of warm popcorn. My young man bought some, offering me yet another novelty. After the film -- I have no memory of its title or actors -- we ate pizza and drank Cokes. I knew this was what dating etiquette required; I had overheard many lunchroom discussions of the subject.

My date was polite and pleasant. When he had walked me to Aunt Mary's front door, he took my hand and said, "You are very nice, and I like you. But we can't ever get serious about each other. My parents expect me to go out with Jewish girls and marry within my faith. I want to do that too, so we better not have any more dates. You won't take it personally, will you?"

It was such an honest speech that I could not feel hurt, and I told him so. I could not put it into words, but I had not really expected him to ask me out again. "Getting serious" had an ominous sound; I was relieved that it was out of the question. For me, the joy of the evening had been the new experience -- going to a movie, eating popcorn and pizza, drinking Coke -- doing exactly what the American girls did on a Saturday night.

"It was perfect," I said. "Everything was perfect. Thank you for a lovely evening." This was the proper phrase to say. I congratulated myself on having memorized it.

As I began to see that I was keeping up with the classwork despite my still imperfect English, I relaxed and became more comfortable socially. I gradually made friends with two girls in my homeroom. One, Harriet, was the daughter of Swedish immigrants. She was not particularly pretty, was a serious student, played the cello in the school orchestra, and did not go out every Saturday night. The other, Lois, had American parents and grandparents and had very blue eyes and shiny, straight, shoulder-length blonde hair. I heard the words "cute" and "fun" applied to her by both boys and girls. But Lois made it clear that she was not to be considered "easy," which I learned meant promiscuous. She was a devoted churchgoer and sang in the choir. She urged me to join her. It was a good way to meet other young people, she said. As she described the church, I realized it was the same one that hosted Roland's Boy Scout meetings. Lois said all the better -- how nice that I already knew how to get there. She was only surprised, she said, that she hadn't seen me and my family on Sundays. I mumbled something about Mother being tired from working all week. I liked to sing so I agreed to try out for the choir. If I was admitted, that meant singing for Sunday services.

Tante would have been pleased, but I had mixed feelings about church, due to my encounter with the lecherous priest. I was also aware of my own growing skepticism about God. I carefully kept quiet about all of this and privately hoped the sermons would not last too long.

Harriet suggested I join the school chorus, which often performed with the orchestra. She sounded happy about the prospect that we would be in rehearsals and concerts together. Harriet's invitation was much more enticing than Lois's. But I could not have refused either one; they were my first real girlfriends. They were offering to share their favorite activities with me. They were not mean like perfidious Dorothea in Dachau.

I joined both the church choir and the school chorus. I have a good memory for melody and learned to follow the conductor and to sing in tune. I even learned to read music at an elementary level. But most of all, I enjoyed having friends.

CHAPTER 13

The Dream: Independence

I attended Senn High School for three and a half years. Thanks to credits I earned by taking extra courses in summer school and at the Art Institute of Chicago, I was able to graduate one semester early, in January 1955.

Those years were busy ones for me and the family. In school, I took every opportunity to improve in academic subjects as well as in practical skills like typing and stenography. The art classes were a happy discovery. They were suggested by the art teacher, who taught weekly lessons in drawing, watercolor, oil painting, linoleum cuts, and wood sculpture. This teacher mentioned a figure-drawing class that was available at the Art Institute. It was offered free to qualified high school students. A recommendation was needed. Our teacher stressed that this offer was to be taken seriously. If she recommended one of us, that student was expected to attend the sessions consistently and to turn out the best work possible. The teacher did not want to be embarrassed by a no-show. My hand went up immediately.

"See me after class," the teacher said. When we had our conference at the end of the hour, the teacher asked if I was considering a career in art.

"No," I said, "I am hoping to study journalism, but I love to draw. And -- I think the Art Institute is wonderful. Free lessons!"

The teacher smiled and gave me a slip of paper with the date of the first lesson. I was surprised that I was the only one in class who wanted to go.

I am happy to say that I did not disappoint my teacher; I went to each and every class at the Art Institute, that year and the next. And in her class at Senn, I improved so much that I won a place in a regional scholastic competition, for a balsa wood sculpture of an owl.

The certificate was a wonderful confidence booster but did not change my mind about my ultimate career; I had my heart set on writing and journalism.

As my English language skills got better, I felt more at ease in social situations. I went out on occasional dates -- to the movies, to the zoo, or to the lakeshore. Mother scrutinized my dates carefully. Each boy was required to come into the living room for a polite interrogation before we were allowed out the door together. Boys who did not care for this did not ask me out a second time, but I accepted that. Mother said not to worry; there were plenty of young men in the world; cowards who couldn't answer a few simple questions were not worth my while.

The school-sponsored a number of student clubs. When some classmates mentioned bowling, I was intrigued but hesitant.

"I don't know how to bowl. Do you think I could go anyway?" I asked.

"Sure," several kids said. "You'll learn how. It's fun. Anybody can do it."

I was good at gymnastics, but I did not know anything about American sports. In Germany, the boys played soccer, but the girls had no teams. Here, when we played softball in physical education class, no one -- not the teacher, not the team captain nor any of the other students -- explained the rules to me. I was the last girl picked for a team and was sent to the furthest outfield, where I stood bewildered and terrified, fervently hoping the ball would not come my way. When it did, occasionally, I panicked and threw it to the nearest person, whether she was on my team or not. I got yelled at, but no one told me how to play correctly.

Thankfully, the bowling club was friendlier. I went with a few girls I already knew, and we were joined by some boys. At the bowling alley, the experienced kids showed me how to rent shoes and how to pick a ball of the right weight. I was put on a team; rules were explained. I was allowed practice time, during which I rolled a great number of balls down the gutter but eventually succeeded in knocking over a few pins. I liked this game. I saw that it could be learned far more easily than baseball. Teammates encouraged each other instead of yelling incomprehensible instructions. I decided to go bowling with the club as often as possible.

In time I became quite competent. There were enough students in the club to form several teams of four or five players each. We competed against each other, writing down detailed scores. When I saw all the cards and small pieces of scratch paper we collected to keep track of team scores and future matches, I had an idea.

"Should we have a newsletter?" I asked. "Would it help? We could announce the meeting schedules and list the teams."

My teammates liked this proposal. "Good idea," they said. "But you better ask the advisor."

The faculty advisor did not come to the alley, but he was kept abreast of our doings. When I made an appointment and went to see him, he approved my plan and offered to show me how to work the mimeograph machine. I was taking a class in touch typing and now I could use my newly acquired skills to write the copy. I wanted the page to look like a newspaper, so I painstakingly arranged the text into two columns, using different margin settings on the machine. I drew a few bowling pins and a ball to serve as a logo. When I had everything ready, the advisor showed me how to type on the green mimeograph stencils -- a tricky business because mistakes were extremely hard to correct. Fixing a wrong letter involved painting on a smelly, sticky correction fluid that had to dry so as not to gum up the typewriter. Sometimes it would have been easier to simply start over, but I was afraid to waste materials. I remembered my early school days with pen and ink, and my efforts not to mess up the precious writing paper.

When a stencil was finally cut, complete with typed copy, ruled lines between the columns, and my drawing, I learned to put it onto the drum of the mimeograph machine and cranked out copies. Though it took many after-school hours, the result was worth it to me. I was proud of my work. It wasn't the *Tribune,* but it was a publication-- in blue ink -- with news in it.

Mother worried about Roland being alone after school when I spent time at extracurricular activities, but I was able to assure her that Roland was safe. He had found a hobby he loved -- making model airplanes from kits. With his natural dexterity, he learned how to assemble the delicate balsa wood parts according to the plans. He understood how to connect the rubberband-driven propellers and adjust the wings for the best aerodynamic performance. When he occasionally made a mistake, he improvised and called the result a hot rod.

While my brother and I expanded our horizons with new friends and activities, we also grew physically. Each of us added several inches to our height and gained weight in proportion.

Mother often told us how pleased she was to see us happy and in good health. At the same time, she felt she had been forced onto a dead-end road. Living with our relatives and working in the factory gave her no opportunity to improve her English or to find friends. She longed for a place of our own, and for a less restrictive, better-paying job. She did not speak of her feelings at the family dinner table, but in private she told me that things had to change--somehow--because she was getting depressed.

That was a new word, coming from Mother. I could not remember her saying it before, not in all the war or postwar years. She had always known what to do and had handled the most serious issues -- divorce, emigration, resettlement -- with cool decisiveness. I did not know what to say to her now. She must have seen my worry because her very next words brought back the mother I knew and loved.

"I have a plan," she said.

Mother explained that ever since we had arrived in Chicago, she had corresponded with Wolfgang, the young artist who had been at the Russian front. He had been one of the few survivors of the disaster at Stalingrad and he had managed to make his way back to his home in Munich after many months.

"His parents thought he was dead," my mother said. "It was a miracle; he walked for weeks on end and found almost nothing to eat, but he made it!"

Wolfgang was back in Munich with his parents, but he wanted to come to America. Mother said that he was now on the list for a visa, and waiting times were shorter now. Aunt Mary and Mother had discussed this and had agreed that they would be his sponsors; they would claim he was a cousin. Once Wolfgang was here, Mother went on, he would find a job and he could share an apartment with the three of us. We would make sure that it was close to Magnolia Avenue so that Roland and I would not have to change schools.

This was the mother who had *Mut*. My courage rose along with hers; I had no doubt things would work out. They did, but it took many months and two strokes of fortune, one bad, one good.

The bad luck was an accident Mother had at the factory. She was operating a drill press. The jig, a heavy metal block that held the workpiece--in this case, a small disc that was to be fitted with a central hole-- had not been locked down properly. It came loose and began to whirl around with the drill. As Mother, panic-stricken, reached up with her right hand to turn off the power switch, the out-of-control jig gashed her forearm. She was taken to the emergency room. The doctors found that although there was a lot of blood, it was a flesh wound. No bones or major arteries had been injured. She was sent home, with instructions not to use her right arm until the wound healed.

It never became clear who had been at fault. It was the foreman's job to see that the machines were set up properly. Had he been careless? Should Mother have double-checked the jig before turning on the power? Uncle Anton's insurance paid for Mother's medical treatment. Aunt Mary felt sorry for her sister; I was shocked that Uncle showed little sympathy.

"If you weren't sure about the jig, why didn't you call over the foreman?" he asked repeatedly. Mother did not try to argue the point. She was not an experienced factory hand; she had turned on the machine as she had been taught; it had always been all right before. By an unspoken family agreement, she never went back to the factory. To me, she said that as soon as she found a different job, even if it was in another factory, we would leave Uncle Anton's house, no matter how poor we were.

The wound on Mother's forearm healed over the next two months. It left an ugly red scar that would take years to become less visible. While Mother was recuperating, Aunt Mary consoled her, saying the accident had not been her fault. She promised that she and Anton would cooperate to find a better job for Mother-- a job that did not involve heavy machinery. In the meantime, Mother was to study her English phrasebook. Mother, of course, agreed readily. She knew that she was qualified to work in an office once she acquired more fluency in her new language. Roland and I were asked to speak English at home; we were happy to do it. It was beginning to feel natural to both of us. Mother liked the song "America the Beautiful" and wanted to learn it. The melody was no problem for her musical ear, but she worked hard to memorize the lyrics.

Uncle Anton kept his word. He knew other manufacturers in Chicago and found an opening in a small company that made phonograph needles. He recommended Mother and she was hired. She learned to take a bus to the plant, where her job was to operate a machine that cut the needles to size, readying them to be packaged for distribution and sale. The work was easy, Mother said. The operators sat at their machines, which were safe to use because the cutting tool was inside a housing; their fingers never had to touch it. Mother was able to use her hand to work the machine without straining her whole arm.

The company employed mostly women. Mother said they were a friendly, chatty bunch. Many were housewives whose children were old enough not to need a mother at home after school. The women enjoyed earning some extra money for themselves or for their children's education.

Once Mother became adept at running the machine, she worked so fast that her coworkers told her to slow down. "If the foreman sees you turning out so many pieces, he'll want all of us to speed up," they warned. "Take it easy-- study your English book for a while."

Mother laughed when she told this story at home. "Imagine that," she said. "This would never happen in a German factory, but they were serious. So, I'll follow their advice. America the beautiful!"

With this new job, Mother's spirits lifted and her ambition to take an apartment for us went into high gear. She wrote many letters to Wolfgang, urging him to haunt the consulate and get his visa with all possible speed. She enlisted Aunt Mary to ask around among the neighbors for an affordable rental. Aunt Mary supported her sister's drive for independence, but she cautioned Mother to consider the economics of such a move. Uncle Anton was agreeable as well. He may have been relieved that his immigrant relatives would soon cease to be his responsibility, but he did not say so openly. He did tell us that he was on the lookout for an office job for Mother; perhaps he could identify a company that needed a German-speaking employee. Whatever his motives were, he eventually proved to be a great help.

I caught the independence fever. I thought if I was lucky enough to get a room of my own, I would have one wall that was painted terracotta, with the other three covered in flowered wallpaper. I visualized earth tones and greens.

Good luck visited us in the person of a neighbor who had an apartment for rent; her house was only four blocks away. It was a second-floor apartment that her married children had lived in until their second child arrived, and the young family wanted more space. They had recently moved to a house of their own.

Aunt Mary and Mother worked out the arrangements. Fortunately, the neighbor lady had a kind heart and understood that our family -- a single mother with two children, all recent immigrants -- was not able to pay top price. Aunt Mary vouched for us.

"They deserve a helping hand," she said. They all work hard and are clean and responsible. The two kids go to school and get good grades. You can trust them not to make any trouble."

It made me happy to hear my aunt say this. She was not usually demonstrative or lavish with praise. I knew that my brother would be as happy as I was to live in a home of our own. I did not know what sort of trouble the adults feared, but whatever it was, we would not cause it.

We made the move to our new quarters just in time. Wolfgang's papers had come through and he wrote that he would be joining us before we had spent a month in the new apartment, which did indeed have enough space so that Roland and I each got a bedroom to ourselves for the first time in our lives. I was fifteen; Roland was ten. The rooms were small, but they seemed palatial to me.

Wolfgang, the young artist, arrived. He was a handsome, dark-haired man of thirty. Mother said I had met him back in Saarburg, but I could not remember. Wolfgang had already renamed himself Lincoln. That was his legal middle name, he explained. His grandfather had visited the United States in the 1890s and had been so impressed by what he learned of the legendary American president, the Great Emancipator, that he had insisted his own grandson bear that name. Our Lincoln now said his grandfather had done him a great favor; the name had helped him sail through his immigration interviews. Mother smiled through her tears.

"Now we'll do well -- together," she said, "Oh beautiful America!"

CHAPTER 14

Love Children

When we were sixteen and in our junior year at Senn High School, my friend Lois became pregnant. I could not believe it. Lois! Lois the pious churchgoer and choir singer! Lois, who had once cautioned me not to swing my hips when I walked. "You will give the boys ideas," she had said.

Lois, of all people! I stared at her when she told me the news. Her chubby body was thicker in the middle, but the bulge was not yet large enough to signal a pregnancy.

"Are you really sure?" I asked.

"Yes," Lois said, "I felt it move--yesterday."

Lois was starry-eyed with happiness. I was horrified.

Before I even asked Lois who the father was, I blurted out, "But that means you can't stay in school. You'll be expelled!" I knew this because there had been a recent rumor about a senior who had left suddenly. To me, being kicked out of school seemed a greater misfortune than bearing an illegitimate child. Lois did not share my dismay.

"It's OK," she said. "We are getting married. He has a job and our parents will give permission."

"But--"

Outrage had built up inside me to the point where I did not know which of my many protests, cautions, or questions I wanted to voice first.

"Who is he?" I finally asked. Lois and I had never double-dated. I had never seen her with any young man who looked like a serious boyfriend.

"Eddie. He's not in school here. He's nineteen; he works -- and it's a good, steady job," Lois said. "We're putting a down payment on a house," she added.

"But you'll never get to college! You're throwing away all your chances -- your education--"

"Who needs school?" Lois countered. "I'm going to have a baby--a beautiful baby-- and a husband. We're in love-- don't you get it?" Lois sounded irritated.

I did *not* get it. Did she really prefer a husband to university? I thought about my mother and August, his loud voice, the coldness of their relations, and their divorce. I thought about how lucky I was to be on my way to higher education and eventually to a career. I was convinced that Lois had made a grievous mistake. While I prepared a self-righteous speech to point this out to her, Lois went on.

"The wedding is going to be in church -- my mom helped me find the perfect dress--Eddie's going to look so handsome, you should see him in his gorgeous suit!"

Of course, I would go to the wedding if she invited me, and later, after the baby came, I would visit Lois in her new home. I promised all that. She was my friend, after all. But we were only sixteen! Why, why, had she done such a thing? And why wasn't she sorry? It was beyond my understanding. I had had no experience with sex. In fact, my puberty had arrived late; I had started menstruating only a few months before. I had no idea how Lois felt, how it felt to be in love, or to have a new being forming inside you.

I put my arms around Lois. I was in a daze. She talked on.

"I think it'll be white roses, or maybe pink-- my mom's dress is lilac, maybe pink to go with that--"

Lois had no idea how I felt.

When I told my mother how Lois had ruined her life, Mother responded with surprise but did not seem angry. "Who is the boy? Is he a responsible young man? Will he marry her and provide for the child? Do they both want the child?"

"Yes, yes, yes," I answered to all the questions. "Lois said her parents gave permission for them to get married. She has it all planned. But--"

"But what?" Mother asked.

"But she won't get to finish school! She won't ever get to university! You can't stay in school pregnant!"

"Yes," Mother agreed. "They are both very young. Did Lois want to go to university? What did she want to be?"

I had no answer to that. I had to admit that I had never heard Lois mention any ambitions regarding higher learning or a future profession. "Who needs school?" Lois had said, to my horror.

"You say they are happy about the baby?" Mother went on.

"Yes, I know Lois is, and they are in love, she says, and he has a job, but--"

"I know how you feel about school," Mother said. "And I think Lois should have waited, but when two people fall in love, and when a child is born, and this child is loved and wanted-- that child is a lucky child. Even if it's not the proper time."

Mother's eyes were shining; her voice was warm. She did not know Lois well, but she was obviously happy to hear that this baby would have loving parents.

I was puzzled because I had expected more disapproval. I was disappointed that my mother did not seem as concerned about the school issue as I was. I did not guess then that unplanned babies had special relevance in her life--and in mine.

Lois and Eddie were married in the Lutheran church where she and I had sung in the choir. It was a short ceremony attended by the two families and a handful of friends. Lois wore a white gown; layers of tulle floated above the now unambiguous bulge that no one mentioned. The choir was not needed, so I was simply a guest. It was the last time I attended any sort of service in that church.

A week before the wedding, I had told the choirmaster that I was dropping out. I have not joined any congregation, of any denomination, since.

The baby was born in the summer between junior and senior year. Lois sent a printed card, announcing the birth of a healthy, eight-pound boy. She included a handwritten note urging me to call her and make a date for a visit soon.

I was not excited about the baby and I had never visited a new mother who was my age. I still felt critical of Lois, and I did not think to bring a gift when I made the longish bus trip to the suburb where my friend now lived. If Lois noticed my indifference, she did not let it show. She was all pleasure and housewifely bustle when she welcomed me for our lunchtime visit.

"You made it! Welcome, welcome," she laughed as she ushered me into the living room of the modest one-story house. "And here's Eddie Junior!" She presented the fat, smiling infant as if he were a coveted prize she had won -- an Olympic medal, perhaps.

I leaned over to give him a pat. He smelled of sour milk and diaper.

"Do you want to hold him?" Lois asked.

"No--no thanks," I stammered. "Let's go sit down first."

"Good, we'll sit in the kitchen. I can't wait to show you--it's beautiful, we have a brand-new refrigerator and everything," Lois said. "We'll eat a little later--Eddie's taking an extra hour for lunch and coming home to join us."

Eddie Junior wailed.

"Oooh, this one's hungry now," Lois added, dropping into a chair, and unbuttoning her blouse.

Lois had gone from plump teenager to fat *hausfrau* in the space of a few months, I thought. Her breasts were enormous; her belly had not lost its roundness. Her shiny blonde ponytail had become a dull, straggly bun held not quite together with an ordinary rubber band. I was glad she was busy nursing the child; it gave me time to come up with the compliment I knew I had to give but had a hard time putting into appropriate words.

"He has a good appetite," I finally said. "He must be growing fast." It sounded lame to me, but Lois beamed as if I had awarded her another medal. She detailed for me all the pounds and ounces the baby had gained, and all the inches he had grown since his birth eight weeks before. I thought about my brother Roland at that age, and how he had reminded me of a giant larva. I could not remember what he had weighed, in kilos or pounds. Mother had nursed him; he had grown bigger. I did not recall much adult fuss about it. Lois's baby was awake and was waving his fat little arms but aside from that, he too resembled a larva. I felt a familiar boredom.

Lois's husband, a young man of medium height with brown, curly hair and blue eyes, burst into the kitchen, calling out, "Where's Daddy's big boy?"

He kissed Lois, scooped the baby into his arms and then turned his bright smile on me. "Hello, welcome," he said. "You're Barbara, sure, I remember you. Pleased to see you again. What's for lunch?"

Lois bounced up from her chair and flitted about the kitchen, bringing dishes to the table-- salad from the refrigerator, a casserole from the oven, bread and butter. She measured water and coffee into a percolator and set it on the stove to boil.

"The bread is from the bakery Eddie works at," Lois said. "And we could have gotten a cake too, but I made one myself--angel food!"

I had meant to get up and offer help, but Lois was too quick for me. As she served the dishes, she kept up a running commentary about who had given her each pot, pan, serving plate, or salad bowl. "Wasn't that nice of them? Weren't they generous to give us that?" she kept asking. I said yes, it was wonderful--but I had little idea who these relatives or friends were. I did not know how to apologize for not having given them a present; I hoped they would chalk it up to my ignorance of American ways.

Lois talked but asked me no questions about school or about my family; she was completely wrapped up in her new life. She showed me all the baby's little shirts, hats, and blankets, and the small mother-of-pearl teething ring that had been hers when she was an infant. I admired everything, praised her lunch and the cake--from a mix, she confessed without apology. My mother would have scoffed but I thought boxes of premixed pastry were quite a clever invention. I could hardly wait for Eddie Senior to go back to work so that I could ask Lois the question that lurked like an unexploded bomb in my brain.

"Do you feel bad about not going back for senior year?" I asked Lois as soon as her husband had breezed out the door. "If you could go back, would you do it differently?"

"What are you talking about?" Lois asked, clutching little Eddie to her chest, and planting noisy kisses on his sleepy face, "Do you mean trade *this* for more boring school? Never. I wouldn't trade -- I wouldn't trade this for anything!"

There was nothing I could reply, so I thanked her again and took my leave. At home, I sat down and wrote a short story titled "I Wouldn't Trade." It was written as a first-person narrative by a young woman who has made a fatally wrong choice, but who refuses to see her error. It was my first short story; it relieved my feelings. I no longer have the text and that may be a good thing. I will not be embarrassed by the sanctimonious voice of the highly prejudiced author. I can only plead that I was very young.

By the time I started my last year at Senn High School, in the fall of 1954, our family was happily settled into our new apartment. Lincoln, after showing his paintings to several gallery owners, had been told his landscapes and still lives were not avant-garde enough for the market, where the Abstract Expressionists claimed the attention of collectors. Practical Lincoln did not mope about being rejected. He asked how to find a job as a commercial artist and was told to try one of the large printing firms that produced mail-order catalogs. With his good command of English and charming manners, Lincoln quickly found a position with the firm that produced the Montgomery Ward catalog-- a thick tome from which you could order everything from ladies' wear to plumbing parts. It was work on a professional level and paid well; in his spare time, Lincoln painted beach scenes featuring Lake Michigan. Eventually, he even sold a few of them.

Mother also had found employment more suited to her skills. Her boss at the phonograph needle plant had referred her to a business connection of his, the head of an import-export firm that traded in German merchandise. Mother went for an interview and was hired as a bookkeeper and secretary. She was to handle all German-language correspondence. It was a responsible position; it paid twice as much as cutting phonograph needles.

Mother was elated. It was time for a nicer wardrobe if she was going to work in an office, she declared. She bought two dresses at the thrift store where we often shopped and refurbished them to look fashionable. Aunt Mary had said she had no use for her sewing machine and had given it to Mother.

"I know I should be grateful, but I should never have sold my Singer," Mother said. "These American machines are terrible-- old-fashioned, clumsy. Why ever did she tell me to sell my good machine?" We were to hear this complaint for decades to come. My children remember it to this day. Despite the machine's inferiority, Mother's office attire was elegantly tailored and stylish. She bought high-heeled shoes and said that finally, she was beginning to feel like her old, prewar self again.

At Senn High School, I had accumulated good grades and extra credits. I knew that I would have only half of a senior year, graduating in January 1955. The question of what our next step would be was much discussed by all my classmates. Many looked forward to entering the workforce; a few had college applications to fill out; boys who had been in the ROTC program expected to go into the military. Girls who were "going steady" hoped to get engaged and then married. I knew what I wanted -- college and journalism -- but I did not know how to go about making that a reality. My mother agreed, as she always had, that I should go on with my studies. In Germany, she would have known how to proceed but in Chicago, she was at a loss.

Aunt Mary was not helpful. "What does the girl want with college?" she asked. "She's old enough to work. Let her get a job and help with expenses. Or she could get married."

It was neither my homeroom teacher nor a designated advisor who would provide the help I needed. Senn High School was recognized for its excellent academics. I do not know why no guidance counselor ever talked with me about my future plans. Was there a guidance counselor?

It was my friend Harriet and her parents who offered the advice that showed me a path I could follow to my goal.

Harriet was an accomplished cellist, but she did not aspire to a career as a soloist; she wanted to become a music teacher; she had already applied to a teachers' college. Harriet was an only child. She often invited me to dinner; her parents were always friendly and were interested in my progress. When they asked, "What next?" I told them about my dream of studying journalism at a university.

"Which one?" Harriet's father asked.

"I don't know--how do I find out where to go?" I must have looked as panicked as I felt. I did not know how the system worked--that there were state schools and private universities--that the fees differed significantly. I knew I was expected to make a decision but, so far, I had no idea how to go about it.

Both of Harriet's parents were immigrants. They had arrived in the United States before World War II. They understood my problem and probably surmised that my family was not wealthy.

"There is Wright Junior College," Harriet's father suggested. "It's run by the city and tuition is free. You can live at home and commute."

This was good news. "Please, can you tell me more?" I asked. Mr. Petersen explained that the junior colleges offered two years of liberal arts studies and awarded an Associate Bachelor of Arts degree at the end. One could then move on to a four-year college, either the University of Illinois or a private university like Northwestern. The state schools charged less tuition than private colleges, he added.

I said, "I think I can pass the test for Wright Junior College." I was expecting an entrance exam like the German *Abitur,* which is required for high school students who wish to enter a university.

Mr. Petersen said he was not sure there would be tests; he thought a transcript from Senn might be sufficient. In any case, he urged, I should make an appointment with the admissions office. I should do that soon, he added, and I should ask whether I could enter in the winter semester, right after my January graduation. Harriet said she knew where the college was located. "We'll take a bus over there this weekend," she offered. "We can walk around, and you can see the buildings."

I wished I had a father like Harriet's -- kind and sensible and helpful. I was so grateful to her family that I tripped over my tongue thanking them: "*Danke*, thank you, thank you, *dankeschön!*" I didn't often mix my languages, but emotion had overtaken me. If I had known the Swedish word for *thanks*, I would have thrown that in too.

After telling my mother that I now had a plan for college and that it would not involve tuition fees or moving to a dormitory that would cost extra money, I felt that the rest of my high school year would be a breeze. Final exams were coming up, but I did not fear them. I planned to study hard, pass them, and move on.

I followed up as soon as possible with Wright College, made an appointment with the admissions office, and was interviewed. I don't remember exactly, but I don't think there was an entrance exam. I was told that I could register for the spring semester. I asked whether the school offered a journalism course; I was thrilled when I heard that indeed there was such a program and a student newspaper as well. What a wonderful opportunity! I resolved to add at least ten new English words to my vocabulary every week so that I could try out for the newspaper.

Relieved of worry about the next step in my schooling, I enjoyed the rest of my stay at Senn High School. I knew that with early graduation, I would miss the senior prom. I cared very little about that. In past years, I had gone to a number of Saturday night dances with Harriet, where both of us sat on one side with the other wallflowers and were never asked to dance. We never went anymore.

When I was a junior, I had a family-approved boyfriend, a German-American boy named Ernie. He was a serious student with the kind of good manners my mother liked. He was unfailingly polite and respectful. He gave me chaste kisses and never took liberties. We did our homework together. He did not care for the school dances, so we went to the movies instead. After a while, without emotion, argument, or recriminations, we drifted apart. I think Ernie felt as bored as I did.

Now, as a senior, I was free to go on dates if I so chose. Mostly, I was more interested in studying or staying home with the family. My best male friend at Senn was a Japanese-American boy who was in my algebra class. He lived in my neighborhood. I don't remember which of us suggested it, but we began walking home together. We often took the long way, wandering up and down the lake shore or strolling through the local parks. Alan was one of the very few non-Caucasian students at Senn. Perhaps we were drawn together because we were different -- he because of his race, I because of my foreign birth. We did not talk about this, but somehow, we felt very comfortable with each other. We chatted, we held hands, and we sat on the grass. Alan had a metal flask that looked like my brother's Boy Scout canteen. Alan claimed it contained whisky and offered me drinks from it. I thought he was telling tall tales; I did not believe him. Lukewarm water from a metal canister did not appeal to me, so I always refused.

On a lovely autumn day, we sat on a patch of lawn near the lake, breathing in the cool, brisk air. Alan reached for my hand. "Want to get married?"

He said it in such an ordinary voice, so casually, that I thought I had misheard him. "What?" I asked, looking into his face for a clue to his feelings. He smiled his usual lopsided smile. "We could get married," he repeated.

"No, we couldn't! We can't! We're in school! We don't want to get married!" I shouted. It occurred to me that there might be something other than water in Alan's canteen.

"OK," Alan said, looking not at all upset. "Want a drink?"

I did not. He walked me home. And he continued to walk with me, day after day. We held hands. Neither of us ever referred to his offer of marriage. I never found out what liquid was in his canteen. We remained friends until I graduated; after that I never saw him again.

My romantic heart had been touched by Alan's impossible proposal; my rational, practical brain warned me to feel amused rather than sentimental. I could not help feeling a little pride; I was not quite eighteen, and here was a young man who wanted to marry me. I needed to talk about this new experience. A week or two after the encounter, I looked for an opportunity to tell the story to Mother. It must have been a weekend because we were at home. I wandered into the kitchen, where Mother was preparing to bake an apple cake with her special topping -- a delicious soft custard she made without a written recipe. I sat down at the table and picked up an apple as if I was planning to help, but I talked instead. When I had finished my tale, I expected Mother to say, "Silly boy," or "What a ridiculous idea."

Mother gave me a searching look and put down her paring knife. "Let's go to your room and talk," she said.

I led the way, still expecting a humorous reaction to my news. I was not prepared for what my mother was about to tell me -- revelations that would hit like a bolt of lightning out of a clear blue sky.

Mother closed the door, sat down on my bed, and patted the coverlet to indicate that I should sit next to her. The bed was neatly made, the pale blue chenille spread pulled tight. I took great care to keep my room tidy because I was proud of it. With Lincoln's expert artistic advice and help, I had got exactly the look I had imagined -- one wall was painted a warm shade of terracotta, and flowered wallpaper in complementary colors covered the other walls. Lincoln and Roland and I had done all the decorating ourselves. We had hung my portrait in its white frame and a landscape by Lincoln on the painted wall. Opposite the bed, a simple student desk and a dresser with a framed mirror completed the furnishings of my happy little kingdom.

I settled down close to my mother as she began to speak.

"If what happened to Lois should ever happen to you," she said as she turned to face me, "I want you not to be afraid. Don't be ashamed. Tell me, and I promise I will not be mad at you. If you have a baby, a child of love, I'll take care of you, of both of you -- I know about love children."

"No! It's not like Lois!" I was shocked-- my mother had misunderstood completely. I thought I had explained it clearly -- I had refused Alan; there was no more to the story.

"No," I said again. "I'm not like Lois, there is no baby! Alan and I don't-- we never did anything; we never even kiss each other!"

"No baby? You're certain? Well, *Gott sei Dank* if that's true. You are too young-- still a schoolgirl --and --" Mother stopped suddenly and gave me a sharp look. "Who is Alan? Why have I not met this boyfriend?"

"Alan Nakamura. You haven't met him because he just walks me home; he doesn't come in," I said.

Mother stared at me. "Nakamura? What kind of name is that?"

"Alan is Japanese -- I mean his parents are -- he was born here," I replied.

"A Japanese! *Gott im Himmel!* What are you thinking, child? Did you think about it at all? If you have a baby--"

"There is no baby! We never--"

"It will be a baby of mixed race. Mixed race -- that is dangerous -- a Japanese!"

I grabbed my mother's hands and looked hard into her face. "No baby!" I yelled. "I am not having Alan's baby! Nobody's baby! No baby -- *kein Kind!*" I added in German to make absolutely sure she got the message. I could not remember screaming at my mother, not since I was two or three. Ashamed of myself, I burst into tears.

Mother put her arms around me. "Let me tell you about love children," she said, as if she were starting on a fairy tale.

"Your father said children born out of pure love are special, better than other children," she began.

"Father?" I asked. I thought of August and could not imagine him saying anything like that. I had never heard him say he loved anybody.

"Father?" I asked again.

"I mean *your* father. Not August -- he is Roland's father, not yours. *Your* father was someone else--a man I loved -- and he loved me more than you can imagine. And I will love him forever--beyond this life -- until I see him again on another star."

I sat there, stunned. August was not my father! In the midst of my confusion, I felt a surge of relief. That cold-hearted, loud-voiced, tyrannical man was not my father. I had never felt love for him; he had never offered me any affection. I had been glad to leave him back in Germany and I had never missed him. On some subconscious level, I thought, I had always known what Mother was telling me now. August had not loved me as a father should. Because he was not my father.

"Where is my father -- my real father -- is he dead?" I asked Mother. I imagined that he must be. Otherwise, he and my mother would be together, now that she was divorced from August. She had been free for years, and though she was admired by men, there was no special friend in her life. Where was my father? And who was he?

Mother told her story. It was like a fairy tale -- not a long one.

"He is gone, most likely dead, yes. He disappeared shortly after you were born. His name was Hans," Mother said in a soft, reminiscent voice, as if she were indeed speaking of the dead. "The moment we met we knew we would love each other for the rest of time. We wanted to be together. We wanted a child, even before marriage. Your father said that children should be born of love -- conceived in the first blaze of passion--a love child was a lucky child, he said. Each of us, separately, had longed for a child. I had been married but there was no baby. With Hans, I was in another world. I became pregnant with you--I could hardly believe how soon it happened--"

"And you got married," I said, eager for a happy ending.

"No. You were born. We were ecstatic. You were a wanted, longed-for child. We were so happy. We knew we would love you always and forever."

Before I could ask another question, Mother hugged me. "You are my love child," she said. "I loved you as a baby and I love you now.

You see why I would not punish you if you found yourself in the same situation?"

"Yes, yes," I struggled to say between sobs. "But what about then--did you and Hans get married?"

"No. He was already married. I found that out later--there was a wife -- there was a reason they could not get divorced--I did not know what it was. He never told me. I sent him away. He disappeared."

"Disappeared?" I asked. "How could he? Just leave you. When you loved each other so much? He left you--and he left me!" I was angry now. Sad for Mother, but bitter about his abandoning me.

Mother's tone when she answered was mild. "He disappeared. It may not have been his fault. It was a terrible time -- the Nazis murdered people -- it happened in those days."

I listened as Mother told me of the Nuremberg laws Hitler had instituted the year before I was born.

"With those horrible laws in place," Mother said, "illegitimate children could be declared Jewish, or part Jewish unless you could prove Aryan ancestry. Even one Jewish grandparent put the whole family at risk. Everyone had to have a family history -- it was a strict rule -- you had to show documents. I could not name your real father. I did not. I have never revealed any details about Hans."

I should have asked if Hans was Jewish. I did not think to do it. I was enraged, upset, and consoled, all at the same time.

"And so, I married August," she said. "You can't remember. You were not even one year old. You got his name and a proper birth certificate; you were safe. You will always be my love child. I will see Hans in another life--somewhere on another star."

CHAPTER 15

Flying

I never did learn to make the special topping for the apple cake. After our emotional conversation, Mother returned to the kitchen. I stayed in my room, curled up on the bed. The love story my mother had told me and the secret about my father that she had revealed took on a physical presence -- as if a small child nestled against my body.

I thought about my brother. We had different fathers. I would never know my father; I did not think Roland could remember August, who had not been part of our life since 1945 when Roland was three years old. Roland was my half-brother, but that concept made no sense. Roland was not half of anything! He was a whole boy -- a tall, strong thirteen-year-old now. I loved him with my whole heart, and I would never love him less. I wondered if Mother would ever speak with him as she had with me, or if I should share the secret. Roland and I were as close as ever, but we rarely talked about the past; we were busy growing into our future. Nothing would change between the two of us. I decided to keep my new knowledge to myself.

By the time Roland and Lincoln came back from their adventures, I had washed my face and gone to help Mother prepare dinner. In my mind, I had constructed the beginning of a heart-stirring tale -- a romance in which my new identity played a role. I was the Love Child.

January 1955. The family admired my diploma from Senn High School and the Scholastic Art Competition award I had won the year before. To keep my important documents safe, Mother gave me a red leather portfolio with a lock. I still have this folder, and my diplomas are still in it, though the key is lost, and the lock broken. Aunt Mary gave me a beige leather jewelry box with gold trim and a green velvet lining. I admired its clever design--the hinged lid that popped up an interior tray for rings and other small items, and the shallow drawer that slid out from the bottom of the case. This charming vintage keepsake takes pride of place on my bedroom dresser; I have carried it through many moves.

Wright Junior College is named for Wilbur Wright. As soon as I had heard the name from Harriet's father, I had gone to the library to look it up; I had learned about the two brothers, America's aviation pioneers, and their flying machines. I took it as an omen. I too wanted to fly, to soar. Like Orville and Wilbur, I was willing to endure a few nosedives along the way.

I started at Wright in the spring semester. The college then was located on North Austin Avenue, about twenty-five minutes from our house via city bus. It was a large brick building in neo-Gothic style that contained classrooms, lecture halls, libraries, a gym, and a cafeteria. There were no dormitories. It was a commuter school that offered evening classes in addition to the regular curriculum. Because tuition was free for city residents, Wright was an attractive choice for students from middle- and working-class families, as well as the sons and daughters of immigrants. Chicago had a large Greek population; I was to meet many young men who were the first in their family to go to college. A number of veterans of the Korean War were catching up on their education.

I enrolled in the liberal arts curriculum. English, composition, American history, and journalism were my major subjects. I also registered for typing as an elective. Physical education was required. and I quailed at the thought of suffering through more games I did not understand. To my relief, I was offered badminton as a choice. This, I knew from my brother, was easy to learn and not strenuous. I signed up. In time, I began to see the humor of the game. It was an uneven contest -- a bunch of heavy-footed teenagers trying to beat a tiny, feathered pincushion to death.

Professor Crist, the journalism teacher, was a slender man with bristly eyebrows and merry dark eyes. I guessed him to be in his thirties. He won my heart on the very first day of class.

"I am Mr. Crist -- short *i* --" he announced. "Please don't address me as Christ, as in Jesus. I am no saint, believe me!"

I could not imagine a German university professor introducing himself in such a relaxed manner.

"In this class, we will study the basics of newspaper journalism-- how to write news or feature stories, proofreading, and editing. Everyone will work on our student newspaper; you will learn about the various jobs that go into a periodical," Mr. Crist said. He added, "If your major interest is journalism, I will be happy to act as your advisor. See me after class."

Most of the students in the room were male. Three of the men, one other young woman, and I approached Mr. Crist when class ended. He asked us to sit in the front row of desks and to write our names on a form he handed us. He gave us copies of the current issue of the paper, a tabloid of eight pages with an imposing name-- something like *The Herald.*

"I know you have to be at your next class in a few minutes," he said. "So just tell me briefly what particular area you're interested in -- writing, advertising, sports, and so forth."

"Some of everything," most of the others said.

When my turn came, I said, "I want to write for a newspaper. As a reporter -- maybe a foreign correspondent."

Mr. Crist gave me a brilliant smile. "Aha! You want to be the next Marguerite Higgins!"

I blushed. He had exposed my heart's desire. Of course, I wanted to be like Marguerite Higgins! I did not know then that this brave reporter had been an eyewitness to the liberation of German concentration camps, including Dachau. When I had started reading American newspapers, I had followed her dispatches from the battlefields of Korea and read every other article of hers I could find. She was one of the very few women then in the profession, a heroine.

"Well, you will start as a reporter on our own newspaper here," Mr. Crist said. "We'll go from there. I will do my best to advise you. And I wish you luck."

I floated out of the classroom. Mr. Crist had said he was not a saint, but I blessed him anyway, along with Wilbur Wright. Both were offering me wings; I vowed to work hard so that I could fly towards my dream.

My first semester at Wright raced by. I felt comfortable among my fellow students. I sensed that many had set goals for themselves, and they did not mind working hard to achieve them. I made a few friends and I did well in my courses. I worked especially hard for the journalism class. Mr. Crist kept us busy. Beginning with the fundamental *who, what, where, why, and how,* we practiced writing articles that would grab the reader's attention and impart information as well as background -- the *why* and *how* of the matter.

"Space is not unlimited; there are only so many column inches," Mr. Crist would remind us. "The story needs to fit in with all the other material on the page. Put all the important information in the first few paragraphs. When the story is edited, cutting starts from the end."

The newspaper had its own office -- a room furnished with desks, typewriters, and even a telephone. Both first- and second-year journalism students used this room to work on the semimonthly issue. In addition to scheduled class time, we were allowed to come in during our lunch and study periods. Mr. Crist believed in hands-on learning. When all the articles had been typed, proofread, and given headlines, we made a "dummy," a paper paste-up of the copy for each page. We did not have the technology to print photographs. One or two line drawings -- often cartoons by one talented young man in our class -- could be engraved and printed. These were called "cuts."

When our dummy was complete, Mr. Crist took the editorial staff downtown to the firm that did the composition, layout, and printing of the final product. I loved these visits. I stood as close as they would let me to the linotype machines, watching the nimble fingers of the operators fit the words into columns as fast as they read them. The men chuckled at my fascination. One of them made me a linotype slug with my name on it. I kept it for years.

Another fascinating feature of our class was Mr. Crist's practice of inviting reporters from the *Chicago Tribune* or *Sun-Times* to speak to the class. Sometimes students were allowed to go along on an actual assignment. I was lucky enough to be chosen for a number of these field trips.

On one occasion, I accompanied a reporter from the *Sun-Times.* We met at a community center that had recently opened in a poor South Side neighborhood. Its mission was to provide after-school sports and other activities to the underserved young people who lived in the area. I stood by, notebook and pencil in hand, as the reporter, an African-American man, spoke with a counselor whose enthusiasm reminded me of my brother's Boy Scout leader.

"It's a God sent," I wrote down. *Godsend* was a new word that my mentor would later correct. Now, having thanked the counselor, he hailed one of the boys engaged in shooting baskets on the small, paved court outside the center's door. The two had a lively conversation of which I understood only about a third. I was totally unfamiliar with basketball; I had no grasp of street slang.

"Well, are you ready to write up the story?" the reporter asked as he walked me to the bus stop. I showed him my pitiful notes.

"I'm very sorry," I said, "I'm sorry my English is not good enough yet. I am still learning."

"Yes, I hear an accent," the reporter smiled. "Something European -- is that German?"

I disliked having an accent. "I am trying hard to overcome," I answered, "but yes, I was born in Germany and I have been in the United States for about five years."

"Oh, don't worry about it; it's very slight, and your English is almost perfect. You just need to catch up a little with the way kids talk. And I was only kidding -- you don't have to write a story. You just watch and learn."

When Mr. Crist asked how my assignment with the *Sun-Times* had gone, I told him I had done poorly. My English had not been adequate. "I am obviously still an immigrant with an accent," I said, wanting to cry.

My teacher was smiling. "Now Barbara," he said, "you should stop feeling sorry for yourself. You speak English better than some native-born students I have; your grammar is better too. Your accent is charming. You sound like the perfect understudy for Lotte Lenya -- why don't you sing me something from *The Threepenny Opera*?"

I had to laugh. "Will I ever be good enough to be a real reporter?"

"Yes, of course, give it time and relax, will you? First, you have to pass Journalism 101 at Wright College. I predict you will, with flying colors!"

I added "flying colors" to my new list of colloquial phrases. "Shooting hoops" joined it soon after.

As the long summer vacation drew near, I felt sad. If only classes would keep meeting year-round! Summer meant finding work; the jobs I had landed every summer through high school had nothing to do with journalism, and they were not particularly rewarding.

As it happened, I did not have to search the Help Wanted ads. Before the semester ended, my mother told the family that she had decided to realize a long-cherished dream of her own. She was about to start on an entirely new venture. It would require assistance from the entire family. It was exciting; she hoped we would work with her.

"But you have to understand," she said, "that until the business starts to generate income, nobody can get paid."

CHAPTER 16

My Mother's Dream

My mother was speaking German, as she did when the subject was serious or complicated; English words did not come to her mind quickly enough to keep pace with the thoughts she wanted to express.

When she was telling us about the new business venture she wished to embark on, the family was sitting at our dining table. It consisted of two bridge tables pushed together and covered with a damask cloth that Aunt Mary had given us as a housewarming present.

"I think you should use oilcloth," she had remarked in her practical way. But she must have known that Mother would have nothing to do with oilcloth; we washed and ironed the white silky table covering every week.

As I listened to Mother, German suddenly sounded like another language-- one I understood and spoke well, but *different*. I snapped to attention. Up until that day, I realized, my brain had made no distinction between the two languages; I was not always aware which one was in use. For the first time in my life, I understood that I was living in two worlds.

At the same time, I saw that for months, I had not paid any attention to one of the worlds-- the family. Immersed in my studies and activities at Wright College, speaking only English and reading textbooks written in English, conversing with my friends in English, I had been living exclusively in my other world. I was not purposely neglectful; when Mother asked me to help out with cooking or shopping, I did it as a matter of course. And the family ran smoothly enough. Mother and Lincoln had full-time jobs; Roland and I went to school. We spoke English with each other. At home, I read and wrote papers for my assignments; Roland finished his homework as quickly as possible and spent the rest of his free time completing projects for his Boy Scout merit badges. He was almost up to Eagle Scout.

Now I gave my full attention to Mother as she laid out her ambitious dream for us.

"You know that I've always loved to sew. When I was young, I wanted to become a dressmaker--not just a seamstress but a designer creating original fashions. How I would have loved to study in Paris! My parents ordered me to go to business school instead-- my mother, especially. She said sewing was a menial occupation--why did I want to be the hired help, called in to let out milady's dresses when they got too tight? She did not understand at all. So, I went to secretarial school and learned bookkeeping and typing."

Mother smiled and went on, "It wasn't a bad thing, as we can see. I understand how an office works, and I had years of experience in Munich with the textile market. I know about American import duties. Now I want to combine fashion and business, and I have an idea! The German people who live in Chicago--the immigrants and their children--would love to see some genuine, quality German clothing they could buy. Nobody sells it. I think there is a market for imported German clothing--traditional *dirndls, lederhosen,* those wonderful hand-knitted ski sweaters. You can't buy that at Sears or Montgomery Ward. There is a storefront for rent on Lincoln Avenue."

"*Lederhosen?*" Roland asked. "With suspenders and knee socks? Not me! I won't! Never!"

I did not speak up, but I agreed with him. I had no wish to wear a *dirndl.* I craved blue jeans lined with plaid flannel and shirts to match.

Lincoln said to Roland, "Don't worry; we won't force you. But I hope you'll help me with carpentry and painting--the store needs some fixing up. We have to build shelves and a new counter, and we need better lights."

I looked at Roland. He was smiling and nodding; building things appealed to him.

Lincoln winked at me. "And for you, your mother is already knitting the sweetest little hat to go with a sweater."

Clearly, Lincoln knew a lot more about this store than Roland and I did. He sounded as if this new venture had already begun, while I was full of confusion and questions. Who would run this store? Mother already had a job; what about that? Wouldn't there be rent to pay and electricity? I did not know the term "venture capital," but I wondered how these extra expenses would be covered. I was not aware of any savings account Mother might have.

"There is some money," Mother said. She often read my thoughts. "Enough to start, anyway. Lincoln is a partner, and I have a small fund I can draw on."

Lincoln said, "I am keeping my job, but your mother has given notice at her office. She will need all her time for the business. Here's to good luck and success!" He raised his coffee cup to salute our entrepreneur.

We talked more. Mother explained that she was in touch with her cousin in Munich. He was helping her to connect with firms in Germany who could supply the merchandise she wanted. He had also put her in contact with a group of knitters who worked in their homes, producing one-of-a-kind sweaters in traditional colors and patterns; they were willing to make items in different sizes if desired.

As the conversation went on, a question that I had not asked was answered in my mind. I had been puzzled by the "small fund" Mother had mentioned. What had she meant by that? Suddenly I saw: The extra capital must be a gift from Karl, a gentleman who had been keeping company with her for the better part of a year.

Karl was a semiretired businessman who was separated but not divorced from his wife. He visited often but did not live with us. The son of German immigrants, he had built a profitable business on a rather simple invention -- a metal perfume flask the size and shape of a cigarette, with a rollerball tip. The flask was easier to use than a spray bottle and was marketed as a must-have for every girl or woman who carried a purse. The product had been successful enough to let him retire at an early age.

Roland and I liked Karl. He was pleasant and quiet and undemanding. He adored Mother; everything she said, wore, or cooked was *wunderbar.* On Sundays, he often took the family on outings in his Dodge sedan, driving to a forest preserve or nature trail. Sometimes he paid for a canoe rental so that Roland and I could practice paddling this Native American craft we had read about in our adventure novels. Sometimes he gave Roland driving lessons on a little-used road.

Karl was not with us this evening; if he had been, I might have figured out his role sooner. Now I thought, of course! If Mother wants a store, she shall get one. *Wunderbar!*

Grandly named, Parkway Sweater Import opened late in the summer, shortly before school started. The store's location was excellent; Lincoln Avenue was a busy street in the heart of a large German-speaking community. The building, on the other hand, was less than grand. It was a small, one-story, shabby storefront. It had a wide front door and a large show window. Inside was a salesroom at the front, with a smaller storage room, a bathroom, and a tiny kitchenette behind it. All of Lincoln's free time, plus countless hours contributed by Mother, Roland, and me, had gone into painting, cleaning, and refurbishing the premises, with little support from the landlord.

In addition to building a counter and putting up partitions and curtains for dressing rooms, Lincoln had created the hand-lettered sign that hung over the entrance, and an attractive window display that featured several of his landscape paintings as backdrops for sweaters of creamy wool embroidered with edelweiss and gentian flowers, a bevy of hats designed and knit by Mother, and, of course, a colorful *dirndl* and a stack of *lederhosen* accompanied by their accessories.

Bouquets of flowers from neighboring businesses and the Chamber of Commerce arrived on opening day. Mother wore a neat business suit and her high heels. Lincoln, in a white shirt with a silk ascot artistically tied around his neck, drew admiring glances. With his dark hair and eyes and slim figure, he was a Rudolf Valentino look-alike--the Latin Lover who was a popular romantic ideal at the time. To please Mother, I wore a *dirndl*. Roland had said that if his Boy Scout uniform was not good enough, he would skip the opening and go to the movies instead. He looked adorable in his uniform -- the very picture of clean-cut American youth.

Customers crowded the store, admiring the unusual offerings, reminiscing about their young days in the Old Country, buying cardigans with carved horn buttons. Older women promised Mother to bring their American daughters-in-law to see the *dirndls* with their sexy, waist-cinching, laced belts. Opening day was a success.

The family was exhausted. None of us had had the energy to go to a film or to read a book for the past four or five months. Lincoln, who enjoyed female company and had no trouble finding it, had neglected his social life. I did not have a steady boyfriend, so I did not have to apologize to anyone. I missed school more than dating.

Roland was thirteen and was in love with an "older woman" of seventeen. Jutta was a German immigrant, working as an *au pair* in one of the northern suburbs. She was petite and shapely, with blonde hair cut in pageboy fashion. I liked her unself-conscious smile. I envied her teeth -- they were healthy and white; mine had never lost the brown tinge of the iron tonic.

The age difference between Jutta and Roland was not noticeable. Even at thirteen, and without facial hair, Roland looked mature. He was slim but well-proportioned and strong. His voice had settled into a pleasant tenor. I had reached my adult height of five feet, six and a half inches; he was only half an inch shorter. By the time he was eighteen, he would stand a full six feet tall.

I had not been in the store when my brother and Jutta had met. Roland told me that she had walked in one afternoon, attracted by the pretty things on display. It was her day off, she had explained, and she had decided to spend it window shopping in Germantown. Her employers allowed her one free day every other week.

Mother had asked about Jutta's family and had learned that Jutta was an orphan who had made her way to America by herself. Predictably, Mother's heart melted. She began to treat the courageous young woman as if she were the third child in the family.

Ever since their first meeting, Roland and Jutta had spent all of their free moments together. Jutta enjoyed coming to the store and helping with whatever activity was taking place. All through the summer, while we had been getting the space ready, she had insisted on lending Roland a hand with whatever chores were on his list, from washing the display window to waxing the floor of the salesroom. As I watched the two of them chatter and laugh, I realized that Jutta was not a *sister*. If there was going to be a permanent relationship, she would be my sister-in-law.

When the store closed at the end of its exciting first day, Roland and I looked at each other.

"Too bad Jutta couldn't be here," I said. "It looks like Parkway Sweater Import is a success."

"Right. For all the hard labor that went into it, I hereby christen it 'Parkway Sweat Port'," my brother said.

CHAPTER 17

Gaining Altitude

Like a growing infant, Parkway Sweater Import gobbled up family time and attention. Mother watched her dream project grow and was rewarded when new customers praised the high quality of the merchandise and thanked her for bringing it to the neighborhood. Compliments inspired her to add extra items, such as knitting yarns and needles so that customers could copy the hats and scarves she created when the store was not busy. This led, inevitably, to knitting lessons for the less experienced crafters. Many evenings, Mother sat up long past closing time, patiently taking beginners through their stitches. The extra hours did not bring in a profit because Mother never charged for her time. "I am building up goodwill," she said when anyone questioned the practice.

Roland and I went back to school in September. Roland was in the eighth grade at Hayt Grammar; after graduation next year --in 1956 -- he would start his freshman year at Senn High School. I was looking forward to the new academic year at Wright Junior College, where I would continue in journalism and work on the school's newspaper. Although we both had full course loads, it was expected that we would help out in the store when Mother needed us. We accepted this, not always graciously.

"The Sweat Port gets sweatier," Roland groused.

"Smellier too -- especially the cleaning and blocking," I added, naming the chore I most despised. Because the hand-knitted sweaters needed special care in laundering, Mother had added yet another sideline to the business--a dry-cleaning franchise. Customers could bring in their garments to be hand washed and blocked, or dry-cleaned, as appropriate. If a button was missing, or if a stitch had been pulled out, Mother would throw in the small repair gratis.

Before we turned over the items to the wholesale cleaning firm, the sweaters had to be measured and tagged so that they could be returned to the customer without any shrinkage or distortion. I was the delegated measurer because the numbers had to be noted down in inches and Mother refused to work with the American system.

"Outmoded, illogical, stupid," she scolded. "When you have a perfectly good metric system a two-year-old can understand!"

So, I measured: width across the chest, overall length, sleeve width and length from shoulder to cuff, width of the neck opening. I wrote the information on a form, added our business name, address, telephone number, and the customer's name, pinned the slip of paper to the garment, and added it to a bag to be collected by the bulk cleaners. There, the sweaters would be hand washed, remeasured, and pinned to a padded board to dry to their original size and shape.

I hated the chore, but the laundry service proved popular with Parkway's customers. They cheerfully paid us a minimal handling fee. I thought our cleaning business was about as profitable as growing wheat and grinding it in a mortar in order to bake and sell homemade bread.

On the plus side, in my opinion, was the new line of less folksy fashions Mother had added to our inventory. I liked the elegant cocktail dresses made of soft, drapey jersey fabric. Tight-fitting stirrup pants-- precursors of today's leggings--were fun. I still admired Mother's inventive wool caps and scarves that she knitted without following any pattern.

Lincoln said these hats were attractive enough to feature in a newspaper advertisement. He wanted to take photographs of me modeling various styles. I was camera shy and ashamed of my teeth; they still bore brown stains from a medicinal iron tonic I had been given years ago. When I smiled, I did not open my lips.

"You will have to put on lipstick and eyeliner," Lincoln offered. I did not wear makeup except for very special occasions when Mother allowed a dab of lip color and a few grains of face powder.

"And mascara," he added.

I was intrigued by mascara. It came in a shallow red plastic box about two inches square. The box contained a black cube, the size of the paint blocks in a watercolor set, and a tiny brush with the bristles set at ninety degrees to the handle. To apply the mascara, you wet the cube and stirred up a thick paste; then you used the brush to coat your upper lashes. I had sometimes watched Mother perform this magic ritual, and I had wished I could try it. Had Lincoln guessed?

I gave him a startled look. He was smiling, his dark brown eyes on mine. His lashes were long and thick without benefit of mascara. I wanted to touch them.

At Wright, my journalism class became ever more exciting. My assignments on the newspaper grew more challenging and rewarding as I wrote faculty profiles and learned proofreading and copy editing. Mr. Crist praised my progress; he hinted that I might be named copy editor before the semester was over.

Mr. Edwards, the reporter from the *Sun-Times* I had met the year before, visited our class again and gave a presentation about Junior Achievement, an organization that taught high school and college students the fundamentals of business. He was on the advisory board, he told us.

"The young people learn how to set up a business, how to buy and sell a product, advertising, and basic accounting," Mr. Edwards went on. "Junior Achievement holds an annual convention where all the student businesses exhibit their wares, and the organization publishes a magazine that includes the program for the convention," he explained. "The magazine uses student writers. It's good experience. The convention is coming up in a few months. If anyone here is interested in working on this, talk to Mr. Crist and me."

A few hands went up but mine was the first.

My teacher smiled at the journalist and said, "Told you! This young lady is very determined."

I was full of excitement when I announced my news at home.

"A magazine! Lots of pages--pictures--advertisements! Over a thousand copies to be printed!"

"A good opportunity, I'm sure. But with a lot of extra work, will you keep up with your other classes too? You don't want to skimp on those," Mother said.

"I'll keep up, don't worry," I answered. "Mr. Crist will let me use class time to write some of the articles. But Mr. Edwards--he's the advisor--will have to meet with the other kids and me after school because of his job at the *Sun-Times*." I hoped Mother would understand that I would have less time for Parkway.

"It's education," Lincoln said. "This sounds like a very professional group. Good luck!"

Roland held up a finger in mock prophecy: "Keep on making junior achievements and one day they shall be senior."

My semester at Wright whirled on. I loved it all -- studying, writing, proofreading, the editorial meetings with Mr. Edwards. I marveled at how many hours he spent with me and my fellow students. I learned that in addition to Junior Achievement, he was on the boards of several community outreach groups; I admired his good humor and his generous nature.

I was not the only one in the family who worked overtime. Mother put in long days at the store; Lincoln and Roland helped after work or school. At home, we still used our formal tablecloth, but Mother's well-planned meals were a thing of the past. We ate tuna noodle casserole--the first American dish I had learned to make -- or hamburgers fried by Roland. We bought bratwurst and potato salad at the German deli. Lincoln did not cook, but, once a week, he brought a carefully selected bottle of Riesling to the table. Roland and I were given half a glass each.

That fall, time passed so quickly that before I knew it, it was Christmas. The holiday season was a good time for the store. Mother and Lincoln decorated the show window with posters of snow-covered Alps, traditional glass Christmas tree ornaments, colorful pullovers and vests, knitted ear warmers and hats. A plaster mannequin wore a beige party dress with a long black fringe at the bottom. Customers loved the unique merchandise. Mother was too happy to notice how tired she was. Her only complaint was that she could not close up shop early on Christmas Eve. In Germany, the festive meal is served on the evening of the twenty-fourth, the tree is lighted, and gifts are exchanged. This year, our celebration would be delayed, and it would lack some of the traditional elements.

"I didn't have time to bake even one cookie," Mother lamented. "All these late shoppers! That's one American custom I don't like!"

After the winter break, I plunged back into my exciting studies at Wright, concentrating on Mr. Crist's class, the newspaper, and the Junior Achievement magazine, which was due to come out in time for the June convention. I paid little attention to how my mother's venture was going. I helped in the store when it was necessary, but my mind was elsewhere. I failed to notice that after the holiday rush, business had fallen off, and the store was often empty.

Mother sat and knitted. "We'll bring in some spring fashions-- something fresh," she said.

An objective observer would have seen at a glance that Parkway would never make a significant profit. The quality, and therefore the cost, of the merchandise was high. Our markup was small. The sweaters were so durable that there was little repeat business. Specialty items like *lederhosen* were a loss. After the folk dancing club had purchased a few pairs, sales stopped; no American teenager would be caught dead in them. Import duties took their toll. Customs inspectors were not above hinting at bribes, including sexual favors. Mother was often harassed; when I went to the airport with her to receive a shipment, I got appraising glances as well. One official went so far as to call me at home and suggest an assignation. I told Mother. She gave me a disgusted look. "You too?" she sighed.

None of us was experienced enough to analyze the business, or to come up with a long-term, profit-oriented management strategy. But Mother and Lincoln did some creative thinking. And they came up with an idea: fashion shows.

"Showing the clothes on real people is the best advertising," Lincoln said. "Barbara and Jutta can be the models."

"Do I have to?" I whined. Mother and Lincoln ignored me and went right on to detail their plan. The fashion shows would be offered free of charge to German-American social clubs; there were many in Chicago. The clubs held luncheons in various restaurants, so the shows would serve as entertainment that would invigorate Parkway's sluggish sales. I was dubious but I could think of no good argument against the plan. Mother's adventuresome ideas had worked remarkably well so far. It was worth trying, I thought. I knew that Jutta would be willing. She thought of us as family, and she would do anything to help.

With her characteristic energy, Mother organized a show for a good-sized *Singverein* -- a mixed choral group. Lincoln designed new stationery and business cards and had everything printed in time for the show, which would be held in about one month.

When the date arrived, I felt apprehensive; but there was no help for it. We drove to the restaurant where the club was to meet. We did not own a car; Mother's friend Karl had lent us his Dodge; Lincoln knew how to drive. I could tell that Mother and Jutta were nervous as well, but they tried heroically not to show it. Roland, as stage manager and carrier of boxes, looked calmly amused by all the excitement.

Lincoln said, "Everything will be *wunderbar!* Don't worry; they're just regular people -- it's not Paris."

The luncheon was held in the restaurant's banquet hall. The management had rolled out a length of red carpet to serve as a runway. The tables arrayed on both sides of it were already occupied by the *Verein's* members. Not surprisingly, they were mostly ladies, all attractively dressed, some wearing hats. The main course was being served.

The club's president came to meet us, introduced herself, and greeted us in German: "*Willkommen!*"

When introductions were complete, the president said to Mother, "Feel free to do the narration for the show in German; everyone here knows it."

I could almost hear Mother's sigh of relief. She was much more comfortable in her native language, although her English was competent.

The president showed us the way to the ladies' room, where we would put the boxes of clothes and where Jutta and I would change outfits.

"Don't mind the other women going in and out," the president said. "It's the only restroom for ladies, but it's quite large, as you see." To Mother, she said, "Before dessert is served, I will make a pause and introduce you to the guests. And while they have coffee and cake, you can start to bring out your models."

Jutta and I looked at each other and at Mother. We had no experience as fashion models. Mother and Lincoln had instructed us to walk to the end of the runway, to pose for a moment, then to pivot and walk back, then to pause once more before going offstage. Mother had added one short directive to this minimal training: "Stand up straight; don't slump!"

"Which of us is first?" I asked. "And which costume first?" In my panic, I had completely forgotten that we had made a list. Mother had one copy for her announcements; we had another -- but where was it? I headed for the boxes piled in the lounge area of the room.

Jutta, who had recovered her poise, pulled the typewritten sheet of paper out of the box of sweaters. "Here -- remember now? We packed the outfits in order--and the first one will be on top, remember?"

"Right, right, I got it now," I said, wishing I were somewhere else. "We'll get dressed and stand outside the door so we can see when you want us to walk out."

"No slouching!" Mother said as she left the ladies' room.

To reach the improvised runway, we had to make our way between a number of tables, to the lectern where Mother stood. Jutta was first, in a pair of charcoal grey stretch pants and a low-necked blouse of angora wool that intensified the color of her sea-blue eyes. Because I was already dressed in my beige jersey sheath--the one with the fringe-- I was able to watch her walk. She looked so natural that I took a deep breath--my first in about an hour, I felt.

The audience was friendly and vocal in two languages. "So cute -- adorable -- *niedlich,"* I heard; then there was applause.

Jutta came back. "Go!" she said and ran off to change. I started walking. I remembered to keep my neck and chin up and my shoulders back; my knees were shaking.

When Mother introduced my outfit, she said, "My daughter is wearing…"

The audience applauded and called out, "Pretty girl --that's an elegant dress --she has lovely long hair." The compliments made me blush. I kept walking but I wanted to run.

The show was not as embarrassing as I had feared it might be, but it did not go flawlessly either. Jutta and I had little time to change. We struggled with zippers and buttons, with stockings that came unfastened from garter belts, with hems that refused to hang straight. Once or twice, Mother had to improvise when one of us did not appear at the door of the ladies' lounge on cue. Once, at least, we mixed up outfits and came out in garments different from those Mother expected to see. We were limp with relief when it was over. The president of the club thanked Mother and congratulated us. "The audience was impressed," she said. "It was a wonderful idea you had."

Lincoln had distributed more than fifty business cards. Several ladies had invited him to call them if he found himself lonely, he told us later.

"You were good," Roland said to me and Jutta when we had packed up our boxes. "For a while there you looked like you wanted to find an air raid shelter and hide, but then you calmed down. You looked nice."

I would have been happy to forget all about fashions and devote my time to the Wright College newspaper and to the Junior Achievement magazine, but our first Parkway show, amateur as it was, brought new customers to the store. Mother was inspired to build on her success. She soon received an invitation from a different club whose ladies wanted a preview of our spring dresses.

"This time we should show more outfits," Mother said at dinner. "And I wish we had one more person to help; it's hard for the girls."

"Perhaps a professional model?" Lincoln suggested. "Someone with experience could help Barbara and Jutta--show them some tricks of the trade."

I was glad to hear this. Help would be more than welcome, especially if Mother planned on showing a larger number of items. I seconded Lincoln's suggestion.

"There might be times when Jutta can't come because of her job," I said. "I couldn't do it alone; it's hard enough with two of us."

Mother and Lincoln agreed to search the Yellow Pages for an agency that could provide us with a model.

"God knows what they'll charge," Mother said.

"If it helps sales, you'll see it's worth it. You will only have to hire her for a few hours, after all," Lincoln reassured her.

On a Saturday, about a week after this family conference, the tallest, most beautiful woman I had ever seen walked into the showroom of Parkway Sweater Import.

Her mane of glossy brown hair fell to her shoulders in sculpted waves; her dark eyes were wide as a gentle doe's. Her slender hourglass figure was dressed in a tailored suit over a white silk blouse. Her arms were elegant, with long-fingered hands tipped by crimson fingernails. The black pumps on her feet had high heels. She carried a leather portfolio in her left hand and stretched out her right.

"Good day. I am Wilhelmina," she said in German. "From the agency," she added in English as four people stared at her, stunned.

Roland, Jutta, and I said, "Pleased to meet you," ... "Welcome." Admiration and envy competed in my heart. This woman was so sophisticated, so elegant, so--*tall!* I thought she must be much older than I was. Years later, when I looked up her biography, I learned that she was actually three years younger.

Mother explained her plan for the fashion show and asked Wilhelmina to look over the dresses, slacks, and sweaters that would be featured.

"Barbara and Jutta will be models, too," Mother said. "Would you spend an hour now to see which outfits would be best on them?

And, of course, choose yours. But then, everything looks good on you!"

"Thank you," Wilhelmina answered. "First, I will show you my portfolio -- pictures from other shows I have done; it may give us some ideas."

The photos were all glamor--head shots of Wilhelmina's beautiful face flawlessly made up; Wilhelmina in a backless evening gown, her swan neck encircled by pearls, chestnut hair piled on top of her head. An agency letterhead gave her statistics: Height - 5'11". Measurements: 38-24-36. Hair - brown. In the fifties, it was not unusual to describe women by their physical dimensions.

"I have just started with the agency," she said. "My parents and I came to Chicago in 1954; originally, we are from Holland. I love high fashion. I want that to be my career."

I could see that my mother was charmed. Here was another immigrant with a dream.

Wilhelmina looked at the dresses Mother had brought into a dressing room and chose a number of garments for me. My favorite was a white, two-piece jersey knit ensemble -- a slim skirt, a matching short-sleeved top with a square neckline that was trimmed with black braid. Jutta had already put on stretch pants and a fluffy pale blue sweater; it was one of the outfits she had worn at our first show. Wilhelmina approved and put aside a pile of sweaters and slacks for her.

When I had changed into the black and white dress, Wilhelmina looked at me and said, "Quite nice. Of course, you will wear a girdle with it; it's necessary. And now, *Aufrecht stehen* -- stand up straight."

I squared my shoulders and stood at rigid attention.

"That's a start," Wilhelmina smiled. "But you need to breathe, too. I will show you an easy way to get the right position."

She demonstrated. "First, take a deep breath and raise your shoulders. Breathe out, lower your shoulders, and relax them; relax your arms, lift up your chin. See? Now you are ready to walk. That's really easy, isn't it?"

Jutta and I practiced while our instructor watched us like an indulgent older sister.

Mother suggested we walk through the showroom for practice. Wilhelmina pointed to my feet.

"Where are your shoes?" she asked.

I pointed to my loafers. "I have my shoes on," I said, puzzled.

"I don't mean those! Where are your dress shoes?"

"Dress shoes?" I asked. "I don't think I have any."

"I see," Wilhelmina said. "I mean shoes with heels, like mine. You have to wear heels with dresses. Here, try mine." She stepped out of her black pumps and I took off my loafers. It was not a fit. Wilhelmina's shoes were a size too large for me. The heels made me feel as if I were walking on stilts.

Wilhelmina looked at Mother, who always wore high heels. "She does need shoes; I know you will agree. Perhaps you have an extra pair?"

I knew Mother's shoes were too small for me. We would have to go shopping. I hoped I would not break my ankles.

Before Wilhelmina left, she added another item to our to-do list.

"Barbara has a nice natural wave to her hair," she said. "She does not need a permanent, but it should be styled. I can recommend a good salon."

My hair had never been cut in a *salon.* I went to the neighborhood beauty parlor -- infrequently -- where a motherly lady cut my bangs and trimmed the split ends.

"Gott im Himmel, this is costing a fortune! And we haven't even had the fashion show yet!" Mother said at dinner that night. "Do you know this agency wants twenty dollars an hour? And we need shoes--haircuts--"

And a girdle, I remembered. I did not say it out loud; I didn't want to mention undergarments in front of Lincoln. He had not met Wilhelmina because he had been on a painting excursion. Mother showed him the publicity photos Wilhelmina had given her to keep.

"I think the expense will prove worth it," Lincoln said. "This model is sensational. She should be in Paris. She will be helpful, you'll see. In a few years, we'll see her on the cover of *Vogue.*"

How right he was! Wilhelmina was to become a superstar. Her aristocratic glamor defined the look that was valued in the nineteen-fifties and sixties. She would appear in countless magazines, and on twenty-seven covers of *Vogue.* In 1967, she would find her own agency, which still exists and has branches from New York to Singapore.

Back in the mid-fifties, at Parkway Sweater Import, Wilhelmina was the warmhearted, unselfish immigrant who aided another. And even when she became world-famous, Wilhelmina never forgot my mother.

The fashion shows given by Parkway after Wilhelmina came into our lives looked much more professional and stimulated enough new business to justify the extra expense. Jutta and I learned the art of changing costumes in less than two minutes. We learned to use lipstick and hairspray. Wilhelmina showed us how to put a net bag over our heads when we slipped dresses on and off. This kept makeup from smudging the garments. We dutifully wore girdles over our flat stomachs; we breathed in and out and relaxed our shoulders and arms. We never quite achieved Wilhelmina's studied languor, but we felt fairly comfortable on the runway.

Mother followed Wilhelmina's burgeoning career. When articles or photos appeared in the women's pages of the newspaper, Mother cut them out and started a scrapbook. With our business going well, I felt free to pour all of my energy into my studies.

When the Junior Achievement convention was held, I dragged the whole family to visit it with me. I was beside myself with joy to see tall stacks of the magazine at every entrance and throughout the hall. I had written the lead article and several others -- all with bylines -- and I had made small drawings to fill the white spaces between stories. My name was listed on the masthead. I made sure we visited every booth, whether they sold yo-yos, clock radios, or dictionaries, and when we left the hall, I collected a number of magazines that had been dumped in the trash bin.

"So much hard work," I said. "How can they just throw it away?"

"They read it first -- and think of how many magazines they've taken home," Mother said as she put her arm around me.

"Our art is not always appreciated as it should be," Lincoln added. "The point is to create it."

My heart gave a lurch when I realized that he had referred to me as an artist. I had never thought of myself that way. I took his hand, feeling grateful -- and something else. It was something that had been stirring inside me lately.

Sexual desire flickered between me and Lincoln. I was frightened by it and did my best to stamp out the spark. I thought of my friend Lois and wondered if she felt trapped; I did not want to end up like her. I was afraid of sex because I had only a vague understanding of how contraception was supposed to work. I was happy knowing that I was a child of love, as Mother had so eloquently explained. But I had no wish to bear a love child myself.

At present, I was glad to step out with a beau who asked for nothing beyond time to look into my eyes. He was a fellow student, a handsome young Sikh from the mountains of Kashmir.

"Your eyes are the color of the skies of my homeland," Surendra had said, the first time we said hello to each other after American History class.

CHAPTER 18

Hullabaloo

As the spring semester of 1956 drew to a close, I was excited by the success of the Junior Achievement magazine and happy that my mother had found Wilhelmina to help promote Parkway Sweater Import. My teachers at Wilbur Wright College commented favorably on my term papers; Mr. Crist praised my progress in journalism class. Life at home was pleasant; the family looked forward to Roland's eighth-grade graduation in June. He spoke English by preference and his reading was up to grade level. Except for spelling, which he would never master, his marks were good.

I was happy with Surendra. Our friendship had begun shortly after the winter break when he had surprised me with that poetic compliment about my eyes and the sky of his homeland. I had not taken special notice of the tall young man before that and I had not known he was from a foreign country. He was clean shaven and wore the same kind of American clothes the other male students dressed in -- cotton or flannel shirts, sweaters, casual slacks, and windbreakers. His hair was black and straight, his eyes dark brown. His skin was the color of cinnamon sugar. I thought he might be from one of the Mediterranean countries, perhaps Greece.

"Your homeland?" I asked after he spoke to me. "You aren't from here? Where is your home? And I don't know your name?"

"I am from Kashmir -- that is in the north of India -- a very beautiful land! May I introduce myself? My name is Surendra Singh." He spelled the names for me.

"Surendra," I repeated. "I'm Barbara, and I am from another country as well."

With that, we had to rush off to different classes; American history was the only one where our schedules overlapped. We did not let that stand in the way of our growing friendship. From then on, we found time to chat during lunch breaks or study periods, or after the last class of the day.

My childhood images of Kashmir and India were of exotic, legendary lands where maharajas hoarded vast treasures of rubies and diamonds, where princes rode on elephants, and sacred cows strolled freely in the streets. Of course, I knew it was not like that in 1956. India had gained its independence; much blood had been shed in the struggle over its partition; hostilities between Pakistan and India had not ended. A fierce territorial dispute about Kashmir was often in the news.

We came from such different backgrounds and cultures, but wars had marked our childhoods. We talked and talked.

Surendra was in the United States on a student visa. At Wright, he wanted to perfect his English -- which I told him was perfect already -- and study social science and economics. He hoped to move on to earn a degree in political science.

"With a degree from a prestigious American university, I have a chance for a position in my country's government. That is what my father wishes me to do," Surendra told me.

"And you-- do you wish that too?" I asked.

"Of course. I honor my father," he said. "Except now, here, I am a disobedient son. I have cut my hair and shaved, and I do not wear my turban as required. We belong to the Sikh religion and there are rules. I hope my father never sees a picture of me like this!"

"I can understand wanting to look like the others," I said. "I don't walk around in a traditional Bavarian dress. Luckily, my mother doesn't make me."

"I am sure it is very pretty," my gallant new friend said. "Tell me about Bavaria."

A week or two later Surendra asked, "Will your mother allow me to call on you and to take you out to a film?"

"I'm sure she will, but I don't have to ask her, you know," I answered. "I decide for myself."

"I see -- American girl!" Surendra smiled, his black eyes aglow.

Mother was enchanted when Surendra arrived to pick me up for our date. He was dressed in a suit and tie and presented an extravagant bouquet of long-stemmed flowers in improbable colors-- emerald green chrysanthemums, neon pink carnations, daisies sprayed with glitter. I thought he would hand me the flowers, but he gave them to Mother with a bow.

"Thank you for welcoming me to your home," he said in his formal, British-accented English.

I made the introductions: "My brother, Roland, and this is Lincoln, our cousin."

Mother offered coffee as everyone was shaking hands. I quickly said, "No thanks, we want to get to the eight o'clock movie; we have to go."

Surendra looked surprised, but I hustled him out the door. I remembered Mother's habit of grilling my high school dates and did not want to watch another interrogation.

On the way to the theater, Surendra said, "I am happy that you have two brothers to protect you. I will do the same. I will not allow any harm to come to you. You are precious. I want to call you *Deva*. It means divine--goddess-- in Sanskrit."

I did not correct him about the relationships. Let Lincoln be my brother. I loved being a goddess. In Sanskrit or English.

We went out on many dates that spring and a few during the summer, when Surendra was taking evening courses and I was working. We went for walks or to the movies. We talked, telling each other about our families, our hopes and dreams, our native countries, our other friends past and present. We talked about the wars that had shaped our childhoods.

Surendra brought flowers every time he came to our house.

"Should I tell him not to spend so much money?" I asked Mother.

"No, no, don't do that," she said. "It might shame him. It will look to him as if you think he's poor and that will hurt his pride. Accept the gift, say thank you, and let him be."

"On the other hand," Lincoln spoke up, "Don't feel you have to give him kisses in return. You are not obliged to join his harem for a few garish flowers."

"What if he gives me a bag of rubies?" I teased, to punish Lincoln for his peevish tone.

"Oh, stop it, you two!" Mother said. "What nonsense. Surrender won't ask anything improper. Surrender is a *nice* man!"

She always got his name wrong. But she was right about the rest of it.

In the darkened theater, Surendra would hold my hand but go no further. On our walks, we did not touch. Sitting on a park bench or on the rocks on the shore of Lake Michigan, he would gaze into my eyes and murmur, "Deva." I liked our relationship as it was. He made me feel beautiful, treasured. I felt warm affection but no passion for Surendra. The dangerous spark that lurked between me and Lincoln was absent.

In Journalism class, Mr. Crist told the class that it was not too soon to think about our future plans. He encouraged us to visit the library and the placement office, where we could look through brochures and college catalogs. "If you have questions, I will be happy to schedule an appointment with you during my office hours," he said.

I had already pored over the catalogs. They were enticing, but even the application fees that were listed were unaffordable. I did not see how I would ever get to a university. I needed to discuss the matter with Mr. Crist; I made a note to follow up as soon as possible. Before I could do so, my teacher had thrilling news for me. It came one day after he had reminded us to give thought to our future education.

"Barbara, please come to my office during lunch hour, if you possibly can," he said when class was over. "I have something to tell you. Something that may be to your advantage."

I was happy to skip lunch for this special conference with my advisor. What had he found?

"Come in and sit down," Mr. Crist said. I took the chair in front of his desk.

"There is an opportunity for a temporary position with the Associated Press this summer during the Democratic National Convention," Mr. Crist said. "You know the convention will be in Chicago, in August?"

"Yes, yes, I do," I said. Thanks to Mr. Crist, I was now an avid reader of newspapers, including the *New York Times,* which he subscribed to and had made required reading for our class. I was well informed about the presidential election of 1956. If I had been old enough to vote and a United States citizen -- I was neither -- I would have chosen Adlai Stevenson over President Eisenhower, the incumbent.

Mr. Crist continued, "The job description says 'dictationist' in the AP newsroom. This is a person who types out the stories the reporters call in from the convention center. The copy then goes to the editing desk; speed is of the essence. You need to be a rapid typist-- eighty words per minute. Can you do that?"

"Yes!" I said without even thinking about it. I had learned touch typing and was good at it, but I had no idea how many words per minute I could produce.

"There is a test," Mr. Crist said. "You need to make an appointment with a personnel agency downtown. They do the hiring. Do you want the information? With your interest in politics and news, I think you may want to try."

"The Associated Press! International News Service!" I said. "Please, yes, I want this job. May I go and try out?" It was like being offered a ticket to the Promised Land. If they wanted eighty words per minute, I would simply have to move my fingers faster than I ever had before.

"A recommendation is required as well," Mr. Crist now said. "I'll be happy to provide one. You are an ambitious student, and this will add valuable real-life experience. Best of luck on the test!"

I used a payphone to call the employment agency and took the first available appointment, although I knew I would miss classes. I was anxious to take the test because I imagined hordes of journalism students would rush downtown and get ahead of me. The appointment was three days away; I would have some time to practice on the portable typewriter my mother had acquired for her business correspondence.

The family congratulated me on the job opportunity and Mother said that of course, I was welcome to use the typewriter.

"Boy Scouts are always helpful and kind," Roland said. "I'll read the manual out loud and time your performance."

It was a fine plan, but it could not be carried out. In my excitement, I had forgotten that Mother's machine was a German brand not made for the American market. The letters on its keyboard were arranged differently from those on the Remington or Smith-Corona typewriters we used here. On English-language keyboards, frequently used characters like *y* and *q* are placed in the top row in easily accessible positions. On German typewriters these two characters occupy places on the lower rows. On Mother's machine, the *z* was where my right forefinger expected to find the *y*. Mother could probably manage eighty words per minute, but I couldn't.

On the appointed day, armed with Mr. Crist's letter of recommendation and what courage I could scrape up, I took the El train to the Loop and found the address of the agency, in one of the tall office buildings on LaSalle Street. I took an elevator, my nervousness increasing with every floor we passed.

When I presented myself at the reception desk, I said, "I am here for the typing test--for the job with Associated Press."

A middle-aged woman who did not give me her name asked me to sit down and fill out an application form while she read my letter. When she had checked over my completed form, she showed me into another room and told me to sit at a desk with a typewriter on it. A dictaphone stood on a table to my left. The woman handed me a set of headphones.

"You will put these on," she said. "When you are ready, I will start the machine for dictation. You will type out the text you hear. If you make a minor mistake, don't backspace and try to correct it.

Don't worry too much about commas and semicolons; just put periods when appropriate. The voice you hear will tell you when to start a new paragraph. At the end of five minutes, I will stop the dictation and we'll determine your score. Ready?"

"Ready," I said, while I tried to breathe normally.

The test began. The male voice spoke rapidly but clearly. The story it read was a generic news article that contained a sprinkling of well-known names and places -- President Dwight D. Eisenhower, Adlai Stevenson, Washington, D.C. For the first few sentences, I lagged behind the speaker. I caught up briefly when I remembered that I was allowed to skip commas and to write "Ike" instead of the president's full name. This helped but I fell behind again; I struggled on. The speaker had come to the end of a sentence; I was still typing the first phrase of it when the machine stopped.

"Stop," the examiner said at the same moment. I wanted to complete the sentence because I remembered the words, but the test was over.

"Sorry, that is only seventy -- well, seventy-three words," the examiner said when she had taken my page out of the typewriter and checked it. "That's not fast enough."

I wanted to die, but that is not what brave reporters do when faced with obstacles. Working for the Associated Press demanded grit -- and, right now, perhaps a bit of groveling, I told myself.

"I -- I'm sorry, really sorry," I said. "I know I can do better. I am so nervous--"

"Yes, I know that. All the girls get nervous," the woman said in a softer voice than she had used before. "If you want to take a break and retake the test in ten minutes, I'll let you. I don't have another appointment waiting for me."

I thanked her for giving me a second chance and took the test again. This time I passed--barely.

"That's seventy-eight words, but I'll say OK," the woman said. "Practice!"

A salary was mentioned but I hardly listened; my head was swimming with relief and happiness. I was told to wait for a phone call at the beginning of August, when I would receive further instructions about the exact date and time to report for work in the Associated Press newsroom. This was not at the convention center -- the International Amphitheater on Chicago's far South Side -- but in one of the large downtown hotels. I believe it was the Conrad Hilton.

During the remaining weeks of school, I typed all of my assignments in the newspaper office. Mr. Crist smiled. He knew why my fingers were leaping about like startled rabbits.

In July, Mother took a booth at a trade fair for imported goods from many nations. Roland and I and Jutta, when she had time, helped staff the Parkway Sweater Import display table. In addition to the German sweaters and the *Lederhosen* that stubbornly refused to sell, we now carried Tyrolean loden jackets and ski sweaters from Norway. When the booth was not too busy, we took turns walking around the vast exhibition space to admire the colorful variety of merchandise.

Surendra came to visit. As we were strolling through the aisles, we discovered a booth that sold fabrics and clothing from India. The vendor showed us a sari of royal blue silk with black elephants woven into the border.

"Your color!" Surendra said and pulled out his wallet.

"No, thank you. I can't let you do that," I said, opening my purse and taking out money. I paid for the sari.

"I see -- American independent girl," Surendra said, shaking his head and smiling. "Will you wear it?"

"My mother will make me a dress when she has time," I said. There is plenty of material for a shawl too, so it will still look like a sari."

"I look forward to seeing you in it, beautiful Deva," Surendra said.

A week before the Democratic National Convention opened, I received the promised telephone call from the Associated Press.

"Hello, this is the newsroom manager, Marian Miller," said a brisk female voice." I will be your supervisor. You will start work on Monday the thirteenth and report to me, at the Conrad Hilton. Please come in no later than three p.m."

I assured Miss Miller that I would be there. I wrote down "basement newsroom" and the hotel's address on South Michigan Avenue. I thanked Miss Miller, hung up the phone and jumped up and down like a hysterical three-year-old.

When I stepped into the basement headquarters of the Associated Press on the first day of the convention, it was like stepping into a memory. Here was the purposeful chaos I had seen from the observation platform of the *Chicago Tribune* -- and I was in it, as if dropped by a magician's hand. Here were men sitting at desks, talking into black telephone receivers -- a dozen conversations going on at once; here were copyboys speeding between the clacking teletype machine and the editors' desks. Typewriter keys tapped out irregular rhythms; little bells pinged, signaling the end of a line and the imminent *ka-chunk* of the carriage return. Phones rang. Voices called out to one another. The only silent element was the cigarette smoke swirling above it all.

Miss Miller was a trim young woman with short, curly, brown hair. Dressed in a white blouse and a dark blue skirt, she wore lipstick but no other makeup. Her only item of jewelry was the small gold pin in the shape of a leaf that she wore on her collar. When I introduced myself, she shook my hand with a pleasant smile.

"Your shift is from four until midnight," she told me as she walked me to the typing desk that was my station. A sturdy Remington sat in the middle of it, flanked on the left by a telephone connected to a headset. On the right, a wire basket held a stack of pale-yellow copy paper. One sheet was rolled into the machine, ready for action.

"When this phone rings, press the Answer button and put on the headset. Give your name. The reporter will say his -- type his byline, start a new paragraph to begin the story," Miss Miller instructed.

"After the last paragraph, type three number signs to indicate the end of the story. When you're done, signal the desk and an editor will take over and prepare it for the teletype operators."

I tried on the headset and adjusted the metal clip to make the earpieces fit snugly. They reduced the background noise but did not eliminate it. I took the set off again and listened to Miss Miller repeat the ground rules: Speed is important -- ignore minor mistakes -- use abbreviations as long as the meaning of the word remains clear.

"Don't be surprised if they say 'OGL'," Miss Miller said. "It stands for 'Our Glorious Leader' and refers to the president. When they say that, type 'the president.' And if you have to go to the bathroom, for God's sake do it when the other girl is in the room. I can help out in an emergency, but let's not create one!"

I did not see the other dictationist. Her shift began an hour later than mine. From the time she walked in until eight o'clock when I had a break, we would not exchange a greeting. This was the opening night of the convention. It would be relatively quiet; Miss Miller had said when she left me at my desk. I did not think so; it was busy enough for me.

The first sound from my telephone almost threw me into a panic. For a second, I could not remember what to do first--push the button? Grab the headset? I did both, said hello and my name, and listened as the reporter gave me his, spelling it out. I typed his byline. I forgot to say "ready."

"You there?" he asked. "You OK?"

"Yes, I'm ready -- fine," I gasped.

The correspondent -- he was from the Washington Bureau, I later learned -- spoke rapidly but he paused briefly at the end of each sentence, giving me a few precious seconds to catch up. All went well until I came to the end of my page and had to roll a second sheet of paper into the machine. I had to ask for a minute to do this.

"OK. Hurry up," the reporter snapped. "I've gotta get back in there."

I inserted the paper straight into the machine. I knew that if it got on a slant it would jam. Luck was with me. We resumed. At the end, the reporter said, "Thanks," and disconnected. I pushed the Intercom button to let the editing desk know that new copy was ready. I could not remember what the story was about -- not a word.

At the convention center, a few miles south of the hotel, the keynote speech was given, delegates scurried about, caucuses met, senators and congressmen gave interviews and they all issued statements to the press. Reporters from the Associated Press, United Press International, Reuters, the *New York Times,* the *Chicago Tribune,* and other major newspapers raced to the telephone booths outside the hall. The AP correspondents called, and I took their dictation. I must have typed a great deal of history that night, but if anyone had asked me what was happening, I would have had to confess that I had no clue. I had become part of the transmission line. Information flowed into my ears and out through my fingers, on its way to the editors who would ready it for the machines that would wire the news to the far corners of the world.

When I went upstairs around eight o'clock to buy a cup of coffee and a roll, I passed the hotel's bar. I was too young to drink, so I did not go in, but I stopped by the door to catch a glimpse of the television. I saw what millions of viewers were watching -- live coverage of the convention. The sight of the enormous arena, crowded with thousands of delegates, the multitude of signs and posters, the noise from competing megaphones, all made for a gripping spectacle. Good thing we don't have a TV set downstairs, I thought; it would be impossible to concentrate; it's difficult enough already.

A man passing by offered me a cigarette. I refused, although I sometimes shared an illicit smoke with my brother. I hurried off to find the coffeeshop, bought myself a snack and quickly made my way back to the newsroom.

It was past midnight when I completed my shift. There had been no disasters, but I felt I had not performed as well as I should have. I had been slow. I was not used to the background noise and the static on the telephone line, and sometimes I had to ask for a word to be repeated. The reporters complied, impatiently. Only one or two had said thank you at the end of a job. When I passed the supervisor's desk on my way out, I looked at her nervously, wondering if there had been complaints.

Miss Miller looked up. "Goodnight," she said. "See you tomorrow. It'll get more interesting."

Mother was still up when I got home. "I worry about you, out alone this late," she said.

"It's all right," I said. "Downtown, it could be lunchtime--lots of people walking around, lots of cars, taxis coming and going. You know, the Hilton is right on Michigan Avenue, near the Art Institute. The buildings are all lit up and the streetlights are bright. It's only a block to the El station."

"Be careful. I wish you could get a daytime shift."

"All the important speeches are at night," I told her. "When the evening news is on and everybody's watching television."

"Evenings should be for the family," Mother said.

"Sometimes we all watch," I reminded her. We now owned a second-hand television and when *Your Hit Parade* came on, we sang along with the popular songs of the day. Mother liked "How Much Is That Doggie In The Window?" I was fond of "Love Me Tender," sung by Elvis Presley.

On the second night in the Associated Press newsroom, I was halfway through my shift when a reporter whose name I had not heard before called in.

"This is Sam," he said when I had answered and given mine. "The last name has an unusual spelling; here goes…"

I typed the byline and said, "Ready."

Sam dictated, "Amid the hullabaloo on the convention floor--"

"The huh--the--sorry, could you repeat and spell it?" It was a word I had never seen or heard before.

Sam began to spell it out, but with our poor phone connection and my rising panic, I could make no sense of the multiple vowels and consonants.

"Never mind -- put 'hubbub' instead," Sam said. "Or leave it -- just put an '*h,u*' and I'll tell the guy at the desk later."

Precious seconds, if not a whole minute, had been lost; I feared my job was over too. And it was only my second day!

Sam continued, at a moderate pace. I expected a swear word or two, but his voice betrayed no anger. Surprise and relief made me concentrate all my attention on every syllable in the rest of the story. Fortunately, there were no other landmines. Before Sam could disconnect, I tried to apologize.

"I'm really, truly sorry," I said. "I'll do better next time."

"Don't feel bad. So, you can't spell 'hullabaloo.' Can you wait for me at the end of your shift? I'm staying at the hotel. I'll come by and explain it to you."

Who was this wonderful man? Instead of asking Miss Miller to fire me instantly, he had thrown me a lifeline. I told him I would wait for him at twelve o'clock -- and that I was thankful, so very thankful.

"See ya," he said. "Hullabaloo!" I could have sworn I heard a laugh.

By eleven o'clock the pressroom had quieted down. Many of the correspondents had left their desks to go upstairs to the bar or to their rooms. The editors put their feet up on extra chairs and reached for a cigarette to smoke at leisure. I got up from my chair, stretched, and walked back and forth, staying close to my telephone. I did not want to make any more mistakes.

I recognized the voice that greeted Miss Miller at her desk near the entry. "Hi Marian, how's things in the asylum tonight?"

"Pretty good, Sam, just the usual crazies," she answered.

I turned towards them and saw a red-headed man in a beige sport jacket, white shirt, and tan slacks. He wore a white shirt with the top button undone. He had loosened his narrow, knitted tie, which was patterned in red, white, and blue squares that looked like a child's building blocks. Blue-tinted glasses shaded his eyes; an impish smile hovered on his full lips. He walked towards me. He was about my height.

"Hullabaloo! It's me -- Sam," he said when he had reached my desk.

"Uh, hello -- and I'm Barbara," I said and reached out to shake his hand. It was warm and soft. I guessed that Sam did not spend much time out in the sun; his skin was paler than mine.

"Sorry about the shades," Sam said, taking off his spectacles. "My eyes are extremely light-sensitive. His eyes were the palest shade of blue, almost grey, like rain clouds.

"And I'm sorry I was so slow about the hull--"

"Oh, no tragedy, we got it right," Sam laughed. "Did you figure it out? It means noise and confusion, uproar, sound, and fury -- it's what the convention is. When eleven thousand people get up on their feet and yell at each other at the top of their lungs, you have hullabaloo. Here's how you write it." He took a notepad and pen out of a slightly frayed jacket pocket, wrote HULLABALOO in large capital letters, tore off the page, and handed it to me.

"Thank you! I promise to get it right next time. I'm sorry my English isn't better," I said.

"You're not a native speaker; I can hear that," Sam said. "But the accent is barely there, and I can't quite place it. Not French. Polish? Hungarian?"

"German," I said. "I have been in this country since December 1950. I am a journalism student."

"In-ter-esting," Sam said, drawing out the word. "Now I know what a pretty girl like you is doing in a place like this -- I was going to ask, but that's a stupid line so I didn't."

I laughed, feeling relieved that he had not held my ignorance against me. Everything about this man was relaxed -- his easy conversation, even his clothing -- the unbuttoned shirt and coat, the dangling tie, the belt that had sagged below the waistline to accommodate a small potbelly. I wondered how he managed to stay so calm in his high-tension job. I wondered how old he was. I could not tell.

"Can we go up to the bar and talk?" he asked. "I think Marian will let you go for the night--there's not much happening at this hour."

"You ask her," I begged. "I don't want her mad at me."

"Okay," Sam said as he put his sunglasses on. "Grab your purse; let's go."

Miss Miller gave us a cheerful wave when we passed her desk. "Have a drink on me!"

Sam and I sat in the dark cocktail lounge that was crowded with news people -- mostly men; the few women I saw were part of a couple. Sam ordered a double vodka with ice for himself.

"I'm not twenty-one," I said. "I'll be twenty in November."

Sam and the bartender laughed. "Ginger Ale for her," they said together.

"Well," Sam said. "You know my name. I work out of the Washington Bureau; I live in Alexandria, Virginia -- that's a suburb. Besides covering the White House, I write a weekly humor column that gets picked up by various papers. I don't suppose it's reached Chicago?"

"No, I've never seen it. I wish I could read it," I answered.

"I'll send you some clippings," Sam said. "And now tell me about you. All I know so far is, you're an immigrant and a college student. That's not a feature story yet. Tell more!"

"I'm at Wright Junior College and journalism is my major--it's what I want to do when I finish my education -- I want to work for a newspaper, or be a wire service reporter, like you--"

"How many women work in the newsroom?" Sam interrupted.

"Three," I said after a long pause. "Miss Miller, the other typist, and me--I should say and *I* -- that's correct English."

"And what do they do? They're typists or secretaries. How many female reporters call in to your phone?"

"No females."

"It's a tough business," Sam said, patting my hand. "You want to think before setting your sights on it. It's a lot of travel, a lot of sitting around in the proverbial smoke-filled rooms. It's hard on families. You might get married and have kids and -- do you see the problem?"

"I am not getting married," I said. "I want to work. I know I have to finish school first, but I don't want to get married. My dream is to be a journalist."

"Hmm--no boyfriend? Bet you have a boyfriend." Sam was smiling.

"Yes, I have but he has to go back to India; we are not getting married."

Sam said, "If you say so. Meanwhile--"

I heard the national anthem playing on the bar's television. It was midnight, the end of the broadcasting day.

"Sam, I have to get home," I said. "My mother worries."

Sam reached for his glass, swallowed the rest of his drink as if it were water, signaled the bartender for the check, and got up.

"Time. Yes. I'll walk you to your bus stop."

"Thanks, you don't have to; I'll be fine, but thanks," I said.

"I want to, and a little air will do me good after the day I had."

"How do you stay so calm with all the tension and hullabaloo?" I asked, trying out my new word.

"I love my work; I get carried away by it. And -- and the vodka helps." Sam said.

At the El stop, my newfound friend shook my hand. "I'll come by again tomorrow night. I like ambition. I want to know more of your story. And I'll tell you more about the real world, but you won't believe me, and I'll tell you anyway because you're nineteen and I'm thirty-eight -- exactly twice your age. You'll have to listen to an old man."

There were three days left until the convention's end. As he had promised, Sam came to the newsroom every night when the breaking news had been covered. In the lounge, Sam would make me laugh by describing the antics of delegates wearing tall Uncle Sam hats and holding aloft signs with slogans in support of their chosen candidate for vice president.

"Adlai hasn't announced a running mate. They're all going nuts, trying to get in front of the TV cameras," Sam said.

I told Sam about my family, about arriving in America, about high school, and about my courses and the newspaper at Wright College. "I'll be graduating next January. Then I want to continue at a four-year college, but I don't know which school. It costs so much money," I said.

"Your advisor should help you-- I'm sure he will, from what you've told me," Sam reassured me. "He can find some scholarship money; don't be shy; ask him."

I asked Sam about his life when he was not working.

"I'm married and have two little kids," he said. "And I won't insult you with the bromide 'my wife doesn't understand me' -- she understands me all too well."

On Thursday, Adlai Stevenson, now the Democratic Party nominee for president, told the convention that he would not name a running mate. The convention was to decide between five possibles, including a young politician from Massachusetts named John F. Kennedy. The scramble, as described by Sam, was the perfect illustration of "hullabaloo."

After multiple ballots, the convention delegates chose Senator Estes Kefauver of Tennessee as the party's nominee for vice president. This was the major news story on Friday, August 17, the last day of the convention. It was also my last day of work for the Associated Press.

My typewriter stayed so busy that my fingers ached. I survived all the fast-talking reporters but one who barked, "Put me through to Marian, now!" I was relieved when Sam came on the line and spoke, not slowly, but at a pace he knew I could manage.

"Wait for me tonight," he said when the story was complete. "We're celebrating."

"Call your mom. You'll be home late but I'll see to it you get there safely," Sam said when he came to the newsroom. "We're going to go hear some jazz -- and don't start looking down your aristocratic nose at it -- it's an American art form and part of your education!"

I knew nothing about jazz. Music, to my family, meant Beethoven and Mozart. American music was Patti Page and Doris Day singing popular hits, or Vic Damone performing "On the Street Where You Live," from the recently opened show *My Fair Lady*.

Chicago's Loop in the fifties was alive with legendary jazz. I don't remember which club we visited that August night, but I know it was Erroll Garner who played piano.

At first, I did not know what to make of the unfamiliar music, but I listened attentively. Hadn't Sam said it was educational? Gradually, I began to enjoy the melodies that flowed in and out of each other and the rhythms that varied from hypnotic to exciting. Sam sipped vodka and smoked; everybody in the room smoked. I asked Sam for a cigarette and he lit it with his Zippo lighter. I felt very sophisticated -- and very tired.

"I don't know if the trains run this late," I said into Sam's ear after an hour or so.

He sat up in his chair. "It's late, isn't it? Don't worry, I'll put you in a cab and send you home safe. No El train. Tell your mom I'm sorry I kept you up. But I'm glad we had this time together. Unless Ike decides to make a trip to Chicago, we won't see each other for -- for I don't know how long!"

"Could I have a piece of paper?" I asked. "I want to give you my address and phone number. Maybe you'll get an assignment in Chicago sooner than you think."

"We can always hope. I don't want to lose track of you. I'm interested in you. Please write to me. I want to know all about your school and your family, your ambitions, and dreams. Will you write? Here -- this is my address."

I thanked Sam as we exchanged papers. I thanked him for everything -- for being patient with my typing, for the visits to the newsroom, for the wonderful music tonight. For being kind.

Sam smiled and said, "Enough of that. Just be sure to write-- everything. Even if you marry that Asian youth of yours. Do you know what 'youth in Asia' sounds like? 'Euthanasia'!"

We left the smoky bar and stepped out into the hot Chicago summer. Sam flagged down a taxi, made sure the driver understood the address I gave, stuck two ten-dollar bills into my hand -- how had he guessed I did not have that much cash in my purse? I protested but he said, "Don't argue. It's to keep your mom from worrying."

I was about to close the cab's door when Sam stepped up close and said, "One more thing. I'll make a bargain with you. If you still want to be a journalist a year from today, and if you can manage a trip to D.C. then, I'll show you all around Washington and take you to the White House press room. Deal?"

"You will? Deal!" I said, not quite believing I had heard right. In my tired, dazed condition, I thought I had slipped into the realm of fairy tales, where promises are fulfilled "in a year and a day."

CHAPTER 19

Flight Plan

"I didn't do anything special for your birthday; I'm sorry I forgot," I said to my brother when I reconnected with my family after the hectic week of night shifts in the Associated Press newsroom. Roland's fourteenth birthday had been on August 15, 1956. The year before, Mother had taken the family out for dinner at the Bismarck Hotel, where a photographer had taken a picture of our elegantly dressed group. Had this year's birthday been celebrated without me?

"It's all right," Roland said. "I went out with Jutta; I really dig that chick."

Mother asked for a translation.

"Girl," Lincoln supplied, smiling. "He likes the girl."

"Tomorrow is Sunday; we can have cake and coffee just for the family -- assuming we are all awake at normal hours again," Mother said, giving me a look that meant "don't sleep until noon!" She had felt uneasy about my working hours even though she understood that I had not been given a choice. An early riser herself, she had little patience with people staying in bed after eight in the morning.

"We've barely seen you -- it seems like a month," Lincoln said. "So, tell! How was it? What did you do? What did you learn? Did you meet Mr. Stevenson?"

"No, not Adlai Stevenson," I answered. "I wasn't at the convention center; we worked at the Conrad Hilton. The reporters went back and forth; I met a bunch of them, and I saw some of the hullabaloo on television."

I had sprung the new word on them on purpose. As I had expected, everyone wanted to know what it meant. While recounting the story, I felt the excitement of the newsroom all over again.

"I didn't know my fingers could move so fast -- I really had to hang on to their every word to get it right, especially at first. The reporters were calling from phone booths outside the hall and it was so noisy -- and they talked fast. I was lucky with that word 'hullabaloo' -- I had no idea how to spell it. Sam -- that's the reporter who used it -- was so nice -- he let me skip it and then he asked the desk guy to fix it. Sam asked for me to take dictation after that and came in to say hello. He's the one who took me to the club Friday night -- Erroll Garner is a jazz pianist; I never heard this kind of music before," I related, all in one breath.

"Wow. Some story!" Roland laughed. "Can you slow down? Who's Sam? New boyfriend?"

"Oh no, no. He's a senior correspondent from the Washington Bureau. He covers the White House. I told him I'm studying journalism and he's friendly and helpful. He wants me to write and tell him about my classes next year and what university I'll apply to. But no romance," I said. It was true; I felt no physical attraction to Sam. I admired him the way I admired Mr. Crist, as a mentor -- a guide who could help me achieve my goals.

Mother's watchful face relaxed. Lincoln said, "Your mother says you came in extra late because you went to a bar with him. I suppose he fed you whisky?"

"We went to hear music; I didn't drink alcohol!" I wondered if Lincoln was jealous. The thought gave me a thrill.

"I'm glad we are back to normal -- at least what's normal for this family," Mother said. "School starts soon. Roland will go to high school and you are in college. I can't believe how time flies by!"

"On wings of song," Lincoln quoted with a smirk.

I decided not to mention Sam's promise and the trip to Washington I would take next year. The family seemed a bit suspicious, but I knew no one would mind my writing to Sam. I sent him a long letter. It was not answered until mid-September, when an envelope full of newspaper clippings arrived. They were samples of Sam's humor column. "How is school? Keep sending your news," was penciled in the margins. After reading each article at least twice, I passed the clippings along to the family.

"Don't lose them or throw them out," I said sternly. "They're mine. I want all of them back."

Sam's columns poked fun at politicians, pretentious intellectuals, UFO sightings, and stories about ranchers being abducted by aliens who had landed in the New Mexico desert. Mother became a fan; she loved Sam's understated humor. When she gave the precious clippings back to me, she said, "Be sure to ask for more."

Roland seemed to be comfortable at Senn High School. He told us that the English teacher had recognized our last name because I had been in her class.

At Wright, Mr. Crist wanted to hear all about my experiences with the Associated Press. "We should schedule a conference," he said. "We also need to talk about the future--you want to transfer to a four-year school. Is that still your intention?"

"Oh yes! I do want to go to a journalism school, a university -- but I've looked at the catalogs and it looks impossible."

"Why? You have the grades. If they stay as good as they have been, you'll graduate Phi Theta Kappa."

My face must have shown that I did not know what the Greek letters signified.

"That's the scholastic honor society for junior colleges; four-year universities have Phi Beta Kappa. Students with the highest grade point averages are invited to join; it's very prestigious; admissions counselors look at these things," Mr. Crist explained.

"I didn't know about that," I said, feeling embarrassed by what I had to tell him next. "It's also a matter of money. My family can't afford it."

"Your mother owns a business; didn't you tell me that?"

"Yes, but she doesn't have money saved up. The business takes care of our rent and food. There never seems to be anything extra. Mother doesn't pay herself a salary; she only takes out what we need for living expenses," I said.

"I see, I see -- you will need financial aid, a scholarship. That will take some searching. I won't say it's easy, but it's certainly possible, especially for a hardworking, smart student like you."

"Is it really?" I asked. What Mr. Crist had just told me was news to me. I knew the word "scholarship", but I had defined it as knowledge, academic achievement; I had never connected it with money.

"Yes," my advisor reassured me. "A scholarship will grant you money for tuition, sometimes even room and board. Of course, it is a competitive process. You have to apply and show that you are qualified to receive it."

I mentally drew angel wings on Mr. Crist's suit jacket. And I again blessed the spirit of Wilbur Wright, who had led me to this college from which it was possible to keep flying towards my dreams.

"I want to hear about your job at the AP newsroom. I'll work on the scholarship research with you, but now tell me how it went," Mr. Crist said. I was more than happy to give him a full account, including my meeting with Sam.

"When I finish school, I want to go to Washington and try for a job with the AP or one of the other news services. I think Sam will help me," I said.

"It's certainly good to know someone in the field," Mr. Crist said. "But I approve of your plan to get a university degree first. I gather your family is of the same opinion?"

"Definitely. My mother always says education is a very important goal. She is all in favor of my going on to get a university degree," I answered.

"We'll do our best. Go to the library and look at the universities in the area -- Northwestern, the University of Chicago, University of Illinois. Miss Clarke will help you," my advisor said.

I went away full of hope. Like Mother, I had a plan. And at the first opportunity, I visited the library. Miss Clarke surprised me by greeting me by name.

"You're Barbara, Mr. Crist's student," she said. "I hear we are looking at universities?"

"Yes, Miss Clarke -- I hope to find a school that will take me -- I will need financial help. How did you know?"

"Oh, Mr. Crist likes to help his students; he is a very dedicated teacher; I like to help him -- and you -- if I can."

"Thank you; thank you very much. I didn't know about scholarships until Mr. Crist told me," I said.

The pretty, dark-haired young woman smiled. "No doubt it's different where you came from. You are still a newcomer, aren't you? You aren't expected to know everything about the American system just yet."

Cheered on by this kindly librarian, I studied the available catalogs and made notes. My most interesting find was the Medill School of Journalism at Northwestern University, in Evanston, north of Chicago. I knew Evanston was reachable by elevated train. Would they let me transfer after I graduated from Wright? Would they have scholarship aid? Would it be possible to commute and save the cost of a dormitory room? I did not have time to ask Miss Clarke because my study period was over, and I had to hurry to a class. I thanked her quickly and left, resolving to talk with Mr. Crist.

"Can't hurt to try," he said a few days later, when I had told him about my visit to the library and asked whether I should seek an interview at Northwestern. "I can't answer your specific questions," Mr. Crist said. "You want to ask at their admissions office. Phone them or go in person."

I felt nervous about this new venture, but I reminded myself that I had gone alone to my entrance exam at the *Luisenschule* when I was only ten. Now I was nearly twenty and was a serious student of journalism. I thought of my mother's word *Mut.* Show some courage, I told myself in English.

My appointment was on a weekday, so I had to excuse myself from classes. From home, I reached Northwestern University in less than an hour. Located on the shore of Lake Michigan, the attractive campus impressed me with its multitude of buildings and tree-lined pathways, the archways, and fountains. Wright College was one massive building on a city street; this was a miniature city!

I was glad that I had allowed enough time to find the administration building and the admissions office without having to rush. A receptionist handed me a form.

"Fill this out -- name, address, current school, date and place of birth, et cetera," she said. So far, this was a familiar procedure; my nervousness started to diminish.

In addition to requesting my data, the form asked for information about parents -- name, address, current status (living or deceased). I wrote in the answers, but the next question brought me up short. "What is your family's annual income?"

I did not know what Mother took from the earnings of the store. I did not know what those figures were. The fingers holding my pen went numb. There was no number I could put down. I wrote, "Family owns business. Parkway Sweater Import," and I added the address on Lincoln Avenue.

The receptionist glanced at me. "If you're finished, you may come this way," she said as she got up from her chair. I followed her into an inner room, where a middle-aged lady with a bouffant hairdo sat behind a large desk. She said her name -- which I have forgotten -- and told me to take a seat. She scanned my form; her expressionless face told me nothing. I waited.

"Hmm, I see. Wright Junior College; January 1957 graduation. Journalism major," the admissions counselor finally said. "So, you would be applying as a transfer student, junior year?"

"Yes, I hope so," I said.

"You did not give an adequate account of your financial resources. Do you, does your family have savings you can use to defray the costs of tuition and room and board? Do you have a college fund?"

"I'm sorry, but I have no savings account, no college fund. We have the business; it pays for all the family expenses. But I would need financial aid. My advisor at Wright told me it may be possible to apply for it," I answered.

The counselor repeated, "No savings, no family income--"

I held my breath, hoping the next words would be an encouraging remark about scholarship money.

Instead, I heard, "Sorry! The University cannot admit destitute students."

I was so taken aback that I could only stare. I knew the definition of "destitute." It meant penniless, indigent, totally without means. Surely that did not apply to me? True, I needed financial assistance, but I had a home, food, and clothing; I was a student in good standing, with the means to buy the textbooks I needed. I earned money from summer jobs. Surely, I was not a pauper, a bum.

I hope I said thank you and goodbye; I do not remember. Back at home, I decided to look up "destitute" again, just in case. I now owned my very own dictionary, a Merriam-Webster. I found the word. I had not mistaken its meaning. There it was -- "penniless, indigent...."

By the time I described my interview at Northwestern University to Mr. Crist, I was no longer tearful; I was indignant.

"I am too poor. They said I am destitute. That isn't right. I didn't even tell my mother because she would consider it a deadly insult," I said, concluding my tale. "You don't think I'm a penniless bum, do you?"

Mr. Crist looked concerned. "No indeed. That's obviously ridiculous. I'm sorry you had to go through such a disappointing experience. Medill is an old, established school; they can probably fill it with the sons and daughters of alumni -- students who have generous trust funds. They may not be interested in transfers either. But Barbara, do *not* give up hope. There are other possibilities. Northwestern is just one school There are others. We have to keep looking, and we will! Who said, 'We have only just begun to fight'?"

"John Paul Jones?" I tried, pulling up a half-remembered quote from American history classes.

"Franklin Roosevelt." Mr. Crist smiled. "He said it in a speech. Admiral John Paul Jones said 'I have *not yet* begun to fight' -- he is often misquoted. However -- the meaning is the same. You keep up the good work in class and at the paper -- and keep up your spirits."

I wished I believed in heaven as unequivocally as Tante did. I wished this heaven would shower blessings upon my advisor. Not when he was old and his earthly journey was done, but now. Today. This minute.

Final exams were still two months away, but I settled down to study extra hard for all of my classes. Now that I knew about the honor society, I wanted to qualify for it and improve my chances of winning a scholarship. Whenever I went to the library to research a term paper, Miss Clarke gave me a friendly greeting. She showed me multipage, printed lists that, she explained, contained information about grants available at different schools.

"If there is scholarship money around, we'll find it," Miss Clarke said. "I am helping several other students too."

My work always went better after seeing the librarian; I couldn't thank her enough. I wrote to Sam, praising my advisor and his helpful colleague. I wondered if they were a couple; they were about the same age and both were unmarried -- as far as I knew.

In October, Mr. Crist called me into his office for a conference. "Good news," he said. "There is a scholarship established by an alumnus of the University of Chicago -- a Polish gentleman, I believe -- it is specifically intended for a deserving foreign-born student. The scholarship will pay full tuition for one year and is renewable if the student's grades remain at a satisfactory level. The curriculum may be in any field the student desires -- liberal arts, science, mathematics; there is no restriction. I think you meet the criteria for this grant. If you agree, we should apply right away."

My teacher handed me the list he had been consulting. "Here, see -- this is the named scholarship, and the details of the application process, and the dates for submitting the transcripts and other paperwork. Do you want to go ahead?"

"Yes, Mr. Crist," I said and burst into tears.

My teacher let me calm down for a few minutes; then he had some "practical questions," as he put it.

"This means you will study at the University of Chicago, one of the finest schools in the world. Do you know much about it? Do you know where it is? And the scholarship is for tuition only. You will need to pay for room and board, as well as books and health fees and such. Can you manage that? How will you do it?"

I gathered my wits and started to answer. "I've never been to the campus; I know it's on the South Side. I'll take a train there as soon as I can and walk around. I'd guess the train ride is at least forty-five minutes. Do you think that's about right?"

"I think so," Mr. Crist replied. "When you go, you might ask for a tour. Be sure to look at the library and Rockefeller Chapel --they're magnificent; in fact, the whole place is."

"I've heard the U of C is very *serious* -- no football team, no fraternities, no sororities," I continued. And my Uncle Anton calls it 'that pinko place -- nothing but a commie hangout.'"

Mr. Crist laughed. "A common perception among our more conservative citizens. The influence of the Cold War. Liberalism is often taken for out-and-out communism. You'll be able to judge for yourself once you're a student. I personally don't see an institution of higher learning as a threat. As for 'serious,' it is that. You will be working hard; be prepared."

"About money," I went on, "I work every summer and save my wages. My mother lets me keep everything I make. I can also find a part time job--maybe at the University -- to help out. If I get the scholarship, I'll probably live at home for the first semester and then work all summer. I know my mother will be happy to hear that tuition is paid for. And she'll find extra money if I need it for living expenses; she wants me to have this opportunity."

Mr. Crist gave me a questioning look. "It's a long commute from the North Side," he said. Are you sure?"

"It's the University of Chicago! You just said it's one of the best in the world! If I win this scholarship, I'm going. I took a train to my school in Munich; that was worse than the El; I never got a seat on it," I said.

Mr. Crist reached out and shook my hand. "Good. We'll get started on the application forms. I will add the word 'dauntless' to my letter of recommendation. And best of luck!"

I guessed at the definition of "dauntless." I looked it up at home; Merriam-Webster said I was right.

After telling the family my news, I could hardly wait to see Surendra. I knew he would be happy for me. To my disappointment, he did not show up for the next history class. I wondered if he was ill and thought of calling him, but I realized that I had no phone number for him. I didn't even know where he lived. A week passed before we met again, in the hall after class.   There was something different about my friend, and at first, I could not identify what had changed. Then, when I was standing close to him, I saw that his brown cheeks were covered with short, curly black hair. A twist of fear pulled at my innards.

Surendra took my hand in his. "Yes, Deva," he said quietly. "I am going home soon. My father wants me. The political situation is tense -- there may be trouble about the plebiscite -- he wants me home with my brothers and cousins. If it comes to fighting--"

I reached up to touch his face. "Your beard hasn't grown. You can't go yet! Don't go and get killed!" I cried.

"Deva, I am not going tomorrow -- I have another two weeks to settle things here. And as for fighting, I am young and strong. The Sikhs are warriors, you know. I will never forget you. I will write to you," Surendra said.

"Yes, please, please write and I'll write you back. I'll miss you so much."

"I will miss you."

Surendra's eyes glistened, but not with tears. My warrior friend would never cry. It was happiness I saw. He was going home to the land he loved, to a father who wanted his son by his side.

On November 6, 1956, Dwight Eisenhower won a second term as president of the United States, defeating Adlai Stevenson by a large margin. Richard Nixon became vice president. On November 11, I celebrated my twentieth birthday. I received a note from Sam, typed on yellow Western Union Press Message paper.

"OGL wins second term no surprise," it read, and the note continued, "Happy Birthday! Legally, you are a minor until you turn 21. As far as I'm concerned, you are already a Major Barbara!"

In place of a signature, Sam had scribbled, "G.B. Shaw," at the bottom of the page. This puzzled me for a while. Miss Clarke at the school library was kind enough to explain the reference.

Shortly after Thanksgiving, Mr. Crist asked me to come to his office when I had a free period.

"Good news again," he said as soon as I entered. "Things have moved faster than I expected; your scholarship was approved. I am happy for you -- congratulations!"

My knees felt weak; I sat down quickly.

"Yes, yes, sit down -- I know it's a surprise," Mr. Crist said. He sounded as excited as I felt. After he had again gone over the details of the grant with me, I asked how I could send a thank-you letter to the sponsor. Mr. Crist gave me an address to copy; I composed a heartfelt message of gratitude.

University! Barbara gets financial aid! A dream comes true! My family treated me like a heroine.

Mother asked, "Is this university only for people who live in Chicago?"

"No," I answered. "There are students from all over the country and the world, in liberal arts, history, humanities, archaeology -- and they have a famous medical school. The science department is working on nuclear physics -- they have a connection with Argonne National Laboratories -- I read about it in the catalog."

Lincoln and Roland congratulated me. Roland said, "You like to study; you'll do fine."

Lincoln asked, "Is your friend Surendra going too?"

"No, he has to go home," I said and told the story.

Roland said, "What a drag! I like him."

I did not look at Lincoln's face. I did not want to know what it was saying.

Mr. Crist had a telephone conference with the admissions officer at the University of Chicago and made an appointment for me to be interviewed. I made my second visit to the campus; the first had been a little more than a month before. I allowed myself time to walk around the campus before the appointment. Although it was a freezing winter day, I spent most of an hour admiring the large, handsome greystone Gothic buildings, topped with graceful spires. Although I had never seen the great English universities, I thought that Oxford and Cambridge must look like this.

The grass on the wide promenade called the Midway was brown and was dusted with snow. The campus buildings, especially the chapel with its stained-glass windows, evoked German cathedrals. I was struck by the thought that I had never seen the ancient city of Munich intact. When I went to school there, I had walked among ruins.

In the red-carpeted admissions office, I was received by a gentleman wearing a dark suit and heavy, black-rimmed glasses. He waved his hand at the chair in front of his desk.

"You are the scholarship student from Wright Junior College, correct?" he asked.

"Yes, Sir. I have a letter from Mr. Crist, my advisor," I said, offering him the envelope.

"Good, good. I see you will be graduating in January and you want to enter in the spring semester."

"Yes, if I can. If it's possible. I'm a journalism major and I want to continue in that field," I explained.

"I see. Your transcripts are here, except for your final grades. Be sure those are forwarded to us. Your major is journalism. Yes. We do not have a school of journalism here; you are aware of that, I believe?"

I had not known, but I was ashamed to admit this. I said, "I understand that my scholarship has no restrictions about curriculum. I could take courses in--"

"What you want is political science! You want to work as a reporter? You can learn to write a news story in six weeks. What you need to study here is political theory, history, government -- it's the background, do you see, not the mechanics," the admissions counselor said. He spoke firmly, as if I should have known all of this before even coming in the door. I did my best to look bright and agreeable.

"Yes, yes. Political science! I love history -- American and European history --"

"Excellent. We will work out a schedule of courses for you. Your B.A. degree, if you complete the curriculum, will be given by the Division of Political Science. You will, of course, take economics and the humanities requirements as well."

"Of course," I agreed. I was so excited by this new direction for my studies that I would have agreed to badminton if this wise educator deemed it a requirement. And, come to think of it, I did know how to write a news story already, thanks to Mr. Crist and the Wright College paper. How different this interview was from the one at Northwestern University!

"Call this office after the Christmas vacation," the counselor instructed. "We will work out the rest of the arrangements. Congratulations on your grant, and, if all goes as well as we expect, we will welcome you to the University of Chicago for the spring semester."

The few students I saw as I walked to the train station were moving fast, bundled in heavy parkas and ski hats with earflaps. Warmed by the gift I had just received; I did not feel the cold. Christmas had come early.

CHAPTER 20

Commencement

The exhilaration of receiving a scholarship and the excitement I felt about the new direction my studies would be taking at the University of Chicago kept my spirits high as the close of my last semester at Wright College approached. I studied for the final exams with energy and looked forward to graduation at the end of January 1957.

My mother asked if we could invite Mr. Crist and Miss Clarke to have dinner with the family. "You talk about them so much and they've done so much for you. I would like to meet them and thank them before you leave that school," she said.

"Yes! Could we? Let's do it during the Christmas vacation. I'll help with cooking and baking. I'll ask when they can come," I answered, surprised and happy that Mother was making this offer in the midst of the holiday shopping season when the store was at its busiest. I should help in the Sweat Port too, I thought; I'll do it during the break.

I lost no time conveying our invitations to Mr. Crist and Miss Clarke. Both accepted and we set a date.

I asked Roland to join me in making our apartment look as festive as possible.

"Who's coming? The Three Kings in person?" he teased. But good-natured as he was, my brother helped me to drag a tall, sprawling spruce tree up the stairs and to set it up and decorate it. He made several trips to the hardware store and to the specialty store for the white wax candles Mother used every year and the metal holders fitted with clips that secured them to the branches.

"You know, they have electric lights -- in colors too. Less danger of fire," Roland remarked.

"Yes, but Mom thinks it's only Christmas with real candles," I said. "Read your Boy Scout manual; see what to do in case of fire."

"Throw a rug over it," Roland said, prepared as a good scout should always be.

On the evening of the party, Mr. Crist and Miss Clarke arrived separately, within a few minutes of each other. Lincoln, Roland, and I greeted them at the door; Mother came from the kitchen a moment later. As I introduced the guests, Miss Clarke handed Mother a bouquet of holly and evergreens and Mr. Crist gave me an envelope.

"Just a card to congratulate you," he said. "From Virginia and me."

I thanked him, realizing he had said Miss Clarke's first name. I had seen it on her nameplate at the library. His given name, I knew, was Edward. At school, teachers and staff were addressed by their titles and surnames.

Lincoln, as host, seated the guests and asked if they would take "a refreshing glass of wine." It was characteristic of him to embellish nouns with adjectives. The guests accepted; Lincoln poured. Mother joined in a toast to "a happy and prosperous New Year" before she returned to the kitchen. Roland put the bouquet in a vase and placed it on the dinner table.

I opened the envelope and took out the greeting card. It was not a commercial one. On the front was a pencil drawing of Gothic buildings with a wide avenue in front of them. Inside was a poem, handwritten and signed, "Ed and Virginia." I no longer have all the words, but my favorite lines were, "From the towers of the Midway peal out paeans to greet Barbara -- Who is halfway towards her B.A."

Before we served the food, Roland lit the candles on the Christmas tree. The guests said, "How lovely...so beautiful." If they had misgivings about open flames, they were too polite to voice them. Mother had stuffed and roasted a capon. She had a low opinion of turkeys; their meat was too dry and stringy, she said. The meal received the praise it deserved; more toasts were offered – "to the honored Professor Crist," and to "Miss Librarian Clarke." Mother thanked each of them for the help and encouragement they had given me. I added my thanks. Mr. Crist wished everyone happiness and success.

After the main course, we drank coffee and nibbled on cookies -- a truly impressive array of *Pfeffernuesse, Zimtsterne,* gingerbread men, and sugar cookies in a dozen fanciful shapes. Although Roland and I had helped, the bravura performance was all Mother's.

Conversation flowed easily despite the formal titles Mother and I could not bring ourselves to abandon. Lincoln, Roland, and Mr. Crist, on a first-name basis, chatted amiably. Miss Clarke asked Mother for a business card so that she could visit the store someday. Mother asked what course of study was required to become a librarian, and what degree was given.

"Would it be something Barbara should study?" she wondered.

"Library science is a rewarding profession," Miss Clarke answered. "But I think Barbara has chosen a different path. Political science, and writing, and literature -- should she become interested in that for its own sake -- are fascinating fields. She is intellectually ambitious; the University of Chicago is ideal for her. She will blossom."

When our guests left, it was again separately, within a few minutes of each other.

"Nice couple," Lincoln observed. "They didn't have to be so secretive about their romance. Nobody minds if they're going to the same place."

Worldly-wise Lincoln! He had answered my question. And I agreed with him; Ed and Virginia were perfect for each other.

In January, I was jittery before the final exams, but I managed to steady myself and passed my courses with high marks. I was inducted into the honor society with about a dozen other seniors. The ceremony made me feel successful and happy; the small gold Phi Theta Kappa key I was given remains a treasured keepsake.

It was a proud family that sat in the Wright auditorium for the Commencement ceremonies on February 1, 1957. On the stage, I was placed in one of the front rows with the Phi Theta society members and the speakers. In addition to my Associate of Arts diploma, I was presented with the Wilbur Wright Junior College Journalism Award -- a check for one hundred dollars.

As I took off my rented cap and gown in the lobby, Mr. Crist and Miss Clarke came over to congratulate me and to shake hands all around. I held back tears.

"Commencement -- as you already know, and we repeat it often -- is a beginning," Mr. Crist said. "Don't think of today as an ending. It's the start of a whole new adventure. And I expect a report from you once you've settled into your classes at Chicago."

Miss Clarke gave me a hug. "Ditto," she said.

Senn High School, Wright College, and the University of Chicago all divided the academic year into two semesters and a summer session that was optional. Because I had graduated a semester early from Senn High School two years before, in 1955, and had entered Wright College in a spring semester, I was allowed to transfer to the University of Chicago in February 1957, as their semester was just beginning.

I had decided to live at home and commute, at least until the summer vacation started at the end of June. As a junior, I was permitted to live off campus; I wanted to save the cost of dormitory accommodations. If I could earn a decent salary somehow -- somewhere -- during the summer, I thought, I could move to the campus in the fall.

Mother gave me warm sweaters and slacks from the store. "Months of winter still to come," she said. "Are ski pants allowed?"

"I don't think there is a dress code," I answered, judging by what I had seen the students wearing when I had visited. Chicago winters were brutal, but I had made it through five of them by now without a major illness.

"For most of the trip, I'll be on a train, out of the wind," I assured Mother. With the fire of ambition burning within me, I gave no thought to the discomfort of the long walk to and from the El station.

I had another meeting with the admissions counselor I had seen in November. He helped me plan a course of study and told me which classes I needed for my degree program. I walked from one of the cathedral-like buildings to another, through corridors lined with colorful leaded-glass windows. I couldn't resist sitting down in a few of the velvet-cushioned alcoves and admiring the view of the snow-covered campus outside. I found the Registrar's office, where I signed up for courses in political theory, history, and economics, and for History of Western Civilization, which was the required core curriculum for Humanities.

The reading lists I was handed would keep me busy for ten semesters, I thought. I felt awed -- intimidated. But along with my trepidation came a joyous curiosity. What would I discover in these new fields?

Courage! I admonished myself once more. This is *commencement!* You are beginning your studies at the University of Chicago -- one of the finest institutions of higher learning in the world! You are one lucky immigrant!

Because I was not an incoming freshman, I had not been offered an orientation session or a tour, so I explored the campus on my own. I found the Harper Memorial Library with its acres of underground stacks; I visited the Student Union and its coffee shop. Outside, at midday, I was greeted by bells, their harmonies as crisp and clear as the winter air. I walked over to the Rockefeller Chapel and gazed up at the bell tower. I felt I was living inside the poem on my graduation card.

I located the rooms where my courses met and began my life as a University of Chicago student. I saw that the schedule was organized differently from that at Wright. Instead of sitting in one classroom for every lesson, students met once or twice a week for lectures in large halls and in smaller seminar rooms for discussion on other days.

My political science professors were Hans J. Morgenthau, Herman Finer, and Kermit Eby. Each assigned reading material and gave lectures that were an hour or an hour and a half long. Small groups of students then met for seminars led by the professor or, sometimes, a graduate assistant. I quickly found that it was necessary to take extensive notes at the lectures because the questions asked in the seminars were probing. Answers were required to be thoughtful and founded on what we had read.

Professor Morgenthau explained that our readings would consist mainly of original sources-- the historian Thucydides on the Peloponnesian War, the philosophers John Locke, Thomas Hobbes, David Hume, and Nicolo Machiavelli on the theory of government and the rights of citizens. All this was new territory for me; I felt both excitement and dread. I hoped that I would be up to the challenge.

The Humanities course -- History of Western Civilization -- included studies in the music and art of past centuries. Students were sent to the library to explore books on Greek and Roman architecture, painting, and sculpture, Renaissance and Baroque art. We were asked to listen to recordings of Gregorian chant, and of the music of Monteverdi, Bach, Gluck, and later composers. I loved these assignments, losing myself in the elegant tangle of madrigals or the stark progressions of Bach that came through my headphones. Although my family loved classical music, I knew nothing about early styles; I was most familiar with Mozart, Beethoven, and Verdi.

I did not have much time to socialize with my fellow students. When classes were over for the day, I would spend one or two hours in the library and then start on the long trip home. Often, it was dark when I got there. After dinner, I would help with the dishes and then settle down with one of my textbooks. I did not get much reading done. After half an hour or forty-five minutes, I would find myself staring at the pages without comprehension.

"Better to read it over in the morning," Lincoln would advise. "The brain needs rest; it works much faster after a restoring sleep. *Gute Nacht!*"

At school, I had brief chats with people before or after class. A more relaxed venue was the coffee shop. It was a welcome haven during the day, between classes; it was warm and informal and was filled with lively chatter. You could sit at any table and join in the conversation that was already in progress. I did not have a room or locker on campus, so I carried my books and notepads with me in a large satchel. I carried my coat or jacket-- hat, scarf, and mittens stuffed into the pockets. My baggage turned out to be a conversation starter.

"Are you just coming from the airport, or are you going on a trip?" someone would ask.

"Just a long trip from home on the North Side," I would say and the group around the table would go on to exchange information about families, countries, and courses. I did not mention that I had never flown in an airplane.

Over coffee and sweet rolls, I met Sayid, who was from Beirut; his major was International relations. Rita, a statuesque blonde from North Carolina, was studying Comparative literature.

One morning, an African man introduced himself: "Hello, I am Babatunde from Uganda; I am a gun runner."

"Nice to meet you," I responded, trying to look nonchalant -- as if I met revolutionists for breakfast every day. I wondered who needed the guns. Guerillas in neighboring Kenya? I knew little of the Mau Mau revolt there, but I had the impression that the country was more or less at peace now. Someday, I might ask Babatunde why a university student would deal in guns. For the moment, I preferred small talk and hot coffee. I thought about the Athenians and the Spartans; they had laid down their arms -- and their lives -- centuries ago. Their war was over. I did not want to hear about contemporary conflicts.

I picked up a copy of the student newspaper, the *Maroon,* and wondered if there might be a place for me on its staff. I put the idea aside almost as soon as it entered my head. A glance at my schedule and the textbooks that weighed down my bag told me that I had no time. I had term papers to research and write, midterm exams to prepare for. I headed for the library, where I needed to work on an assignment about the theories of Thomas Hobbes and John Locke. What were the natural rights of man? Were there absolutes, such as Hobbes' right to self-preservation at the expense of liberty, or should the social contract include Locke's "natural rights" to life, liberty, and property? Which views had been adopted by the founders of the American republic? I began to make notes, but I soon pushed the heavy tomes away. I decided to take a break so that I could write a letter to Sam.

"The library is very big and very quiet," I wrote. "No hullabaloo here!"

Seven or eight weeks into the term, I was exhausted. I slept on the train in the mornings and evenings; I sat down for a five-minute rest in the ladies' restroom and fell asleep on the hard bench there. I dozed in the library, and, worst of all, during one lecture, I could not keep my eyes open. My hand kept moving, scrawling a page full of hieroglyphics. I was deeply embarrassed when I came to, hoping my lapse had not been noticed. Fortunately, I was seated in the back of the room. I drank too much coffee; it upset my stomach but did not keep me alert.

At home, Mother looked at me and said, *"Kind"* -- she called me Child when she was concerned -- "You look like you did when we came over on the ship. I'm worried. This is not healthy! Can't you move into a dormitory or a room in somebody's house nearby? Remember when you had pneumonia after falling into the Saar?"

"I fell asleep in class," I confessed. "It's no good. I think I'd better find something. You're right. I'll fail the course if this goes on; I'm so tired!"

"We'll find enough money; don't worry," my mother said.

Mother's practical suggestion about rooming with a family prompted me to search the bulletin boards on campus before visiting the housing office. It was easier than I had expected. On the board outside the coffee shop, a handwritten notice was posted, "For Rent -- Room for female student. Three blocks from campus. Share bathroom and kitchen. Reasonable. Call after 4 P.M." I wrote down the telephone number and used a pay phone to call when my last class ended at four-thirty.

"Leah speaking, are you calling about the room? It's still available," a businesslike voice said.

I gave my name and asked, "Is it all right to come over now and see it? I'm at the library."

"Sure, come on by; it's on the second floor," Leah replied and gave me the address. As the notice had said, it was just a short walk away. I hoped the "reasonable" rent would be something I could afford.

Leah was a tall, dark-haired young woman with large brown eyes and full, red lips. The kimono-style housecoat she wore over blue jeans and a sweatshirt had seen better days; so many loose threads hung from the edges of the sleeves that they looked fringed. Mother would have wanted to mend them on the spot.

"Come in," Leah said as she led me into the living room. It was very warm; I wished I could move in immediately. The room was furnished with a daybed covered by a multicolored quilt, two overstuffed chairs, several small tables, and bookshelves made of boards resting on bricks. The shelves were heavily populated with what looked like textbooks. Like Leah's sleeves, the cloth bindings trailed strands of green or brown linen. Lamps that did not match and ashtrays full of butts sat on the tables.

Leah walked across the room and pointed to a doorway.

"That's the bedroom; I sleep in there," she said. "This is your room. The daybed's more comfortable than it looks and you can have extra blankets -- that's if you want it. Do you want it?"

"Yes," I said. I wanted to ask for the blanket and lie down in the warmth of that room without further ado-- but of course, there was business to be settled first. We settled on a price; I had no idea what this apartment share should cost. The figure Leah named was affordable, and I made a down payment with cash Mother had given me.

"There's one condition," Leah said. "I gave you a discount on the rent in return for a small daily chore you have to do--"

"What?" I started, but Leah went on with hardly a pause.

"I like my morning coffee early because I have to go to work. I like it freshly ground -- I buy good beans -- and brought to me hot. I'll show you how to make it and you'll set the alarm clock for six. All right?"

"Uh, yes, all right. I can do that," I said. Leah's request reminded me of my mother's ritual counting of coffee beans when we had received our first post-war package from Aunt Mary, in 1946.

What really convinced me to take the room was that bed with its quilt and the promise of an extra blanket. I wanted to sleep in this room. I would gladly brew the coffee, even if it meant leaving my warm bed at an early hour.

"Fine," Leah said. "My husband used to make it, but he left. We're divorced -- good riddance to bad rubbish!"

I had meant to say that I was sorry about the divorce. Evidently this was not necessary. I added Leah's colorful phrase to my growing stock of colloquial English.

"I'm working on my thesis," Leah said. "But it's going slowly because I have to work almost full-time. My no-good husband's supposed to pay alimony but he pretends he doesn't have enough income -- the jerk!"

"What are you studying?" I asked.

"Anthropology. God knows when I'll get finished."

"Where do you work?" I asked. "What do you do?"

"It's a factory; they make shitty souvenirs -- kitschy little teacups and saucers, garden gnomes -- they're handpainted. I'm one of about twenty women who do it. Stupid job, but I need the money," Leah explained.

"I understand," I said. "When we first came to America my mom and I worked in a factory. We're immigrants."

"It's a country of immigrants," Leah said, taking my answer in stride and asking no further questions.

"I'll be going home most weekends. And in the summer, I need to find a job. I'll be living at home," I said. "I won't need the room; hope that's okay."

"I have no idea where I'll be myself during the summer," Leah said. I keep thinking I'll get assigned to do field work somewhere, but who knows. If I'm here in the fall, we can talk again."

Everyone in my family was much relieved when I told them about my new living arrangement.

"Be sure to come home every weekend," Mother urged. "You can sleep late, and you should eat too; you're much too pale!"

I smiled because that was a complaint I had heard all my life, even when I was in perfect health.

"I'll miss you," Lincoln said. "But I miss you even when you're here. You're too busy or too tired. We haven't been to a film or a play in a long time."

"I have a lot of studying to do," I said. But maybe we can go out some time soon." I admitted to myself that I missed him as well. I wasn't sure when it had started, but there was a new warmth to the relationship between Lincoln and me. The air between us seemed to heat up when we sat close together. It was frightening and exciting at the same time.

"Watch out for the Mau Mau gun runner," Roland said.

I collected clothes, shoes, and pyjamas and brought them to Leah's apartment. I slept well there even though she kept late hours and talked, without lowering her voice, on the wall telephone that was installed over the kitchen table. I was used to sharing quarters; it made me feel safe.

Staying attentive in class became much easier because I was rested in the mornings. At lunchtime I would eat a sandwich and then go to my afternoon lectures and to the library after the last class. I would make my way back to Leah's in the early evening. The apartment had a tiny kitchen with a two-burner gas stove and a small refrigerator, but we rarely cooked. Dinner might be another sandwich or soup purchased from a local deli. When Leah had a guest -- which happened only once or twice in all the time I shared her apartment -- she made spaghetti and meatballs with a tomato sauce concocted from ketchup and Italian herbs. She was fussy about the cheese. It had to be imported Parmesan and it had to be freshly grated. The after-dinner coffee was brewed extra strong.

My mother never cooked spaghetti; I thought Leah's meal was a delicious example of American cuisine.

My classes were challenging, but I was fascinated by the material. Much of the subject matter was new to me. My previous studies in history had dealt mostly with facts and events, not with the theory of government, or the influence of religious beliefs on nations. The assigned readings took a great deal of time; I had to read slowly in order to understand the complex ideas and the different writing styles of the seventeenth- and eighteenth-century authors. One day, after class, I asked one of my professors to clarify a particularly difficult passage. He obliged, and then asked, "You are new to the university, aren't you? You transferred from--remind me?"

"Wright Junior College," I said.

"How are you doing? How do you find life here?"

"I am a little -- overwhelmed -- I guess is the word," I confessed. "But I think my courses are the most interesting ones I ever had."

The professor smiled. "You must have done well at Wright. You were probably a big fish in a small pond. This pond is much bigger. Nevertheless, you'll do well -- I know that. Don't worry yourself unduly."

After thanking my teacher, I rushed to the nearest bench so that I could record his words in my notebook. The metaphor of the big fish in a small pond was new to me, though I had instantly understood what it meant. And I had never before heard anyone say "unduly" in casual conversation.

Spring arrives late in Chicago, but as the days got longer and the weather became balmy, it was possible to actually enjoy the Friday walk to the train station. I liked my weekends at home, when I could spend time with Roland and sometimes with his girlfriend. Roland told me in confidence that he and Jutta were lovers. I was not surprised because I had seen that they were attracted to each other from the first.

"Honest?" I asked. "Be careful! You don't want to get her in trouble."

That was the current euphemism for getting pregnant.

"I won't. We both know what to do," Roland said with a grin. I believed him, remembering that it had been Roland who had explained the sex act to me when he was six years old and I was eleven. Mother spoke unabashedly about love children, but she had never offered to explain the facts of life to either one of us.

On many Saturdays, I spent time at Parkway Sweater Import, helping Mother with sales or lending Lincoln a hand while he made small changes in the show window. He treated the displays like works of art -- swapping a pink sweater for a bright red one because the color was more vibrant, sliding a champagne flute between the rigid plaster fingers of the mannequin wearing a cocktail dress, adding a small painting in a corner that needed an "accent."

Mother said the store was doing well; some new, pretty summer fashions she had ordered were due to come in any day. Lincoln was good at advertising, she added. Customers mentioned seeing Parkway ads in the local *Pennysaver*.

Although these weekends were relaxed, I brought my textbooks home to study. When a written essay was due, I typed it on Mother's German typewriter, moving my fingers slowly so as not to get trapped by the different arrangement of the keyboard.

In the evenings, Lincoln urged me to go with him for "a cooling promenade," as he called a walk by Lake Michigan. These strolls were a pleasant counterpoint to Chicago's sometimes oppressive temperatures. However, they generated more heat than comfort between us. Brush fires broke out. We could not keep our hands off each other. We looked for secluded park benches or deserted stretches of beach and covered our explorations with a beach towel.

"I dream of possessing you -- fully," Lincoln would whisper in German. "Please, let's be together--maybe in the store after hours."

The idea excited me, but the terror of it made me sick with fear.

"I can't! Mom could walk in any minute. I can't face it. We should just stop."

"I would never hurt you, you know that," Lincoln said. "It would be so lovely. Promise you will make it possible!"

"I want to -- only not now; I can't; I'm too scared."

Despite our perpetual frustration, our promenades would continue throughout the spring and summer. I was certain Mother already knew what we were up to, because she suggested that we take Roland along on our walks. Roland was busy every time we made a show of asking him.

Towards the end of the semester, work on term papers and studying for exams took up almost all of my time. I loved the stacks of the Harper Library and spent hours reading and researching there. I went home to the North Side less frequently, drawing woebegone looks from Lincoln when I appeared.

One Saturday morning in May, when I was at home, Karl, my mother's longtime friend, walked out of her bedroom, dressed as we always saw him, in a three-piece business suit, white shirt, and tie. Lincoln and I were eating *muesli* for breakfast. Karl took a few steps towards us, stumbled, and gasped; his face and hands turned blue. Mother, who had come through the door right behind him, rushed to his side and tried to steady him. Karl tottered and slid to the floor. His lips moved but no sound came out.

"*Gott im Himmel,*" Mother shouted. "Quick, to the hospital!"

She plunged her hands into Karl's jacket pockets in search of his car keys, found them, tossed them at Lincoln, and repeated, "He has to go to the hospital, now! Get him in the car!"

Lincoln was already at Karl's other side. Together they half-carried, half-dragged Karl downstairs and muscled him into his car. Lincoln drove to the hospital.

I stood in the kitchen, stunned and ashamed that I had not done anything to help. What had I just witnessed? Was that how a heart attack happened?

An hour later, Mother and Lincoln returned.

"It was too late," Lincoln said.

Mother sat down at the table and wept.

"The hospital will notify his family," Mother said after a while. "There'll be a funeral. I wonder if we can go. I had no chance to say goodbye."

Karl's divorce had never been finalized. I did not know what had caused the delay. He must have talked about it with Mother, but the rest of the family accepted their arrangement without question or comment. Karl had been a quiet, kindly presence in our family. He had slipped out of our lives as quietly as he had lived.

About a week later, our family went to a Catholic church for Karl's funeral. I did not know how Mother had found the information about it; perhaps there had been a death notice in the neighborhood newspaper.

Karl's family sat in the front row; we took a pew at the back. The embalmed body lay in an open casket in front of the altar, flanked by a meager array of slightly wilted yellow chrysanthemums.

"Barbaric custom -- dressing up the dead," Mother whispered to me. "When I go, promise you won't put me on display like this! Give me a shroud and close the coffin--promise!"

I promised, clasping her hand tightly.

When the service concluded, we joined the dozen or so other mourners and went up to the front of the church to pay our last respects. I looked at the pale figure in the coffin. Karl's body was dressed in a three-piece suit, starched white shirt, and tie, exactly as he had dressed in life. His glasses were tucked into the breast pocket of his suit jacket.

A woman dressed in black -- Karl's widow, we assumed -- and a middle-aged man who might have been a brother stood at the foot end of the coffin and accepted condolences. They shook everyone's hand and said to everyone who approached them, "Thank you...so kind." The widow's face was stony behind her black veil. I could not tell if she knew who my mother was. Was she aware that Mother had held a special place in Karl's life?

Back at home, Mother opened her purse and took out a pair of rimless glasses.

"They put his eyeglasses in the coffin," she said. "What a stupid idea! What good are spectacles to a corpse? These always worked better for me than for him. He won't mind my taking them. If he'd known what was going to happen, he would have given them to me anyway."

Roland, Lincoln, and I had stood very close to Mother in front of the casket. None of us had seen her palm the glasses.

My first semester at the University of Chicago had begun with much nervousness on my part. It ended in June, on a high note. My grades were good enough to assure me that my scholarship was safe. For the course in European political history, I had written a term paper on David Lloyd George, the British Labour Party leader. Professor Finer had awarded me an A for it, and had added a handwritten note that said, "You write well because you think well."

When I had cleared my few possessions out of Leah's apartment and had said goodbye and good luck, I found the El train far too slow. I would have liked to *fly* home to my family. Alas, my wings were only metaphorical.

CHAPTER 21

The Lies of Summer

I knew that the summer of 1957 would not be as exciting as the previous one. There would be no political convention and no adventurous visits to jazz clubs with Sam. He answered my letters with short notes typed on the familiar yellow Western Union press message paper, or with clippings of his column. I wondered if he remembered his promise to take me on a tour of Washington, D.C.

However, it made me happy just to be back with my family after school ended, and I enjoyed a week of leisure--swimming in Lake Michigan, and spending time with Mother at the store without any particular schedule. Parkway Imports was doing well, although sales in the summer months were never as brisk as they were around the winter holidays.

Roland had finished his freshman year at Senn High School. He was not a brilliant scholar, but his grades were satisfactory. The school offered a woodworking shop class, and this had been his favorite activity. He was looking forward to receiving his Eagle Scout badge, having completed almost all of the required projects.

I learned that in addition to the purloined eyeglasses, Mother had received another legacy from Karl -- his car. This inheritance seemed to be accidental rather than planned. After Karl's sudden death, Lincoln and Roland had searched the vehicle for documents with an address so that the car could be returned. They found nothing. Expecting that someone in Karl's family would call to claim it, they had left the Dodge parked at the curb in front of our apartment building. No request came -- for weeks, then months. Mother had no home address or telephone number for Karl. Long ago, she had given him a key to our apartment. Sometimes he had called to say that he would be visiting; sometimes he had simply dropped in. Karl's last name -- Burger -- was so common in Chicago that the telephone directory would be useless for finding a listing. Perhaps his family did not know about this car, Mother speculated. Maybe it had belonged to his business and was registered in a corporate name? Lincoln had driven Karl to the hospital; he still had the keys. He began driving the car to work, rather than letting it sit in the same space in front of our building week after week. If the police noticed and considered it an abandoned vehicle, they would tow it away as a nuisance.

The car would remain in our possession. Eventually Lincoln managed to register it in his name. Perhaps he found an official willing to accept a bribe. It was not unheard of; it was Chicago, after all.

Mother missed Karl. Riding in the Dodge with Lincoln for an occasional Sunday drive reminded her of happy days with her friend. Roland, with Lincoln supervising, learned to drive. It did not take him long; he was a natural. I was not. I learned the basics, but I was hesitant and nervous. After a few lessons, I decided to leave the driving to Roland or Lincoln. Mother had no interest in operating an American car and she never did learn.

Mr. Crist had given me his home telephone number and had asked that I let him know how I was doing at the university. I felt shy about the phone, but one afternoon I picked up my courage and dialed his number.

"Great to hear from you," the familiar voice said. "Tell me all about it!"

I related all my news, including my temporary move to Leah's apartment on the South Side.

Mr. Crist congratulated me on my successful semester and asked, "How are you spending the summer?"

"I have to find work and save money for housing in the fall," I said. "I can't commute; it's too exhausting. My mother can't pay me to work in the store, so I want to find an office job. I can type; I'm looking at the classified ads."

"How is your mom's business going?"

"She says customers like the imported fashions, but business is always slow in summer," I said.

"Let me wish you good luck and please say hello to the family for me," Mr. Crist said. "And I will tell Virginia you called. She'll be glad to hear from you too. Do call again and keep me posted, won't you?"

I promised to do so and again thanked my teacher -- and Miss Clarke -- for their help. I felt a twinge of guilt because I had said I was checking over the want ads, but I had not yet bought a newspaper. I went out to get the *Tribune* and the *Sun-Times.*

I needed a job for the summer months until school started again; I wanted to find a clerical position that would pay better than babysitting or waiting on tables. This almost certainly meant that I would be applying for a full-time job, which in turn meant I would have to tell a lie. Unless a firm just happened to need a temporary worker, I would have to pretend that I was looking for permanent employment. If they asked about schooling, I could show my high school diploma and not mention the university. I told my conscience to take a nap.

I began to peruse the listings. One advertisement in the *Tribune* attracted me:

Help Wanted - Clerical Secretarial

Typist - accurate - correspondence dept.

Downtown HQ of nationwide firm.

Apply in person….

I knew I had the typing skills for correspondence. I wondered if stenography would be required as well. I had taken only one semester of Pitman shorthand at Senn; it was probably not enough, but I had also learned some speed writing. With that and my good memory, I thought I could get by. I liked the mention of "downtown" and "nationwide." That might mean a successful business and an air-conditioned office. I telephoned to make an appointment.

A female voice chirped, all in one breath and at a rapid pace, "Good morning Relaxasizer business is wonderful how may I help you?"

Before I could answer, the receptionist asked, "Can you hold?"

Recorded music came through the receiver.

After a pause, the cheerful receptionist came back on the line and said, "Good morning, Relax--no, no, wait a minute, you're on hold -- how may I help you?"

"Good morning. I'm calling regarding the help wanted ad in the *Tribune*--the ad for a typist," I said. I wondered how many times a day she had to recite her speech and whether business was always wonderful. Did she ever announce that business was sluggish?

"May I have your name, please? I will connect you to the personnel department -- spell that last name?"

"P-i-t-s-c-h-e-l," I said. "Like Mitchell, but with a *P*; one *l* at the end."

The receptionist said, "Thank you, please hold while I connect you." Again, music played.

At length, I was able to talk with the personnel manager and to request an interview. She too spoke briskly, giving me an appointment for the very next day. The firm's address was on North State Street, in the heart of the Loop.

I could not guess what sort of gadget this company manufactured. Was a "Relaxer" an easy chair or a drink? Or an inflatable mat to use at the beach?

For my interview, I dressed in a dark skirt and white blouse, nylon stockings, and the black pumps I had worn for Mother's fashion shows. Because I left home after the morning rush hour, the El train was not crowded and it was comfortable, despite the muggy July heat. The company's headquarters were easy to find. They were in the Stevens building, a high-rise close to the El station.

I checked the directory in the lobby and found that the firm's name was written Relax-A-Cizor; its office was on the fourteenth floor. I was more curious than nervous.

When I entered the suite, I recognized the voice I had spoken with the day before. The receptionist was a pretty young woman with a great deal of makeup shadowing her bright blue eyes. A black headset, like a tiara with earflaps, sat atop her abundant blonde curls. She raised a hand, signaling me to wait. "...business is wonderful, how may I help you?" she said into the instrument, completing the company's telephone greeting.

"How may I help you?" she asked me as she pulled wires out of sockets and plugged them into others.

"I have an appointment for an interview," I answered. "About the job as a typist."

"Name? Just a second, I have to answer this. Good morning Relaxacizor business is wonderful how may I help you?"

Business is certainly *busy*, I thought while I waited. I said my name as soon as the receptionist stopped to take a breath.

"Right. Personnel--I'll call them and let them know," she said, smiling at me.

The receptionist took another call as a tall woman in a navy-blue suit came towards me. I was glad I had dressed appropriately.

"Hello. This way," she greeted me, pointing to a cubicle on our right.

As I had expected, there was a form for me to fill out. The woman, who introduced herself as Miss Bernardi, sat down behind her desk while I took the visitor's chair placed to the right of it.

"Do you have previous office experience?" Miss Bernardi asked while I was writing out my name, address, and telephone number.

"I was a typist for the Associated Press last summer. I took dictation for the news reporters," I said.

"Why did you leave that employment?"

"It was a job at the Democratic convention, in the newsroom -- it was temporary, two weeks in August."

"I see," Miss Bernardi said. "List that on your form. And anything else?"

"My mother owns a retail business," I said. "I've worked there." I hoped that this unsmiling manager would assume I had typed letters in an office, but my answer was not complete enough for her.

"What sort of business? What was your function?"

I could hardly admit to measuring garments for dry cleaning, so I said, "Imported fashions. Sales and modeling for shows."

Miss Bernardi looked at her gold wristwatch and touched the charm bracelet next to it. "I see," she said again. "And why are you not staying there? Why are you applying here?"

"Working for my mother is only part-time," I said. "I am looking for something full-time -- for the future." I had prepared myself for this lie. It came out quite smoothly, without a blush.

"What are your typing skills? Can you type at least forty words per minute accurately?"

"Yes, ma'am. Fifty. My spelling is good," I said -- this time truthfully.

"I think we can use you in the customer service department," Miss Bernardi said. "It involves typing letters to clients who have questions about the product. The working hours are nine to five, Monday through Friday, an hour for lunch and a mid-morning coffee break. We are looking to fill this position immediately. Can you start next Monday?"

"Yes, I can. And thank you very much, thank you," I said. "Uh, could you tell me how much per hour?"

Miss Bernardi named a dollar figure. It was slightly higher than my pay in the Associated Press position. Two months of this salary would more than cover the cost of a room--Leah's or some other -- close to the campus.

"That will be fine; thank you again," I said. "I will be here on Monday morning."

My future was as a student, not as an office slavey, but the personnel manager was not to know that. I could now spell Relax-A-Cizor; I still did not know what it was.

My mother was impressed that I had landed a job on the first try. My brother and Lincoln congratulated me as well.

"They'll expect you to dress nicely," Mother said. "If you need anything from the store, don't spend your money downtown; just ask. You should buy extra nylons though; they get runs. I don't know why the Americans can't produce a stronger thread. Remember the parachute? You needed an axe to make a rip in that!"

"Maybe you're going to like Relax-A-Cizor so much you'll get to be the boss," Roland said, with characteristic deadpan humor. "What kind of a thingamajig is it anyway?"

"Tell you Monday," I said.

I made the most of the weekend although it was extremely hot. Chicago weather is rarely moderate. Our apartment did not have an air conditioner. Roland and I swam in the lake as early in the morning as we could get ourselves out of the house. On Saturday afternoon, we went to Parkway Imports with Mother; the store was pleasantly cool thanks to a room air conditioner Lincoln and Roland had installed.

After dinner at home, Lincoln suggested we all go with him for a drive. "With the car windows open, it will be refreshing," he said.

"Sitting in the car is hotter than sitting here," Mother said. "I'll do some sewing."

Roland and I said yes. The three of us got in the Dodge and set out. A few blocks from home, Roland asked to be dropped off.

"I'll walk over to Bruce's-- see you later," he said. Bruce was his Boy Scout troop leader; the two often spent time together.

Lincoln and I looked for a secluded place to park. It was not easy to find one -- it seemed as if all the young couples in the city were on the same quest.

It was nearly midnight when we returned home. We sneaked into our bedrooms without turning on any lights. As always, our tryst left me feeling disheveled, thrilled, and wanting more than I had been willing to risk.

Of course, my late-night adventure had been noticed by Mother. On Sunday, she took me aside. When she said, *"Kind,"* I knew I was in for a serious talk.

"Are you involved with Lincoln? Is he bothering you? Don't -- don't give away your heart to him. He's charming, oh yes -- but he is a playboy. He does not want marriage or children. He has one girlfriend after another. When he moved in here, I warned him to keep his hands off you. Is there something between you now?"

"No! Nothing is between us. We like to go to the lake, where it's cool. We talk," I said. I was becoming quite a liar.

"What do you talk about?" Mother asked. It was hard not to cringe under her skeptical look.

"Art. He knows a lot about Italian art -- Botticelli, Michelangelo," I improvised.

"You could go to the Art Institute to learn that," Mother said. "In the daytime!"

Mother let me go with a warning. She reminded me that I was still in school and that if I wanted to finish university, I should avoid "complications." It was clear that she meant love children. I felt embarrassed that Mother had seen through my denials. And I was uncomfortable about the relationship with Lincoln -- it felt wrong, vaguely incestuous. We had been living together as a family for a long time and in the beginning, I had thought of him as an older brother. Now that had become impossible. Mother was right, I thought. I had to keep myself under control, difficult as it might be.

On Monday morning, I made sure that I arrived at the Relax-A-Cizor office fifteen minutes before nine o'clock. The switchboard was silent. The receptionist's head popped up behind it.

"Oh, good morning," she said. "I was just changing my shoes. I wear sneakers on the street; no sense wearing out your dressy ones, you know." She held up one skinny-heeled, pointy-toed pump. "I keep these in the bottom drawer -- you can do that too if you want. You might need a light sweater too. Sometimes the air conditioning gets to be a little too much."

"That's good to know, thanks," I said. "Hi, I'm Barbara; I'm new."

"I'm Georgette," the receptionist said. "Your supervisor will be here in a minute. Customer service, right?"

"Yes, I think so. That's what Miss Bernardi said."

"Well, good luck. Ask me if you need the key to the ladies' room. It's down the hall." Georgette sat up, adjusted her chair, and reached for her headset. She smiled as she glanced up at the wall clock. "Five more minutes of peace and quiet," she said.

I was grateful for the advice about shoes. I would feel much more comfortable on my commute in my well-worn penny loafers.

At one minute before nine, a slender woman who looked to be in her forties came out of the inner office. Her dark hair was cut short in a severe, almost mannish style; a few wisps of grey showed at her temples. She wore glasses.

"You're Barbara, I assume, and you are on time. That's a good habit, in my book; keep it up, all right? Nine o'clock means nine o'clock and not fifteen minutes after."

"Yes, ma'am, I will," I answered. Mother and my teachers in Germany had insisted on punctuality since my earliest days; it had become second nature.

"Come this way and I'll show you your desk and introduce you to the other girls and explain what you have to do. Did Georgette show you the employee door? That's the one you should use from now on. The door in front is for the public," the supervisor said without waiting for me to answer her question.

I followed her into a large room filled with desks and typewriters. It was brightly lit by fluorescent tubes on the ceiling, although there were windows on the far side of the space. A number of women were already busy sorting through papers or typing. Others were still settling down, taking cloth covers off their machines, opening drawers and reaching in for paper. I did not see any men in the room. This was very different from last summer, I thought. The press room at the Hilton had been full of men and smoke. Here, not a single cigarette was in sight.

"You will sit here," said my boss, pointing out a desk. It was one of a group of four, set slightly apart from the rest of the typing pool.

"Next to you is Christine, in front of you is Donna, and next to her is Elaine. Say hello to Barbara, everybody!"

The three young women turned to me, waved, and smiled.

"Welcome," Christine said. "I go by Chris; ask me if you need any help."

"Hello. Same here," the other two added.

I said, "Thanks, nice to meet you."

"Now. See this folder? This is some information about the product and a couple of current advertisements for it -- the Relax-A-Cizor; you should look this over, but you don't have to memorize it or copy from it. The letters you are going to type are basically form letters, but they are personalized with the customer's name and address. Your job is to type the letters I'll put in your basket -- here -- and you will use the paragraphs I specify. There is a sample letter in the folder too. I'll give you a few minutes to read it," the supervisor said. "My office is over by the windows. I'll be back shortly."

I opened the folder and took out a booklet with a picture and the words "Relax-A-Cizor -- Effortless Exercise" on the cover. I could not make much of this paradox, so I studied the illustration. It was just as puzzling. It showed a box with dials and electrical cords. Belts and round pads were shown next to the box. I turned the pages and gradually learned that the Relax-A-Cizor was a reducing machine made for home use. It promised "Slimming while you rest...instead of going to a sweaty gym." Users were to strap a belt and two or more electrode pads around their waist or hips and connect the belt to the control unit which was plugged into an electrical outlet. Turning on the power caused the belt to vibrate, with the intensity of the pulses regulated by dials. The electrodes stimulated muscles to contract -- "exercising" them, and "slimming contours."

Once the belts were in place, the user was to sit in a comfortable chair or stretch out on a bed -- and -- RELAX! "It's easy! Let the machine do the exercise for you!" the brochure urged. "Use the Relax-A-Cizor for 30 minutes a day to reduce problem areas on hips, waist, and thighs! No need for calisthenics."

I was still engrossed in the manual when the supervisor returned.

"Got the idea?" she asked. She continued, "Now I'll go over the form letter with you. Here's the sample, and here is the list of paragraphs to use." She put several sheets of white bond paper with the company's letterhead in front of me." All of the letters sent by this department are to customers who have a question about the product -- they often say complaint-- but it's mostly that they don't understand how to use the machine. So, the answers are prepared; all you do is insert the relevant paragraphs. The paragraph numbers will be on a sheet of paper stapled to the customer's letter."

I said, "I see." It was not entirely true. I thought I might have to watch Chris or Donna do a letter before trying one on my own and spoiling a piece of the expensive-looking stationery.

"And here are the letters you'll be answering," the supervisor said, handing me a clutch of papers. "You put the date, then the customer's name and address, then type the body of the letter, using the paragraphs indicated. Bottom left, put 'Sincerely,' and sign it 'Clara Dexter.' Bring the finished letters to me."

At last I knew my new boss's name!

"Yes, I'll get started right away. Thank you, Miss Dexter," I said.

"What? Oh no, you misunderstood. My name isn't Dexter; it's Miss Hodges. There is no *real* Clara Dexter. The initials stand for 'Complaint Department.' All you girls sign the letters the same way. Below the signature, put 'CD' in caps, colon, then your initials in lower case. It's the standard business letter format. Is that clear?"

"Yes, Miss D-- Hodges."

At ten o'clock, Chris got up from her chair, straightened her skirt, turned to me, and said, "Break time! There's a coffee shop on the sixth floor. Do you want to go with me? We get fifteen minutes, but the service is fast."

I hesitated. I had finished only one letter because I had spent quite a bit of time reading over the suggested answers, looking at the brochure again, and studying the sample reply to the customer.

"Do you think it's OK? Maybe I should stay and do a couple more? I'm slow because it's all new to me," I said.

"Get your purse. It's fine," Chris said, walking ahead of me towards the door. "It's your first day; you'll get up to speed real quick; don't worry. Everybody goes for coffee break. Half of the room now, half at ten-thirty."

In the bustling coffee shop, the waitress set a cup of coffee and a sweet roll on the counter in front of Chris even before we sat down.

"Same? Are you new?" the server asked me.

"Yes, thanks, coffee, and roll; yes, I'm new. I work next to --"

But the waitress had sped off. Half a minute later -- no more -- my coffee and pastry appeared. They took time seriously here.

Chris was about my age, I guessed. She looked a bit like Lois, with shoulder-length blonde hair and hazel eyes. But she was much slimmer and better groomed than my high school friend had been the last time Lois and I had seen each other. I wondered, once again, if Lois regretted her choice.

"Have you worked here long? Do you like it?" I asked Chris, after enjoying my first swallow of the hot, fragrant coffee.

"About a year -- year and a half," Chris answered. "I like it. It's good experience, but I'm not planning to stay forever. I want to learn shorthand, maybe in an evening class, and then go for a job as a secretary. I'd like to work in a law firm, eventually. Meet a nice man with some education and earning potential, as they say."

"I don't know much shorthand either," I said. "Good luck with it -- with your plans." I hoped Chris would not ask me about my future; I would have to tell another lie.

To keep the conversation focused on office matters, I asked, "Have you ever seen a Relax-A-Cizor machine? Did you ever try one?"

"No, nobody I know in the office has-- maybe the executives get to try, but we don't, not that I know of anyway," Chris answered. "But you and me don't have to worry; we don't have 'problem areas,' do we?"

I laughed, thinking that if I had a problem, it was the reverse of what Relax-A-Cizor's clients complained of. I did not wish for smaller body parts; I wished my breasts were larger.

Chris took a compact and a lipstick out of her purse and touched up her lip color. My purse contained only transit tokens, money, a handkerchief, and a house key. All through the school year, I had not worn any kind of makeup. I decided that at lunchtime, I would find a Woolworth's. It would be fun to buy myself a lipstick -- cherry red, like Chris's.

Back at my desk, I tackled the letters Miss Hodges had assigned to me. The first two were from women who had recently bought the devices, tried them -- following all the instructions, they said -- but had found that the machine was not performing as promised.

"I measured my hips before the first treatment and I measured them yesterday, after about six weeks. It was 46 in. before and it's still 46!! I'm writing to your customer service dept. because I want to know what to do," one letter said.

Clara Dexter's reply was soothing. The first paragraph thanked the customer for writing and assured her that the company cared deeply about all of its clients and wanted them to be happy with its excellent product.

After typing this opening, I looked at the sheet of paper stapled to the client's letter. Miss Hodges had written, "Use these," and a series of numbers. I copied the corresponding paragraphs from her master list. The customer was advised to read the manual again, to make certain that all the cords and belts were properly connected. Further advice was about placement of the electrode pads, the proper length of time per treatment, and the need to use the device "consistently."

A concluding paragraph assured the customer that her Relax-A-Cizor was a smart investment and that she would soon enjoy compliments from her friends on her new svelte looks-- once she had learned to operate the machine correctly.

As Chris had predicted, my efficiency improved as I became familiar with the preset sentences I copied into letter after letter to customers who found fault with the machines' performance, or who complained that the results they obtained were not worth the hundreds of dollars they had paid for the devices. I typed the boilerplate responses, signed them, "Sincerely, Clara Dexter," and brought them to Miss Hodges for final approval.

At the end of my first day at Relax-A-Cizor, I thought that this work was a hundred times easier than the Associated Press job had been. But I wished I could be back in the press room, smoke, and chaos and all.

Thinking about last summer's hullabaloo reminded me that I had not heard from Sam in a while. Before my first week at Relax-A-Cizor was over, I wrote him a letter describing the fictional Clara Dexter and the strange machine that jiggled your muscles by sending electric shocks through your body. I asked how things were going in Washington.

Sam replied in his usual telegraphic style: "D.C. hot as hell. Not much news in summer. Congress out on recess. I still want you to come and visit but don't do it now. Can you manage in spring? Cherry blossoms. Club on U Street has a band plays wicked Dixieland. Do not send me a Relaxa-whatsis. When I feel like exercising, I lie down until the urge passes (that's a joke -- old one)."

He had remembered his promise! I was elated. I had no idea when next year's spring break was scheduled, but I resolved to make that trip. Dixieland was a name for the American South, and it was also jazz music. Was it like Erroll Garner's? What made it "wicked?" I would ask Sam in my next letter and tell him I was looking forward to seeing the cherry blossoms with him.

A few days after Sam's letter, an airmail envelope arrived, addressed to me. I found it in the mailbox when I came home from work. It was marked "AIR MAIL - PAR AVION" and was postmarked with characters written in an exotic alphabet. Could it be from Surendra? I raced upstairs and let myself into the apartment. I was the first one home.

I wanted to tear the letter open, but I knew that would destroy half the words on the fragile paper. I grabbed the sewing scissors Mother had left on the table. They were very sharp; cutting paper with them was strictly forbidden. Without even thinking, I slit the aerogramme at the top and sides and saw "Dear Barbara -- "written in blue ink.

"I am thinking of you and thinking how much you would enjoy this summer day, Deva. The sky is so blue…."

Surendra went on to say that his family was happy to have him at home, and that they were safe. The border war had not come close to their village. He was preparing to sit for civil service exams. He hoped I was well and that my mother and my brothers were well.

I wondered if he had come home to find a bride his parents had chosen for him and whether he was already married. His letter did not say. I realized that I had never seen Surendra's handwriting. It was neat and graceful; the characters were well formed without flourishes. Like Surendra himself, his handwriting had an unselfconscious beauty. The ink he had chosen was the very same shade of blue as the sari we had bought at the trade fair.

It was not a long letter. The last sentence read, "I wonder, Deva. Will I ever see you again?"

I went into my room, took the sari out of the bottom drawer of my dresser, and pulled aside the tissue paper wrapping. I feared that Surendra would never see me in the dress I hoped to have made from it. Kashmir was so terribly far away! I quickly covered the sari again and thrust it into the drawer. I did not want tears to spoil the lovely silk.

Later, when I showed the letter to the family, Roland said, "Look, here's his address, on the outside of the sheet. It looks like something written in a secret code -- no, I guess it's another language. What do they speak in Kashmir? Let me look at it. I'm good at codes."

"When you figure it out, let's copy it down on another sheet of paper. I'll write him back and we'll mail it just as soon as we have something we can take to the post office," I said.

If Surendra and I could stay in touch, perhaps it was not so impossible that we might see each other again, I thought.

By the beginning of August, I was weary of repeating Clara Dexter's evasive answers to Relax-A-Cizor's unhappy customers. I barely glanced at their letters now because they made me feel sad. I pitied the women who had trouble meeting the payments on machines that did not bring them any benefits. Would the company please take the thing back and refund their money, they asked, sometimes adding, "My kids need school uniforms and shoes. I never should have bought this."

Clara Dexter answered that financing could be arranged, but that "Company Regulations" did not permit taking back used devices. "Your sales consultant will be more than happy to demonstrate the proper use..."

One day, I felt so tired of the stock wording that I paraphrased a sentence or two in several letters. I thought I had conveyed the meaning of the refusal; I had tried to soften the language by inserting a few words -- "We are sorry to hear the machine is giving you trouble."

I left the letters for Miss Hodges at the end of the day. At five minutes after nine the next morning, I was told by Georgette to report to the supervisor's office.

When I entered her cubicle, Miss Hodges held up several letters. "These are wrong!" she snapped. "You have changed paragraph twelve, here -- and paragraph eighteen, here. That is not allowed! Your job is to copy the wording exactly. Did you lose your template?"

"No, Miss Hodges. I'm sorry, I just changed a few words. I have the list. All the other paragraphs are exactly the ones you said to use."

"It is not your place to change anything," Miss Hodges lectured. "Our legal department has carefully drawn up these responses and the secretaries are to follow them exactly. That means word for word!"

"I'm sorry," I said again. "I didn't realize. It won't happen again. Please excuse me."

"Be careful in the future. Don't make me waste my time correcting your work. Other than this, your work has been satisfactory." My boss sent me back to my desk. I did not hate her; she was doing her job. I hated Clara Dexter.

I meekly accepted Miss Hodges' scolding and went back to copying the approved responses. I wanted to keep this job for a few more weeks and hoard my salary, as I had been doing. I had spent very little money. Train fare, morning coffee, lunch, and an occasional pair of nylons were necessary expenses. My luxuries were minimal -- a small box of face powder, an inexpensive compact, a pocket comb. I did not have a bank account; I signed my checks over to the Parkway bank account for deposit. Mother, always the conscientious bookkeeper, insisted that I keep a list of my earnings.

The month of August dragged on. I disliked the work, but I enjoyed the convivial coffee breaks. The girls -- female office workers of all ages were always referred to as "the girls" -- did not seem to mind the monotony of the work as much as I did. They looked forward to dates with their boyfriends at the end of the workweek. Many hoped for a day when they would marry these boyfriends and become "homemakers," a title they preferred to "housewives." None of my coworkers seemed to worry, as I did, that the Relax-A-Cizor company lied to its customers. Poor product performance, Clara Dexter insisted in paragraph after paragraph, was the customer's fault. Complaints came in by the hundreds, yet prospective customers called Georgette's switchboard all day long, every day. The machines must be selling by the thousands. Business was wonderful indeed.

I never mentioned my scruples to anyone outside the family and in the third week of August I told Miss Hodges that I would be quitting at the end of the month.

"But you just started a month or two ago! What is your reason for leaving? Are you getting married?" Miss Hodges asked.

"No, Miss Hodges," I answered. "It's that my mother needs me at her store. It's open six days a week and too much work for her. She really needs my help. She asked me. I'm sorry--"

The lies came easily. After all, I had been participating in a fraud all summer. I had impersonated a compassionate customer service representative who told customers they mattered. That sympathetic person did not exist. Clara Dexter was part of a cold-hearted, profit-oriented scheme. I had begun to suspect that this company knowingly sold a faulty product. If I had been a seasoned reporter, investigating and exposing Clara Dexter would have made a noteworthy story. In August 1957, I was not equipped to write such an article. I was a college student eager to get away from corporate America and go back to classes.

I had lied to get this job. I had taken the company's money, for which I had performed my assigned duties satisfactorily. I did not feel guilty. But I was heartily glad that I did not have to continue as one-fourth-- or any fraction -- of Clara Dexter any longer.

CHAPTER 22

Horizons

I looked forward to my second semester at the University of Chicago, and I was thinking of calling Leah to ask whether I could rent space in her apartment again. When I mentioned this to Mother, she surprised me with an alternative suggestion.

"Aren't there apartments close to campus that a family could rent?" she asked me one day in late summer. "Why should you pay money to squeeze in with somebody when we could live close to your school? Why don't we look for a large apartment and rent out a bedroom or two ourselves? I wish you'd take me to the neighborhood and show me around."

This new idea of Mother's was unexpected. Living close to campus in a place of our own would certainly simplify my life. But what about the others? Mother had never seen much of the city beyond our neighborhood and Lincoln Avenue, where the store was located. How would she feel living far away from the German-speaking district she was used to?

I asked, "What do you mean? Do you want to move to the South Side -- all of us -- the whole family?"

"As a matter of fact, it would not be *all* of us," Mother answered. "I've been thinking about this for quite a while and I've discussed it with Lincoln; he's been wanting more space for his painting -- and for himself too -- more privacy. He thinks he could take over this apartment and you and I and Roland would move."

I realized that Mother's idea was not a brand-new inspiration; it was more like a plan in its early stages. And Lincoln had a hand in it. I wondered if "privacy" meant distance from me.

I said to Mother, "You haven't had a chance to see my school or the neighborhood. I can show you around and we can look at where

Leah lives. There are apartment buildings. On some streets, there are stores with apartments on the top floors; it's kind of a mix. The neighborhood is called Hyde Park-Kenwood; it has some nice old houses and some not so nice ones. The city and the university are working on improvements."

So as not to alarm Mother, I did not mention the blighted, dangerous sections immediately adjoining Hyde Park. Mayor Daley and the trustees of the university were committed to urban renewal and had made a start, but segregation, poverty, and crime still dominated large territories on the South Side. Like the other students, I knew where not to go.

I brought up Mother's plan at dinner. "If we get serious about a move, we should do it soon," I said. "Because registration is in a couple of weeks and once classes start, I'll be busy. And Roland can't go to Senn if we live on the South Side. He has to change to a different district; I don't even know which high school that is."

Roland said, "School is school. I don't mind. If there's a Boy Scout trip or special meeting, I'll take the train. I know my way around pretty well. I might have to lend Jutta my compass so she can find me in the wilds of the South Side."

"What about Parkway?" I asked Mother. "Speaking of trips, you'll be the one with the long commute. It's not much fun in the cold, as I found out."

"That's so, and it may be inconvenient. I may have to find part-time help." Mother paused for a moment and then a happy smile lit up her face. "You know what? Just the other day a lady stopped by and said she used to work in a fancy boutique in Germany. She's been here many years and speaks perfect English too. Now that might be a possibility!"

Lincoln had listened quietly so far. Now he said to Mother, "Good that you are giving some thought to yourself! It's a six-day workweek for you. I think Parkway is doing well enough, thanks to all your efforts. You can count on me to keep on helping, but an extra person would make a difference for the better. She might even bring in some new customers. Surely she has friends…"

"So, let's go apartment hunting as soon as possible," Mother said.

"Want me to bring my bow and arrows?" Roland asked, and the family council concluded with groans and chuckles.

I was happy. I loved the university, but I had no close friends there. Living with my brother and mother and fellow students appealed to me much more than sharing Leah's cramped quarters. The only drawback was that I would miss Lincoln. Would he miss me? He had not said a word about that! As soon as we had a minute alone together, I would have to ask him.

The opportunity did not come until before breakfast the next morning. Lincoln was preparing his favorite *muesli,* adding a sliced banana. I took a cereal bowl out of the cupboard and held it out.

"Some for me?" I asked.

"*Natürlich!* Anything else I may get for you?" he answered, courteous as always.

"Yes," I said. "But not food. I'd like to know how you feel about me moving away. I'll miss you. How about you? You haven't said."

"Of course, I'll miss having you close! How can you even question it? I'll miss seeing you -- or touching you -- every day. But think! I'll have the apartment to myself. You aren't going to forget the address, are you?"

Mother came in before we could move into a passionate embrace. Fortunately, I still had the cereal bowl in my hands so our standing close to each other looked natural. Lincoln poured *muesli* and winked.

"*Danke,*" I said. "Thanks."

Once the decision had been made, our move to the South Side was accomplished with remarkable speed. We found an apartment offered for rent on East Fifty-Fifth Street, in a four-story building whose brickwork showed signs of age. However, when we were led inside by the superintendent, Mother remarked on the clean hallways and well-lighted stairwells. "That's a good sign," Mother said. "The landlord cares about safety."

"We do our best," the super said.

The third-floor apartment was on a front corner of the building. Large windows admitted plenty of daylight, although the views were not elegant -- a fish store, a tavern, a convocation of old cars at the opposite curb.

A smattering of used furniture -- rickety dressers, bedsteads without mattresses, an enamel kitchen table, a few wooden chairs -- came with the apartment, which had been inhabited by students who had moved on. I saw that if we followed Mother's plan to sublet, we would have no problem finding other tenants, given this convenient location only a few blocks from the Midway. At that time, while undergraduate enrollment was at a low of just over two thousand students, there were more than three thousand graduate students. Most of them lived off-campus.

I had told Mother to use the money I had deposited in the business account over the summer for whatever was needed -- a security deposit, rent, or additional furniture. I was proud that I could contribute. A deal was struck on the day of our visit. Mother had noted that there was a bedroom and a maid's room off the kitchen that we would not need for ourselves.

Mother left enough furniture and housewares in the North Side apartment so that Lincoln would be comfortable. We packed up the rest of our possessions; Roland and Lincoln, with a rented truck, would transport them to Fifty-Fifth Street -- a distance of about fifteen miles. Using Lake Shore Drive, the most direct north-south route, they would take forty-five to fifty minutes, bypassing the Loop halfway through their journey.

"I didn't know we had collected so many things!" I said to Mother, looking at the pile of boxes and suitcases, assorted pieces of furniture, the sewing machine, and the typewriter in its maroon carrying case.

"*Ich hatte nichts als einen Stab als ich über den Jordan kam. Nun bin ich zu zwei Heeren geworden,*" Mother recited, quoting one of her favorite biblical passages. It was the words of Jacob who led the Israelites across the river into the land of Canaan. ("I had nothing but the staff in my hand when I crossed the Jordan; now I have become two armies.")

While it never reached the poetic heights of a promised land, our new apartment was to become a warm and pleasant mini-community where I lived happily for the rest of my time at the university.

Before school started, I went with Roland to Senn High School, where we asked for the address of the district school that served the neighborhoods around the university. The principal's secretary asked for our new address and then gave us the information. She said she would send a transcript of Roland's grades in time for him to register for his sophomore year at the South Side school.

"Should we go and look at it?" I asked my brother.

"No, I'll just go when it opens. Don't want to think about school until I have to," Roland answered.

I knew he was not eager to face his continuing problems with certain subjects, particularly English composition. He spoke without an accent now and could read adult books, but his spelling was chaotic -- he reversed letters, left out vowels or inserted incorrect ones. Words like "who" and "how" were interchanged. Trying to memorize assigned vocabulary lists was hard work and he often gave up in frustration. We did not know about learning disabilities at the time; most teachers simply assumed that such students were slow learners and urged them to work harder. Meanwhile, Roland had barely passed his English courses.

"There's still a lot to do at the apartment," I said to cheer him up. I knew that if he had a choice, he would spend all his days at the lumberyard and at the hardware store instead of in a classroom. In the new apartment, he was busy repairing the furniture we had inherited, and he had started putting up extra shelves in the kitchen, where Mother had complained of too little storage space. I remembered the pocketknife Roland had mysteriously acquired when he was four or five years old and recalled how easily he had mastered the art of assembling model airplanes. I marveled at the natural way he handled tools and at the advanced level of his self-taught skills.

Until school started, both of us enjoyed furnishing and decorating our new dwelling. It was a friendly building, we found. Neighbors -- a young married couple, both graduate students -- and several other tenants stopped by in the evenings to introduce themselves and offer advice about local stores and pubs. Mother wanted to invite everyone to a dinner on an upcoming weekend and asked me what foods she should cook for these young people.

"Let's make it a potluck instead," I said. "Do you know how that works? It's an American tradition; everybody brings something, and everybody shares. It will be much easier on you."

"What? We ask guests to bring food? That does not sound polite. Are you sure?" Mother asked.

"Yes, it's a custom; perfectly all right. We'll make a main dish and maybe cookies, if that's okay with you. Did we bring the cookie cutters?"

"Of course, we have the cookie cutters! Would I leave them behind? Find the box!" Mother said.

A lively crowd attended our potluck supper. I had told the neighbors to bring friends from other buildings, if they wished, and several did so. There were three or four international students, an artist who lived across the street, and the people we had already met. The guests brought salads, macaroni and cheese casseroles, bread and fruit, and a bottle of Chianti in a straw wrapper. Mother, nervous about the potluck concept, had simmered enough beef stew to feed all of Hyde Park and she had baked cookies besides.

We did not have enough chairs or a table large enough to seat everyone. To Mother's horror, a number of guests plopped themselves on the floor, cradling plates of food in their laps.

"Gott im Himmel!" Mother said, nudging me. "This is horrible! How poor have we become now?"

"This is fine! It's America! Everybody here is used to it," I said. "That's how we do it at a party. It's potluck. Look -- everybody's having a good time," I shouted over the noise.

The guests left with many special thanks for the homemade cookies.

"Our housewarming party was wonderful," I said to Mother.

"Do you think they had enough to eat?" she asked. "Young people are always hungry."

Roland pointed to the kitchen. "There's one pot of stew still sitting on the stove. Enough for next week!"

"People say the U. of C. is where fun goes to die," I said to Roland while we were cleaning up.

"Can't prove that here," he answered. "I thought we all had fun."

From my laconic brother, that was high praise.

Classes started in September. My curriculum now included economics and anthropology in addition to continuing political science courses. I was excited by the new disciplines, but I found economics difficult. I struggled to understand the theories of John Maynard Keynes and Chicago's own Milton Friedman. Supply and demand seemed simple concepts at first, but the subtleties of their influence on the cost and prices of goods were complicated; I struggled with charts and statistics. I was glad that we lived so close to the campus that I could enjoy time with the family after an arduous day of studying.

Roland did not say much about his school. When asked, he would answer, "It's going okay," or "It's different, but all right."

Before long, one of the graduate students who had been brought to our housewarming party by neighbors asked his friends about a room he could rent. They remembered that I had mentioned extra space and made the connection. The young man, a physics major, was from India. Mother interviewed him and agreed to sublet our extra bedroom. When she learned that Ravi was a vegetarian, Mother remembered her youthful interest in *Rohkost* and offered to prepare meals for him when she had time. Ravi accepted gratefully, offering to pay for the extra consideration.

"Vegetables aren't very expensive," Mother said. "If you want special ingredients, imported things for instance, I will ask you to supply them."

Ravi moved in. When he ate with us, all of our diets benefited. We bought more fruits and fresh vegetables. Mother combined chopped nuts, buckwheat, and herbs into patties that tasted better than any veggie burger I have eaten since. I should have watched her and learned the recipe, but I did not take the time; I was busy reading Machiavelli.

I thought about the economics of our household. Even with extra income from a boarder, the family budget could use a boost. I did not have to draw a chart to see that. There had been moving expenses and if Mother followed through on her plan to hire a saleslady for Parkway Imports, the store's overhead would increase. With a part-time job on campus, I thought, I could earn enough to pay for my textbooks and school supplies. I visited the student employment office to check out the offerings.

A middle-aged woman gave me a friendly greeting and handed me an application form. "We need your name, current address, and telephone; also, please check off what skills you have -- typing, filing, and so on," she said.

I had filled in about half of the sheet of paper when the counselor leaned over her desk and said, "You have very neat handwriting. I think I have something for you! Would you be interested in working in the library -- it would be in the bindery and repair section?"

The library was one of my favorite haunts.

"The library! Oh yes, I would be very interested," I said. I wondered what handwriting had to do with it.

"Good. They have been looking for someone. The bindery repairs books that are damaged or that are threatening to fall apart. When these books come back with new covers, they need to have the spines labeled with the title and author of the book, and with the Dewey decimal number. The information is written on the spine using transfer tape and a hot stylus; you will be trained to do it. As you can understand, accuracy is important and legible writing is essential."

"I think I can do that. I would really like to apply for this job," I said. "Is a hot stylus like a soldering iron? I have experience in using them."

"Soldering iron? Really?" The counselor sounded surprised. "Yes -- well I personally have never used either of these tools, but I suppose they are similar. The stylus is thin, like a pencil. It is heated with electricity. Shall I give you a slip of paper to take to the repair department so they can talk to you?"

"Yes, please -- and thank you!" I answered, hoping no one else would snatch this unusual job before I made my way across the campus to the library. Working with books was honest and useful, unlike the evasions and obfuscations of Clara Dexter.

I was hired for the bindery job. Quite a few students worked there part time so the hours were flexible to accommodate class and lab schedules. I was able to arrange work times on several afternoons per week; the wages were not grand, but I hoped to add extra hours during vacations.

Miss Gregory, the department's supervisor, was a tall woman with long grey hair looped into an elegant chignon. On my first day, she demonstrated the tools and method for labeling the book spines. The tape was a silver ribbon about two inches wide; the stylus was a pen connected to an electric cord. A holder for the pen when it was not in use sat on the worktable.

"First, copy the title of the book and the author's name on a piece of paper. Then spread the book on the table, spine up, and lay down a length of tape on it. You will find it a bit tricky to keep the tape straight," Miss Gregory said. "Be patient. Copy the information accurately; that is more important than speed. At first, anyway."

As the supervisor had said, it was finicky work. I wished I had three hands, but with practice I learned to print the required words in a straight line along the book spines. I loved watching the silver pigment as it liquefied and flowed onto the linen binding; it was magical.

Not all the books in the stack on my worktable were written in English or in the Latin alphabet. I had to ask Miss Gregory to identify the different scripts and to point out which clusters of words on the title page I was to copy. I liked the elegant curves and loops of Arabic and the intricate characters of Sanskrit. It was difficult to work on these volumes. I concentrated hard, determined to duplicate the lettering as exactly as possible.

One afternoon, as I was bent over a book in a foreign language, a voice at my shoulder said, "If this is hard for you, you can give it to me. The language is Bengali, and this is a book of poetry--lovely poetry."

I looked up. It was the student who sat at the other end of the room. I had waved hello to him several times, but we had never been introduced. I thought he might be from India.

"Thank you -- I'm sorry, I don't know your name -- thanks, but I'm almost finished here. I hope I did it right?"

My colleague's smile was friendly. "They call me Gogo," he said. "No one can pronounce all the syllables in my name; it's long and complicated. Be glad you don't have to write it on a book--I haven't written one yet!"

"Hello, Gogo; I'm Barbara," I said. "I wish I could read these books--the poems. They must be beautiful--the characters of the alphabet are beautiful too."

"Yes, we are rich in poets," Gogo said. "And you did the lettering perfectly. Still, if you want help anytime, my table is over there by the door. I am happy to assist."

"When you write your book, will it be poetry?" I asked.

"Nuclear physics -- it has its own kind of poetry. Let's go for coffee sometime and I will tell you more. Right now, I had better get back to work or Miss Gregory will chase me down."

"Thanks for offering to help. I know I'll be needing it," I said. "I'd like to have coffee too; that will be nice. See you soon."

Over time, Gogo became a friend. We sat in the coffee shop or the student lounge and talked about books and our studies, about our families and the Chicago weather. He was from Madras, in the south of India. He was acquainted with Ravi, our boarder, but they were not close friends. Both were pursuing research projects at Argonne National Laboratories. Gogo gave me glimpses of the beauty he saw in physics -- the lively, invisible dance of protons and electrons, the mysterious neutrino which was a particle that might or might not exist. He was in love with the tiny moving parts of the vast, unknowable universe; it was poetry, as he had said.

I was thrilled with my new international acquaintances. I thought back to Germany, where I had not known a single person who had been born in another country, or who came from a different religious tradition. Until 1945, when the two ex-prisoners came to live with us and the American GI Prima threw Hershey bars to the children, I had never heard a language other than German or seen a person with a skin color other than white.

In America, in high school and junior college and now at the university, I had made friends who were Japanese, Indian, Kashmiri, African, and Middle Eastern. They were Christian, Jewish, Hindu, Sikh, and Muslim. I doubted that a German university I might have attended had my path been different would have offered me such wide horizons. I remembered my long-ago wish to learn ancient Greek; now it was Sanskrit I wanted to study. If only I had time.

A week or two later, while looking for a required text at the bookstore, I leafed through a copy of *The Chicago Review*, a slender, perfect-bound paperback. I was fascinated. I liked the look and feel of the journal -- the artwork on the cover, the quality paper, and the crisp printing. I was an avid reader of newspapers, but this elegant publication offered a glimpse into another world-- a world of poems and stories, essays, and book reviews.

"Is this published here?" I asked the salesclerk.

"Yes, he said. "It's a quarterly run by students; they feature new writing. It's seventy-five cents."

I bought the textbook and the *Review.* It was a purchase that was to have fascinating consequences.

CHAPTER 23

Beat Poets and Zen Buddhists

When I looked at the table of contents of the *Chicago Review* I had bought, I realized with a shock that I did not recognize a single name. Here was new writing indeed -- and one immigrant who needed to catch up with contemporary American literature!

My German childhood had familiarized me with the heroes and villains of Brothers Grimm and the exploits of Wilhelm Busch's bad boys, Max, and Moritz. Alice in Wonderland and Tom Sawyer were strangers.

In high school and at Wright, I had read the classic poets taught in English classes -- Shakespeare, Keats, Byron, Shelley, and Longfellow -- as well as stories by Mark Twain and novels by John Steinbeck and Ernest Hemingway.

"Marjorie Morningstar," by Herman Wouk was the most recently published fiction I had taken out of the library. I liked this 1955 novel because its heroine was a Jewish girl about my age. Born Marjorie Morgenstern, she wanted her life to take a different path from that of her parents and the family's traditional community. I had no close friends who were Jewish, so Marjorie's adventures had intrigued me.

Even a casual look at the stories in the *Chicago Review* revealed that they were not about teenage romances with predictable happy endings.

At the time, I spoke and wrote English fluently although I could still get tripped up by colloquialisms. I loved and admired the power and beauty of my adopted language. If the editors of this journal would have me, I thought, I would join the staff.

I wrote a letter to the *Review*, asking for an interview. I explained my interest in journalism and my experience at the Wright College student newspaper. A short time later, I was invited to meet with Irving Rosenthal, the editor, at the magazine's headquarters in the Reynolds Club. I had never been inside the Reynolds Tower; I pictured an office suite as grand as the imposing Gothic exterior of the building.

The red carpet and the dark oak paneling of the staircase to the second floor of the Reynolds Club were as elegant as I had imagined. The large office I entered had no carpet. A number of massive desks stood against the walls; bookcases held stacks of magazines and boxes filled with folders and binders. Some of the desktops overflowed with papers; some were organized, with open-topped cartons full of bulgy envelopes standing on them.

Irving Rosenthal, a lithe, dark-haired young man with huge brown eyes, was alone in the office.

"Welcome," he said. "People come and go at different times so there's no one else for you to meet right now. Take a seat and let's chat."

This job interview was so relaxed it made me nervous. Perhaps the *Review* did not need any additional staff at the moment. Would I be sent on my way after a few minutes of conversation? I began talking about my political science courses and about my ambition to become a reporter.

"But I want to learn about literature as well -- I mean creative writing as an art," I explained. "I haven't read much for pleasure. Some of the books for my courses are very dense. They take a lot of time."

"True," the editor smiled. "If you want to join us, there's a box of submissions over there that we're reading and commenting on. When we've all gone over them, we have a staff meeting and the editors make decisions. You'll like our poetry editor, Paul Carroll. He's very hip -- in touch with all the new young poets."

"Do you mean I can work on the *Review*?" I asked, not quite believing I had been accepted so casually.

"Yes, if you have the interest. It's all voluntary, you know. Nobody gets paid; you get no course credits. It's a great group of people though."

"Thank you, Mr. Rosenthal," I said. "Thank you. I'm more than happy to join if I can help. I didn't think I had enough experience," I babbled. "When should I start? I have to work at the bindery this afternoon, but tomorrow --"

"Call me Irving," the editor replied. "Come in whenever you have a couple of hours. Before you start reading manuscripts, look over the back issues we have on those shelves. Familiarize yourself with what we publish. When you're ready, the submissions are in the envelopes the authors send us. There's a sheet of paper for comments in each one. Write your thoughts on that and keep everything together so the manuscripts don't get mixed up."

"Yes. I see; I'll be very careful," I said. I felt like an inexperienced swimmer who had just jumped into the English Channel, determined to make it to France. Without knowing the crawl stroke.

The large windows in the *Chicago Review's* office offered views of the spacious campus quadrangles. When the windows were open the breeze carried in the smell of autumn leaves and mown grass. In past years I would have spent all my free hours at the lakefront; now I sat inside, poring over manuscripts. I was as conscientious about course work and my job at the bindery as I had always been. These and my new, self-imposed effort to understand avant-garde literature kept me so busy that I spent little time with the family. I went home in the evenings for dinner and afterwards prepared class assignments. I collapsed into bed late and rose at an early hour the next morning.

I asked my brother about his school and received noncommittal answers. I almost forgot about Lincoln. We saw each other at Parkway Imports on occasional Saturdays when he and Roland would be renewing the window display or organizing the inventory. Lincoln and I would embrace, but the urgency of our summer encounters had died down. We never called each other during the week. I was grateful for this new calm; I was too tired for anything else.

At the *Review*, I learned that Irving Rosenthal was a doctoral student in human development. I could not imagine when he pursued his studies or met with his advisors because he seemed to spend twenty-three out of twenty-four hours at the office. I met Paul Carroll, the poetry editor, and six or seven other staff members, most of them graduate students. Paul, a tall, genial man, was older than the rest of us. He was a professor at the University of Illinois at Chicago and a published poet. As a non-student, he could not hold a staff position, so he was listed as guest editor. He and Irving Rosenthal, who was a native of San Francisco, regularly corresponded with Allen Ginsberg, Jack Kerouac, Lawrence Ferlinghetti, and other members of the group called the Beats.

I had never heard of these authors and I was relieved when other students confessed that they had not either.

"What does 'beat' mean?" I asked Irving.

"Kerouac came up with 'Beat Generation.' He says they're not the lost generation or the found generation -- they're just *here,* just *beat.* He also says you can think of it as *be-at,* meaning open to the moment -- beatific," Irving replied, and he added, "We're going to have a bunch of their work in one of the next issues; you'll see what they're about."

I did my best to be open to the moment. As I read poems by Philip Whalen, I noticed references to Zen Buddhism. I knew that Buddhists were a major religious community, but I did not know what Zen was. Hesitant about asking too many questions, I waited for enlightenment. The poems were written in free verse -- so free that in some, the words seemed to have been poured onto the page, landing wherever there was room. Careful rereading did reveal rhythmic phrasing and there were evocative images of nature. These poets lived in California, where I had never been. I wondered whether the open form of the poems reflected the spirit of the place. The spaces between the poems' words looked like deep breaths.

As decisions were made about the forthcoming 1958 issues, Irving asked me to help with copy editing, which I had listed in my letter as one of my jobs on the Wright College newspaper. I happily agreed. It was a task I could do with confidence and feel useful.

In back issues of the *Review*, I read poems by Isabella Gardner -- great-niece of the art collector Isabella Stewart Gardner -- fiction by Philip Roth, and essays that dealt with the works of J. D. Salinger, Saul Bellow, and Nelson Algren -- author of *The Man with the Golden Arm*, and *Chicago, City on the Make*.   Gradually, I was becoming familiar with new writing. Still, I felt very much at sea when asked for an opinion on the merits of the current contributions, especially the works of the San Francisco poets Paul Carroll and Irving Rosenthal had already chosen.

One of my first tasks shortly after I became a staff member was to help out at a *Review*-sponsored event that was not about literature but about architecture. A lecture by Frank Lloyd Wright was scheduled for November, to celebrate the university's decision not to demolish the 1909 Robie House and replace it with a dormitory. The threat to the beautiful historic building on the university campus had caused a major outcry. Thanks to pressure from the public, and from historical and architectural organizations, the trustees had second thoughts and the building was saved.

Irving planned to have the *Review* host a festive dinner at Robie House before the famous architect's lecture at Mandel Hall. At a staff meeting to discuss plans for this, Irving asked if I would like to be part of the team.

"It will mean helping with the food and the kitchen stove; can you do that?"

"I would love to help. I've never been inside the house. And Frank Lloyd Wright will be there in person," I said promptly. As Irving wrote my name on his list, I remembered that no family lived in Robie House at present. I knew it was an old structure. When had someone last fired up the stove? What if it didn't work and we had to serve a cold dinner on a November night in Chicago? I looked around anxiously to see who else was volunteering. On that special evening, I would need rescuers nearby because I had jumped into deep water again.

The *Review's* staff was not large, but enough help was on hand to make the evening with our famous guest a success. Frank Lloyd Wright, then in his ninetieth year, sat by a crackling fire in the living room with its handsome wood paneling and stained-glass windows. The architect talked with his young hosts and sipped his favorite Scotch, provided by Irving.

In the kitchen, three or four of us struggled to keep the large cast-iron stove up to temperature. Despite some defiance from the monster, we managed to produce a hot meal, and everyone sat down to dinner. Our guest, who was very serious throughout, spoke about the spread of urban ugliness and about the need to design homes in a style suited to the people who would live in them. I was too shy to say a word; I listened respectfully. After dinner, we accompanied Mr. Wright to the lecture hall, which was filled to capacity.

Frank Lloyd Wright died in April 1959. Robie House is a historic landmark.

At home, my mother told me that she had hired a saleswoman to work part-time at Parkway Imports.

"The holiday season is here, and the store is -- *Gott sei Dank* -- busy. Mrs. Beckman has experience in Germany and here," Mother said. "It's a great relief to have her there for the mornings and on Saturdays, especially."

I felt guilty because I had not been to the North Side for weeks. I was consumed by my new activities in addition to class work and my job at the bindery.

"Winter vacation is coming up," I said. "I'll come to the store with you."

"You will like Mrs. Beckman. She is very competent. But don't overtire yourself. You look terribly pale." It was true that I was sometimes tired, but I had not been ill all year; I wished Mother would stop worrying about me.

Although I spent considerable time at the *Review* office during the winter break, I kept my word. Roland and I went to Parkway, where he and Lincoln installed a Christmas tree in the show window. For safety reasons, this tree was decorated with a string of electric lights.

On Christmas Day, Lincoln and Roland's girlfriend Jutta came to the South Side. After a festive meal, we listened to classical music on WFMT radio. I felt that my family was complete and wonderful.

As Lincoln was saying goodbye, he kissed my cheek and asked in a whisper, "You have not forgotten me? We want to be together -- even just one night -- won't you make it possible?"

"I didn't forget. I want what you want," I whispered back. I meant it. All my desire for him had rushed back. But the idea of traveling to the North Side, staying away from home for a whole night, and returning to face my family the next morning, scared me more than the Grimms' witches had done when I was a preschooler. What excuse could I possibly invent? I had no girlfriends who might invite me to sleep over. My mother knew that; and she had so easily seen through my previous lies.

To take my mind off this conundrum, I wrote a lengthy letter to Sam. Avoiding any mention of family events, I detailed my experiences at the *Review* and my efforts to expand my acquaintance with contemporary literature.

"Suggest you read the great American poet Ogden Nash," he wrote back on a postcard. "Know what he says about inexperience? 'You are only young once, but you can stay immature forever!'"

CHAPTER 24

Adventures

S hortly after the beginning of the 1958 spring term, my academic advisor told me that if I passed the courses I was enrolled in, I would meet the requirements for a B.A. degree in political science and that I could graduate in June. I was happy to hear this and I thought it was an achievable goal. I had earned good grades so far; I was confident that I could manage my course work for the semester even though I was deeply committed to the *Chicago Review* and spent a great deal of time working on the magazine.

Looking forward to receiving my degree was exciting -- but so was the *Review*! Two special issues were in preparation, one devoted to the San Francisco Poets and one to writings about Zen Buddhism, Irving Rosenthal's most recent enthusiasm. I was fascinated by all of this novel material, which would be published during the coming year. I had also been talking with Irving about a future issue that would feature German Expressionist literature and poetry. I had become interested in the dramatic writings of the painter Oskar Kokoschka and the work of the Austrian-born poet Georg Trakl. I wanted to research little-known material and perhaps try my hand at translating it. Irving thought it was an ambitious project, but he encouraged me to go ahead and explore the subject.

When I had started at the university, my plan had been to look for an entry-level job in the news media immediately after graduation. Now that time was approaching, and I did not want to leave the campus. I wondered if I could take courses in literature in the fall semester and whether I could use my tuition grant if I changed my major. Before going back to my advisor, I talked the matter over with my mother. I recalled that she had gone to work as soon as we had arrived in Chicago, that she had built a business with very little capital, and that she had supported my brother and me as a single mother from 1945 on. She had encouraged us children to do well in school and she had never complained. If she now felt burdened and needed me to contribute more than my meager part-time wages to the family budget, I thought, I would go to work -- only not at Relaxacisor.

"We are managing all right now," Mother said when I had presented my question at the family dinner table. "As long as the store continues to do as well as it has been doing, and if we keep the two extra rooms rented out, we can pay our bills; nothing will change."

"My scholarship will pay for another semester, I think. I will be studying literature, and possibly translating some German poets and playwrights," I said and went on to explain my project at the *Review*.

I felt a little embarrassed by this piece of salesmanship, but I knew that the idea of publishing German poetry would appeal to my mother who regularly quoted Goethe and who could sing all the words of Friedrich Schiller's "Ode to Joy" in Beethoven's Ninth Symphony.

"I'd rather work than be in school," my brother said. "Why don't I quit and make some money? I'll be sixteen in August and it'll be legal."

"Out of the question!" Mother said, her cheeks turning red with anger. "You are only in high school -- not finished -- you need to study and go on to university!"

My brother looked at me and shook his head. Because I was sitting next to him, I could see his downturned thumbs. I sensed his unhappiness and I felt guilty that I had been too busy with my own life to pay attention to his. The family's move to the South Side had been made on my account and I loved being close to my school, but I began to understand that it might not be the same for my brother. The two of us would have to talk in private.

"You can get a job this summer," I said to Roland. "It's not that many months."

"School first! That's most important," Mother repeated.

To defuse the situation, I said, "Roland, you can come over to the campus in the afternoons. I'll meet you at the library and show you where I work. You can have my library card and take out whatever you like -- and if you want, I'll introduce you to the guys at the *Review.*"

"Good idea," Mother said. "Without a proper education, you will always be stuck in a low-class milieu. Go with Barbara."

When Roland and I were alone, I was shocked by what he revealed about his high school.

"I don't learn anything there. I hate the place," he said.

"Why? Are the classes too hard? You always kept up before and you're really good at math and science."

"It's not the subjects -- it's getting to the rooms -- up the stairs --"

"I don't get it," I said. "What's wrong with the stairs? Are your legs hurting? Do you have pain?"

"No, it's not me -- or yes, it *is* me. They shove me. I take two steps up and they trip me or push me down. They're big and tough and I can't fight them all."

I was still bewildered. "You mean there's a gang? What about the hall monitors?"

"They don't *see* anything," Roland answered. And complaining would be stupid; I'd end up in Cook County Hospital. The whole school is one big gang-- I'm the foreigner. I'm a white kid; I don't belong. Don't tell Mom! She'd come marching in the principal's office and make it worse."

I agreed with my brother. Our mother was used to German orderliness and respect for rules, especially when it came to schools. On the North Side, we had lived in a homogeneous, middle-class neighborhood and the schools had reflected that. Nothing in Germany had prepared us for the racial and economic divisions that were a fact of life here. School desegregation was years in the future. None of us had been exposed to the racial animosity that -- as I was beginning to see --Roland now had to deal with every day.

On the South Side, the public high school Roland attended was in a district that included Hyde Park, directly adjacent to the University of Chicago, as well as a large swath of a historically poor area with a high crime rate. Children growing up in this neighborhood faced daily threats to their very survival; no wonder they were tough. The more affluent and/or professional families of Hyde Park sent their children to private schools that we could not afford.

I saw that Roland understood this reality. He simply said, "We can't do anything about it. I just have to get out of there. If the truant officer comes after me, I'll tell him I'm a student at the U. of C. -- where my sister goes."

"Fine," I answered, "I'll back you up, but can you try and stick it out until June? Once summer vacation starts, you can get a job and just keep it -- not go back to high school. We won't tell Mom anything until it happens."

My brother said he would try, and he did. But I began to see more and more of him on the university campus, where no one questioned that he belonged. He was a tall young man dressed in jeans and sweatshirts, rather quiet but friendly when engaged in conversation. He could be found in the Harper Library reading Dostoyevsky or in the office of the *Chicago Review*, talking with staff members or drawing on pieces of scrap paper.

A letter from Sam arrived, once again inviting me to visit Washington, D.C.

"We have a guest room. My little boy is excited about meeting you. His sister is too young to have an opinion, but she'll like you. You should come during the week -- want to show you the hallowed halls of Congress and the White House press room. Of course, you can stay for a weekend too. Pick a date -- cherry blooms await."

The thought of attending a real-life press briefing brought back all of the ambitious excitement I had felt a few years ago when I had stood on the observation platform at the *Chicago Tribune*. I checked the calendar and looked at a map to find out the distance between Chicago and the District of Columbia-- it was almost six hundred miles, I learned. I called the Greyhound bus terminal for information about schedules and fares. While I was listing possible dates for my adventure, I realized that Sam's letter had not mentioned his wife -- not even her name. She had two small children and a house to run. What did she think of her husband's inviting a young woman student she had never met to stay with them? What if she felt annoyed and imposed upon? When I wrote to Sam again, I mentioned that I could make myself useful as a mother's helper; I had experience.

"Susan says not to worry. She is not expecting to entertain you. I'll take you out to work with me--leave her alone. Sometimes I think she's happiest that way. Young Patrick (son) is really looking forward to your visit so don't disappoint," Sam wrote back.

We set a date. I would travel to the nation's capital during the spring break. I felt both thrilled and panicked, wondering what Marguerite Higgins, my journalist heroine, would have advised.

"Calm down; nobody is shooting at you," I imagined her saying.

At the *Review*, we continued to work on the spring and summer issues. I made appointments with my advisor and with the chair of the Humanities department to discuss changing my major to comparative literature. Both conferences went smoothly. I explained my involvement with the *Review* and my wish to take literature courses in the fall; I asked whether my scholarship would cover tuition. I received permission for the curriculum change, and I was assured that my tuition grant would extend to one more semester. After that, I would have to reapply for financial aid.

The fall semester was still in the future, but I was happy to have a plan in place for my new course of study. I told the news to the family and I shared my excitement about the present -- my planned visit to Washington. On a Saturday, when Roland wanted to help Mother at the store, I went along with them to Parkway. We found Lincoln there with Mrs. Beckman, the saleslady. They were arranging the display shelves and chatting with customers.

"As soon as spring vacation starts, I'm going to Washington, D.C." I said when we had all greeted one another.

"Washington? Is this a school trip? Are you going with a group?" Lincoln asked.

"No, I'm going by myself. Sam invited me -- I'll be staying at their house and he'll show me the Capitol and the White House and the press room--" I rattled on.

"Sam -- what Sam?"

"Sam the reporter. Remember? Two years ago, when I worked for the Associated Press -- he's a news reporter who covers the White House. He invited me back then, but I couldn't make the trip last summer, so I'm going now."

Lincoln smiled. "Oh yes! The one who took you to the after-hours place and poured whisky into you. I remember him."

"It was a jazz club and I didn't drink, but otherwise you're right," I corrected and couldn't help adding, "This year I'm twenty-one so I *can* drink if I want to."

"*Jawohl!* The young lady is of age; that is important -- she makes her own decisions now," Lincoln said.

Before we left Parkway late that afternoon, Lincoln called me into the back room and gave me a business card. "It's my new phone number. Will you call me before you leave? I have a souvenir I want you to bring me from Washington, something very special. You'll call me? Promise to an old friend?"

"Of course," I said. "But what is it? How do you know I can get it in Washington -- you've never been there, have you?"

"No, but I will explain when you call me -- from a payphone," he answered, dropping his voice.

As usual, it was impossible to resist the seduction of those dark eyes. Our dialogue began to feel like a movie script. I promised.

For my trip to the nation's capital, I packed what I imagined an American girl reporter would wear -- slacks and a turtleneck top, a skirt and a white blouse with a collar and French cuffs. I did not own a blazer, but I brought a man's tweed jacket that I had found at a thrift store; it fit me well and had roomier pockets than women's garments normally did -- a plus, because I planned to carry a notebook like Sam's. Just before closing the suitcase, I added a pair of bright red knee-socks. I needed a splash of color to give me *Mut* -- my mother's word for courage.

The ride on the Greyhound bus would take eighteen hours; I boarded in the late afternoon. I had not traveled much since we had settled in Chicago and I looked forward to seeing the landscape outside the city. From my window seat, I had a view of the steel mills and oil refineries of northern Indiana, followed by stretches of flat farmland. It was exciting at first, but the state of Ohio seemed endless as the bus rolled on for hour after hour, lulling me to sleep. Some time after midnight, the bus stopped, and I jumped up to gather my belongings. I thought we had arrived -- but it was only at a rest stop in Pennsylvania.

"You'll get to D.C. for a late breakfast," the driver told me.

When the bus arrived at the terminal, my body felt stiff from sitting scrunched up in my seat for many hours. I was awake, but one of my legs was still asleep. I limped down the step and saw that Sam, wearing his blue sunglasses and a rumpled, beige sport jacket, was standing there with his right hand extended, ready to help. He looked the same as he had two years ago, in the basement newsroom of the Conrad Hilton Hotel. Even the loosely knotted tie was familiar.

"Welcome, fearless traveler," he said as he put his arms around me. "Do you want to walk around for a bit before I stuff you into my car for another ride? This one won't be long. I thought we'd go downtown -- no point going all the way out to Alexandria and then back again. I'll put your bag in the trunk."

I hopped up and down to chase the pins and needles out of my leg.

"Whatever you say. If downtown is where the White House is, I would really love that -- and can we stop in at your office? Is Miss Miller still the secretary?"

"Yes to all of the above -- onward!" Sam said.

It was April and the famed cherry blossoms were in bloom. Sam parked the car near the Washington Monument, and we strolled around the Tidal Basin. The warm, fragrant air was a welcome contrast to the dank body odor that had surrounded me all night on the bus. Sam pulled a small camera from one of his jacket pockets.

"Go perch picturesquely on that lower limb; you look so pretty in this light -- let me snap a photo," he said.

"Do you know something? We've never seen each other in the daytime before," I said to Sam. "We were working nights at the convention."

"That's true," Sam laughed. "We're going to fix the situation right now. Are you up for a walking tour of downtown D.C.? You can come out of your tree now!"

Sam explained that the city had been carefully planned, with its wide avenues named after states laid out like spokes of a giant wagon wheel, its monuments and parks clustered around the most famous address in the country -- the White House at 1600 Pennsylvania Avenue. As we walked and paused to gaze at all the famous sites I had only read about or seen on television, I thought Washington was the loveliest place I had ever visited. I had no idea what time it was, and I could have wandered around for the rest of the day, but Sam decided it was time for lunch.

"We'll get the car and go to the luncheonette for a burger and then I'll take you to visit the office. I told Marion you were coming," he said.

The sandwich shop was a bar, dark and smoky. Sam was known there. As soon as we seated ourselves at a small round table, a waitress brought over a glass filled with ice cubes and a clear liquid. Was that vodka? I wondered, remembering the club in Chicago.

Sam took a swallow. "Join me?" he asked.

"I'll have coffee, please, regular," I said to the waitress, who gave me a smile and the menu.

We ordered club sandwiches. I had not realized how hungry I was after an overnight bus ride and a sightseeing tour. I ate everything on my plate and half of what was on Sam's before stopping to apologize.

"Sorry," I said. "I took your food. Please let me pay for it -- I'm sorry."

"That's okay; I'm not that hungry. Finish -- here comes my dividend anyway -- thanks, Kitty," Sam said as another drink was put in front of him.

The Washington Bureau of the Associated Press was on one of the grand avenues, in a modern building with huge plate glass windows flanking the entrance on the ground level.

"All we need is a large sign saying 'Fish -- 39 Cents,'" Sam said as we approached. "AP -- A *and* P supermarket -- what's the difference?" Sam joked as we went into a large, bright room. It certainly did not resemble the subterranean press area in Chicago, I thought, but this was the national headquarters!

Marion Miller, the young woman who had been kind to a nervous typist two years ago, beamed as we walked up to her desk. She gave me a hug.

"Welcome to Washington," she said. "Ready to go to work?"

"That would be great -- thank you -- I could start as a typist or anything, really. Only I have to finish school first," I answered.

"The girl is conscientious to a fault," Sam commented.

A subversive question invaded my mind. Why *did* I have to stay in school? What if I simply found a job here instead of returning to Chicago? The sobering answer was, of course, the university degree that I had dreamed of and that I had worked so hard to earn. Not finishing my courses would be a major disappointment for the whole family. Besides, I had projects at the *Review.* How could I forget?

"...take her to meet some of the guys?" Marion was saying as I woke up from my musings.

"Right," Sam said, giving me a sharp glance. "Let's go and say hi to the boys in the back room."

The correspondents working at their typewriters, as well as the messengers who picked up and delivered copy from the teletype machines, were all male. Sam introduced me as a family friend who was studying journalism.

I received polite handshakes accompanied by inquisitive looks.

"Do you want to write for the women's pages?" one of the men asked.

"Well, actually, I'm interested in the news -- the political and international news," I replied.

"Really? That's a tough beat -- bunch of roughnecks. Just look at the gang in this room! It's not a job for women-- well, there's Helen Thomas. You don't want to be like Helen, do you?"

I knew that Helen Thomas worked for United Press. She wrote about important personalities in Washington and about news from the Capitol. Her stories were published in major newspapers along with those of her male colleagues. I had never seen a picture of her. Was she some kind of monster? Why should I not want to be like her?

Sam moved along towards another group of desks. I leaned close to him and whispered, "What's so wrong about Helen Thomas?"

Sam laughed. "Nothing. She's a feisty little lady -- cranky -- doesn't take any guff from these cowboys; they think she's uppity."

Maybe I would be lucky enough to catch a glimpse of her this week, I thought. My sympathies were with Helen Thomas.

After making the rounds of the newsroom, Sam said that he had a column to finish and we walked over to his desk. He pulled over a chair for me.

"Sit -- take a rest -- or you can read today's paper; it's here somewhere. I won't take long and when I'm done, we'll head home," he said.

I sat down and breathed in the busy atmosphere of the office. I daydreamed of my future as an intrepid female reporter who took no guff -- whatever that was -- from anybody.

Sam pulled the sheet of copy paper from his machine and handed it to me.

"Done! Want to read it?"

"I do -- yes, please," I said.

It was one of his clever humor columns about earthlings who had been captured by space aliens. Little Green Men were a hotly discussed topic in 1958.   The previous October, the surprise launching of Sputnik 1 by the Soviet Union had sent the nation into collective shock and had precipitated the space race. Sam's fictional humans had been kidnapped and transported to a distant galaxy. "Take us to your leader," the victims demand. The otherworldly creature complies. The leader is a woman.

"My mom would love this! Do you think I could have a copy when it's printed?" I asked.

"Sure. Remind me tomorrow, would you?"

Sam's wife, a petite brunette, came out of the front door of their two-storey house when the car entered the driveway. She held a squirming toddler in her arms. Before Sam and I were fully out of the car, a small, red-headed boy burst out of the door and hurtled down the front steps.

"That's Patrick -- hello, son -- stand still for a second so I can introduce you," Sam laughed. "Shake hands with Barbara -- don't run her over!"

The little boy had Sam's fair skin, liberally sprinkled with freckles, light-blue eyes, and enough energy for a gymnastics team. He bounced at my side as we walked up to the rest of the family.

Sam's wife smiled. "Hello -- welcome. I'm Susan, and this is Mags -- short for Mary Margaret. Come in so I can put her down and shake your hand properly."

Mags scampered off as soon as Susan released her inside the carpeted living room. "She hates to be confined," Susan said, "She's going to learn to run before she can walk."

Sam, who had gone back outside for my suitcase, now brought it in and offered to take it upstairs.

"I'll show you your room and the bathroom," he said.

Patrick raced past him. "Me! Me! I show her -- my room too," he shouted.

In the guest room, Patrick came up to me with a huge grin. "This is for you," he said, holding out a tiny yellow bulldozer. "It's a steamshovel. For you. Daddy says you dig everything!"

"Wowee -- thank you, Patrick! A steamshovel -- that's just perfect for digging. Your dad's right -- I dig it!" I gave Patrick a hug and said to Sam, "I wish I'd brought *him* something. I didn't think; I was so excited about the trip."

"That's okay. These kids have more than they need already. Patrick is good at sharing, aren't you, son?"

"Dinner's almost ready. We'll just eat in the breakfast nook if nobody minds," Susan said as the three of us came downstairs again.

"Formal dining and two-year-old just don't go together," Sam said. "Kids are easier to corral in the kitchen."

"Please don't do anything extra for me," I said. "I'll help you after dinner and tomorrow."

We sat down. Sam got up again, went to a cupboard, took out a bottle, and poured himself a drink.

"Susan, Barbara, do you want to join me?" he asked.

"No thank you," I answered.

Susan asked, "How many did you have at work?"

"None. I don't drink in the office," Sam said with a straight face. "A partial truth is a lie by omission," my religious *Tante* said in my head.

Dinner conversation was pleasant; Patrick wanted to hear all about the bus ride, Sam said we could visit the Capitol tomorrow; Susan told me to enjoy the sights and not worry about a particular dinner time, explaining, "It happens when it happens; schedules don't mean anything in this house."

The little girl fell asleep in her highchair halfway through the meal. Susan readily accepted help with the dinner dishes. I was glad that she treated me like family -- or perhaps a trusted *au pair*. Sam took the children upstairs. I thought I heard Susan murmur, "More than he does most nights." But I wasn't sure; the water was running.

"My knee has been bothering me again; I'm going upstairs to put a heating pad on it. Feel free to sit up if you want -- or go to bed early. You must be tired," Susan said as soon as we had dried the dishes.

"I'm beat, I admit," I said. "Thank you for everything. The bedroom is so nice; I didn't realize how tired I feel."

In the guestroom, I found a piece of pink construction paper lying on the bedspread. Printed on it in pencil was, "Dear Barbara I like you. You remind me of Kim Novak -- love PATRICK"

Kim Novak? I did not think I looked like the blonde actress. I knew that her recent films had won critical acclaim, but I had not seen any of them. I also knew that they were not movies a six-year-old would be admitted to. And how many first-graders knew how to spell "remind"?

In the car the next morning, I said to Sam, "That was a cute note Patrick left for me last night--but I don't look like Kim Novak. I'm surprised he even knows about her. Did he get a little help with his spelling?"

"Well--maybe a little, Sherlock," Sam admitted, looking straight ahead with a sly smile on his face.

"I said thank you to him this morning -- and now, thank *you!* But I don't see any resemblance to Kim Novak. She's blonde."

"Hair color can be changed. But you have things in common; do you know that?" Sam asked.

"No, I don't know anything about her. I haven't gone to the movies in months," I said.

"Kim Novak is a native of Chicago; she is the daughter of immigrants; she attended Wright Junior College; she worked as a model at trade shows before her film career took off," Sam recited, as if he were reading from a fan magazine.

I sat up straight in my seat. "What? I didn't know any of that -- I never met her at Wright; at least I don't think so," I exclaimed.

"She's three or four years older than you," Sam said. "You can look all this up. Research is an essential ingredient of journalism. End of lecture."

"I promise to remember," I said. "I have a lot to learn."

"So, do we all" Sam reassured me and added, "Look -- we're almost downtown. Today's itinerary takes us to the United States Capitol, where your illustrious lawmakers are holding forth upon weighty matters. We'll go sit in the visitors' gallery for a while and see what's happening -- there are no major debates today that I know of -- and then I'll show you the rest of the building. Are you game?"

"Ready!" I said. "Excited -- and just so happy to be here!"

When we walked into the public gallery, I saw that we were in luck. I recognized the speaker from newspaper photos. It was Senator Everett Dirksen of Illinois.

"He's been in Congress since before you were born," Sam told me in an undertone. "What the hell are they discussing?"

Senator Dirksen was holding up a bottle with a colorful picture on its label.

"Four Roses!" he thundered in the voice that the newspapers described as operatic. I had never heard it.

"Four Roses -- surely you cannot contemplate adopting a state flower named after an inebriating beverage!"

"Bourbon," Sam whispered in answer to my astonished look.

I listened carefully, completely bewildered. I began to understand that the debate concerned a state's official flower.

"State flowers are adopted by law," Sam murmured. "So, they can only be changed by law. What? Did you think you were going to hear about war and peace?"

We left the gallery and spent the rest of the morning touring what Sam called "The Corridors of Power." In the afternoon, we walked around the National Mall and paid a visit to the Lincoln Memorial.

"Is it all right for you to spend so much time out of the office? What about your assignments?" I finally asked Sam.

"I have another column, for next week. No current newsflashes or interviews; no deadline today," he said. "We should stop by, though -- just in case. You never know. Somebody might croak."

In the AP newsroom, Marion Miller, cheerful as always, greeted us.

"Ready to file your story?" she joked. "What do you think of Washington?"

"I'm coming back, definitely. When I finish school, I'll come and ask if you need a dictationist or a copygirl or whatever job people start with here," I said.

"I can't manage to discourage her," Sam commented.

"You're taking her to the press conference tomorrow? I got her a pass, as you requested. She's your student assistant, if anybody asks," Marion said to Sam.

"Press conference?" I nearly shrieked. "You mean like the press conference -- the one where the reporters--"

Sam laughed and said, "At the White House briefing room. Tomorrow's Friday. You're not leaving until Saturday, did you say?"

"Yes -- Oh, I wouldn't miss this for anything! I'm so glad I can go!" I wanted to cry with happiness. Sam had remembered the promise he had made on a July night in Chicago, when he had put me in a taxi on the last night of the Democratic National Convention.

I did not think I would sleep that night, but I did. Touring Washington had tired me more than I realized, and I had taken the drink Sam had offered me before dinner.

For the press conference, I wore the tweed jacket and a skirt. I tied my shoulder-length hair into a ponytail, hoping to achieve a businesslike look. I tried not to gawk when we entered the White House and Sam led the way to the briefing room in the West Wing. I willed myself to be calm as credentials were checked and we joined the group of reporters already waiting. They all knew each other; Sam exchanged greetings with his colleagues and introduced me to one or two by name before they took their seats.

Sam walked me to the back of the room. "I have to sit in my assigned chair in the middle," he said. "Sit here in the last row, on the end; you can see and hear everything. See ya later!"

Everyone stood up as the President Eisenhower, followed by his press secretary, James Hagerty, walked through a doorway at the front of the room and walked to the lectern.

"Good afternoon, gentlemen," the president said and the reporters, dressed in suits and ties, resumed their seats.

"The president will make a brief statement before taking questions," Mr. Hagerty said. A steno pad was in my pocket, with a pen and a pencil. I forgot all about them -- too riveted by this marvelous experience to take notes.

When it was time for questions, many hands went up. The president pointed. The designated reporter stood up, identified himself by name and affiliation, and asked his question. After an answer, and in some cases, a short follow-up, the reporter sat down. I watched as correspondents from Reuters, United Press, the *New York Times,* the *Baltimore Sun,* and other publications took turns. There was even a reporter from the German magazine *Der Spiegel.* Sam had told me beforehand that he had no particular question prepared; he was there to listen and if a topic struck him as possible material for his column, he would note it.

After about forty-five minutes, Mr. Hagerty picked up a sheaf of papers from the lectern and said, "That's all we have for today; thank you."

A tall reporter in a grey suit rose from his chair and said, "Thank you, Mr. President."

"That was Merriman Smith, from United Press," Sam told me a moment later. "We call him Smitty -- he's the senior correspondent, so he gets the honor of saying thank you. Come with me and meet him; he's a good friend."

Mr. Smith shook my hand and asked Sam, "Your relative? Showing her the sights?"

"She's a journalism and political science student. University of Chicago," Sam answered.

"I'm happy to meet you, sir. I hope to work in news reporting," I said.

"Call me Smitty -- it's okay. Has Sam told you life with the press corps is not like it is in books? It's not that pretty -- a hard-drinking crowd and not always as well-spoken as they were today."

This response no longer surprised me. I did not want to sound argumentative. "I still have to finish my degree at the university," I said. "But some day, I hope to turn up in D.C."

"You have time. Think about it," Smitty advised.

The next day was Saturday and time for me to thank Susan and Sam for their hospitality. My bag was packed, ready for a bus that left shortly after noon. I promised Patrick that I would dig up half of Chicago with the toy steamshovel. Susan pulled Mags off a stepstool that the toddler was not allowed to climb on and shook my hand. "I hope you had a pleasant visit," she said.

"It was wonderful. Thank you for letting me stay in your home."

In the car, Sam looked downcast. "I wish I could move the U. of C. to the George Washington University Campus! That way I could see you every day," he said.

"I know; Chicago is such a long trip," I agreed. "But what about Susan? She'd hate that kind of an arrangement, wouldn't she?"

"Don't be so sure. I don't think she has much use for me. She has the kids -- all her energy goes to them. I'm often traveling; I'm not her ideal of a good suburban dad."

"It was wonderful being here -- I never thought I'd see so much -- learn so much! Thank you a million for everything," I said, feeling embarrassed by the personal tone we had fallen into. "And I'll write you as soon as I get back."

"Yes, keep writing me letters. Long letters. I want you to think of me as your best friend," Sam said as he reached over and squeezed my hand.

"I will. I've been writing, and I'll keep it up," I promised.

At the Greyhound bus terminal, I told Sam to drop me off.

"I'll cry if we say goodbye one more time," I said. "And look at the traffic. Let me go inside and get on my bus and before you know it, it'll be time for another visit."

"I agree. No crying! Real life is not for sissies. Be careful and be good," Sam said, stopping at the curb. He lifted my suitcase out of the trunk and put it down next to me.

We hugged and then I watched him drive off before I entered the terminal. Where I bought a ticket -- not for Chicago, but for New York City. I was headed there because I was going to meet Lincoln at a hotel. Because *I* was the souvenir he had wanted me to bring from Washington.

It was just like the movies. I was Kim Novak, playing the lead.

CHAPTER 25

A Degree and a Revolution

"*Es ist so schőn wie ein Traum,*" Lincoln said, "You have kept your promise -- it is like a beautiful dream."

"Are we really in New York? Together? And Chicago is eight hundred miles away? Maybe we *are* dreaming," I replied.

"Say twelve hundred kilometers -- that sounds even further away," Lincoln laughed as he drew me into an embrace that felt reassuring and enticing in equal measure. "Do you know how dreams become real? Will you let me guide you?"

Would Kim Novak cringe with stage fright now? She would not! And -- after all my trepidations and anxieties and even panics over the years -- neither did I. I felt joyful and brave. And eager.

Lincoln laughed at my story about 1945 when some of the boys at the Moosschwaige had paraded an intriguing new toy -- a transparent rubber tube that could be blown up into a balloon. He chuckled when I described the adults' horrified reaction.

"Oh, that's funny," he said. "How old were you -- eight, nine? You couldn't be blamed; you were far too young! But -- now that you are an adult woman of twenty-one, let me demonstrate the correct use of this item -- where and how it goes. You can help if you wish..."

I reached out to touch.

"It was so smart of you to think of meeting in New York and to work out all the arrangements," I said later.

"It wasn't difficult. Your mother and Roland think you are in Washington through the weekend because you told them so. They don't expect you to call home because long distance is expensive. If anyone should ask me why I took a few days off work, it's the most natural thing in the world. I am an artist; I have never seen the great museums of New York; I went. It was *wunderbar!*"

"You're *wunderbar*," I said and kissed him.

"You're beautiful," he replied.

"Really? No -- I'm too skinny and I have no bosoms."

"Wrong! Next time you're in the library, look up Lucas Cranach -- Sixteenth-century German master, as you may know -- or go to the Art Institute. You might have been one of his long-legged models."

I decided not to dispute an expert's opinion and Kim Novak agreed with me.

"A souvenir is something beautiful that you keep. We'll both remember this weekend--this happy weekend. It is ours alone. No family, no obligations," Lincoln said and added, "Do you agree?"

"It's beautiful now," I said. "And do you know -- I wasn't scared? How did you do that?"

"*You* did it! You trusted me; you let go of the *angst*. You know that you can trust me always. And as for the future, don't be afraid. There will not be consequences; you were protected."

The long bus ride to Chicago gave me time to return to my everyday self after the heady adventures I had enjoyed during the previous ten days. I arrived home on the day I had said I would, and I had stories to tell about Washington and the White House press conference and Senator Dirksen. I gave the clipping of Sam's article about the little green men to my mother.

"We should start a scrapbook. These stories are so funny," she said.

I went back to my routine -- classes, work at the library and at the *Chicago Review*. It seemed that no one noticed anything different about me, but I felt the change my romantic escapade had brought about. I was full of *Mut* -- confident, optimistic -- free!

The Spring 1958 issue of the *Review* featured the work of the San Francisco poets. It represented the first exposure, in a major national journal, except for some work that had appeared in the *Evergreen Review*, for poems by Allen Ginsberg, Lawrence Ferlinghetti, Philip Lamantia, Michael McClure, and others. It also contained an excerpt from William S. Burroughs's *Naked Lunch.* The issue was well received. Our business manager reported an increase in the magazine's circulation.

Irving Rosenthal was confident our summer issue would be equally successful. This one was devoted to writings about Zen Buddhism -- a discipline that had captivated Irving but was unfamiliar to most Americans at the time. On a balmy spring day, as I was walking across the quadrangle towards the Reynolds Tower, I heard a voice from above.

"ZEN!"

I looked up. Framed in an open window on the second floor stood Irving, arms outflung, repeating, "Zen!"

"Zen!" I shouted back, adopting the new ritual greeting.

Irving's prediction was proved right when the summer issue, with its lovely Japanese cover art, was published to good reviews and excellent sales. As the weather warmed, I noticed students wearing a new style of sandal with straw soles and cloth thongs. They were called zoris -- later to be mass-marketed as flip-flops.

For me, the summer of 1958 brought the fulfillment of a dream. At the end of June, I received my Bachelor of Arts diploma, granted by the Political Science department. It was a proud moment for my family. I felt that we had reached a milestone in our journey towards the American Dream. We were settled; we were not rich, but we were financially independent; education had proved to be achievable, thanks to perseverance and a good deal of luck.

Lincoln called and congratulated me. I thanked him and told him that I would be going back to school for at least one more semester. He said, "*Wunderbar!* Don't forget to look for Cranach's *Eve* in the library."

"I won't. I will never forget her -- or you," I answered. Fortunately, no one else was in the room to overhear those words. There had been no disagreement, but we had not continued our romance. Without discussing it, we were content with shared memories.

I was happy about my degree and equally glad that I would be continuing my studies in the fall. Although I needed a paying job for the summer, I planned to spend as much time as possible with the *Review*. I felt the excitement of the literary revolution that was unfurling before my eyes and I wanted to be part of it.

I found a position with a commercial magazine that published an extensive weekly entertainment guide. My work consisted of keeping the listings up to date by calling the hotels, nightclubs, and restaurants that offered music or other entertainment, obtaining information about the featured performers, showtimes, prices, and cover charges. The magazine's offices were on the third floor of an older building whose electrical system was unable to support an adequate number of air conditioners.

"Don't bother with stockings or long sleeves; it gets really hot up here," my boss advised.

The work was prosaic and tedious -- so different from the *Review*, which was anything but.

Irving Rosenthal planned to include another section from *Naked Lunch* by William Burroughs in the Autumn 1958 issue, along with works by Philip Whalen, John Logan, David Riesman, and other authors previously published by the *Review*. I knew little about Burroughs. I had not seen the unedited manuscript of the excerpt that had run in the previous issue. Paul Carroll and Irving had prepared that for publication.

"Burroughs is brilliant, but raw," Irving asserted, pointing to a cardboard box full of paper. "We need to get this in shape."

I looked at the manuscript. It was a mess. Typed on flimsy onionskin paper, the text was littered with erasures, crossed-out phrases, overwritten words, and miscellaneous comments in the narrow margins. I could find few pages that were numbered and when I began to read, I asked if the pages were in sequence. "Not always," Irving answered.

The story, if it was a story -- I couldn't seem to find a plot -- was a nightmare. Drug pushers, boy prostitutes, sadistic doctors, and desperate addicts scrambled through episodes set in the slums of Tangiers. It was a dark, dark world, slashed by lightning bolts of gallows humor. The characters were like tortured figures painted by the gloomiest of German Expressionists.

Naked Lunch was the exact opposite of the Zen writings I had begun to like, I thought. Instead of celebrating the beauty of selfless emptiness, this author plunged the reader into frenzy and despair, graphic violence, and predatory sex. Instead of being invited into the calm of introspection, the reader was assaulted by obsessive, chaotic sensuality expressed in vulgar language. It was astonishing that Irving could find these vastly different styles equally attractive and meritorious. I helped him with the monstrous task of copy editing, thinking that this revolution was wide-ranging indeed.

I wrote to Sam regularly, reporting my impressions.

"Your guy Burroughs killed his wife. Tried to shoot an apple she put on her head. Missed. Ain't no William Tell. What do *you* do for entertainment these days?" Sam wrote on a Western Union Press Message message form.

Before replying to Sam, I asked Paul Carroll if the story about Burroughs was true. Paul confirmed it, adding, "That's why he's in Tangier, hiding from the police."

"I went to a movie with my brother and his girlfriend," I wrote in my next letter to Sam. "We saw *Daddy Longlegs* with Fred Astaire and Leslie Caron. The dancing is wonderful, and nobody gets shot. I'm sure you know all this. The movie has been out for a couple of years. Haven't had too much spare time lately."

Sam's next few communications were postcards with plaintive messages that troubled me because they lacked his usual jocular tone.

"Wife and I don't go to movies. She's tired. Back hurts. Too much lifting of kiddies but she won't hire a babysitter. Tells me to get lost. Wish you were here. Patrick likes you; I like you," read one. Another postcard asked, "Will you be in Chicago forever? Would you try to make a go of it here? Miss you."

I thought about Washington and the cherry trees. My friend sounded so sad. Could you be lonely even though you were married and had cute children? I wished I could take a walk with him and hold his hand.

When the new school year started in September, I was excited by my literature classes. The professor who taught modern German literature announced that we would be reading Thomas Mann's *Death in Venice* in German and that class discussion of it would be conducted in German as well. I looked forward to this, but I was a bit frightened, wondering if my vocabulary was up to the challenge of Thomas Mann's erudite language.

Roland did not return to high school. He had turned sixteen in August and had declared that he would keep working at his summer job; his employer had agreed to make it permanent. Siegel's bookstore was a well-known literary meeting place, where local authors gave readings and avant-garde books were prominently displayed in the show window. The store carried the *Chicago Review* and similar journals.

I knew why my brother had made this choice and I thought it was a good one. Our mother was furious.

"Stock boy! Nothing but a common laborer," she scoffed. "If you just worked a little harder and finished high school you could apply to the university and make something of yourself!"

"*You* run a store, Mom!" Roland retorted. "Is your saleslady a common laborer? Would you rather have me at Parkway, selling *lederhosen?* No, thanks! I think books are better. Educational, in fact."

"Not everybody wants to go to the University of Chicago," I said. "There's nothing to be ashamed of at the bookstore. They sell all the best modern literature."

Mother said, "I need a cold compress on my forehead. This is bringing on a migraine." She left the room.

"The dig about *lederhosen* was too much," I said to Roland. "But I'll stand by you. Going back to school is impossible and we can't explain that, so let's just give her time to get used to the new plan. You can still spend time on the campus here, as much as you want."

Mother would not speak a word to either of us for the next two days.

The *Review's* autumn 1958 issue was published that month, with the excerpt from *Naked Lunch* advertised on the cover. Irving's plan was to introduce the unorthodox new writer by publishing short segments in three consecutive issues. Burroughs' work would be accompanied by that of less controversial writers -- and before they knew it, the reading public would have been presented with a brilliant new talent.

At first, we thought the scheme was working. There was no adverse reaction to the new feature. The staff continued to put together the winter issue, which was to contain a second, larger portion of Burroughs and pieces by Jack Kerouac and Edward Dahlberg.

And then, in late October, a *Chicago Daily News* columnist exploded into a tirade.

"Filthy Writing On The Midway," blared the headline of Jack Mabley's column. "Do you ever wonder what happens to little boys who scratch dirty words on railroad underpasses? They go to college and scrawl obscenities in the college literary magazine," Mabley continued.

Without naming the *Review,* the columnist berated the University of Chicago for publishing "one of the foulest collections of printed filth" he had ever seen. The editors, whom he called "juveniles," were not only "beatniks," but "evidence of the deterioration of our American society ... dangerous."

Mabley concluded that the editors were too "immature and irresponsible" to be blamed. However, he strongly recommended that the trustees of the university take a long, hard look at what was being published. Not surprisingly, Chancellor Kimpton was alerted to do just that in short order.

The Furies, in the form of outraged trustees, a nervous administration, and a faculty advisor who had so far paid scant attention to us, were upon us within a week. Irving was told that the Winter 1959 issue we had laid out could not be published as it stood. We could go ahead only if we removed the works by Burroughs and all the other "offensive" material and published a magazine that "a sixteen-year-old girl could read without blushing."

The alternative was to resign.

"Blatant censorship!" Irving and Paul responded. Others added, "Suppression...Denial of free speech."

Multiple meetings were held. Irving Rosenthal met with the dean of the Division of Humanities and with the *Review's* faculty advisor; the trustees confronted the chancellor, who demanded to know how the *Review* had gotten away with publishing the controversial material. The editors were reminded that material considered obscene could not be legally distributed through the United States mail. The magazines could be seized by the post office; publishers and even printers were subject to fines and jail sentences.

All of us were aware of these dangers as we met to discuss our individual options. In an emotion-filled conference in mid-November, Irving, Paul, and three other staff members who held the rank of editor said that they would resign if the administration held to its ultimatum. Rather than scratch the planned issue and return the manuscripts to the authors, they would find a way to publish the contents without the university's imprimatur. The business manager sided with them, saying that he would begin selling ads for the future publication immediately.

I thought about censorship -- about the paintings that the Nazis had condemned as "degenerate," and the writers and poets my mother had told me about who had been silenced. The university was not a police state, and this was America -- but in my opinion, those two facts made it doubly wrong to forbid the publication of a work of art, distasteful as it might be. My choice was clear: I could not stay on at the *Review* under the conditions the university was imposing. But there was one fear I could not banish--the worry that I might become embroiled in an obscenity trial. I was not yet an American citizen. Unlike the other staff members, I could be deported as an undesirable alien if the case went against us. I resolved to ask Irving to leave my name off the masthead of the new magazine, if and when it could be launched.

With that small reassurance to myself, I said, "I will resign with you."

Only one senior staff member -- Hyung Woong Pak, the Korean student -- decided that he could produce an innocuous issue if he were named to stay on as editor. I had been friendly with Pak; we had gone to the theater together and he had taught me to write my name in Korean characters. I sneered that he was an opportunist. Later, I regretted my harsh attitude. In the heat of the moment, I did not think about how hard it was to be a foreigner trying to make your way in an alien land.

I called the Associated Press Bureau in Washington and left a message with Marion Miller. "Sam will be interested in this story about the University of Chicago," I said. "It's important."

When Sam telephoned the next day, I described the situation at the *Review* and the university's demands. "Irving and all the senior editors except Pak have sent in their resignations," I said. I'm with them. I only hope they won't take away my scholarship; I want to finish the semester."

Sam reassured me. "If you all resign from the *Review*, they'll have achieved their objective. I wouldn't worry about anything more personal," he said.

I asked, "Can you help us? Can you get a story on the wire about this suppression? It's an outrage -- the University of Chicago of all places!"

"I'll try. Give me names and facts -- who is that scandal sheet columnist you mentioned? Spell his name --"

I could see Sam's ever-present notebook, the pen he fished out of his pocket, and his puckish smile as he took down the details of my story. I wished I were sitting next to him.

"I can't promise a story -- Chicago isn't exactly my beat -- but I'll bring it to the attention of a couple of people I know. In the meantime, you rebels need to make as much noise as you can in the press. Someone should call the *Saturday Review,* and so on," Sam advised.

"We've started," I told Sam. "We've alerted the *Maroon* -- that's the student newspaper-- and the student government and I think the *Tribune* is picking up the story. We can't let the university just bury this issue. We're determined to get it out somehow."

Sam laughed. "Comes the revolution... you *will* eat strawberries and cream!"

I had to laugh too. Sam's offbeat humor was back.

In November, the *Chicago Tribune* picked up the story and ran an article and a photo in its Sunday magazine supplement.

"*Chicago Review* is midwest outlet for writings of beat generation," the caption reads. Irving Rosenthal, who had grown a beard that made him look like a Russian saint, is shown in the foreground, hugging a copy of the controversial magazine to his chest. Eila Kokkinen, the art editor, and I -- by then the managing editor -- stand behind Irving. We look quietly defiant, with a hint of amusement. Also, in the background is essay editor Hyung Woong Pak, a serious Korean student. In front of him, Doris Nieder, the editorial assistant, smiles impishly.

The *Tribune* article's main point was that beatniks were a nuisance, but fortunately, most of them were already leaving Chicago and were on their way to the West Coast.

The ex-editors -- who were not on their way to San Francisco -- spent the rest of the year "making noise" -- protesting to the media that the University of Chicago, an institution renowned for liberal thought, had engaged in censorship. We let it be known that the suppressed material would be published in a new, independent magazine. Irving and Paul Carroll were in constant contact with Allen Ginsberg and Jack Kerouac, who supported the rebel venture with readings and benefit appearances. As we brainstormed about a name for the magazine, Jack Kerouac suggested *Big Table* -- supposedly because he had left himself a note to get a bigger table.

Irving and Paul Carroll were enthusiastic about the name-- *Big Table* it was! For the first issue, Irving wrote a preface recounting the sequence of events that had led to its creation. A cover was designed in red, white, and blue -- broad stripes on the front, white stars on a blue background on the back. Paul agreed to become editor for subsequent issues of *Big Table* because Irving had decided to move to New York to pursue his own writing.

A nonprofit corporation was formed to publish the magazine and now we had a new problem -- finding money to print it. We no longer had access to the services of the University of Chicago Press which produced the *Review*. I joined in the search for a printing firm that would take the job at a price we could afford. It was difficult because the material was obviously controversial and vulnerable to the censorship laws. Our funds, contributed by donors who believed in our cause, were not ample enough to tempt print shops to take a chance on our venture. It would be many weeks before Irving was able to make a deal with a company in New York, The Profile Press.

Amidst the fundraising, the publicity efforts, and the practical tasks of launching a new magazine, I went to my literature classes -- where the *Review's* fate was never mentioned. We were studying dead authors; I wrote a paper about symbolism. I became more and more certain that this was not destined to be my life's work.

I talked with Sam on the telephone when he called me. I was still shy about disturbing him at work and I never even considered calling his home. I wrote to him instead. I thought about the plot of *Daddy Longlegs*, in which Fred Astaire, as the eccentric millionaire benefactor of a young woman in an orphanage, receives letters from her that eventually lead to their falling in love. Would our story develop like that? From the time we had met, we had been friends despite the differences in our ages and experience. Was our relationship becoming something more now? I remembered our carefree tour of Washington and about eating half of his lunch. It had felt so natural -- as if we were a couple already used to intimacy.

Sam's missives to me were typically short, like news bulletins or one-liner jokes. Sometimes, they asked a single question: "What after you leave UC?"

It was a hard question to answer. I was twenty-two years old; my birthday, on November 11, had passed almost unnoticed in the chaos caused by the dramatic events at the *Review.* Much as I had loved being a student at the university, I knew that I would not continue after the current semester ended. Working for *Big Table* was not a career for me; it would always be a nonprofit operation in all senses of the word, and I had to earn my keep.

I was drawn to Washington, D.C. How wonderful it would be to work there, and to be close to Sam! Was that possible? What would happen to my family if I left -- especially to Roland? He was only sixteen and though he was capable and responsible, he still looked to me for the emotional support our mother now withheld from him; she would never understand why he had dropped out of school.

One of Mother's favorite German maxims popped into my head: *Kommt Zeit, kommt Rat.* It means "In time, good counsel will come." That, I thought, was a wise saying. It reassured me. At the moment, *Big Table* concerns demanded all of my energy; my attention was focused on solving immediate problems.

I would give it time; I would think about my future, but I would not make a hasty decision.

Shortly before Christmas, I received a letter. It was from Sam and it contained not advice, but a single sheet of pale-yellow paper without a date, salutation, or signature.

love poem

she should be draped
    in evanescent silk forever
        fed delicately by blind eunuchs
        in my altered image
            on brandymarinated grapes.

          like hell she should
          she should be out
              ploughing my fields
              fetching my firewood

            whelping my pups.

she should be shod
    in gossamer spiderwebs golden
        having bathed in purplescented bubblebath
            having stroked on invisible nylons

          like hell she should

          she should be out

              trampling my grapes

              raping my olives

              rounding up my steers.

CHAPTER 26

Another World

I could not show the poem to my mother or to Roland— not before talking with Sam. And I couldn't call Sam before questioning my own heart and trying to put my feelings into words. While I procrastinated, I read the poem over and over again, thrilled by the sensuous images. The man was in love with me; it was like the tale I was so fond of, *Daddy Longlegs.* Sam was the older man; I was the girl who felt grateful for his friendship and guidance. We had known each other for two years; we had spent little time alone together and those meetings had been in public places or in his family home. And yet— all of our letters and conversations made me feel that we already had come to an intimate understanding. A physical relationship would deepen that into abiding love. How often had I longed to reach out and straighten his tie, or to take off his blue glasses and brush my lips over his eyelids?

If Sam should ask me to move to Washington, I knew that I would say yes. I was free and willing. It would be the happy ending our fairytale romance called for. And, as a modern heroine, I would also pursue a career. But Sam was married; I had met his wife and children. What would happen to them? I hoped Sam had an answer because I didn't.

The last month of 1958 was almost over. I had not yet found the courage to talk with Sam when he took the initiative and called me.

"You know how I feel about you; I wrote it for you, but you must have known for a long time," he said after I had filled a few minutes with chatter about Irving Rosenthal, *Big Table* magazine, and the difficult task of finding a printer for it.

"Yes, I— I know. That is the most beautiful poem— I don't know what to say," I stammered.

"You can say you love me. Do you? I love you," Sam said. He chuckled and added, "Simple English words. I don't know how it goes in German or I'd translate it for you."

"I know the words, Sam— and I do. But I'm shy about saying it on the phone— people are in the house— I'll write a letter."

"Oh, baby! That's so wonderful and great. I'm very happy. Can you listen to me and let me explain a few things and say yes or no?"

"Yes, please! I have no idea how to go on from here. What about Susan and Patrick and Mags and your house? What about— "

"Hold on a second. I *can* tell you a few things; but first things first, so answer another question before we go on. The question is, will you come to D.C. if Susan agrees to a separation? I think she will; I think our marriage is pretty much over— it's been that way for a long time," Sam said.

"I didn't know," I answered. "If you think that will happen, I'll come to Washington; I'll have to figure out how— when— "

"I'm sure you saw how things are at our house when you came to visit," Sam said. "She loves the kids, but I'm superfluous. She was perfectly happy to shoo the two of us out of the house in the mornings and at night she went to bed early with her bad knee."

Sam was right; I had noticed the coolness between husband and wife. On the other hand, I had also seen the love and hero worship little Patrick had for his father. What would happen to that?

"Hello? You there?" Sam asked. "Do you need time to think it over— to talk to your mother? I can't ride over on my white horse and formally ask for your hand— at least at this time, I can't."

I was relieved that Sam's lighthearted humor had not deserted him, even during the most serious discussion we had ever had.

"I definitely have to talk to my mom and to my brother, but I won't let them talk me out of what I want. And that's the same thing as you," I said. "I think the horse is funny— but right now I'm afraid I'm going to cry."

I was shaken. After years of knowing Sam as a mentor and friend, I had just admitted to myself and to him that I had much deeper feelings. I wanted to move to Washington to be with him. I was excited by the idea and I was scared— but not enough to call Sam back and refuse him. I believed in the power of love.

I already knew that the coming year would bring change to my family and friends. I had decided not to sign up for any more courses after finishing the current semester. I did not see a future for myself in literary scholarship. I would not be working at the *Review.* Though I was disappointed by the university's not standing up for the principle of free speech, I looked back at the education I had received as a gift of lasting value.

Friends I had made were also leaving Chicago. Irving Rosenthal had found an apartment in New York, where he wanted to pursue his own creative career. He had written an introduction for the first issue of *Big Table,* recounting the events that led to its founding; it was his last editorial responsibility, he said. Paul Carroll had agreed to take on the responsibility of the new publication, knowing that battles with the censors were almost certainly in his future.

What would happen to my family if, or rather when, I left?

I asked Roland before talking to Mother.

"You and Sam are in love. He's separating from his wife and you want to go live in D.C. to be near him. I never met the cat— but if you think it's right for you, you gotta do it," my brother summarized calmly after listening to my tale.

"I want to *work* in Washington. I'll find a job with a paper, or the AP if I'm lucky, and a room to rent. I'm not going as Sam's kept woman," I added.

"That's my sister," Roland smiled. "I know all that. But are you sure he really is going to leave his wife?"

"I believe him. How long it'll take I don't know," I replied. I did not doubt Sam's word, but as I talked with Roland, I saw that I was describing an uncertain and possibly perilous situation.

"What about you— I wish you could come with me— and what about Mom— I haven't told her yet?"

"I wouldn't mind visiting Washington, but I'm fine here. I might look for a different job than the bookstore— that's mostly gift-wrapping these days. I think I'll check with the bindery; that's interesting work," Roland said. "And I think Mom is all right. The store is doing okay. I think she has a new friend."

"Really? A friend as in male friend? Who's that? Do you know him? I haven't met him. Has he been here for dinner and I was out someplace?" I asked.

Roland laughed. "Well, you sure are out a lot, but she hasn't brought him over yet. He's a businessman— some kind of grocery store, lives on the North Side, either retired or semi— anyway, they met at a Chamber of Commerce open house or a luncheon."

"I'm really curious. Let's tell Mom to introduce him, okay? I'd be happy for her if he's a nice man."

I felt encouraged by Roland's understanding and by the news about our mother. I thought that if she had found a new friend, an adult companion, she would not mind so much if I left the nest.

The day after my talk with Roland, I went grocery shopping and had dinner prepared when Mother returned from work at Parkway. I took care to make the meal more formal than the catch-as-catch-can fare we ate when all of us came home from work or school at different times.

"This is nice," Mother said as we sat down. "*Gemütlich*— how do you say in English— comfortable?"

"It's a busy time of year. Did you have a lot of holiday shoppers at the store today?" I asked.

"Yes, *Gott sei Dank*, it was very good. Mrs. Beckman wouldn't even take her lunch hour," Mother answered.

"I can't believe Christmas is next week already," Roland added. "I *should* believe it because I must have wrapped a hundred books today. I can tie bows in my sleep."

"You can show me how to curl up the ribbons; that material is so slippery. I do better with the old-fashioned satin," Mother said to Roland. I was glad to see her chatting in a friendly way. Was she beginning to accept her son as a young working adult rather than criticizing him as a failed student? I hoped so.

When I had served coffee, I raised my cup. "*Prosit Neu Jahr*— an early toast to the new year," I said. "Next year is almost here and we should talk about how things will change. The semester is over at the end of January and I won't be a student anymore after that. I've handed in all my term papers. I have nothing to do with the *Chicago Review* anymore—and— we talked about this before, right? "

I hesitated, unsure of how to move on to the news about Sam and the changes this would bring to my life.

"One moment, *Kind.* Go a little slower. The American schools are so different— I don't understand the system. Have you completed all required work at the university?"

"Yes, Mom, I have my Bachelor of Arts degree. That was in June, remember? And then in the fall, I took courses in literature. That semester will be over shortly after New Year's. I could stay on, but it's not required."

"That means she's a University of Chicago graduate. She's done a great job. And now it's time to go out into the world," Roland said. He was smiling. Mother still looked confused.

"That's right. I went to Wright Junior College and then got the scholarship, and then I had really wonderful professors here. And getting on the staff of the *Review* was so different from political science— it was all worth it— but now it's time for the real world, as Roland said," I rambled.

"A degree from the university is a title you can be proud of; you have worked hard for it," Mother said. "And now?"

And now I had to come to the point. It was time— time had been mentioned often enough.

"And now I will find a job in journalism— what I've been studying for all this time— a professional job. And it may not be in

Chicago. There's something else I have to tell you. Sam— you know Sam— will help me find a place in Washington. I want to move there. He's my friend. Well, more than a friend, to be honest."

Mother picked up her coffee cup, took a sip, and grimaced. "Too cold. Never mind. I know Sam; he has a job in Washington. But what do I hear about moving and what does it mean, more than friends?"

"I mean that Sam will help me to get settled in Washington. We've been friends from the time we met here at the convention, when I was a typist. And now we feel more than friendship for each other. We want to be together; it's love," I said and took a deep breath, relieved to have given voice to my new truth, shocking as I knew it to be.

"I'll do the dishes," Roland said. My brother should have been a playwright, I thought; he had crafted a perfect exit line.

I told Mother about what Sam had said about his marriage and about what I had seen for myself on my visit. I tried to explain how we had fallen in love over time, getting to know each other through dozens of letters.

"Sam thinks his wife is ready to agree to a separation. He wants me to move to D.C. because he knows I've wished for that too. He's well known in the news business. If anybody can help me, he can," I said.

Mother's face had the same expression I had seen years ago, when she had told me that I was her love child. She seemed to be looking beyond me-- back at her own life before I was born. Speaking German, as she often did when the subject was the past, she said, "I can't forbid you to go. If you two love each other, you will go where your heart leads you. You are of age and not engaged to anyone else. The only thing I can say, *Kind,* is that the circumstances are very difficult. I know; I fell in love with a married man. I am not sorry, but it is a hard world. People will talk and some will call you ugly names. I will never blame you if you want to come back home— even with a child—"

"There will be no child!" I interrupted. "He *has* children and as for me, I don't want babies. I want Sam."

Mother hugged me, cuddling me as if I had turned into an infant again.

"You can't know what happens in the future," she said.

We celebrated New Year's Eve at home with a festive family dinner and a special guest— Mother's friend Ernst. He was tall and broad-shouldered, with white hair and a deeply lined face. He looked much older than Mother, who at fifty-six still had the unwrinkled skin and bright eyes of a thirty-year-old.

Ernst had brought a gift— the largest jar of honey I had ever seen; it must have weighed ten pounds.

"From the store," he explained. "I sell wholesale and retail, you know."

Mother thanked him, exclaiming that we would never have to buy honey again in our lifetimes. I thought that the unwrapped gift he had pulled out of an ordinary brown shopping bag and the prosaic presentation reflected an honest nature— a generous man, a practical provider, who would never be a poet.

Dinner was pleasant, with Mother drawing out Ernst for Roland's and my benefit; she knew that our social skills did not match hers. We learned that Ernst had been born in Germany and that his family had come to Chicago when he was a teenager. He had taken over his father's grocery business and still lived next to the store on the North Side; he was a widower; he had no children. He was financially comfortable enough to retire but was not in a hurry to do so. What would he do with himself all day long?

We all laughed at this. Mother will never have this problem, I thought and looked at Roland. His smile said that he agreed with me.

After the first of January 1959, events in my life began to move with bewildering speed. Sam wrote to say that Susan had agreed to a six-month trial separation.

"She says that if we all feel the same about things six months from now, we can move on to get a divorce. If not— I guess she thinks I may come to my senses. I'm in my right mind now; I've never been saner. Will you come as soon as your course is over? When is it? I'll call soon," his letter read.

"I can't believe it's really going to happen! I can move in February or March. But where to live? I need to rent a room, or is there a YWCA?" I wrote back.

Sam phoned before my letter could have reached him. I greeted him enthusiastically. "I talked with my mother and Roland. They were surprised but they say they understand— my mom was so good about it; I'm amazed, really," I told Sam.

"I said before you were a major Barbara," Sam answered. "Your mom is an admirable woman. I want to meet her. She should see for herself that I'm not an axe murderer or a white slaver. And I don't want your brother to shoot me. Before you move here, I'm coming to Chicago. Just give me some possible dates when you'll be free."

"I will. That's a wonderful idea. Can you really do that? My brother is an Eagle Scout. He doesn't have a gun; and my mom admires you. She says you write great stories. What about work? Can you take time off?"

"There's always an assignment I can pick up if I need a reason to travel," Sam said. The best story is that you agreed to join me in a very different life. It must be a little frightening for you. Is it?"

"Yes," I said. "It's like moving into another world."

We said goodbye and agreed to talk again in a day or two. It would be about practical matters, Sam promised. I went to look over my clothes and books I had acquired, wondering how I was going to transport my belongings to Washington. I did not own enough to fill a truck, yet it was more than I could carry on a Greyhound bus; the books would be heavy, but I never even considered leaving them behind. When Mother came home, I would ask her how much money I had on deposit. I had put my summer wages in the business account rather than opening a checking account of my own. I used the smaller amounts from the job at the library repair department for daily expenses. I knew that my mother's ledger could tell me to the penny what my balance was. It was good to think about these mundane matters; it kept me from worrying about unanswerable questions. For instance, would Susan regret the agreement she had made? Would Patrick hate me when he learned that his father and mother were splitting up?

At the end of the month-- and the semester-- I said goodbye to Gogo and my other colleagues at the library's repair department. My studies at the university were over, but I was still active with the group of ex-editors who were launching *Big Table.* Irving Rosenthal reported that he had at last found a printer for the publication in New York. I relayed the news to Sam by leaving a message at the Associated Press office; he had told me that news about the *Review* could be considered official business.

Early in February, Sam called me. This time the conversation was personal.

"Good news, Major Barbara," he began. "I have a plan and a number of suggestions, and I think you'll like this. Ready?"

"Ready," I said. "Or is 'shoot' the right thing to say?"

Sam laughed. "Funny, but no shooting, okay? What I called to tell you is that I found an apartment for you. It's on Massachusetts Avenue, Northwest, near Dupont Circle. You don't know the neighborhood yet, but you'll love it; it's pleasant and not far from downtown. I'm paying the rent because you don't have a credit rating--"

"Wait, wait," I interrupted. "An apartment-- that sounds wonderful. If you like it, I will too. But I want to say that I'll pay my share just as soon as I find a job. Can we agree on that?"

"If you say so," Sam chuckled. "We're not there yet. When the time comes, we'll talk finance. For now, understand that you don't *owe* me anything for the apartment. It's yours to live in. I can stay there with you during the week-- I agreed to spend Saturday and Sunday with the kids in Alexandria -- but if ever you feel you're getting too much of my company, you just say so and I'll bunk with a friend."

"Too much of your company? I haven't had *any* of it yet! Not that kind of company, I mean," I answered, feeling very bold.

"It will be a pleasure. For us," Sam said softly. After a moment, he continued, "Uh, where were we? I have more news and plans. Can you keep talking? Are you on your way somewhere?"

"No, I'm home, cleaning up my room so my mom can rent it out when I'm gone," I said.

"Which brings me to my next point. About two weeks from now, I'm planning a trip to Chicago. As I said, I want to meet your family before you move out. I'll have a rental car; we can load up your suitcases and drive back to D.C. together. The apartment is furnished; you don't have to bring anything besides your personal stuff. Sound good?"

"It sounds great! You know I don't have a license? I barely know how to drive," I replied. "It's a very long trip, as I found out on the Greyhound Bus!"

"We'll work it out. We can stop overnight somewhere. The main thing is I want your mom to know that I'm not some criminal. My intentions are as honorable as they can be under the circumstances; I know that's not saying much. Can you be ready to make the move that soon?"

"It will be more than a move -- it's a big adventure. Yes, I'll tell mom and Roland. I'm so happy you can come," I said.

"Me too--I'm very happy. I love you. Can you say it now that nobody else is listening?"

"Yes. I love you too."

Sam's flight arrived at Midway Airport late in the afternoon on a weekday. A hurried call from a payphone informed me that he was renting a car and would drive to our apartment.

"I'm home," I said. "And the others will be shortly. Can't wait to see you!"

I had gone to the supermarket early in the day and had bought the makings for a simple dinner. I wanted Sam's first meeting with the family to be informal and comfortable.

A few minutes after Sam's call, Mother and Roland came in and sat down in the kitchen to take off their wet boots and galoshes.

"The sidewalks are horrible-- nothing but slush," Mother complained.

"It's February in Chicago," Roland pointed out. "We should move to California."

The doorbell rang. There was no intercom buzzer, so Roland and I ran downstairs to open the front door. Sam--hatless and wearing one of his light sports jackets-- was taking a small overnight bag from his car. I hurried to grab Sam's hand and to lead him into the building as fast as possible. Roland took the bag.

"Welcome--hello -- where's your coat?" I asked.

"Hello," Roland said. "I'll get whatever's in the car. You don't want to leave anything in there."

"Thanks. Coat? Oh yes, my raincoat is in the back seat. Thanks, Roland," Sam said and added, "I don't think anybody'd steal it."

"I see I don't have to make introductions," I said and kept hold of Sam's hand as we walked up the stairs.

"*Willkommen!*" Mother greeted us at the apartment door. "I am pleased to meet you, Mr. --"

"Please call me Sam; I am more than pleased to meet you, Mrs. Pitschel," Sam replied as he shook hands.

"Come in, please; come in out of the cold," Mother said. I could tell she approved of Sam's formal manners; she did not feel at ease with people who addressed her by her first name without permission.

"Let's sit down and relax in the living room for a while," I said. "It won't take me long to make dinner."

Before taking a chair, Sam walked over to the carryon Roland had put down by the front door. He unzipped the bag and pulled out a bottle.

"A little drink before dinner -- you'll join me, I hope?" he asked as he presented the bottle to Mother.

"Thank you," she said. "What is this liqueur? Is it Schnapps? How is it served?"

"Vodka," Sam said. "It's not as strong as brandy. Just a regular glass and some ice for me. If you don't want it plain, I can mix it with orange juice for you -- that's called a screwdriver."

"A screwdriver? That is very new to me. I would like to try it. Will you come with me to the kitchen and fix it?" Mother was intrigued, I could tell.

We all stood around the kitchen table while Roland brought tumblers, Sam opened the bottle, and I opened the freezer compartment to find -- no ice!

"Oh, no! We forgot to fill the trays again," I said. "We never put ice in our drinks. I'm sorry, Sam."

"Not to worry," he laughed. "I'll have it neat, as I understand they do in Europe. What can I fix you?"

Roland and I wanted to try screwdrivers -- the American drink.

Back in the living room with our glasses, Mother took a cautious sip and said, "Refreshing -- thank you for showing me."

I excused myself to start dinner. As I walked towards the kitchen, I heard Mother say, "You wore no hat, no gloves, no overshoes. Is there no snow in Washington?"

Sam replied and I could hear the conversation continue, with both Roland and Mother asking questions and chatting. I hoped Sam would recount some of his funny anecdotes about the often-nonsensical debates in Congress. It was not a complicated menu I was preparing, and I was about to rejoin the company in the living room, when Roland came in and said, "Sam needs a refill. Do you want a hand with anything?"

"You could set the table when you've delivered," I said. "You might as well leave the bottle with Sam."

"Washington is an interesting city. Your friend has been telling us stories about the parties at the embassies of other countries and about when Mr. Truman was president," Mother said when we had sat down to eat.

I asked Mother if she wanted a glass of wine.

"No thanks--I am still drinking this orange juice cocktail; it's quite strong," she answered. Her glass was half full, as were Roland's and mine.

Sam complimented me on the meal, but he ate little. He reached for the vodka and offered to pour refills. The three of us refused.

"Just a splash for me then," he said.

Dinner was a success, I thought, as Sam entertained us with gossip about senators and congressmen and described how beautiful Washington would become in a few months, when the cherry trees would be in bloom again. My spirits rose. I had seen the flowering trees the year before -- and now I would be lucky enough to see them again-- perhaps for many years to come.

"Can you tell us about the apartment?" Roland asked Sam.

"Your sister will like it, I think," Sam replied. "It's a one-bedroom, furnished flat on the second floor. It has a balcony that overlooks Massachusetts Avenue. Washington has an early spring; as soon as it gets a little warmer, that balcony will be a great place to sit."

"Chicago snow doesn't melt until May," Roland said. "I think they put some special ingredient in it to keep it hard."

"I hope you'll come and visit," Sam said. "And speaking of visits, I am enjoying being here with you all--or 'y'all,' as they say in the American South."

Mother smiled and said, "It's so good that you could come. I hope you will be our guest tonight. No need to go to a hotel; we have a room you can sleep in-- it's the small one off the kitchen. It isn't rented out. All we have to do is move the ironing board out of the way."

"That's most kind. I wasn't looking forward to driving to the Hilton, I have to admit," Sam answered.

"Stay as long as you like. You are very welcome," Mother assured him.

"Thank you. But I'm afraid I need to get back to work. Barbara said she has packed her things and is ready-- are you?" Sam asked, turning to me.

"Yes, I am. We can leave tomorrow if that's the plan," I said. My voice sounded steady; in my stomach, a large flock of butterflies was making merry.

"It's a long trip, isn't it? Barbara said she felt like she spent a week on the Greyhound," Roland said.

"Not quite that bad--but the road trip is twelve or thirteen hours, depending on traffic." Sam looked at Roland and continued, "You drive, right? I have an idea--would you consider coming along to escort your sister? I'd really appreciate having another pair of hands on the wheel. We could spell each other. What do you think?"

"Uh-- well, I can do that. Actually, I like the idea if it helps you out. I just have to call my boss and tell her I'll be taking a couple of days off. I don't see a problem. The bookstore isn't that busy with the holidays over. They can live without me for a little while."

I reached for Roland's hand as the butterflies folded their wings.

"Thanks!" I said.

"I am in favor of this plan too," Mother said. "Roland can see where Barbara will be living and tell me about it. That will help me to have a picture of her new life."

"Sam will write down the address for us before we leave," I said.

Roland went into the hall to make his phone call and I showed Sam the spare room and the bathroom. I took him to see my bedroom, where bags and boxes were stacked up.

"I didn't think it was that much when I started to pack. I hope it all fits -- if not, Roland can send some of the books to me later by Railway Express," I said.

"We'll do our best. As long as you get enough space in the car-- that's what I care about," Sam laughed. "You may have to leave the

Peloponnesian War behind for a few weeks; you won't miss it, will you?"

"As long as there isn't a test coming up," I said. The word "test" stirred up my nerves again; tomorrow's journey would be a test of my courage, requiring plenty of *Mut*. I thought of my mother and her decision to take two young children to the New World. Suddenly, Washington, D.C. didn't seem all that far away.

The morning of our trip was clear and bright. Excitement woke me early and I got up, dressed, and went to make coffee. Mother was already in the kitchen; coffee was bubbling in the percolator on the stove and oatmeal was simmering in a pot beside it.

"Did you sleep? Or did you have *Reisefieber?*" Mother was asking if I had been kept awake by feverish anticipation of my trip.

"Both-- I slept but I was excited too; I still am," I answered. *"Reisefieber"* is difficult to translate, I thought, but you know it when you have it.

Sam and Roland joined us. Mother asked what they would like for breakfast--cornflakes or oatmeal?

"Something hot," she advised. "The sun is shining, but it will be cold outside."

Sam asked for coffee. "Just black. Nothing else, thank you."

Mother looked disapproving but held her peace. Her code of etiquette did not allow one to argue with a guest. Roland and I helped ourselves to oatmeal garnished with generous dollops of honey. The kitchen was warm and smelled delicious. Four people sat around the white enamel table, sharing breakfast. It was as normal as could be, I thought. And in half an hour or so-- it would be very different.

Sam asked for some orange juice he could pour into his canteen. "It's a good pick-me-up for the trip," he said as he thanked Mother. An image of my teenage friend Alan Nakamura zipped across my mind--Alan and his canteen that supposedly contained whisky. I had not believed him. I watched Sam pouring juice. His hands were trembling slightly.

We loaded the car, with Roland doing most of the carrying and arranging. Several boxes did indeed have to be left behind. Mother came downstairs to see us off. She shook Sam's hand and said, "I wish you luck. I know you will be good to my daughter."

She hugged me. "*Geh mit Gott, mein Kind,*" she whispered. I couldn't speak, but I kissed her cheeks.

Sam drove. Roland asked to sit in the front seat so that he could study the dashboard controls and the gearshift.

"We should fill up the tank before getting on the highway," he suggested. "And I'd like to get a map. I haven't driven much out of state."

At the service station, Sam pulled out his canteen. "Didn't have my orange juice for breakfast, so I'll catch up now," he said. Roland asked the attendant for a map; in 1959, they were free at gas stations. Sam paid for the gasoline and pulled out onto the road. He drove for about an hour. We were in Indiana when he pulled the car over in a rest area and stopped. He took off his sunglasses and rubbed his eyes.

"Driving east," he said. "The light's so glaring; it's hurting my eyes and I'm tired too. Guess I didn't sleep a lot last night -- no fault of the accommodations though. The hospitality was excellent."

"Want me to take over for a while?" Roland asked.

"That would be great, thanks," Sam answered. "It's straight highway--you'll be fine, and I'll catch a little nap."

Roland got in the driver's seat and pulled smoothly out onto the highway. He drove with assurance and skill. I couldn't remember when he had started to drive; it seemed as if he had been born with the ability. Sam slept.

It was early afternoon before we stopped at another service area to use the restrooms and to buy sandwiches and coffee. Sam, revived by his nap, thanked Roland for driving.

"Do you want me to take a turn?" he asked.

"No, thanks, I'll go on. I'm not tired; I enjoy it," Roland answered as we got back into the car. Sam took a swig from his canteen. Roland glanced at him, as if he were wondering why Sam had not ordered juice in the restaurant. I had the same thought, but neither of us said anything.

Even though I had drunk a large cup of coffee, the quiet motion of the car put me to sleep not too long after we left the rest area. I woke up in the late afternoon, wondering why I felt so tired. Perhaps the emotion of the past few days was taking its toll.

When we got to the outskirts of the District of Columbia, Roland asked Sam to give directions to the city and to Massachusetts Avenue. It was after nine o'clock at night when we arrived at the address-- a brick apartment building on a tree-lined avenue. I looked up at the facade and saw a balcony with a wrought-iron railing. If this was my new home, I liked it!

Sam led the way upstairs and opened to door to the apartment.

"Welcome! May it prove to be a happy place," he said. Walking into the living room, he turned on a light and handed me a key.

"Yours-- a new key to a new life," he said.

While Roland was bringing my suitcases upstairs, Sam took my hand and walked around the apartment with me. The rooms were not as large as those we inhabited in Chicago, but the suite was laid out efficiently, with a kitchenette off the living room and a bathroom between the bedroom and the front room. French doors led to the balcony. It was chilly outside, but I couldn't resist stepping outside and gazing at the multitude of streetlights.

"It's late, but would you like to go out for pizza--or should Roland and I go get one to eat here?" Sam asked.

"I think I'd like to stay and unpack my toothbrush," I said. "Do you mind?"

"No, take your time, sweetheart. Your two knights will be back in a jiff. Ready, Roland?"

While Sam and my brother were gone, I opened the small refrigerator in the kitchenette, took the single ice tray from the freezer, filled it with water, and put it back. I resolved that there would be ice cubes readily available every day.

We ate our way through a giant pizza--that is, Roland and I ate more than our share while Sam nibbled. Sam opened a bottle of vodka he had brought and poured himself a hefty measure.

"There's beer for you and me," Roland said. "Thanks for buying, Sam. Cheers!"

When had Roland started drinking beer?

"The couch in the living room pulls out to make a bed," Sam said to Roland. "It may not be the most comfortable mattress you ever slept on, but I hope you'll be okay."

"Thanks. I might sleep on the floor. I'm used to camping out. As a matter of fact, I could fall asleep this minute. It's been a long day," Roland replied.

"We're all tired. I can't keep my eyes open," I said. "I vote we retire."

"All in favor--yes. Let's call it a night," Sam said. Turning to me, he said, "Go ahead, sweetheart; I'll just finish my drinkie."

After the beer and the food and the long car ride, I was too tired to dig through my suitcase for a pretty nightgown; I was too tired to undress; I was too tired for anything. I went to the bedroom, lay down on top of the bedspread and fell into a heavy sleep. I did not know how many hours had passed when I came partially awake to find Sam next to me, also in his clothes. I reached over to pat his shoulder. He did not stir.

This isn't how the first night with your lover is supposed to go, I thought. But I felt deeply happy. He was there, next to me, and tomorrow was another day that would be followed by another night. I went back to sleep.

CHAPTER 27

High Hopes

Morning found all three of us awake before eight o'clock. My fatigue of the previous day had been erased by a refreshing, dreamless sleep. When I walked out of the bedroom, I heard the shower running.

"Sam says good morning," Roland said. "You can have the bathroom next. I'm dressed, as you see."

"So am I--but these are yesterday's clothes; I'll change in a minute. But-- wow-- look at the sunshine!" I said, walking over to the balcony door. I don't see any snow, either."

"It's pretty mild outside; I checked," Roland said. "We're in the South."

"Is there any coffee?" I asked.

"No, I checked that too. Fridge is empty. Want an ice cube? We *have* those."

Sam, dressed in slacks and a shirt, came out of the bathroom, walked over to us, and gave me a hug.

"Mornin', Princess," he drawled. "Welcome to the nation's capital!"

"Thanks. Good morning to you. This is wonderful--you're wonderful. I'm so happy to be here!"

Sam smiled. "I was afraid she'd be grumpy without her morning caffeine," he said to Roland.

"She normally is," my honest brother replied.

"We'll go to the pancake house and I'll feed you kids. When you're ready, Princess."

"So, Roland, do you want to stick around for a few days? See Washington, keep your sister company?" Sam asked when we were drinking coffee and eating grits -- a bland, unfamiliar food that allowed me to add the expression "true grit" to my English vocabulary after Sam had explained the joke.

"No thanks. I'd better get back to Chicago --and three's a crowd, anyway," Roland said.

"I understand. If you don't mind turning in the car at the airport, I'll give you the money to pay for it and for a plane ticket back. It was a big help that you drove, and you're welcome to come back and visit any time," Sam said. He pulled a roll of bills from his pocket and handed some to Roland.

"Wait a minute--airport? Take a plane? We never did that before, Roland. Do you know how to do that?" I asked. I had assumed he would take the bus.

"I'll just need directions to the airport. How hard can it be to buy a ticket? I think I can learn," Roland laughed.

I reminded myself that my brother was sixteen--but what a capable and sophisticated sixteen! "You're great," I told him.

Sam chimed in. "*Wunderbar!*"

Saying goodbye to Roland back at the apartment was almost as hard as taking leave of my mother had been, but I consoled myself with the thought that airplane travel took only a few hours, rather than a day and a half on the bus. I would miss the brother who had been my constant companion since his birth; I hoped we would call and visit each other as often as possible.

Sam had taken off his sunglasses. I caught sight of his raincloud eyes. I looked forward to our time alone together. Love is very powerful, I thought. My love would be so strong that all the obstacles in our path would be cleared away. I felt no nervousness, only joy, and boundless hope.

"I'm not expected at the office today, but I'll call in," Sam said. "I left my car there, in the garage. Tomorrow I can take the bus. What do you say we walk around the neighborhood to get you acquainted?"

My heavy parka was almost too warm as we strolled along Massachusetts Avenue towards DuPont Circle. I admired the ornate columnar fountain and the array of interesting shops and cafés around the traffic circle.

"When it gets a little warmer, there'll be folk singers with guitars and other street performers," Sam said. "And if you feel like *Kultur*, there's the art museum over there-- the Phillips Collection."

"I'll want to go there, for sure. It's a beautiful city, and I've seen only a small part of it so far. Is there something like a grocery store too-- aside from the high art and culture?" I asked.

"What is she going to demand next--a laundromat?" Sam moaned theatrically.

"Let's mosey on over to Connecticut Avenue."

Mosey? No one I knew in Chicago ever took a leisurely stroll in February. I liked this city's mild climate; I loved Sam's relaxed manner.

When we arrived back at the apartment building after our walking tour and marketing expedition, Sam said, "I can't carry you across the threshold; that would make me a bigamist."

I answered, "I'll step across on my own. But hold my hand; don't let go."

My new life was full of wonder and excitement. I was with a man who cared deeply for my happiness. The capital city felt both vibrant and hospitable, with its many parks and plazas, and its busy downtown shopping area. Smaller than Chicago, the District seemed packed with historic mansions, monuments, and imposing government buildings.

The day after my brother left, Sam said, "Time for me to go back to earning a living. Come with me as far as the office, and I'll point you in the way of the major attractions-- the museums and so on. You play tourist and we'll meet up again after work. We'll go out for dinner."

"Did you tell anyone that I've moved here -- that I'm looking for a job?" I asked.

"Yes, Marian knows, and I told Smitty -- he's a good buddy. I didn't spell out the arrangement for them, but it won't take them long to put one and one together. There are no secrets in this town and remember, we're in the news business!"

"I like your friends. I hope Marian will let you know if they need a typist or file clerk," I said.

Sam smiled at my eagerness. "Give it time, sweetheart. Let's just enjoy being together."

"I love being with you," I said. "That won't change even when we're both working."

During the rest of the week, I visited the National Gallery and the Smithsonian Institution's fairytale castle. I stood in Lafayette Square, across from the White House, and wondered when I might get another chance to pass through the gate -- perhaps on a story assignment. "Give it time..." I heard Sam say in my head.

On Friday, Sam reminded me that he would be spending Saturday and Sunday in Alexandria with his children.

"But tonight, it's Dixieland," he announced. "We're going to U Street -- as promised a couple of years ago. I haven't forgotten your education, see?"

"I remember the club in Chicago, that night after the convention, and how it all started when you wanted me to write 'hullabaloo' and I couldn't," I said.

"Well, now you can -- and a whole lot of other things too," Sam laughed. "May the gods bless hullabaloo."

The area around U Street, Sam explained, was often called the "Black Broadway" -- the hub of African-American culture. Settled by descendants of freed slaves in the nineteenth century, it was now a neighborhood known for its many jazz clubs.

"Get ready to add to your American experience," Sam said. "U Street is full of soul!"

I had only the vaguest notion of what constituted "soul," but I decided to wait and find out later, at Sam's favorite club.

As soon as we had walked through the door into the small, crowded bar, a tall, smiling black man carrying a trombone came towards us.

"Hey, look who's here -- Sam, my man -- how you doin'? And who's the pretty friend?" he asked.

"Hey, Kelly; this is Barbara from Chicago," Sam replied as we shook hands.

Kelly led us to a table near the front of the room, where the rest of the band was sitting on backless stools, chatting while taking a break. Besides Kelly, there were men with trumpets, clarinets, and saxophones. I saw a piano, a bass fiddle, an array of drums, and a xylophone. All of the band members waved and called out greetings.

The bartender brought a vodka for Sam and asked what I wanted.

"Let her try a highball," Sam suggested.

"Fine, thanks; that sounds great," I said. I looked forward to this unknown drink. My education was progressing.

The music, when the band struck up, was loud and lively-- part marching band, part dance tune. I had never heard anything like it. There was no sheet music and no conductor or leader. Individual players took turns playing solos, embellishing the melody, or improvising alternate lines. It seemed to be all right to applaud in the middle of a piece, I noticed; it was not like a performance of the Chicago Symphony, where you waited until the end. Because there was no printed program either, I asked Sam what the composition was called.

"Bourbon Street Blues -- but there's always a lot of free association; most of the music isn't written down," Sam said. "Bourbon Street is in New Orleans and what you're drinking is bourbon and ginger ale, very apropos. Like it?"

"Oh, yes; I like it all -- everything is so new," I said, taking Sam's hand. "I'm so happy!"

The musicians completed their set. When they started another, a young woman with tousled hair and rhinestones pasted on her high cheekbones came to the microphone in front of the band and sang, "When I fall in love...it will be completely..."

It was a haunting melody; it was exactly how I felt...

"It will be forever..."

The room was smoky and warm. My drink -- had I had more than one? -- was sweet and bubbly; it had made me sleepy. I was so in love -- it was forever --

I remember getting home to the apartment and falling into bed; I did not know what time it was.

In the morning, I felt almost grateful that Sam would be away for the next two days. I was dizzy and longing for another two or three hours of sleep. I remembered that at the club, Sam's glass had been refilled numerous times. Yet, he appeared to be his usual self, calmly getting dressed and sipping orange juice from a coffee cup.

"Take it slow today, sweetheart," he said, giving me a kiss. "You're not used to the life yet. I'll try to call you, just in case you need anything. But everything will be fine; I'm not far away and you know the kids will like having me visit. Be good!"

By noon, I felt ashamed of my laziness and pulled myself out of bed. I made coffee, showered, and dressed, ready to go for a walk. I thought about the art museum. A look at the crumpled bedding reminded me that laundry ought to be a priority today. Sam had seen to sheets and pillowcases, but there was only one set. I pulled my suitcase from the closet and fished out the cloth bag that held the money I had brought with me. Living on Chicago's South Side had taught me not to keep valuables in an easily accessible place, such as a dresser drawer. We had never had a break-in, but I felt better when my small stash was hidden. I put twenty dollars in my purse. I really need to think about earning a few dollars, I thought; these savings won't go far.

Using a pillowcase as a bag, I set out to find a laundromat and found one a few blocks away, conveniently located next to a stationer's which also sold newspapers and magazines. I bought a copy of the *Washington Post* to peruse while I waited for the washer to gurgle through its cycles.

When my laundry was finished and I had read the news and editorial pages of the paper, I saved the classified ad section to study later. Sam had not given me any news of a job opening at the Associated Press or elsewhere. I thought I had better look for something temporary to tide me over until I could find work as a journalist.

The weather, once again, was sunny and mild. I walked around DuPont Circle and explored the side streets. I stopped to look at the colorful posters displayed in the windows of a travel agency. I went in and asked the smartly dressed lady at the desk if she could let me have an outdated poster. "I can't afford to go anywhere, but I like to look at the beautiful scenery," I said.

The woman leafed through a stack of posters behind her desk. "At least you're honest," she smiled. "I'll give you this one. It's last month's special -- cruises to Bermuda or the Bahamas -- here you go."

I thanked the friendly travel agent and headed back to the stationer's to buy thumbtacks and tape. Asking for posters that would otherwise be thrown away was a student gambit I had learned at the university. It was an easy and cost-free way to brighten up a dorm or rented room.

Here, my poster would go on the blank wall of the kitchenette, a dark space where I would have placed a window if I had been the building's architect. The poster's palm trees, silhouetted against blue sky and pink sand, would give me a view; I could pretend that it was sunrise or sunset -- and my window would never show snowflakes coming down in thick clusters.

On my way back to the apartment I bought bread, cold cuts, and fruit, and I enjoyed the sights and sounds of my new neighborhood. It felt airier than Chicago's East Fifty-fifth Street, whose stolid brick apartment houses lacked architectural charm. On Massachusetts Avenue, several elegant buildings housed the embassies of foreign countries; they were identified by brass plaques or flags. There were trees along the avenue and sparrows gossiped on the sidewalk. In another two months, the cherry trees would start to bloom; the thought made me happy.

I studied the Help Wanted advertisements in the newspaper without finding any openings in writing, in publishing, or even in secretarial work associated with a magazine. The best opportunities for immediate employment seemed to be in retail -- there were several columns that listed establishments seeking salesclerks. The name Garfinckel's caught my eye. I recognized it as a large department store Sam had pointed out on one of our walks downtown. It was on Fourteenth Street, two blocks from the White House, and across the street from another landmark, the Willard Hotel. According to the advertisement, Garfinckel's was hiring salespeople for ladies and men's wear, as well as shipping and inventory clerks. My experience at Parkway Sweater Import, I thought, would give me a chance at an interview. I copied the telephone number to call for an appointment and cut the ad out of the paper. It was Saturday evening; the store and its offices would be closed the following day; my venture would have to wait until Monday. All I could do for now was to find a business card from Parkway that I could present as a reference.

On Sunday morning, I bought another newspaper and turned to the classified ads -- just in case some new opportunities had joined the listings. I did not find any exciting additions, but I did see more Help Wanted ads for Garfinckel's. If I get a job, I thought, it won't be as challenging as working in a newsroom, but maybe I'll meet a customer who has connections and is willing to help an aspiring journalist.

Sam returned in mid-afternoon. "Patrick says hello; he wants to come visit you," Sam said as he gave me bear hug.

"Well--uh--that's okay, I guess," I fumbled. "But what does he know and isn't his mom upset about that?"

"Before I answer, let me say that I am mightily glad to see *you,* and I hope you missed me!"

"I did; I'm so glad you're back. And if Patrick isn't mad at me, that's a relief," I said.

I wanted to tell Sam about Garfinckel's, but he had other plans.

"Come show me how much you missed me," he smiled and led me off to the bedroom.

I let Sam go to work the next morning without discussing my plan with him. I thought that if I landed a job, I could surprise him with the news. If I was not successful today, I would tell him that I had tried, and that I would continue to look for employment. Pleasant as it was to play tourist, I did not feel comfortable being totally dependent on Sam.

I had decided to apply in person rather than telephone for an appointment. When Sam had gone, I took a city bus to Fourteenth and F Streets. It was easy to spot the large, eight-storey Garfinckel building. I entered and looked around. It was Monday morning, but a crowd of shoppers, mostly women, was already looking over the cosmetics, handbags, hats, and other accessories that were displayed on the first floor's counters. I decided to explore for a while before asking directions to the personnel office. The department store reminded me of Marshall Field's in Chicago. The merchandise was of high quality; the displays were tasteful; the salesladies were nicely dressed and wore discreet jewelry -- a pearl necklace, a gold bracelet, or a decorative watch. I took an elevator to the second floor and walked through the lingerie and sleepwear section. Again, I saw well-selected, discreet displays -- Mother would have approved.

Back on the first floor, I found an information desk, showed the clerk my newspaper clipping, and asked where to go for an interview.

I followed the route the young woman pointed out. Another elevator took me to a high floor, where the company offices were located. I half expected a perky receptionist, like Georgette at Relaxacizor, to greet me, but it was a businesslike, middle-aged woman who asked what my name was and why I had come in.

"I came to apply for a position in sales. I saw this advertisement," I said, showing my clipping.

The woman handed me a form and started to walk into another room. "Fill out this application -- sit at one of the desks in here. When you're finished, raise your hand and we'll collect it for evaluation. Stay seated until we call you," she said.

The room looked like a classroom; it was full of young women and a few men, all busily filling out papers. My heart began to sink at the sight. Were there enough jobs for all these applicants? On the other hand, I thought, would the company be interviewing this many candidates if there was no demand for their services? What would Keynesian theory say?

"Fill out the paper and take your chances, *Dummkopf!* It's a job, not graduate school," I answered myself.

I passed what I now thought of as the written exam and was called into another room for an interview. After answering a few questions about my previous experience at Parkway Sweater Import, I was offered a job selling ladies' sportswear.

"I think that will be the best place for you -- considering you are familiar with the type of merchandise -- the fourth-floor sportswear department," the interviewer said. "There is a three-day training program for all new sales staff, in which you learn how to operate the cash registers and we tell you about payment procedures, employee rules, salary and commission arrangements, and so on. You may start the training program as early as Wednesday this week, if you have no other commitments."

"Thank you -- thank you very much," I said, surprised at how easily the interview had gone. "I have no other job because I just moved to D.C. so Wednesday will be fine. Could you tell me where to go and whom to ask for?"

"Certainly," the interviewer said, handing me a printed card. "Follow these directions; use the employee's entrance. Pleased to have met you." No smile accompanied the words. The woman's bland face was already turned towards the door; she was ready for the next interview. Garfinckel's was certainly well organized, I thought, if a little soulless.

That evening, when Sam had come home and had poured himself his customary vodka, he asked how I had spent the day.

"I went to Garfinckel's," I answered.

"Really? I would have thought their styles were a bit too matronly for you. Or were you just window shopping?"

"No; I got a job. Starting Wednesday -- there's a training program first," I said, as deadpan as I could manage.

"What? Job? No kidding -- why? Did your mother call and scold you -- idle hands do the devil's work and so forth?"

"I haven't talked with Mother since I left. And it was always agreed that I'd work; at least I thought so. Until something opens up at the bureau or at a paper -- this is not supposed to be forever," I said.

"You're something!" Sam smiled. "You just moved in and already you're stepping out into the wage-earning world. Brave girl!"

"I'm used to going to school or work, or both. Living here with you is wonderful, but I can't hang around without *doing* something," I explained.

"I see that. But why Garfinckel's?"

"Because they're hiring. And I'm familiar with clothes, thanks to Parkway Sweat Port. It was pretty easy to land the job; I was surprised."

"You know, I do wish there was something more rewarding for you. I haven't stopped asking around at the office," Sam said. "It's just that you can count the female journalists in Washington on the fingers of one hand, to coin an overused phrase."

I laughed and took his hand. "Something will turn up -- I can see it right here," I said, peering at the crossed and tangled lines of his palm.

On the following Monday, I punched the time clock at Garfinckel's, left my jacket in the employees' cloakroom, and was taken upstairs by a supervisor who introduced me to the head saleswoman in the sportswear department. She in turn took me to meet several other coworkers, and two store detectives -- one male, one female.

"If you see anything suspicious about the customer, just give me a nod and I'll step in to help," the man said. He was dressed in a suit and tie and carried a paper shopping bag, as if he were a customer buying a birthday gift for his wife. I wondered how believable his disguise was.

After saying hello to my colleagues, I was assigned a station in the large room and told which cash register to use.

"You get a commission on sales, as you know," Miss Emerson, the head lady, said. "That was explained in the training program. The base salary is small, but you can double it -- it may take you a while to get familiar with the styles."

I felt a bit puzzled by the styles I saw displayed all around me -- pastel-colored shorts and sleeveless blouses with round collars. It was early March and the weather was much milder than it would be in Chicago, but shorts?

"You'll be selling mostly cruise wear at this time of year," Miss Emerson answered my unspoken question. "People go to Bermuda and the islands."

I thought about my travel poster. I was glad it did not show any tourists in salmon-pink shorts.

My first two weekly paychecks were miserably small. I had not earned much in commissions because, although customers bought multiple items, they often returned most of their purchase a day or two later, with the excuse that their husbands had not liked the outfits. I realized that my clients were not career women; they were wives spending money their husbands had given them.

On the other hand, I had spent a chunk of my salary on a new skirt and two blouses that I could wear to work. There was an employees' discount, but I was not able to add much cash to my savings in the closet. I decided to remain hopeful; time would show me how to be a more effective saleswoman. I also started checking the classified ads again on a regular basis. I looked forward to the end of each workday and to the weekend when Sam and I would visit U Street where Kelly played the trombone and I was affectionately greeted as Barbara-from-Chicago.

Sam gave me a cat and a marimba. The cat, a young male, was a stray we had seen wandering up and down Massachusetts Avenue. One evening, Sam brought him up to our apartment.

"Here's Bertram. I tried calling him different names, but his ears went up when he heard Bertram. So, I think he needs to get off the streets and live with us," Sam said.

"Are you sure? Maybe he has a home and his people are looking for him?" I asked, as Bertram freed himself from Sam's arms and came over to me.

"No. He was looking for you, and now he's found you -- isn't it obvious?" Sam declared.

"Well -- he's beautiful. I love cats. In Germany, there were cats, but they lived outside. I think there's some hamburger meat--"

Bertram stayed. His dark grey coat became smooth and glossy with regular meals and the petting we both lavished on him. As the weather warmed, we left the door to the balcony open so that he could enjoy the fresh air. My heart skipped a beat when he jumped up onto the wrought-iron railing. It was barely three inches wide. Bertram paraded back and forth, looking secure and unfazed by the two-storey void at his side. I could have sworn he was laughing at my discomfort.

The marimba arrived with Kelly.

"Surprise for you!" Sam said when he let our visitor in. "Early birthday gift -- do I even know when your birthday is? Anyway, I don't want to wait."

"For me?" What is that -- is that a xylophone?"

"It's called a marimba. It has a lower range than a xylophone and the bars are wood, not metal," Sam explained as he helped Kelly bring the instrument into the living room. "This is a small model. It can fit right over there, next to the door to the kitchen."

"Here, I'll show you how it goes," Kelly said, taking a pair of mallets out of his pocket. "You like 'Bye Blackbird'? It goes like this -- looky here."

"Is there any instrument you *can't* play?" Sam asked.

Kelly laughed. "Tried a whole lot of 'em over the years." He made the mallets dance as he performed the song at a brisk tempo. Sam sang the words.

"I had piano lessons when I was about four," I said. "But they didn't do much good. I didn't keep it up."

Sam and Kelly urged me to try, so I slowly picked out the first four notes. The instrument had a lovely, mellow sound and tapping the mallets on the sounding bars was easier than pressing down piano keys had been.

"Oh! I think I could learn this. It'll take me about a year -- but I love the sound," I said. "Thank you both. It sure is a surprise. I promise I'll practice," I said.

"Kelly -- like to sit down and have a drink?" Sam asked.

"Or a cup of coffee?" I added.

"No thanks. Gotta get movin'. See ya at the club soon, I hope? I'll leave my phone number in case you have a question. You be sure and invite me when she takes her first solo!"

"We'll invite you long before that," I said. "Solo may never happen--not in public, anyway."

"Well, he didn't want a drink, but I do," Sam said after Kelly had gone. "Play something for me; pretend we're at the club."

Although the job at Garfinckel's was a step backward as far as a career was concerned, living with Sam made up for many frustrations. He loved me -- even before breakfast when I was invariably grumpy. He wrote me a poem about it. I never learned the name of his favorite jazz club, but we went there as often as if it were our second home. Sam invited the band to a party at the apartment. I cooked spaghetti and meat sauce on the two-burner gas stove and served garlic bread and Chianti. Kelly and Lewis, the band's drummer, took turns playing the marimba while the rest of us sang along or clapped out the rhythms. A joint was passed around after dinner. I inhaled -- once -- and started to cry. For some reason, the drug did not give me a pleasant high; it brought on a fit of depression instead. Sam walked me to the bed and held my hand until I fell asleep.

"You'll never make it as a drug addict," he said the next morning.

I learned to play "Bye-bye Blackbird" -- inexpertly, but it gave me a feeling of accomplishment. I played with one mallet in each hand; I never quite mastered the art of striking the boards with two per hand.

In April, the cherry trees bloomed, and we walked underneath their fragrant branches. Before they finished flowering, I had found a new job, as a secretary in the office of the dean of the George Washington University Law School. It was pleasant work; I took dictation and typed letters and had lunch in the student cafeteria. I loved being back on a university campus -- especially this one, in downtown Washington, D.C.

Sam gave me a yellow-blonde wig -- a cloud of tight little curls, with lime-green highlights.

"Wear it to the club," he said. "Nobody will recognize you as the *veddy proppa* law school secretary who plays the marimba."

I wore the wig, garnering raucous approval from the band. I stopped asking Sam for news of possible opportunities in journalism. If he knew of any, I thought, he would tell me. If he didn't, I would not nag. I was his jazz-baby lover, not his wife.

CHAPTER 28

Crash

Washington's early summer arrived well before Memorial Day, which delighted me because we could take our two kitchen chairs out onto the balcony and sit there after coming home from work. Bertram would join us, stretching his full length on the outermost edge of the deck. Pushing his head under the railing, he kept a sharp eye on the sparrows flying by and on the foot traffic below.

Our workplaces were air-conditioned, but the apartment was not. As the temperatures rose daily in June, I left the door to the balcony open day and night and put out an extra bowl of water for the cat.

"People call it a swamp, but the city was actually built on the bank of the river," Sam said. "Still, it's beastly hot; it makes me listless. Does it bother you?"

"Not really. I'm used to extremes -- hot summers, cold winters. I'm tired of Chicago winters, but I survived them," I answered.

One afternoon I came home, took off my shoes and nylons, and walked through the living room, calling, as I always did, "Hello, Bertram -- how was your day?"

I did not expect an answer, but I *did* expect to see a somnolent cat. There was no cat. Bertram was not on the balcony; I searched the living room, the bedroom, the kitchen, the bathroom, and the closet. I pulled out dresser drawers, thinking that he might have squeezed in and become trapped. Desperate, I opened the kitchen cupboards and peered in. Bertram was not in the apartment. I put my shoes back on and walked downstairs, looking around and calling his name. It was very quiet in the stairwell. I heard no cat sounds -- not even a tiny meow. I had opened the street door when I remembered that I had not taken the key, so I raced back up, took my purse and keys, and nearly tripped as I skipped downstairs as fast as I could. I walked up and down both sides of Massachusetts Avenue, looking under parked cars and calling. There were no pedestrians to ask. I walked all the way to DuPont Circle and then back: no cat.

"Bertram's gone! I can't find him anywhere. How in the world did he get out?" I wailed when Sam came home.

"Sweetheart -- hello -- you're crying! What's this about Bertram?" he asked, giving me a hug. His arms did not seem to have their usual strength; his chest felt hot through the shirt.

"Bertram's missing. I can't find him. I just hope he didn't fall off the balcony," I said.

"It's the season," Sam said, plopping down on the couch. "In the spring, a young tom's fancy lightly turns--you know how it goes. He'll come back. Meanwhile, I'm limp just from walking up the stairs. I need a drink -- hot days call for cool drinks."

"I can fix a salad and cheese to go with it; you look exhausted," I offered.

"Not for me, thanks," Sam said as he got up to pour himself a vodka. "Do you mind if we don't go anywhere tonight? I'm beat and I'm not even a beatnik -- too old."

"Of course, I don't mind staying home. I wouldn't have gone -- in case Bertram shows up. But Sam, are you sure you feel all right? You're not sick?"

"No, dear. It's just the heat. It bothers me more than it does other people. Don't worry; I'm getting better by the minute."

"Good. If you're okay, I might go out and take another look around. Bertram may be hungry, even if we're not," I said.

"Go ahead. It'll make you feel better. You'll find me asleep when you get back. Sorry I'm not more scintillating company."

Despite my worries, I laughed. "I'm not sure I can spell that," I said.

When I returned an hour later, having found no trace of the cat, no lights had been turned on in the apartment. Sam, wearing only pajama pants, lay asleep on the bed. In the faint summer evening light that came through the window, his bare skin looked ghostly pale -- almost grey, as if it had been dusted with ashes.

A few days later, Sam, who said he was feeling fine now, had got a glimpse of Bertram being let into a house half a block from ours.

"I took the liberty of ringing the doorbell and asking the lady if that was her cat. She said yes, he had been missing for a long time, but now that he's finally home, she's going to have him neutered so he'll stop straying. Poor Bertram, with his manhood--uh, cathood -- gone," Sam told me.

"But he has a home -- he isn't dead. I'll miss him. Does she look like a nice lady?"

"Kind of a sour old biddy. I didn't tell her we had anything to do with Bertram and she didn't ask. Shut the door in my face."

"Oh, dear! Let's hope for the best -- such a nice cat," I said.

That evening, as we were eating sandwiches instead of a hot dinner on the balcony, Sam asked, "Do you want to go to Harrisburg with me this weekend? I've got an assignment to do an interview there."

"Harrisburg--isn't that in Pennsylvania? I think we passed through on the Greyhound," I answered.

"Harrisburg, Pennsylvania. Correct. It's a couple of hours' drive. They want me to interview some guy who is a town constable and the reigning poker champion. Bureau chief thinks that is a funny juxtaposition. You don't usually get law enforcement openly encouraging card games and possibly gambling. Seems only mildly funny to me, but it'll make a story. I have to go on the weekend, so I'll skip the family visit and you can come with me."

"Oh yes, I'd love to," I said. "In high school, some of the boys invited me to play poker, but it was strip poker and I almost said yes because I didn't know what it was. One of the girls dragged me out of the room and explained it meant taking off your clothes. She was mad at me for not knowing the game and I had to tell her I was a foreigner--"

Sam laughed and said, "Saved from a fate worse than death! Nice of your girlfriend to do that. I don't think the police chief or whatever he is in Harrisburg will suggest anything like that. And I hereby swear I will knock his block off if he does. Okay -- are you coming along? I want you to. You can call it another educational field trip."

"Yes, yes, definitely I want to go. It will be fun. I know you'll write a great article," I said.

"Good girl -- thanks. Here's to you, sweetheart!" Sam raised his glass and clinked mine. His contained vodka and ice while mine held ginger ale. Ever since my first experience with highballs at the club and the miserable morning after, I had avoided alcohol, except for an occasional sip from Sam's glass. I liked the refreshing shock of the ice, but not the burning sensation of the liquor. Sam never had a hangover; perhaps men had stronger stomachs, I thought.

"There's some coffee cake for dessert. Should I make coffee to go with it?" I asked.

"Not for me, thanks. I'm not very hungry; it's hot again. Cool liquids are in order. Don't get up -- I'll help myself." Sam replied. I knew he meant the vodka bottle. It had been nearly full yesterday. This afternoon, the level was down by two-thirds. I began to wonder if drinking so much "cool liquid" had something to do with Sam's recent fatigue and the unhealthy pallor that lingered on his skin.

The question must have shown on my face because Sam said, "You haven't got a poker face. You'd stink as a player. What is it? You think I'm hitting the bottle too hard? I don't want you to worry; I can cut down anytime I want. In fact, after this one, I won't have another drink until tomorrow night. Here, give me a pen or a pencil and I'll make a mark on the bottle. You can check it and see that the level will stay the same."

We could not manage to draw a line on the glass, so I used a piece of scotch tape to mark the level. Sam put the bottle in the cupboard.

I hugged him and we went back to the balcony. I hoped Sam had not taken my concern for scolding, but he dropped the subject and chatted about Harrisburg and our planned trip there.

Sam's promise that he could drink less if he chose to reassure me. But my feeling of comfort would not last long. The next day, I came home from work before him and went to the kitchen for a glass of water. Curiosity prompted me to take the vodka bottle out of the cupboard. It looked untouched, with the tape where I had placed it and the liquid level at the height I remembered. I felt ashamed of my sudden suspicion, but I couldn't help myself. I opened the bottle and poured a small amount into my glass that was still empty. I knew that vodka had no smell. And this vodka had no taste either -- no sting, no feeling of heat as it went down my throat. I took a larger swallow. It was water.

When had Sam finished this bottle? I was a heavy sleeper and his getting up to use the bathroom never disturbed me. Was it possible he had consumed a pint of vodka in the middle of the night? I could not understand it. This morning, there had been no sign of any ill effects. We had woken up and dressed for work, as usual. Sam had given my rear end a playful pat as I was bending over to pick my shoes off the floor. We had drunk our morning coffee and he had not wanted anything else. That also was normal; he never ate breakfast.

Now I heard Sam come into the kitchen. I turned to greet him. I did not know how to talk to him about the watered vodka. For as long as I had known him, his daily drink had been part of his routine. I told myself that he was forty years old and that he went to work every day, producing news stories and humor columns. He must know what he is doing, I thought. I did not have the courage, the experience, or the words to confront him. I kissed him instead. I wanted to love him so much that he would not need vodka.

On Saturday, we drove to Harrisburg. Sam was relaxed and chatty and I enjoyed sitting next to him. We cranked down the car's front windows and let the breeze wash over us.

"We'll go past Gettysburg -- this is Civil War country," Sam said. "At Gettysburg, there's a memorial site -- the cemetery, you know. If you like, we can stop overnight in Harrisburg and visit Gettysburg on the way home. We can take a tour -- or not, if you feel it's too sad."

"I'd like to see the memorial park. Of course, we studied the Civil War in school. It's such a tragic history! But I've only read about it. I've never been near an actual battlefield. Can we go tomorrow?"

"Yes, we'll plan on it. It's history, but it was only a little over a hundred years ago. There are probably living great-grandchildren of soldiers still around. And then we had two world wars, and Korea -- seems like we never learn to keep the peace," Sam said.

"My mother is very interested in the United Nations. She thinks international leaders should talk instead of fighting," I said.

"Hasn't worked yet, I'm sorry to tell her," Sam replied. "But let's not be sad today; we're on vacation. Do you know that Harrisburg is on the Susquehanna River? Can you spell that?"

The police officer Sam was to interview had given him an address for the meeting. I had assumed it would be at the man's home or perhaps at the police station, but our destination turned out to be a storefront on one of the town's downtown streets. The sign above the double doors said, "Pool Hall and Lounge."

"A bar?" I asked Sam as we went in.

"Yup. Bar, poker, pool -- and cigarettes and whiskey and wild, wild, women! Are you ready?" Sam laughed.

Officer Pete -- that was how he introduced himself -- was a tall, beefy man with twinkling blue eyes and short, dark hair that stood straight up in military formation on top of his head, leaving his ears and temples bare. He wore a short-sleeved cotton shirt and jeans and was smoking a cigarette.

"Pleased to meet you -- glad you could come. As you see, I'm off duty today. Let me get you folks a drink and then we can sit and talk," he said to Sam and me as we all shook hands. He had a powerful grip.

"Thanks, Pete. I should be buying -- but your hospitality is appreciated," Sam said and added, "Ginger ale for the lady and a vodka for me, please."

"Why don't we take our drinks over to a table and make ourselves comfortable?" Officer Pete suggested, pointing to the right side of the room, where a card game was in progress at one square table.

I did not want to intrude on Sam's interview, so I asked, "Is it all right if I go into the pool room and watch? I've read about billiards in novels, but I've never seen a game played."

"Sure, little lady, you go right ahead. We call it pool. It's played with eight balls. Go ahead; the boys won't hassle you," Pete said, smiling as if I were a curious, somewhat backward child.

"Thanks; I'll be quiet," I said, staying in the character he had assigned me.

Five men were playing; all were smoking, and all had drinks parked on empty bar stools that had been pushed aside. I leaned against the wall, close to the door, and smiled when someone looked my way. One or two of the men gave me a nod, but mostly they ignored me. After a while, I found an empty chair to sit on. I did not know the rules of the game. I watched as balls were knocked into the pockets at the edge of the table and the players moved wooden discs on what looked like a giant string of beads that hung on the wall. I guessed it was a way of tracking their scores, although I had no idea how many points counted as a win.

Half an hour -- or a whole hour, perhaps -- had passed when Sam came into the pool room.

"Came to see what the boys in the back room are having," he said. "I see! I see they're having Barbara!"

The men guffawed. I looked at Sam. I realized he had made a joke; I knew it must be funny, but I didn't get it. I laughed anyway and Sam put his arm around me.

"Nice guy, good interview. It'll make an amusing feature," Sam said. "We can go now and look around the town. Their capitol is a very impressive building -- if you're not tired of American history yet."

"I'd like a walk," I said. "Do women play pool?"

Sam answered, "I don't know any that do. And, you know, unaccompanied ladies are not admitted to most bars. If you see a woman on her own, you assume she's for hire."

Officer Pete had told Sam about a local restaurant he liked and about a decent motel. After our stroll around the city and a pleasant dinner, we slept at the motel and in the morning, we drove south to Gettysburg.

At the battlefield, where so many thousands lay buried, I echoed my mother's perennial question--would there ever be a world without wars?

"The slaves were freed," Sam mused. "But we've got a long way to go towards equality. Neighborhoods and schools are still segregated. How many Negro customers did you have at Garfinckel's?"

"I never saw any at all," I replied.

"They're not welcome there; I've heard they're not allowed to try on clothes."

"Really? That wasn't in our training program; I would remember something like that," I said.

"The supervisors would know, and they would have taken action if the 'wrong' type of customer appeared. But apparently, it doesn't happen. The rules are understood. Washington is a southern city. It's different from Chicago."

"But *you're* here and I'm here with you," I said. "That makes Washington the best city in the world."

Sam let me read his article about the poker champion before turning it over to his editor. The piece was clever, as I had known it would be. Sam had captured the Saturday afternoon ambiance of the bar perfectly -- the card players, the leisurely pool game, and the relaxed police officer who turned into a ruthless competitor at the poker table.

"It's one of your best," I told Sam. He laughed and answered, "You wouldn't be a little bit prejudiced, would you? But thanks; I'm happy you like it."

We had come back from Harrisburg on Sunday. It was the last week of June and the weather continued hot and muggy. I wished the cool waters of Lake Michigan could magically be moved to DuPont Circle, where the fountain was merely decorative and not suitable for wading. By Friday, Sam had decided once again not to make his customary visit to Alexandria. He blamed his lethargy on the temperature.

"The kids wear me out at the best of times. I can't cope with them and a heat wave at the same time. I'll make an effort next week. Let's hope we have some rain or a thunderstorm to cool things off in the meantime."

The week that followed was no less hot. We went to work and sat on the balcony after coming home. We left the lights off in the apartment to discourage mosquitoes. I made salads and iced tea; Sam preferred vodka. He ate little. He did not look well; his face looked puffy and when he took off his blue sunglasses, I saw that his eyes were bloodshot. I wanted to ask him if there was anything I could do, but since he did not complain about any particular ache or pain, I said nothing.

Sam again excused himself from a visit with his family. On Saturday night, he wanted to visit the jazz club. We went, but we left after about an hour.

"Going already? Got better things to do?" Kelly teased when we said goodnight.

"You're going to get bored with me and leave me," Sam said as we were getting ready for bed. "I'm so tired, I can't do anything except go to sleep. I'm useless!"

"I'm never bored with you, sweetheart. I'm tired and it's too hot to make love. Let's rest and save it for another day. We have all the time in the world." Before I had finished speaking, Sam was asleep. I lay as close beside him as I could without making him uncomfortable and soon dropped off to sleep as well.

On a Tuesday in mid-July, I came home from work and saw that Sam had arrived before me. I was surprised to see his jacket and tie carelessly flung on the living room couch. Normally, he hung them up in the closet as soon as he came in. Once I had remarked on his tidy habits and he had said, "I'm well trained -- I've been told to set a good example for the children."

It was very quiet in the apartment. I walked to the bedroom and paused in the doorway. Sam lay on the bed, curled up in a fetal position. His arms were folded tightly over his stomach, as if he were in pain. I walked up to the bed and bent over to see whether his eyes were open. They were shut; he was fast asleep. It must be heat exhaustion, I thought. He had left work early and gone straight to bed. I did not want to disturb him, so I tiptoed out of the room.

I checked on Sam after half an hour or so, and again after an hour had passed. Each time, I found him in the same position, lying very still. I listened to his breathing. It was shallow -- so quiet that it hardly moved his chest. I let another half hour pass and then I tried to wake him. I touched his cheek and said his name; I touched his shoulder, moving it slightly to rouse him. I wanted to give him a drink of water and possibly some medicine for whatever stomach pain he seemed to be experiencing.

Sam did not respond to my touch. I shook his shoulder harder and called his name again, raising my voice. He did not open his eyes or move his body. I was worried now, but I still thought that he was worn out and simply needed a long rest. I went to sit in the living room, willing Sam to wake up and talk to me, but the apartment remained silent. Finally, I could bear it no longer and got up from the couch to check once again.

Before I reached the hallway, I heard the bathroom door slam. And then I heard loud groaning and retching sounds. Terrified, I opened the door and saw Sam doubled over the toilet bowl. He was vomiting a gritty, dark liquid that looked like coagulated blood.

"Sam -- Sam -- let me help! Oh, Sam -- sweetheart -- what is it-- what can I do?" I cried as I went to him. He turned his head and gave me a blank look. It seemed as if he didn't know who I was. I put my arms around his shoulders and held him. The retching abated a little and Sam moved sideways, away from the toilet. He wanted to go back to bed, I guessed. I moved with him. We hobbled across the hall. Sam collapsed on the bed, instantly closing his eyes, and resuming his fetal position. Nothing I did after that elicited any response whatever.

We needed help -- a doctor, a hospital, an ambulance! It was a crisis and I had no emergency phone numbers. I thought of calling Susan, his wife, but there was no time to explain to her what had happened and for her to explain it to their family doctor. I needed to get Sam to a hospital -- now! I had no friends in Washington. Who would help me?

I thought of Kelly, who had left his phone number when he had brought over the marimba. I called, desperately hoping that he would be home.

"My doctor is at Freedmen's Hospital. You sure Sam wants to go there though? Doesn't he have a doc someplace else?" Kelly asked after I had told him that Sam was unresponsive after his bout of vomiting.

"He needs help, and fast. If you can help get him to Freedmen's, please -- let's go. I don't know who his doctor is. Kelly, please help me! Get an ambulance -- I'll give you the address here again -- "

"I'll do it. Try to calm down, girl. I'm gonna call the emergency and my doctor now. You hang up and take care of Sam," Kelly said.

I did not know anything about Freedmen's Hospital. From its name, I guessed that it served the African-American community and that it was in a neighborhood I had never visited. It did not matter how far away it was, I thought. Saving Sam's life was all that mattered at this point. I knew that if Sam were conscious, he would be as grateful to Kelly as I was -- Kelly was our friend in need and in deed.

An ambulance arrived and two attendants brought a stretcher upstairs.

"He's in a coma," one of the medics observed.

"You coming with us? Don't forget to take your purse," the other said.

I was grateful for the advice; I had been about to walk downstairs without it.

Sam, still unconscious, was taken to a room and put into a bed with an oxygen tent over the head of it. He had not woken up. A nurse pulled his wallet from the pants she had removed.

"I'll take this to admissions," she said. "You don't have to come with me. You're family, right? You can stay a little while. Hold his hand. He may not feel it -- but we never know, do we? Visiting hours are over, so you should go home and get some sleep. You can come back tomorrow."

"Yes, I'm family. Thanks for letting me stay. I'll be back in the morning," I said.

The nurse's sympathetic words made me cry. I understood that Sam might not know that my hand was touching his, but I reached under the sheet and gently squeezed his cold, clammy fingers.

I took a taxi home. In the morning, I called the law school office and excused myself for that day and the next, claiming that I had caught some bug or other.

Before I set out for Freedmen's Hospital, the telephone rang. When I answered, the doctor Kelly had consulted introduced himself.

"I've examined Sam," he said. "He hasn't come to; he's in a coma. I have to tell you -- I have to tell you-- it doesn't look hopeful. It's the liver-- an advanced case of cirrhosis--chronic alcohol abuse. There's been hemorrhaging. We're doing what we can, but it isn't much. You can come in, sit with him. Maybe he'll wake up. I'm sorry, Missus."

"Thank you, doctor. I know you're doing your best. Thank you very much for caring for Sam. My name's Barbara," I said.

The moment I hung up, I knew that I had to let Susan know where her husband was and what had happened to him. I was not missus -- or Mrs. -- anything! I was the unmarried girlfriend. I had to call the wife.

But not yet! I went to the hospital and sat next to Sam's bed. He never moved or opened his eyes. I remembered saying that we had all the time in the world to be lovers. Now I knew I had been wrong. We had no time left; time had stopped.

From a payphone in a hospital corridor, I called Sam's home number in Alexandria. It was evening, late enough for the children to be in bed.

"Why Freedmen's?" Susan asked when I had given her the news.

"It was an emergency. Sam couldn't tell me anything different; he couldn't talk," I said. "They're doing everything they can for him. He's in a private room. The doctor is very sympathetic."

Susan hung up.

When I came back into Sam's room, the nurse said, "I've taken out the tubes and cleaned him up a little. He's sinking -- I'm sorry, honey."

Perhaps it was wishful thinking, but I thought I saw Sam's eyelids flicker. I leaned in and saw his lips move.

"...Wife?" It was the barest whisper. I did not know if he meant me.

"She's coming," I said to Sam's expressionless face. His eyes had closed again. I kissed his cold hand and left the room.

In the brightly lit corridor, Susan was walking towards me. I could not avoid her.

"You have to give him back to me now," she said when we were face to face.

I didn't steal him, I wanted to say. What we had been to each other had been out in the open and we had never lied. We had loved each other honestly in the time we had together. But I could not and did not say a word as Susan swept past me on her way to Sam's room.

The next day was Thursday. Smitty, Sam's trusted friend and colleague, called me.

"Sorry, honey," he said. "I have something to say that's awkward -- don't take it ill, okay? I have to tell you that Sam's family don't want you at the funeral."

"Smitty," I said, "I never intended to go. I don't know what day it's going to be, and I don't want to know. You can assure them I won't show up."

"Will you let me take you out to lunch then? We'll go to the Maryland shore and have crabs -- they're a famous regional specialty," Smitty said. At first, his suggestion surprised me -- Maryland crabs were the farthest thing from my mind. But then I understood that Susan didn't trust me. Smitty had been charged with keeping me away. Did she really think I would crash the funeral?

I thanked Smitty and said that lunch at the shore would be fine.

In an obituary that appeared two weeks later, Sam was remembered as a journalist "with a light touch." The brief article reported that he had died on July 16, 1959. It did not say where he was buried.

CHAPTER 29

A Different Course

I spent the weekend after Sam's death in a howling spiral of grief, anger, and guilt. The apartment felt like hell made real. It was hot and close and smelled of vomit. It was empty -- too empty to be borne, but I wanted no one to come over and keep me company. On my first day alone, I did not call Roland or my mother. I missed Bertram -- and at the same time I was glad that the cat was not underfoot; I might have kicked him and made myself guilty of cruelty in addition to all my other failings.

I picked up Sam's jacket and tie and went to the closet to put them away. Why? I asked myself. The garments were useless now. I might just as well have stuffed them into the trash bin. We had shared the only closet in the apartment. It was crowded with both of our wardrobes. I reached in to find an empty hanger, moving my arm to create a little space. When I pushed aside a row of Sam's jackets, I heard the sound of glass clinking. I thought I was hallucinating. Would I hear Sam say "Cheers" next? I pulled the string that turned on the closet light and took out one of the light-colored sportscoats. It felt heavy and the pockets bulged -- because an empty bottle was in each one. It was the same with all the other jackets.

The shock of the discovery made my chest feel constricted, as if I could not catch my breath. I realized that I had ignored what had been in plain view. I had reached into this closet a thousand times; how could I have been so willfully blind and deaf?

Anger at myself and guilt combined to make me feel that I had not loved Sam enough to prevent his death at age forty-one. I had seen him down drink after drink, but I had not asked him to stop. I had not informed myself about the effects of alcohol abuse, nor had I urged Sam to seek help. Because Sam had continued to go to his office and to write regularly, I had told myself that there was no problem. My negligence, I thought, had helped to kill him.

I went to the balcony door and shut it. I did not want any passersby to be alarmed by the strangled sounds I was now making.

My thoughts went in circles as I told myself over and over that Sam was dead. I had failed him, and I could never set it right. I berated myself for all the things I had not done. I had accepted all the happiness he had given me, but I had not told him often enough how much he meant to me. Should I have been a more adventuresome lover? I had let him take the leading role. Perhaps our relations had not been so exciting that he could forget about vodka. I had sometimes remarked on other men's good looks and had not thought to apologize when he felt jealous. I had not asked him whether he missed Susan, whether he had any regrets -- whether he worried about his children. I had not insisted on contributing to the rent. In fact, I did not even know what the monthly fee was, or to whom it was paid!

By coming to Washington, I had placed a burden on him. Because he had asked me to come, he could not admit that the burden was heavy. I should have talked him out of bringing me to Massachusetts Avenue. I was angry with myself for being selfish, reckless, and vain about my power to attract men. I began to feel anger towards Sam for having left me so suddenly. In the next breath, I felt furious with myself for having dared to be angry. Sam had not died on purpose; how could I be so unfeeling?

On my second day alone, I forced myself to call my mother and Roland. There was no answer at the South Side apartment. I remembered that it was Saturday and that both would be at work. Mother would be at Parkway and Roland -- I didn't know if he still worked at Siegel's bookstore. I had not been in touch for more than a month.

To my surprise, it was Roland who answered at Parkway.

"I'm helping out. The place needs some odds and ends of repairs -- as usual," he said when he heard my voice.

"Roland!" I said. "Roland, I'm glad it's you. I have bad news-- about Sam. Really bad news -- the worst!"

"What is it, Sis? You're all upset. Did Sam leave you? Or is he sick?"

"He's dead, Roland. He died at the hospital. I didn't realize he was that sick -- it was liver disease and --"

"Vodka," Roland said. "Poor you. I'm sorry, so sorry. You shouldn't have to go through this."

"I have to tell Mom now. Or is she busy with customers?"

Roland said, "She's busy. If you want, I'll give her the news and you two can talk later this afternoon."

"Don't mention the vodka, please, Roland. She'll blame me for not stopping him. I blame myself enough. It was up to me and I failed him!"

"It was up to Sam," Roland said. "You probably tried, but he had a habit before you met him. Remember he brought his own bottle when he came to see us?"

"Yes. There was always a bottle."

"I'll tell Mom it was a disease. Are you going to leave D.C. and come home?"

"I don't know what I want to do. I have a good job at the law school. I want to stay at least a couple more weeks until I figure out what to do," I answered.

"If you decide to come back, you can stay with me. I moved out; it was getting too hard to live with Mom. I'm renting a coach house -- no heat, but it's cheap. Mom's about to give up the apartment. She's been staying with Ernst a lot; I think they're going to get married."

"Wow, that's a lot of news, Roland. I need time to think. I'll call later, or better, have Mom call me, okay?"

Why had Sam's drinking been visible to everyone but me? Because I had not wanted to see it. I was guilty. If I had confronted Sam and brought the issue out into the open--

And now it was too late.

When I talked with my mother, she said, "*Du armes Kind*--you poor child--come home. Are you all alone there? That's not good. Come home. I know Sam was a good man and you loved him, but you shouldn't stay so far away from your family."

I could feel my mother's arms around me as she spoke. There was no anger or reproach in her voice.

"I will, Mom -- I will, but not right away. I have to give notice at work and take care of some things here. It'll take time," I said.

I went to work at the law school on Monday. Joanne, the other secretary in the dean's office, asked, "Are you really better? That must've been some nasty bug. You look horrible."

"It was bad. I'm all right, though; don't worry, it's not catching. I couldn't eat," I said, giving an answer that contained a major falsehood. I was *not* all right.

When the dean came in, I asked him when it would be convenient for him to talk with me for a few minutes.

"Come in now, Miss Pitschel," he said, opening the door to the inner office.

"I hope this is not a complaint about your miserable working conditions here," he said, smiling. "I know we drive you poor ladies to distraction with our longwinded correspondence."

I looked around the carpeted office with its polished mahogany furniture and the shelves crammed with leather-bound law books. I thought it was the most pleasant environment I had ever worked in.

"Oh, no," I said. "It's not about conditions -- this is a wonderful place to work. It's -- I came to see you because I'm afraid I have to give notice. I have to leave--"

"Really? May I ask why?"

I decided to tell another partial truth. "There's been a death in the family. I have to go back to Chicago, where my mother is. I can stay a few more weeks, until you hire somebody else."

"I am sorry for your loss. Of course, if you must go, I understand. It's a shame, though -- I had been thinking of offering to make you my private secretary. I like the way you deal with my letters. When you hand me the typed copies and I read them over, they sound better than what I dictated."

"Thank you. Thank you for the compliment," I said. I was surprised that the dean actually read the stacks of paper he was given to sign every day. "I don't change anything in your letters, really. I don't know why they would be different. But thank you."

"The position would command an increase in salary also," the dean continued. "Are you certain you won't consider it?"

"Thank you, sir. You are very generous. I'm sorry I have to say no. My mother and my brother want me to come back."

Joanne said she was sorry to see me go. I told her I was staying until the end of July and that I had liked working and sometimes eating lunch with her. She was almost a friend, I thought, but I could not tell her about Sam. If she asked about the death in my family, I would say it was a relative in Chicago.

I cleaned the apartment. I looked in the Yellow Pages for a junk dealer who agreed to take away Sam's clothes. Like my mother, I believed it was wrong to discard items that could still be used by someone else.

"Guy walk out on you?" the junkman asked when he came to the apartment. "I can give you ten bucks for the jackets and pants."

I took the money without answering the insulting question.

Marian Miller called from the news bureau. She had heard the news from Susan.

"Sam was so in love with you. He tried to be secretive about it, but it stuck out all over him," she said. "I was happy for him-- for both of you. I'm so sorry. What are you going to do?"

"I'm going back to Chicago next month. It's too sad here. I talked with my mother and my brother; they say come back," I answered.

"Best thing to do, I agree. Before you go, would you stop by the office? I want to give you my home address and I want you to stay in touch. I loved Sam -- we all loved him -- and I want to know what happens to you in the future."

"I would like that so much. I don't know what to say. Thank you," I said. It seemed that I had made a friend -- through Sam.

Kelly called to give me his and the band's condolences.

"He's with the saints, God rest his soul," Kelly said. "He was a good guy -- a real hep gentleman."

I thanked Kelly and asked him to please come over at his convenience and take the marimba as a remembrance.

Sorting through the dresser drawers in the bedroom, I found Sam's Zippo cigarette lighter and put it in my suitcase. Later, I added a book Sam had given me when I had visited Washington the year before. It was *The Unquiet Grave*, a collection of personal observations, aphorisms, and quotations, written by Cyril Connolly under the pseudonym Palinurus. Sam had told me that Connolly's thoughts about approaching forty years of age were similar to his own. I had found the passage too gloomy and had tried to steer Sam towards a more optimistic outlook. Now, I wondered if Sam had been so depressed by his fortieth birthday -- which we had not celebrated -- that he had overdosed on drink.

Guilt and remorse hit me again. Why had I not been more sensitive to his emotions?

It was almost the end of July. I had not been able to find any documents relating to the rent and the telephone bill -- no receipts, no canceled checks, no business cards with the name and address of the landlord or rental agent. I thought the bills had been paid because there had never been reminders or second notices. Sam had told me he would take care of it and I had trusted him. If there were papers, they would be in his office desk, to which I had no access. I did not know any of the other tenants in the building. It was impossible to knock on a neighbor's door and to ask who the rental agent might be. It occurred to me that I could simply leave when my last week at the law school was up, but I did not want skip town like a criminal. What if Sam had *not* paid the rent? He had not been well; he might have forgotten, or he might have left the task to be done at a future time. If there was an unpaid balance, I wanted to clear it. I decided to stay in the apartment until someone contacted me. I was going back to

Chicago with fewer possessions than I had brought -- my winter jacket, and the summer clothing I had bought recently. I had decided not to take my books, except for Palinurus. I planned to visit the neighborhood bookstore to ask if I could get a few dollars for the used volumes.

I was home, sorting through the bookshelf, on a weekday during the first week in August. I was no longer working. A loud, repeated knock -- what my mother would have called a "Gestapo knock" -- startled me and I ran to open the apartment door.

An angry-looking man in a grey suit moved towards me briskly, as if he wanted to run me over.

"You! You're moving out! I know who you are -- and you're *not* Sam's wife! You're evicted!" he shouted.

I opened my mouth to reply, but he continued to rant. "You're leaving-- you understand plain English, I hope? What d'you think I'm running here? This is a respectable apartment building, not a *house!*"

"I'm leaving," I said. "I didn't know your name -- I don't know your name. I wanted to call you--"

"Never mind your excuses. Just leave. How soon will you have your junk out of here?" The man was not going to give me his name, I realized. I also understood that Susan must have called him. How else would he have known?

"The day after tomorrow," I said, as firmly as I could. I had intended to ask whether a balance was due, but my goodwill had evaporated. The agent was treating me like a squatter, or worse; I decided I owed him nothing.

"Make sure you're out of here. I'm going to check every day," he growled as he turned his back on me and marched out.

I did not have a phone number for Roland; I called Mother at the store.

"Gott sei Dank, Kind," she said when I had told her I would be leaving Washington in two days.

"Could you tell Roland to call me? I'm taking a plane; maybe he can meet me at the airport. He said I can stay with him," I said. The thought of being with my brother and my mother again made me cry.

Suddenly, I felt that I couldn't get out of Washington fast enough. I left the apartment on Massachusetts Avenue the next day. I left my books and Sam's ties that I had not been able to touch because they made me unbearably sad. I left Bertram's water dish on the balcony. Without calling ahead to buy a plane ticket, I asked a bus driver for directions to the airport and made my way there, carrying a suitcase, a duffel bag, and my purse.

I learned that I could fly as a standby passenger, and that the ticket would be less expensive than those for reserved seats.

"Yes. That's nice," I said to the ticket clerk -- as if I were a seasoned traveler who knew all about fares and discounts. I did not mention that I would be boarding a plane for the first time in my life.

Anguish again overtook me when the airplane had lifted off and I saw the Potomac River below us sparkling in the sunlight. I remembered the high hopes I had brought to the capital and the romantic promise of the cherry blossoms. I had wanted to accomplish so much! I had wanted to live happily ever after with Sam, but Sam was gone. I had lost so much. I started to cry and did not feel like stopping. The young sailor in the seat next to mine put an arm around my shoulder and said, "Go ahead and cry. You don't have to tell me anything about it if you don't want to."

I nodded and kept on weeping. When the captain announced that we were about to land at Midway Airport, I woke and couldn't remember when I had fallen asleep. I turned to the sailor to thank him for comforting me. He was dozing, so I simply whispered, "Thanks."

Roland was waiting. He had let his hair grow almost to his shoulders, and he seemed taller than I remembered. He looked handsome. His wideset blue eyes were scanning the crowd when I rushed into his arms.

"How did you know what flight I was on? I didn't know this morning because it was standby and I just left a short message with Mom," I said, feeling faint with relief and joy.

"That wasn't too hard. I called the airlines until somebody found you on a passenger list. There aren't that many flights," Roland said. "I borrowed a car so we can ride in style. Let's get your bags."

My wonderful, practical brother. He was my *little* brother, I reminded myself; I had carried him piggyback down to the air raid shelter. Now he had grown many years older and wiser and more sensible than his distraught older sister.

Roland's new dwelling was on a street north of the Loop, in the area called Old Town. Roland said it was a neighborhood where the rents were affordable for artists and writers. The coach house was an old stable in an alley behind a row of substantial Victorian mansions that had belonged to the owners of the carriages and horse teams.

"Welcome!" Roland said, as we entered through a tall wooden door. "It's a little bare but improving. I'm learning to build furniture."

The main room was two storeys tall, with a sleeping loft -- the old hayloft -- at the far end. A ladder with broad treads led up to it. A kitchen stove, a sink, and a wooden cabinet had been installed on one wall. The horse stalls on the opposite wall had become a bathroom.

"And this is the living room," Roland said, pointing to the large open space in the middle of the room. "I made the couch out of an old bedspring I found in the alley. The legs still need work; they're wobbly, as you'll notice. Or you can sit in the beanbag chair; that's steady."

"It's great -- all of it. I'm glad I can stay with you for a while," I said.

"Stay, relax. It's a rough time for you. I'm sorry it had to end that way with Sam -- I liked him, you know."

Roland boiled water in a dented saucepan and made mugs of tea for us. I sat on the couch while he settled into the beanbag.

"Poor kid--" he began.

I interrupted him. "You shouldn't feel sorry for *me*. Oh, Roland -- I made such a mess! I failed. I failed with Sam -- I should've helped him, stopped him from drinking, I should've seen what was in front of my eyes. I didn't get a job at the AP either -- I failed at that too. I'm not even twenty-three yet and my life is over--"

Roland looked at me with his usual calm expression.

"Not yet. Your life isn't over. It's shitty right now, but you'll find a way out. You loved Sam; *he* didn't think you were a failure! Don't blame yourself so much. Things are going to be different for you now; think of it as putting yourself on a different course."

"And I should stop feeling sorry for myself, right?" I asked, regretting my outburst.

"Yup. If you don't mind," my brother said -- and he not only smiled but grinned.

CHAPTER 30

Into the Sixties

During the rest of August, I did not look for a job. My mother encouraged me to help her at Parkway Sweater Import and I welcomed the offer. Business was slack, as it usually was during the summer, so we had time to talk. Despite my resolve not to give in to self-blame, I often felt angry at myself for not having prevented Sam from drinking too much. Mother, to my relief, was not mad at me; she pitied me.

"You loved Sam. It's so hard to lose someone you love -- and you are so young. Life can be cruel," she said.

I told her about the happy times -- going to the jazz club where Sam had good friends, and meeting his colleagues at the news bureau. I recounted Bertram the cat's adventures and described sitting on our balcony on warm summer evenings.

Mother told me that she and Ernst would be getting married. They had not set a date, but it would be sometime in the spring of 1960.

"I haven't gotten to know him well," I said. "But I'm sure he's a good man. Could we have dinner together soon, so I can say congratulations? He's a lucky man too. Would he mind if I said so?"

"He'll be happy to have your good wishes. He's an honest man and he's been very lonely since his wife died years ago," Mother said.

I noticed that my mother had not said she loved Ernst, but her voice was tender when she described him and his feelings. Perhaps she too felt alone, despite her social nature and her many acquaintances.

Mother took me to the storage area behind the salesroom and showed me a number of large cardboard boxes.

"I brought your books and the other things you left behind in the apartment. Roland packed them up and brought them here. There was no point in my living on the South Side after he moved out," Mother said. "Now that you're staying with him, he can help you take them to his cow shed."

"Coach house!" I said, laughing. "It was for horses and carriages, not cows."

"What's the difference," Mother said bitterly. "It wasn't meant for civilized people. If your brother would only value education more--"

"He's working at the university book bindery. He reads the great Russian novels in his spare time," I said. But I knew my words would not change her dislike of the path Roland had chosen.

A few days later, after Roland had borrowed his friend's car once again and had moved my boxes, I found my blue sari in one of them. I would never see Surendra again, I thought, but I trusted that he was alive and prospering.

My lover Sam was lost forever; he was dead. I dug through the suitcase that held my underclothes and sweaters -- Roland did not own a chest of drawers -- and found Sam's Zippo lighter. When I gave it to Roland as a memento, he promptly lit a cigarette.

"Thanks, Sis. Let's always remember him as a good guy who made you happy," he said.

Roland and Jutta were still seeing each other; that made me glad. Jutta came to visit on her day off and the three of us went out to a neighborhood pizzeria. I felt as if I had been gone for half a lifetime; I had been away for only six months.

Being with my family began to lift my spirits. As September brought cooler temperatures to Chicago, I enjoyed walking through Old Town, admiring its many-chimneyed Victorian houses. September had always signaled the start of a new school year, when choosing courses had been an exciting adventure.

This year, I had to decide on what direction my new life without Sam was to take. I was living in the coach house as Roland's guest.

So far, I had contributed very little towards expenses, aside from buying groceries and an occasional six pack of beer. I had a moderate sum of money saved from my job in Washington, but that cash was dwindling. The first step on my new path was to find a job.

Thinking about newspaper reporting and journalism made me sad; I decided to stay with secretarial work, for which I had the skills and good references. An office job would give me a decent salary while I looked into other possibilities, such as editorial work for a magazine or a publishing firm. Shunning the *Chicago Daily News* whose columnist had caused so much upheaval at the *Chicago Review*, I bought a copy of the *Tribune.* I knew from previous experience that their classified ad section, especially on weekends, would offer employment in a variety of fields.

I had a talk with Roland.

"It's good to be staying here with you," I said. "But I'm going to start chipping in for the rent and expenses -- that's only fair. You don't make enough money to support two people. As soon as I start working, I'll take you out to the Old Town Ale House."

"No objection to that. Take your time though; find something that's better than Relaxarama, or whatever it's called," Roland said.

"I will, definitely. I know I can get a recommendation from the dean of the law school; he complimented me on my work," I replied.

"Onward and upward! In the meantime, if you want to go out this weekend, I know where there's free wine and cheese -- high-quality wine and cheese -- nothing schlocky."

I looked at Roland's face to see if he was teasing. His expression gave nothing away.

"What? You're kidding, right? Who gives out free drinks?" I asked.

"The art galleries on Ontario Street have parties when they put up a new show," Roland explained. "They have a preview -- it's free to go and meet the artist-- and they serve wine and breadsticks and cheese."

"But Roland -- that's for prospective buyers, isn't it? We can't go! We don't look like rich aristocrats looking to buy avant-garde art -- because we're not. We're beatniks," I protested.

"We'll be rich, aristocratic beatniks. German aristocratic beatniks-- the Count and Countess von Hoellenschlund!" Roland stood up, clicked his sneakered heels, and executed a perfect bow, just as he had learned to do when he was four years old. "This is America, land of opportunity," he declared.

What could I answer except -- "*Jawohl!*"

On Saturday, the count and countess from the maw of hell visited the Holland-Goldowsky Gallery, which was opening an exhibition of works by a painter who lived and worked in New York. According to the announcement in the newspaper, he was an abstract expressionist, or action painter.

The gallery, one block east of elegant Michigan Avenue, was a brightly lit space with large windows and a plate glass door that stood open in welcome. As Roland and I walked towards the building we could see huge, colorful paintings on the walls. A crowd of guests was moving about the large room, talking, and laughing and sometimes gesturing with a hand that held a cigarette or a long-stemmed glass.

"They're not looking at the paintings much," I said to Roland.

"It's a party, not the museum," he answered. "I don't know when they pick one to buy. Maybe never -- who's got a living room big enough?"

"You do! The coach house has lots of wall space -- you have to like brick, that's all."

We walked through the door and mixed with the gathering, nodding, and smiling, as if we already knew all the art patrons in Chicago. I did look at the unframed paintings. I knew a little about German Expressionism, so the non-objective style did not shock me. I thought they were landscapes -- but landscapes that were exploding, with bursts of vivid colors flying off the edges of the canvas.

Staying true to our cover, I put that thought into multisyllabic, not strictly grammatical German and turned to Roland, asking, *"Nichtwahr?"*

"Right," he replied in English. "Is that what they mean by 'action,' flinging all that paint?"

We had made our way to the back of the room, where a long table covered with a crisp white cloth was set up to serve as a bar. An ice bucket filled with wine bottles, glasses, a cubic vase filled with breadsticks, and a platter of cheese looked as inviting as Roland had described.

A black-haired man in a dark suit, white shirt, and pale blue tie, came towards us. He had thick, exuberant eyebrows and warm brown eyes. He was compactly built and was about my height. A cigarette, with an ash at least an inch long, was glued to his lower lip.

"Hello, I'm Noah Goldowsky," he said.

"Roland and Barbara von Hoellenschlund," Roland said, bowing slightly.

"Welcome to the gallery," Noah replied without raising an eyebrow at the outlandish name. "I don't think you've visited before. Are you man and wife?"

"We live together, but Roland is my brother," I said, staring at the cigarette ash that had not yet dropped. I looked around for an ashtray. I hated the thought of smudges on that beautiful suit -- it was obviously made to measure; the fabric looked like raw silk.

Noah saw my glance.

"You and everybody else! Don't worry about it," he said, raising two fingers to take the cigarette out of his mouth. At the same moment, an ashtray appeared between the three of us. It was held by a slender, beringed hand attached to a wrist crowded with charm bracelets.

"It *never* drops on his lapel -- I don't know how he does it," a blonde woman in a dark red cocktail dress said. "Extraordinary, isn't it?"

Noah's cigarette was already back in place; he had tapped the ash into the waiting crystal saucer with the briefest of motions.

"Hello, Muriel," he said. "You worry too much. What do you think of our boy's art?"

"It's fantastic! Of course, I knew it would be. Every artist you've chosen is a major talent -- you've got the *eye,*" the lady exclaimed. She turned to Roland and me and added, "Doesn't he?"

I did not want to admit that I knew nothing about this artist or about Noah Goldowsky, but I thought I had better agree with this woman; most likely she was a collector. Judging by her dress and her jewelry, she was also rich.

"Oh, you are right -- he is very knowledgeable," I said. "These new Expressionists must have come from the tradition of the Germans -- Kokoschka --"

Noah's dark eyes turned to me with a look that was either scornful or amused; I couldn't tell which.

"Hmm," he muttered with his lips closed around the cigarette. Then he asked, "Have you had a drink yet, Muriel? Let's all go get one, shall we?"

"*Danke* -- thank you," Roland said.

As we turned to walk towards the bar, Noah and Muriel were pulled into conversations with other guests while Roland and I made our way through the crowd to the bar. We helped ourselves to wine and breadsticks. I admired the appetizers. Toothpicks with paper frills were stuck in perfectly cut cubes of cheese, making the platter look like a giant hedgehog with red spines. With a glass in one hand and bread in the other, I did not know how to pick up a piece of cheese as well; I decided to tour the room and come back later.

I saw that Roland was chatting with a group of people, so I studied the paintings on the walls, noting that small red dots had appeared beside several of the labels that gave the title of the artwork and the year it was produced. All of the dates were recent. I guessed the stickers meant that someone was buying the painting. Noah came up beside me.

"You don't know much about these painters, do you?" he observed, rather than asked.

"Well -- no -- I--" I started, thinking that I might as well admit my ignorance.

"Here's somebody who'll explain it all to you. Meet Aaron Siskind -- he's a photographer -- an *important* photographer. We have some of his work here, in the backroom -- he'll show you."

"Hello, Aaron -- I'm Barbara," I said, turning to the man with Noah. I thought they might be cousins. Except for eye color -- Noah's were brown, Aaron's blue -- they resembled each other. Both were of medium stature and had black, curly hair. Both seemed to be chain-smokers. Noah's cigarette was loosely held by his lips; Aaron's was in his left hand.

"Barbara, hey? Did you hear what he said? You ready to visit the back room with me?" He gave me an exaggerated wink along with a stage villain's cackle. It made me think of Sam's quip about the boys in the back room.

"I'm not scared," I said. "If I need help, my big brother is right over there."

With another jolly laugh, Aaron took my hand and led me towards the rear of the gallery. Just before we reached the door, I quickly put my empty glass on the bar. We entered a large storage room filled with open racks of framed and unframed pictures. Aaron touched a light switch on the wall, walked to one of the racks, pulled out a black portfolio, and carried it to a large desk.

"I'll be having a show here next month," Aaron said. "But for you there's a special preview. You'd like that, wouldn't you, sweetie?"

Aaron's black and white images were striking in their simplicity and power. The pictures showed massive flat rocks balanced on smaller, rounded ones, strands of seaweed like Japanese calligraphy painted on sand, tattered posters peeling off fences or billboards.

"I like these," I said to Aaron. "I've never seen abstract photographs."

"You want bodies, I can show you some," Aaron said, pulling another portfolio out of the rack. "I did a bunch a couple years ago called Pleasures and Perils of Levitation-- kind of a mouthful but that's what it is."

In these photographs, men or boys in swimsuits were caught in midair as they tumbled or jumped into water that was not in the picture frame.

"They make me nervous," I said. "You don't know if the lake is really down there or not."

"Exactly, sweetie! See, you can be an art critic if you want. Nothin' to it. Just use your pretty blue eyes," Aaron said.

With impeccable timing, my brother ambled through the door.

"Hi there," he said. "I've seen one of these photographs. There's one on the cover of *Big Table*. So, I guess you're Aaron Siskind? I'm Roland."

"My brother," I added as the two shook hands. "He does design for *Big Table* and I was on the *Chicago Review* last year until we had the big controversy."

"I know, I know," Aaron said. "You beatnik radicals have been stirring things up here. The bourgeoisie is astonished."

When Aaron and Roland had put the photographs away, the three of us walked back into the main gallery space.

"Are you and Noah Goldowsky related?" I asked Aaron.

"Not directly -- we're both New York Jews -- Russian immigrant parents. We're not family but we've been friends since before you kids were born. Noah used to be in the rare book business in New York."

"And now you're both in Chicago," Roland mused.

"Noah's heart's in New York. Wouldn't surprise me if he packed up and moved back any day now. You watch and see," Aaron laughed as Noah came to join us. Another cigarette, tipped by another perilous ash, was in the corner of his mouth. The gallery had grown less crowded. Groups of visitors came to say goodbye to Noah.

"We'll call you," several said. Perhaps they were the new owners of the red dot paintings.

"Ricardo's?" Noah asked Aaron.

"Sure-- that's a nice place. Can we take these two along? They could use a good Italian meal."

As Noah gave Roland and me a noncommittal glance, Aaron added, "They're part of Paul Carroll's crowd -- *Chicago Review, Big Table.*"

"That right?" Noah asked. "Would you like to join us? A few other people are coming too."

"Thank you; that's very nice of you -- thanks. I hope you were happy with the opening; there were a lot of people," I said to Noah.

"Mmm -- lots of lookers, couple of serious buyers -- the reviewer from the *Tribune* -- the usual," he answered.

Despite their physical resemblance, I saw that Noah Goldowsky and Aaron Siskind were very different personalities. Aaron was a cheerful, extroverted artist; Noah was a thoughtful scholar and critic. I could easily imagine him presiding over a collection of rare books and manuscripts.

I felt drawn to both. It would be easy to chat with Aaron; his longtime friend, however, intimidated me more than a little.

At the restaurant -- an elegant establishment that Roland and I could never afford to frequent -- Noah was greeted enthusiastically by the maître d', and the party of eight or nine was seated without a moment's delay although the dining room seemed to be filled to capacity.

I introduced Roland and myself to the other guests, using our real names. I knew Noah had not believed in our fake aristocratic titles for a minute.

Noah was a generous host, ordering bottles of wine for the table, bourbon for himself and Aaron, and whatever other predinner drinks were wanted. Aaron kept the conversation moving at a lively pace, talking about his projects at the Illinois Institute of Design, where he was teaching, and about the new generation of artists emerging in New York. Noah was engaged with the other guests, but he seemed to listen with half an ear to Aaron, who was asking questions about the *Review* and about Roland's and my current activities.

"Are you an artist?" Aaron asked Roland.

"Not really -- bookbinding and carpentry's what I'm doing right now," Roland answered.

Aaron turned to me and asked, "And you? Still a student or what?"

"I got my B.A. a year ago and then I spent some time away from Chicago," I said. "I'm back now -- I'm helping my mother in her import store, but I'm going to need something that pays a salary soon."

"Maybe I can help you. Or Noah -- he knows the corporate types -- the capitalists, you know."

Before dinner was over, Roland had written the address and telephone number of the coach house on the inside of a matchbook cover for Aaron, and Aaron had invited himself to visit us.

I thanked Noah for including us in his dinner party. "The food was delicious," I said. And much success with the show -- it's off to a good start, don't you think?"

"Thanks. We'll see -- he's a good painter," Noah said. "Come back for Aaron's opening."

"Definitely! That will be great," I said. Noah's serious expression gave way to a smile -- the first I had seen. There was a spark in his brown eyes; he had square, even, white teeth without a nicotine stain on them. Considering how much he smoked, that was a miracle.

We did not have to wait long for Aaron's visit. He arrived less than a week after the preview at the gallery, bearing a shopping bag filled with cheese, salami, bread, and a bottle of bourbon.

"A picnic for the refugees," he declared, looking at the bare brick walls, the kitchen table consisting of two sawhorses and a wooden door Roland had picked from a pile of construction debris, and the low couch with its legs made of aluminum tubing.

"They don't know from bagels in this town," Aaron said. "I got Jewish rye; best I could do."

"Wow! A CARE package!" I said. "Thank you!"

Aaron looked insulted. "Whadda ya mean? It's better than a stupid CARE package -- it's real food, no dried-up powdered stuff!"

"Oh no," I apologized. "You don't know what packages meant to us in Germany, when we didn't have anything but potatoes and turnips. A package was a wonderful and exciting event -- real food like eggs and milk, even if it was powdered. My aunt even sent us coffee beans and our mom was so happy she cried. I didn't mean to criticize. It's a beautiful picnic!"

"I see," Aaron said in a changed voice as he came close and gave me a hug. "Tell me about those times. But pour us a drink first and sit down on that -- what do you call that thing -- *deevaahn* -- next to me."

Roland poured drinks, unwrapped the food Aaron had brought, set it on a large metal tray, and put the tray on the floor in front of the couch -- which I resolved to call by its new name from then on. "Divan" was a word full of oriental splendor.

"You said picnic. Thanks -- this is perfect," Roland said.

I told our story to Aaron, beginning with the day the Americans marched through Dachau and the weeks afterward when we were given Hershey bars by Prima Prima and delousing powder and typhus shots by the army medics.

"I was a little kid," Roland added. "But I remember the big black guy and when the soldiers let me sit inside a tank and Mom couldn't find me and got the whole town to look for me."

"We finally saw his head pop out of the turret," I said. "Our poor mother thought he'd been kidnapped."

"My parents got out of Russia to escape the pogroms and the Cossacks," Aaron said. "The lower East Side wasn't heaven, but it was America. A free country."

I talked on, answering Aaron's questions about our family in Germany and in Chicago. I asked Roland to make coffee and drank two cups. Aaron and Roland smoked while my story went on. I had never talked so much at one time.

After more than an hour of sitting side by side on the couch, all three of us felt ourselves gently sliding forward and down as the front legs of the divan slowly crumpled.

Scheherazade, her bottom now resting on the bare wooden floor, concluded her tale for the night. "I'll tell you the rest next time," she said. "It's cold down here."

Roland repaired the divan by pushing cement blocks under the frame. Aaron visited again and asked me why he had not met me before.

"I've spent some time out of town," I said and talked about Washington, D.C., and the White House press corps and the difficulty in finding work in the news business. I did not mention Sam or our relationship.

"Well, now that you're back, I hope I get to see a lot of you," Aaron said. When Roland left the room for a minute, Aaron whispered, "Actually, I mean I want to do more than *see*, if y'know what I mean, sweetie. I want to *touch* -- you willing?"

I looked at this man whom I had known for all of three weeks. I liked his honest sensuality, his devil-may-care attitude; I was tempted. But wasn't it too soon? I felt disloyal to Sam.

To gain time, I said, "Aaron, they say you have a whole harem of girlfriends -- and aren't you married too?"

"Nah, I'm not married; not anymore. That didn't work out. And girls" -- it sounded like "goils" -- "sure, I like women. Young, pretty ones like you."

Aaron's laugh was irresistible. Sam was dead, I thought. Aaron was full of life. Wouldn't it be good to feel alive and joyous again?

"I'll think about it," I said as my brother came back into the room, interrupting a moment that was about to turn into a movie clinch. I mentally awarded Roland an Oscar for his perfect stagecraft.

Aaron's show of photographs at the Holland-Goldowsky Gallery opened in November, and Roland and I went to the preview.

I had borrowed a dress from the store. Remembering how elegantly dressed Noah Goldowsky and his customers had been at the last opening, I wanted to abandon beatnik threads for the occasion. Mother had suggested a black, sleeveless sheath topped by a white, short-sleeved jacket. "I'll lend you my pearls," she had said. "They're real -- no plastic beads at a party like that!"

"You fit right in -- black and white," Roland said when we walked into the gallery.

"I didn't plan it; Mom's the expert -- black dresses for evening, she says. Like the ladies at Monte Carlo in the twenties when she was young."

The gallery was crowded and noisy, with Aaron's unmistakable laugh frequently cutting through the conversations.

"Stunning -- fabulous --" I heard Muriel, the blonde we had met at the last opening, exclaim.

"It *is* stunning! That's exactly the word for it," I replied, although the art collector had not been speaking to me directly. I did not expect her to remember me, but she gave a nod as if she did and said, "Noah has done it again -- and of course, he's known about Aaron Siskind for years and years."

"And are you speaking of the devil?" Aaron asked, coming up to us. "Here I am -- and here's my sweetie -- how are ya today, Beautiful?"

"Fine, thanks, Aaron; this is so impressive -- it's your work that's beautiful! I'm so glad to be here," I said.

"Thanks; happy you like it. Enjoy yourself-- go get a drink; say 'hi' to Noah on your way. You can thank him for putting up the show; it looks good--"

Aaron was interrupted by a couple who clapped him on the back and congratulated him. Aaron had called me beautiful and had given me a suggestive wink, but he had not remarked on my dress. That did not surprise me. His tweed jacket, like most of the clothes I had seen him wear, looked as if it had come from a thrift store; I knew that fashion was not one of his priorities. Roland and I moved on.

When we drew close to Noah Goldowsky, I caught a look on his face that made me glad I had chosen to wear something more traditional than my bell-bottom jeans. The skepticism -- almost disdain -- I had seen at our first meeting a month ago had been replaced by admiration.

"Good evening," he said. "Like the show? Have you talked to Aaron -- oh, sure you have -- I know you're friendly," Noah said, with a very slight emphasis on the last word. Did he know that Aaron was paying frequent visits to me and Roland?

Before I could reply, Noah added, "Nice pearls."

"Thank you; they're my mother's. I'm just borrowing them," I said.

"Nice," Noah repeated. "Should have your own -- suit you."

This man of few words was full of acute perceptions -- and some surprises as well. In my head, my mother said, "Still waters run deep."

When I next saw Aaron, he gave me a copy of his just-published book -- a handsome folio-size volume of photographs. He had inscribed it, "Barbara - Aaron - October 1959."

"Thank you, Aaron! Thank you -- I've never owned a book signed by the author," I said and kissed him.

"Aw, sweetie, it's nothin'. Read Rosenberg's introduction and you'll see he doesn't even know if photographs are supposed to be like paintings or if they're art in their own right."

"They're wonderful and they're art and I'll keep this book for the rest of my life. So says Barbara the art critic!"

"Aw, sweetie --"

It was November and the unheated coach house became almost impossible to live in. Roland and I slept in the loft, cocooned in goose down sleeping bags. We used his camping stove to warm our hands in the morning and turned on the gas stove full blast, leaving the oven door open and sitting directly in front of it to drink our coffee.

"Time for a new pad," Roland declared. "Help me hunt up an apartment. With heat!"

"I will -- and I'll also find a job, I promise. I can't ask Mom to pay me for working at Parkway; I don't think business is all that great there," I said.

The Old Town neighborhood was not yet gentrified, so we found an affordable rental in a brownstone on St. Paul Avenue within days. The apartment was on a high first floor. A flight of six or seven stone steps led up to a stoop and a massive wooden front door that was flanked by narrow panels of stained glass. Inside, a small foyer opened into a living room with an open kitchen area, a bedroom, and a bathroom. It was partially furnished. Most importantly, it had central heating!

We moved our scant possessions, using a rented U-Haul truck, but we had to leave the divan behind; it was too unwieldy, and the cement blocks were not only heavy but unsightly.

I answered an advertisement in the *Chicago Tribune* and was hired for a secretarial position by an accounting firm in the Loop. The job was temporary, I was told, but it might become permanent. A trusted employee had gone on sick leave; if she recovered, she would return, and I would have to look elsewhere. I agreed to start at the beginning of the coming week, at a salary that would allow me to contribute to the rent of our new apartment. After the interview, I went to the Woolworth's I remembered from Relaxacizor days and bought nylon stockings because you were not allowed to wear slacks at work. Not even pantsuits.

Roland was hired as a part-time bartender at the Gate of Horn, a nightclub that featured talented folk singers like Odetta.

"I'll keep on at the bindery during the week and do the Gate of Horn on weekends," Roland said. Neither one of us thought it strange that the bar was hiring a seventeen-year-old, when the legal drinking age was twenty-one. It never occurred to me to question his new position. Roland was so capable and mature; perhaps no one had asked his age.

On my twenty-third birthday, on November 11, 1959, I said to Roland, "You were right. My life isn't over. In fact, a lot of good things are happening right now and, I hope, will keep on happening."

"Happy Birthday, Sis," said my big brother who was younger than I was.

Aaron and I spent many evenings and nights together. He took me to parties. His show at the Holland-Goldowsky and his book -- the first collection of his photographs to be published -- were bringing his work to the attention of the city's art connoisseurs. Even though he had been working in his abstract style for more than a decade, Aaron had been better known as a teacher than as the creative innovator that he was. Gregarious by nature, he enjoyed the buzz, and I enjoyed watching him being petted by the society hostesses -- all of whom he called "sweetie." Noah Goldowsky -- invariably sporting a perfectly fitted dark suit, a white shirt, and a silk tie -- was a frequent guest at these gatherings. Anxious hosts and butlers stood by with ashtrays at the ready, but his cigarette never dropped an ash on his lapels.

Noah and Aaron talked as old friends; I was included in their conversations because I felt shy about mingling with the other guests on my own and stayed by Aaron's side. At first, Noah showed little curiosity about me, but, prodded by his jovial friend, he began to ask me about my family, my schooling, and my interests in literature. I asked him about his career in the book business. Noah said that it had been a great experience working with his partner, Walter Goldwater, and that he missed New York.

One night, at a birthday party for a friend of his and Aaron's, Noah asked me to dance. I took his hand as we made our way to the crowded middle of the room. I did not know how to dance, but the slow shuffle the couples were doing did not look as difficult as the Viennese waltz my mother had tried -- and failed -- to teach me. I had drunk a glass of punch -- bourbon, vodka, gin, and whatever other alcoholic beverages the guests had brought, all muddled together with orange juice in a huge bowl. The drink had made me feel giddy and relaxed. I leaned into Noah's embrace.

The music was provided by a long-playing record; there were no breaks between songs. Some couples left the floor after one or two numbers; others stayed in place, swaying slightly to the slow tempos. Noah and I danced until the record came to an end -- and then until the record was turned over by the host and the music resumed. I concentrated on moving my feet backwards or sideways so that our feet would not land on top of each other's, accidentally. That would have signaled that I was a bumpkin who did not deserve this handsome man.

"Aaron is too old for you," Noah suddenly murmured into my ear. It was the first thing he had said since we had started to dance.

I moved my head back to ask, "What? Why? I don't think so!"

Noah tightened his embrace around my waist and moved his head so that our faces touched. I slid my left hand, which had been resting on his upper arm, around his back and snuggled into his chest. My heartbeat sped up to way beyond three-quarter time -- it felt like two hundred beats a minute. My cheeks were hot, but I was not uncomfortable. I wanted us to stay entwined like this forever.

"Come home with me," Noah whispered.

"Now?"

"Now -- sooner if you want to."

In the taxi, I felt wide awake -- not at all drunk or befuddled or even tired. I wanted to ask Noah a hundred questions. Why me? Whom you pretty much ignored so far? Why tonight -- when I was your friend's date? What did I do that was different from other times we've been in company together? Why do I feel this is so *right* when I hardly know you? How old is too old? How old is Aaron? How old are *you*?

I did not ask any of my questions because the driver would be listening. It was delicious to just sit next to Noah and keep still, listening to my new, double-quick heartbeat.

Noah's apartment, on Chestnut Street, was as elegant as his wardrobe. From the marble-floored foyer, to the living room with a huge Franz Kline painting on the wall and a bronze Giacometti sculpture standing next to the sleek, leather-upholstered couch, the space spoke of good taste applied with understated opulence. But we did not sit in the living room; Noah led the way to the bedroom, pausing briefly to point out the bathroom.

"I'm so happy here," I said as I took off my dress. "I'm not drunk; the punch was horrible."

"I didn't drag you against your will." Noah smiled.

"No!"

And that was the one and only time I said the word "no."

"It's Saturday. I have to go to work, but you take your time," Noah said in the morning. "Don't get up until I go out the door. I want to remember how you look in my bed."

I would have stayed for a week, or for the rest of my life, if he had asked me to. But I did not say anything. It was not time yet for such momentous questions. I knew what I would answer if and when he asked me.

I felt guilty towards Aaron and dreaded our next encounter. Aaron had never said a cross word to me. He had made me happy. Now I had caused him pain, and I felt deeply sorry for him.

Sorry, but not regretful. What I had done was right and inevitable. Was it fate? God's will? I did not believe in either, but I did not doubt my decision. I would have to face the consequences, explain, apologize -- whatever was necessary. I would have to call up all my good old German *Mut* and be brave.

But I wasn't. I went home to St. Paul Avenue and locked the door. When Roland came back from a morning errand, I asked him not to answer the phone no matter how many times it rang. I told him why.

"Aaron yelled at me for stealing his girl," Noah said to me on Sunday evening, when Roland had had enough of the telephone's shrilling and had finally answered it.

"There was no stealing. I came of my own free will," I said. "I'm sorry, though. I didn't mean to hurt him. I haven't talked to him yet -- I know I have to."

"He has no case," Noah said. "He shouldn't talk about stealing. Has he told you about Carolyn?"

"Carolyn?"

"She's leaving her husband to come live with Aaron; she has a kid," Noah said. "Don't let him yell at you."

I had always known that Aaron had more than one girlfriend and this hadn't bothered me. I had enjoyed our fling without feeling the need for an exclusive commitment. But Carolyn was news to me. A married woman and a child! That was serious. What would happen next?

The unavoidable meeting with Aaron came a few days later. He looked at me reproachfully, but he did not shout at me. I asked him about Carolyn. Yes, it was true, he said. She wanted to move into his apartment. Yes, probably with her seven-year-old daughter.

I asked Aaron if he and Noah were still friends. "I didn't mean to hurt either one of you," I said.

"Yeah, we're friends -- can't help it after all these years. But he shouldn't have stolen my goil!" Aaron started laughing and I couldn't help joining in.

Within a few short weeks, Aaron, Noah, Carolyn, and I and the rest of the art crowd were all as cordial to one another as we had been before. It was like living in a French novel -- Sartre or Simone de Beauvoir without the gloom.

We had entered the decade of the liberated sixties even before the New Year's holiday ushered in its official beginning.

CHAPTER 31

Dreams Come of Age

The 1960s began with new loves and changed relationships that would lead to my family's geographical separation.

In the early spring of 1960, Mother and her friend Ernst were married. Ernst had retired from his grocery business, but Mother still ran Parkway Sweater Import. She had moved into Ernst's apartment on the North Side.

Roland and his girlfriend, Jutta, parted amicably. Jutta had met a man who wanted to marry her and take her to California, where he had family.

"She wants babies," my brother explained. "I'm not ready for that and she understands. I'm happy for her."

Noah Goldowsky and I spent a great deal of time together. It was a happy, compatible relationship even though our ages and backgrounds were very different. Noah was fifty years old and I was twenty-three. He was the son of Jewish immigrants; I had German parents. I didn't know if my birth father had been a Jew. I told Noah what my mother had related about my being a love child.

"I never loved my stepfather, but I love Roland with all my heart," I said. "It makes no difference that we had different fathers."

I knew from Aaron that Noah's marriage had recently ended in divorce. I asked Noah to tell me more.

"Lola had a child by a previous marriage," Noah said. "I adopted the boy and raised him as my own; he's almost eighteen now and he wants to take his birth name back. He wrote me a beautiful letter to let me know that it isn't anything negative -- he thinks of me as his father. It's about his identity. I wrote back to say I'm with him, whatever name he wants to go by."

"Will I get to meet your son?" I asked.

"Sure. When he finishes his semester at college," Noah said. "He's a very fine person. But I wish I could have had a son of my own, with my name."

I looked into Noah's serious dark eyes and felt love wash over me.

"We can have sons," I said. "But there might be daughters too."

For the first time in my life, I thought that a child was something to be not dreaded but welcomed. I thought about my high school friend Lois and the baby that I had considered a mistake, but that Lois had valued as a wondrous blessing. I remembered my mother saying that she had never regretted her choice to bring me into the world, and that I was her beloved love child. Now *I* wanted a child. I was surprised at myself.

Noah took my hands, but he did not say any more. I knew that this quiet, reserved man needed time to get to know me. Still, I felt that I had crossed another threshold.

"How much do you know about Jews?" Noah asked on another occasion.

"I never met a Jewish person until I came to Chicago and went to school," I told him, adding that before the war, my mother had had Jewish friends in Germany and that she was a staunch anti-Nazi.

"My family lives in New York. My mother is dead, but I want my father to meet you; I've invited him to visit," Noah said.

"I'll like that," I said, feeling both curious and nervous. I thought a meeting was important because I did not want my German birth to be an obstacle in our deepening relationship.

Before Morris Goldowsky's visit, I brought my mother to meet Noah in his element. I could tell that she was impressed by the elegant gallery and its well-dressed proprietor. Noah was gracious but not talkative; he let Mother lead the conversation, which she cheerfully did, relating anecdotes about her many artist friends in Munich, and about Lincoln, who now lived and worked in Chicago.

"Some day Barbara will show you the portrait Henri Niestlé did before we left Germany," Mother said. "He is well known in Europe."

As if I were preparing for a final exam, I studied a book Noah had given me -- *Life Is with People: The Culture of the Shtetl,* by Elizabeth Herzog and Mark Zebrowski. By the time Noah's father came to Chicago, I had learned a great deal about the history of Eastern European Jews, and I felt a bit less intimidated by the visit.

Morris Goldowsky, then in his seventies but without a single grey hair in the dark curls that were exactly like Noah's, had been sent to Siberia by the Czar for fighting in the Russian revolution of 1905 but had been able to escape and make his way to America. In New York, he had been a labor activist who had helped to organize the Amalgamated Clothing and Textile Workers' Union. In 1925, he had been elected an alderman on the Social Democratic ticket. I listened, spellbound, to his life story and asked him to tell me about his eldest son, Noah, and about Noah's ex-wife. To my delight, Morris filled the week of his visit with fascinating tales. The questions he asked me moved swiftly from the general -- where was I born, where was my brother born, what was our religion -- to the personal.

"If you and Noah get married," Morris asked, "you will bear him children?"

"I want to," I said, trying not to blush. "Noah and I talked about it; I would like to have a child."

"Is *gut*," the formidable elder smiled. I felt I had passed the test.

In April 1960, I made an appointment at the downtown office of the Immigration and Naturalization Service. It was not far from my workplace on LaSalle Street, so I asked for an afternoon off in order to go and apply for American citizenship. I had expected to stand in line with other applicants, but when I arrived at the bureau, I seemed to be the only candidate. An unsmiling official who sat behind a desk at the far end of the large room beckoned me to come close so that he could hand me a form.

"Do you speak English?" he asked.

"Yes, sir," I replied, having remembered just in time not to sound huffy and not to mention that I had a degree from the University of Chicago.

"Fill this out; you'll have to swear to the answers," the examiner said.

I sat down to answer the questions. I affirmed that I was not and never had been a communist, and that I would not seek to overthrow the American government. I promised to bear arms for the United States if required to do so. I noted that I understood that I could be deported for giving false information, for seditious activities, or for moral turpitude -- which was not further defined.

"Do you write English?" the examiner asked.

"Yes, I do."

"Well, write something. Here, on the bottom line of the form," the official commanded.

I asked, "What shall I write?"

"Write, 'I like the United States.'"

I wrote the phrase and added an exclamation mark. I took the oath. I hoped and wished for a friendly word of welcome to my new country, but there was none.

A week later I received my naturalization certificate in the mail. I showed it to my mother and to my brother; I showed it to Noah and to Aaron; I would have liked to frame it and hang it on a wall. But the precious document had to be kept private and safe.

Another dream had come true. I was an American citizen and I would be able to vote for John F. Kennedy in the presidential election in November -- and I would be able to vote in every election from then on.

I told Noah that my job at the accounting firm was about to end; the secretary who had been on leave had returned. Noah introduced me to his friend Jim Somers. "He and his partner are headhunters," Noah said.

I thought of Karl May's adventure stories and wondered if Jim and his partner went to their office clad in leopard skins.

"Management consultants," Noah explained when he saw my puzzled look.

The headhunters hired me and agreed to pay me a salary that was almost twice as much as I had been earning. I bought a pair of high-heeled shoes in honor of my new position as office manager.

Roland and I still lived in the apartment on St. Paul Avenue, but I was spending most weekends with Noah. On Sunday mornings, Noah and Jim were in the habit of eating brunch and reading the Sunday *New York Times* together. Noah began to take me along to Jim's apartment, which was in one of the new glass-and-steel high-rise buildings designed by Mies van der Rohe, on Lake Shore Drive. I loved the view of Lake Michigan from Jim's huge living room. Walking towards the east wall that was all windows felt like stepping out into space, with no balcony or terrace between me and the blue expanse of the lake. On Sunday mornings, I called my boss by his first name. On Monday mornings, I called him Mr. Somers.

One weekday, I returned to the office early from the coffee shop where I usually ate lunch and sat at my desk reading *Lolita;* I had fallen in love with Nabokov's prose at first sight

Jim's partner walked by my desk on his way to the restroom.

"Don't read that filthy book in public! Ugh! Just looking at it makes me want to take a shower," he snapped.

I looked up at my boss's red face, surprised by his vehemence. The partners had always been polite and pleasant in their dealings with me.

"It's literature," I mumbled and quickly slipped the book into my desk drawer.

The next day I brought in a copy of *Ladies' Home Journal* and hid *Lolita* inside its unimpeachable pages.

In July, Noah wanted me to come with him to visit Martha's Vineyard, where friends of his from New York owned summer homes.

"You'll have to put in a good word with my employers," I said. "I really would love to go, but secretaries don't get vacation time in the middle of the summer -- that's for executives."

"You're right; I'll talk to Jim," Noah said, and on the following weekend, we flew to New York so that Noah could visit with artists and gallery owners he knew before continuing our trip by car.

"When are you moving back here?" was the most frequently asked question.

"I'm thinking about it," Noah replied.

I wondered how soon Noah would make a decision and what would happen to his gallery; as for me, I would be more than happy to live in New York, which was becoming the new art capital of the world.

Noah rented a car and we drove to Falmouth, Massachusetts, from where we would take a ferry to the island. The landscape of the East Coast was new to me; I enjoyed the views and the clean-smelling summer air. Having stopped several times to stretch our legs and eat a snack at a roadside restaurant, we reached Falmouth so late in the evening that we missed the last boat of the day. Noah drove through the town, looking for a place to spend the night. Every motel we passed flashed a red neon "No Vacancy" sign at us. When we failed to spot any rooms to rent, Noah pulled into the parking lot of the town police station.

"Maybe they know something," Noah said. "After all, they won't want us sleeping on a park bench like vagrants."

I laughed, admiring this practical approach to our dilemma.

"Every place is full at this time of the year," the police chief said. "But," he added after a moment's thought, "we've got a spare room at my house; the missus won't mind putting you up for the night. You aren't the first tourists she's helped out."

"Don't tell them we're not married," I whispered to Noah when we were snuggled under the quilt in the chief's guestroom. "They can deport me for moral turpitude, you know!"

On Martha's Vineyard, Noah's friends welcomed me pleasantly and asked how I liked the ocean. Was the Atlantic colder than Lake Michigan?

"I'm used to cold, but the waves are so big," I answered. "This is the first time in my life I've actually *stepped* into the ocean. The only other time I saw it, I was on a ship, horribly seasick. At that time, I never wanted to go near the Atlantic again."

I enjoyed other firsts on Martha's Vineyard, such as using nutcrackers and hammers to get at the delicious flesh of freshly cooked lobsters, collecting clamshells of various sizes, and sitting on the cooling sand to watch the red sun sink into the darkening sea.

Back in Chicago, the rest of the year brought more changes to my family. Roland had met a young woman named Barbara, a graduate student of library science who worked as a cocktail waitress at the Gate of Horn, where Roland was tending bar.

"We're meant for each other," my brother told me. "It sounds corny, but we *know.* And we're both tired of Chicago, so next year we're heading for Frisco. You won't feel I'm walking out on you, will you, Sis?"

"I want you to be happy. I'll miss you, but if you and your Barbara are sure about what you want, you should go," I said. "Why San Francisco?"

"All the hip people seem to be out there -- Irv Rosenthal, for one; and I'd like to see the City Lights Bookshop. If Barbara wants to finish working on her degree, she can do it there. But first, we'll get married."

"Congratulations! Can I visit when you're settled?" I asked.

"Sure. Bring Noah if *you're* married."

In November, I cast my first vote as a citizen, and I celebrated my twenty-fourth birthday with three different parties. My mother and Ernst invited me to dinner at their apartment; Roland bought me champagne at the Gate of Horn; Noah took me to Ricardo's.

In December, Noah was approached by one of his art clients with a proposition to buy a tract of undeveloped land in Albuquerque,

New Mexico. The parcel was to be made into a golf course surrounded by one-family houses. The client promised big returns on investments because, he assured Noah, vacation homes in the Southwest were becoming popular, especially with retirees seeking warm winter climates.

Noah agreed to look over the land and asked whether I wanted to travel to Albuquerque with him.

"Do you think Jim Somers will let me take time off again?" I asked.

"I'll speak to him," Noah said -- and I knew that soon I would be flying off to see another part of America.

In Albuquerque, I admired the view of the Sandia mountains in the brilliant sunshine and the Rio Grande River that flows through the town. A real estate broker showed us the land that Noah had come to see. Sandy lots were marked out with numbered wooden stakes and orange ribbons. The salesman pointed in various directions to show us where the golf course's fairways and clubhouse were to be built.

"It's all sagebrush and sand," Noah said when we had come back to our motel. "Who'd ever want to live here, retired or not? I don't; that's for sure!"

"I like Martha's Vineyard better, though the mountains are beautiful," I said.

At dinner that evening, Noah reached into his pocket, took out an envelope, opened it, and laid a turquoise and silver ring on the table. He handed me the ring.

"Made by a local Indian artist," he said. "Will you wear it as your engagement ring? I know it's not traditional, but I think it's right. Nothing about us is traditional -- do you agree?"

I looked at Noah. "I agree! Yes! Yes, to everything!"

"I've been introducing you as my fiancée all day; you didn't notice." Noah smiled.

"I *did* notice," I said. "But I thought you might be saying it, so we'd look proper in public."

"Well, now it's for real. Let's talk about the date when we get back home. I also want to start planning for our move to New York."

The ring fit my finger perfectly. "Yes, to that too," I said.

"Noah is much older than you. But he is a successful businessman and he will provide for you," my mother said when I told her of our engagement. I hugged her; it made me happy to have her blessing.

When Roland and Barbara left for San Francisco in January 1961, Noah invited me to move into his apartment on Chestnut Street. It was an easy transition because I had been spending most of my time there anyway. I owned no furniture; moving my clothes and books was an easy task. I was excited about entering a new stage of my life, but I knew I would miss my brother, who had shared my life ever since he was born.

Noah and I were married on June 9, 1961, in the living room of the apartment. My mother and Ernst, Jim Somers and his fiancée, Linda, were our witnesses. A business friend of Noah's, who was a Unitarian minister, officiated. My ring was a traditional gold band. After champagne and canapés, Noah and I took a taxi to the airport and flew to New York for a weekend honeymoon.

Noah and his business partner negotiated a buyout agreement that allowed the partner to keep the gallery space, which would be renamed the B.C. Holland Gallery. The agreement stipulated that Noah was not to open a competing art business in Chicago for a number of years.

"All the more reason to move to New York," Noah said. "It's where I belong. My family's there. You've met my father and you'll like my brothers. Their name is Gale; they changed it to sound more American. The army changed mine too, but I went to court when I came out and took my name back."

"I didn't know the army could just change your name. Is that legal?"

Noah laughed. "It's the army. It was too hard for them to spell and they said nobody's named Noah either -- they made me Nathan!"

"I'm happy to be a Goldowsky," I said.

By September, I knew I was pregnant; my family doctor confirmed it and referred me to an obstetrician. Noah gave me a look that clearly said a dream had come true. He was instantly solicitous.

"Quit going to the office. You really didn't have to keep working at all, you know. Be very careful. Are you sure this doctor is the best? I want to go meet him," he said all in one breath. I had never seen him flustered.

"I stayed on because I'm not used to being idle. We eat out a lot and you like your wash done by the Chinese laundry; the cleaning woman comes once a week. There's not much for me to do. But right now, I think staying home will be wonderful. I'm so sleepy all the time," I said and yawned.

For my birthday in November Noah gave me a double strand of baroque pearls with a gold filigree clasp. I remembered wearing my mother's pearls on one of my first visits to the Holland-Goldowsky Gallery. That day Noah had said, "Pearls suit you." And now he had found the most beautiful necklace in the world for me!

The pregnancy would not change our plan for moving to New York, Noah and I decided. The doctor was consulted and agreed that as long as I did not lift or carry any heavy objects, I would be fit for travel.

"After all, it's easier to take a trip before the baby's born," the doctor joked. "It can't run away from you and get in trouble."

Noah seemed relieved by the medical expert's reassurance; I had not given any thought to possible difficulties since I had gotten over my morning sickness. I felt young and strong enough to move mountains. But I knew that I wouldn't be allowed to pick up anything heavier than a teapot.

An apartment in Manhattan became available in December, and Noah sent a deposit to secure the rental. It was a two-bedroom apartment on the sixteenth floor of a high-rise building on East Sixty-third Street and First Avenue. I had never lived on a high floor and when Noah mentioned that there was a terrace, I remembered Bertram the cat sunning himself in Washington, D.C.

I had told Noah much of my life story and I had mentioned Sam as a friend and mentor. I had never talked about the balcony on Massachusetts Avenue.

In January 1962, I said goodbye to my mother and Ernst.

"Go with God, *Kind,*" she said. She had to stand on one side of me to embrace me because my belly was so big. I was in my seventh month of pregnancy.

CHAPTER 32

New Life

The bright, spacious apartment on New York's East Side was so different from any place I had lived before that at first I felt like a tourist in a hotel. I was not used to taking an elevator every time I wanted to step outside, exploring my new neighborhood, and walking along Sixty-third Street to Lexington Avenue, where I found interesting delicatessens, coffee shops, clothing boutiques, and bookstores.

Noah's father was one of our first visitors; he cautioned me not to lift any of the cartons that were stacked in the foyer, waiting to be unpacked.

"Keep the baby safe -- it's very important," he urged.

Noah's brother Joe, an accountant, arranged a family dinner at his home in Great Neck, Long Island, so that I could meet his wife and their three sons as well as Noah's younger brother and sister and their families. I was glad when they received me warmly and congratulated me on the coming addition to the family. Someone asked if I wanted to raise the baby in the Christian faith.

"I'm not much of a Christian," I answered. "I believe in doing what's right without going to church. I've married into this Jewish family and I believe the baby should learn about your faith and traditions -- and about other religions too."

"Passover is in April," Morris said. "We always have a Seder; you'll come? Will the little one be born by then?"

"March fourth -- I think -- is the due date," I answered. "If all goes well, we should make it. Thank you, everybody!"

One of my first errands in Manhattan had been to see an obstetrician who practiced at Mount Sinai Hospital. When the doctor had examined me and had found nothing amiss, I explained that I had read about the Lamaze method of natural childbirth and wanted to sign up for classes. The physician looked skeptical.

"Husbands are supposed to come to the classes too. Have you talked it over?" he asked. Having husbands present to help their wives in the delivery room was a fairly new idea in the early 1960s.

"Yes," I answered. "We've talked. May I have the schedule?" I did not know how enthusiastic Noah was about the Lamaze idea, but I hoped he would agree to the course.

That evening, when I had told Noah about my visit to the hospital, he again showed his nontraditional side; without hesitation, he said yes to the classes.

And when our baby was born--two weeks after his due date -- in the early hours of March 20, 1962, Noah was in the delivery room with me, telling me to breathe and pant as we had learned. I laughed when the nurses repeatedly asked, "Are you all right, sir?"

It was a boy, as my mother had foretold. "We're going to name him Alexander," Noah announced to the delivery team.

"That's a good name for this healthy child. In fact, it's not just good -- it's great," the nurse, who had just swaddled the baby in a white blanket, said, chuckling.

"Your husband was ecstatic; he was dancing on the sidewalk. I saw him when I left the building," the doctor told me later that day.

"Your life will never be the same; everything changes when you have the responsibility of raising a child," the pediatrician said on our first visit. He was right. My life became that of a wife and mother, and I was enthralled by it. But it was a very different life from the future I had envisioned when I had set out to become an intrepid international wire service reporter. The happiness of two other beings was now intertwined with mine. One was the husband I loved; the other was a tiny human whom I nursed and diapered and cuddled and adored.

Noah's father understood that I felt too sleep deprived to come to that year's Seder, but we would attend all the ones in subsequent years.

While he was looking for a commercial space, Noah hung paintings in our living room and conducted his art business from home. Within a few months he opened the Noah Goldowsky Gallery on Madison Avenue, between Eighty-first and Eighty-second Streets. Noah's artist and literary friends were happy to have him back in New York. Soon, we had congenial visitors to our home and the gallery began to receive favorable critical notices for its shows of nineteenth and twentieth-century American masters.

At the same time, Noah's eye for innovative art remained as sharp as ever. He had championed the Abstract Experessionists Willem DeKooning and Franz Kline, buying their work and financially supporting a gallery in New York that showed their work before it became a blue-chip investment. Now there were Pop artists, minimalists, and artists who shunned traditional materials in favor of scrap lumber, crushed car parts, or tubes of fluorescent lights.

The epicenter of the most radical new art was the Green Gallery on Fifty-seventh Street, where Dick Bellamy introduced the public to the soft sculptures of Claes Oldenburg, the monolithic sculptures of Donald Judd, and to the oversized cartoons painted by Roy Lichtenstein. Noah knew Bellamy from previous visits to New York and introduced me to the tall, thin, somewhat enigmatic young man who wore large, thick eyeglasses. Noah and Dick laughed together at the most frequently asked question at the Green Gallery: "But is it art?"

My mother was delighted to have a grandchild and mentioned how nice it would be if she could live nearby to help me take care of the infant. I could almost hear her form plans in her mind; her tone of voice clearly said that she would make them happen. I wondered how she could convince her husband to move from the only American city he had ever lived in and what she would do with Parkway Sweater Import. But, knowing my mother, I felt confident that she would prevail. Ernst didn't stand a chance against her persuasive charm.

The art business in New York City practically closed down in the summer, so Noah and I and our baby spent June, July, and August in Provincetown, on Cape Cod. As Noah had predicted, we saw the same artists and socialized with the same collectors as we did in New

York City; the scene had simply shifted to the seashore. I loved going to the beach; I practiced jumping over or ducking under waves; I built sandcastles. I felt that I was living a childhood I had never had. Alexander went everywhere with me, cradled against my chest in a canvas sling. When people stopped to coo at the baby, Noah's smile made the brightest summer day even brighter.

In the fall of 1963, the lease on our sublet apartment was about to expire. With many new high-rise apartment buildings being constructed in Manhattan, there was no shortage of housing. In fact, landlords were making concessions such as giving a month's free rent or including utilities. Noah found an apartment on Madison Avenue and Eighty-third Street, two blocks from the gallery. In early November, we moved to a fourth-floor apartment in a prewar building that featured glass bricks surrounding the casement windows, central heating and air conditioning, and cork flooring in the apartments. I was impressed by the quiet luxury of our new home, by the shops on Madison Avenue, and by the grandeur of the Metropolitan Museum of Art on Fifth Avenue. The museum was only one block away! I planned to go there, and to the adjoining Central Park, often.

Noah took me to a rug dealer's emporium -- an Aladdin's cave full of Persian carpets -- to choose a rug for our living room. I would gladly have flown away on any of the colorful selections the dealer rolled out, but Noah's eye fell on a beige carpet with a central medallion of light green, blue, and red flowers.

"It is a Kerman," the dealer explained. "Hand-knotted by artisans in a small village. The carpet is of fine wool and the fringe is pure silk."

"We'll take it," Noah said. Looking at me, he asked, "You like it, don't you?"

"Oh, yes, I do! It's like a meadow," I said.

When the dealer named a price and Noah, without any haggling, took out his checkbook and wrote a number with three zeros after it, I could hardly believe my eyes. I resolved to never wear my street shoes when walking on this field of flowers.

On November 22, 1963, our apartment on Eighty-third Street was furnished, but we had not yet hung any paintings or connected our radio and phonograph equipment. We did not own a television. After lunch and Alexander's nap, I put my toddler into his stroller for our daily outing.

Downstairs, the usually chatty doorman sat in a corner of the lobby, staring at nothing; he did not say hello as we passed him. Perhaps he had a stomachache, I thought.

I turned the corner of Eighty-third Street and began to walk up Madison Avenue. It seemed very quiet. It was the butcher in the grocery store I frequented who told me the horrendous news: President Kennedy had been shot. He was dead. Lyndon Johnson had been sworn in as president on the airplane that returned from Dallas.

"It's a bad, bad world, missus," the butcher, who hailed from Belfast in the north of Ireland, said. "It's good your little tyke is too young to understand."

Noah was at home when we returned. He too had heard about the tragedy belatedly, when a relative had called him at the gallery. He had been too stunned to telephone me, but he had rushed out to purchase a portable radio. Now we joined the nation and the world in mourning the first American president I had voted for.

My mother arrived in New York in the early spring of the following year, without Ernst.

"I have a job in Scarsdale--do you know that village, very expensive? -- as a cook," she had told me on the phone before taking the plane. "Ernst will not move until we have a place to live -- near you, of course -- and we don't have the money to stay in hotels. The couple in Scarsdale have a big house, no children, and there is a housekeeper and a gardener. I get a room and private bath. The pay is excellent. I won't spend any of it. Good deal, you think?"

My mother would have made an excellent general, I thought. She had a plan and a strategy for carrying it out. She was establishing a beachhead. When the time came, she would advance her troops, and she would win.

She did. Shortly after we celebrated Alexander's second birthday, in March 1964, Mother and Ernst moved into an apartment on East Eighty-fifth Street, in the heart of Yorkville, the German-American neighborhood of Manhattan. Mother had collected an excellent reference from her Scarsdale employers and had taken a new job as a cook for a couple who lived on Park Avenue.

"They asked if I had any feelings against working for Jewish people," my mother told me. "I explained to them and I think they understand. The hours are good -- I go in time to make them lunch, then cook dinner and leave after cleaning up. I have Saturday and Sunday off -- plenty of time to babysit!"

"How does Ernst feel about New York?" I asked.

"He loves the stores. He goes shopping at *Deutsches Haus* and Paprikas Weiss, the Hungarian specialties place," Mother answered, smiling.

With my mother nearby as a reliable babysitter, I was free to enjoy the pleasures of city living with Noah. We went to the opera and to the ballet, to restaurants, and to concerts. A dressmaker fashioned a cocktail dress from my blue sari. As I had predicted, there was enough fabric for a matching stole; the outfit was much admired.

Noah was invited to every art show at every museum. We attended openings at the Metropolitan Museum's American Wing and the Guggenheim Museum. We watched Andy Warhol, the son of Slovakian immigrants, make dramatic entrances at parties where he became the center of the American art world's attention in a microsecond. With Dick Bellamy and his partner, Sheindi Tokayer, we went to the East Village to hear jazz performances by Ornette Coleman whose atonal improvisations were like an audible expression of the new artistic consciousness.

Collectors sought Noah's expert advice on the most important artists in an art world that was bursting with novel trends.

In 1963, we had begun to spend our summers in East Hampton, Long Island, instead of in Provincetown. I loved the town of East Hampton from the first time we drove down its wide main street lined with elm trees, some of which, Noah told me, were three hundred years old. We would rent a house for the summer and visit with old and new friends as we enjoyed the miles of lovely beaches and trips to the fishing port of Montauk, at the eastern tip of Long Island's South Fork.

Noah introduced me to Willem DeKooning and, separately, to DeKooning's ex-wife Joan Ward and their daughter Lisa.

"When I didn't have money for food, Noah bought my paintings," DeKooning said to me. "And now I'm rich; I'm famous; the neighbors ask me to donate to their charity auctions. I don't; where were they when I offered them paintings in exchange for a sack of groceries?"

While the arts were flourishing, America was confronting its segregationist past. Students I had known at the University of Chicago had joined the Freedom Riders and other civil rights protesters and had braved angry mobs in the South. I had a two-year-old child; I could not take an active part. I sent donations to the NAACP and CORE--the Congress for Racial Equality. I used the checking account Noah had set up for me shortly after we were married. He had given me a sum of money with the stipulation that I visit his investment adviser and learn to invest in the stock market. I also had to read a book about finance; it was like doing homework, but I complied. I understood that Noah was giving me independence. Although I never became a Wall Street whiz, I valued the gift of knowledge.

While life in Manhattan and summers in East Hampton were idyllic, I could not help feeling uneasy about the war that was brewing in Vietnam. Since the early 1960s, American advisers had been present in South Vietnam and in March 1965, the first combat troops entered the country. I looked at my carefree little boy and wondered if his youth would be overshadowed by war, even though this conflict was far from American soil.

I worried about my brother, who was twenty-three, wondering if he would have to serve in the military. Roland and Barbara had settled in San Francisco and they had a new baby, a daughter, born in July 1965. When I talked with them on the telephone, Roland reassured me.

"The draft board hasn't found me. I guess I've had so many addresses that I got lost," he said. "And if they do find me, I'll get a deferment as a married man and the father of a young child. Don't worry, Sis."

I joined Women Strike for Peace, which opposed not only the United States involvement in Vietnam, but also the testing and proliferation of nuclear weapons.

"Where is the United Nations? Why can't they talk some sense into our leaders?" my mother lamented.

"I don't know. It seems to be up to the citizens," was all I could answer.

In 1965, the Green Gallery closed in the midst of a surging bull market for the new art. Dick Bellamy, a visionary when it came to choosing artists, was a failure as a businessman. In addition, Dick's personal life threatened to unravel as he battled addictions to alcohol and drugs. The collector who had supported the gallery had withdrawn his backing, fed up with the disheveled director who cared deeply about his artists but not at all about paying the phone bill.

Noah offered Dick the use of the small side room of the Goldowsky Gallery as a base and safe haven. The space was not much larger than a storage closet. A desk, a chair, and a filing cabinet were moved in. Dick Bellamy told friends that he was very proud to have "a proper office" at last. For the first year of their association, Noah asked for no rent, but Dick agreed to give Noah a cut on sales.

Noah and Dick's association would feature a stunning roster of artists over the next seven years. Dick brokered the first sale of one of Yoko Ono's conceptual vending machines; the sculptors Mark di Suvero, Walter De Maria, and Richard Serra were given a group show; Dan Flavin's fluorescent light tubes were installed. Works by Peter Young, who painted rows of penny-candy colored dots, and Milet Andrejevic, who portrayed contemporary patrons of art as ancient Greek mythological figures, passed through the gallery. All the while, Noah patiently tried to teach Dick Bellamy more prudent business practices, but Dick's lilies of the field nature remained unreceptive.

I had happy news for the family early in 1966: I was expecting again.

"That's wonderful," Noah said. "Is it another boy? But it doesn't matter -- as long as it's healthy." Ultrasonic imaging was years in the future.

"I can tell you," my mother said to me in private. "Lie down; give me your wedding ring and a long hair from your head."

"What's this-- gypsy fortune telling?" I laughed.

"Exactly! It never fails. You tie the ring to the hair -- like this -- and let the ring dangle above the belly. If the ring moves in a straight line, it means a boy; if it goes in a circle, it's a girl. There! See? It's moving up and down, straight -- see? It's a boy!"

"How do you know so much about gypsies?" I asked.

My mother looked sad. "They used to come to town," she said, "before Hitler put them in the concentration camps. There were some in Dachau. They never got out."

Boy or girl, we happily prepared for the child to come. The due date was in early August. Noah asked if we should rent a house in the Hamptons or if I preferred to have the baby at Mount Sinai Hospital.

"East Hampton, of course!" I said. "We can't keep Alexander from the beach. You know how much he loves the water. He'd never forgive us and worse, he'd hate his baby brother or sister for making us stay in the hot city. Southampton Hospital is just fine; we'll find an obstetrician as soon as we get there."

My mother liked her job and wanted to stay in Manhattan, and I knew that Ernst, who had no children, liked her undivided attention. Noah suggested hiring an *au pair,* and with his usual efficiency, he found an agency that in turn recommended a German art student who was fluent in English and who wanted to spend her summer in the U.S. We rented a four-bedroom house with a large yard in Amagansett, the village next to East Hampton.

Once again, I told myself that I was a lucky immigrant. But as I often did, I felt guilty about my luxurious life. I thought of the newspaper photos that showed fourteen-year-old boy soldiers the Viet Cong had recruited to fight and die in the jungle.

Our babysitter, named Barbara, arrived at the end of May and we took her with us when we moved into our rental in Amagansett. Barbara-Babysitter, as we decided to call her, was a tall, athletic young woman. Her hometown was in central Germany, far from the North Sea. She was as excited by her first step into the Atlantic Ocean as I had been. She had learned to swim in lakes and rivers and was a strong swimmer; she quickly learned to deal with waves and surf well enough so that I could trust her with my energetic four-year-old who regarded water as his proper element. While I could have built sandcastles all afternoon, Alexander wanted as little time on the shore as possible, even when he had turned blue and shivery with cold.

"Alexander's mom has a watermelon under her bathing suit," a young playmate of my son's observed. As I grew larger and heavier, I preferred the quieter waters of East Hampton's beaches on Gardiner's Bay. It was bliss to float, weightless, with warm sun as well as a cooling breeze on my face.

I had been floating like that on the afternoon of August 1, 1966. I still had a few grains of sand between my toes when I arrived at Southampton Hospital in the early hours of August second. Noah had driven me, at record speed, because my water had broken, and I had experienced a contraction or two.

"Hold on," Noah pleaded. "Let me get you inside before you push."

As it turned out, we had several hours before our second son was born.

"Healthy and strong," the doctor assured us. "I want a photo of him as soon as you get a chance. I collect pictures of all the babies I've delivered; it's my art gallery!"

Alexander Goldowsky welcomed his brother Boris four days later, when I was released from the hospital. In those days, new mothers were not sent home the day after giving birth.

Alexander had made a mobile of pencils and brightly colored paper squares to hang over the baby's crib.

"Barbara-Babysitter says he can only look at them now. When he's older, he can draw," Boris's big brother explained.

Dazed with happiness, I looked at my two boys. Their eyes were brown, like Noah's. I wondered when Alexander's blond curls would darken, and when the black fuzz on Boris's head would grow into curls. Like the wicked fairy in the tale of Sleeping Beauty, a nagging voice at the back of my mind asked if the war would be over before my sons were eighteen. The *New York Times* had recently reported that there were 400,000 American troops in Vietnam.

When the family returned to Manhattan in September, I joined Another Mother for Peace -- the organization founded by New York's colorful, outspoken congresswoman, Bella Abzug.

My mother was delighted with Boris, and she sewed a plush blanket for his baby carriage. Sensing that Alexander might be jealous, she created one especially for him.

Walter De Maria, who had visited us in Amagansett just before Boris's birth, gave Boris a delicate pencil drawing that illustrated a prose poem: "There once was a boy named Boris / he played, and he grew up..."

When we strolled through Central Park on our way to the children's zoo, Noah always wanted to be the one pushing Boris's carriage and holding Alexander by the hand.

Noah's father visited and sang Jewish folk songs to the children.

"Be sure and bring the boys to every family dinner, even if we go to a restaurant," he instructed me. "Don't leave them with a babysitter-- we want to enjoy them, now that Noah and you finally gave me grandchildren."

"They are very lucky children," I said. "They have a big, loving family; I can't imagine anything more wonderful."

I thought of my mother and the father who had loved me but had left me before I was born, and about the stepfather who had not loved me. I had been happy to leave him in Germany; I was glad that my children would grow up as Americans, with a father who loved them, and was there every day to cherish their American lives.

CHAPTER 33

House and Home

"Now that we have two kids, we should buy a house in East Hampton. That way, you wouldn't need a moving truck to bring out their gear every summer -- not to mention bringing it back, with all the rocks and seashells they collected added to the rest of the stuff," Noah said.

"Not a whole truck. The moving company lets you send a partial load -- if that costs too much, I'll try to cut down on what we take," I answered.

"Don't worry about that. What I'm thinking is a house -- a proper house, where we can be sure the water pump works, and the cesspool doesn't overflow once a season. Wouldn't you like a place we can use not only in the summer, but for weekends all year round?"

I laughed because the disasters Noah had mentioned were not hypothetical; they had happened, and at the most inconvenient times, like the Fourth of July weekend.

"A house! It would be wonderful! The boys could have their own rooms to keep their toys in, and I could buy a coffee maker and some sharp knives for the kitchen. The rentals never have any -- I think they lock up their good ones. I love the idea of a house," I said, "But doesn't it cost a ton of money?"

"Real estate in the Hamptons is a good investment. I'll look into it."

I admired my husband's business acumen. If he thought a house was a good plan, I was sure he was right. I asked him to go to East Hampton without me and to choose a second home for us.

"I don't know the first thing about real estate," I said. "I wouldn't know how to decide between offers. We'd be there for months."

In the early summer of 1968, we took possession of a ranch-style house on a lovely, tree-lined, residential street called Mill Hill Lane, in East Hampton. The house had three large bedrooms, three bathrooms, an L-shaped living room with a fireplace, a large kitchen, and an attached two-car garage. The finished basement had been divided into a laundry room and an open area in which a ping-pong table elicited whoops of joy from the boys. The house had belonged to a local furniture dealer; Noah had bought it fully furnished with American colonial-style tables, chairs, and bureaus, some of which have survived to this day. The lawns in the front and at the back of the house were perfectly groomed and surrounded by a split-rail fence.

"Are we going to live here all the time now?" six-year-old Alexander asked. "I want to!"

I felt the same way, much as I loved our city apartment, the museums, and rambles in Central Park. The grass on Mill Hill Lane must have been mowed just that morning. It breathed out a heavenly smell. And it was a shiny, rich shade of green that was definitely greener than anything in a city park. Much greener.

"Main Beach is about a mile thataway," Noah said, pointing southwards.

"It's heaven. It's magic," I said, remembering the German folk tale about the little   table that appears, fully set with luscious dishes, when the magic words are spoken. Noah had said "house" -- and here it was.

"Magic and a little cash," my practical husband remarked, making me laugh, because there was nothing *little* about this property.

We spent a contented summer in our new home, making friends with the neighbors, relaxing at the beach, and inviting local artists to visit. Alexander was enrolled in a day camp in Montauk, where he easily passed the swimming test, and was introduced to sailing and tetherball, and to eating ice cream every afternoon while the campers waited for their parents to collect them. The whole family learned to play mini golf at a small course adjacent to a gas station on Montauk

Highway, the main road between East Hampton and the villages to the east.

In September, Alexander entered the first grade at P.S. 6, a public school on Madison Avenue, two blocks from our city apartment. Two days into the term, a citywide teachers' strike shut down the entire New York City school system. According to the news, no agreement between the teachers' union and the school board was in sight; parents were advised to find alternative ways to educate their children.

Alexander proposed going to the Natural History Museum or the Hayden Planetarium every day, and I believed him when he said that he would be happier there than in any school. He had been troubled and unruly in kindergarten and at first, I had not understood why. After consulting our family physician and a testing specialist she recommended, Noah and I had learned that Alexander's IQ was in the near-genius range, and that his hearing and his vision were excellent. Why had his Kindergarten teacher called him "slow"? Why had the headmistress of the nursery school told me to enroll him in a school for "the retarded"?

I could find only partial answers. Alexander had difficulty learning to read. When he tried to write words, the letters were often reversed or upside down. I was reminded of Roland's problems; I worried that my bright, intellectually curious son would fall behind in school. As it turned out, the teachers' strike became a blessing in disguise. A neighbor, who had also planned on P.S. 6, called me to say she had found a new private school that was accepting students.

"They're actually *looking* for kids," she said. "Not like Dalton and the others that are impossible to get into now. You should go talk to them right away."

I told Noah. "Make an appointment; take your checkbook; sign up if you can," he advised. And so, I found the Earl Kelley School and its headmistress, Eileen Nelson, who assured me that my son would be in good hands. She asked no questions about his reading readiness. Within a week of Alexander's enrollment, Mrs. Nelson called me in for a conference and told me about a condition called dyslexia.

"It's not surprising that you don't know about this learning disability; few people do," she said. "But the kindergarten teacher should have known. Children's lives can be ruined by such ignorance and indifference. It makes me furious. But don't despair. I'm a specialist in this. You have not heard of the Orton Society, I'm sure, but I trained with them and I assure you Alexander will catch up."

I burst into tears of relief and gratitude. It would take time, but Alexander did overcome his reading difficulty, though spelling remained a challenge, as it had for Roland. Mrs. Nelson did not live to see it, but Alexander went on to earn a doctorate in education from Harvard University.

When the 1968 teachers' strike finally ended, I felt thankful. The hardship it had caused many families was over, and I was grateful for the neighborly phone call that had steered me to the Earl Kelley School. Thanks to Mrs. Nelson's specialized knowledge and individual attention from teachers, Alexander began to learn to read. He continued to do well during the rest of the school year.

In November 1968, Richard Nixon was elected president. He promised that his administration would begin efforts to wind down the Vietnam War by withdrawing troops. Antiwar groups waited for action but were disappointed. Young men were leaving the United States for Canada in order to avoid the draft as protests continued. When I took the children with me to join an antiwar march down Fifth Avenue, I told them that we would be participating in a "peace parade." I said that they were helping to bring about peace, by ending a dreadful war.

In 1969, we set out once again for our summer home in East Hampton, where I planned to start a vegetable garden in the backyard of our house. Noah had also agreed to converting half of the garage into a guest room and bath. These two projects made for a busy, happy summer for all of us, but the greatest excitement was supplied by NASA's Apollo Eleven mission, when astronaut Neil Armstrong set foot on the moon. We followed events on the radio and in the *New York Times,* which Noah bought every day at the stationery store on Main Street. Alexander asked me to help him send for autographed photos of the three astronauts, and I was almost as pleased as he was when the color pictures arrived in due time. I had not believed that a large government organization like NASA would respond to a child's request. In my mind, our letter had been like writing to Santa Claus.

When the guest suite in the remodeled garage was finished in mid-August, my mother and Ernst came to join us until Labor Day.

"So cozy," my mother said. "All it needs is a wood burning stove for the colder nights. We'll buy one -- I like those Swedish ones -- and pay for installing it. That will make it even more perfect."

"We can do that next summer," I said. "Then you can be comfortable no matter what the weather is."

Noah was not an athlete. He could not swim or ride a bicycle. His mother had discouraged him and his siblings from playing on the streets of the lower East Side because she feared for their safety, he explained. There had been no money in the immigrant household budget for bikes.

"Don't let that stop you from teaching them," Noah said to me. "I'll show them how to play chess."

Back in Manhattan, school started in September. Alexander rejoined his home room -- first and second grade combined -- and Boris entered the nursery school. With my mornings now free, I volunteered to help the director of the Earl Kelley School as her part-time secretary.

"That would be a big relief," Mrs. Nelson said. "I love to teach, and answering the phone takes time away from the students."

I had spotted a dusty mimeograph machine in the office, so I asked if an occasional newsletter would be of interest to parents and children.

"It would be marvelous," Mrs. Nelson answered. "Do you think you can make that thing work?"

I laughed, thinking back to my high school publication that chronicled the wins and losses of the bowling club.

"I have experience," I said.

In November, Boris's nursery schoolteacher asked me why our family did not own a television.

"It's the war," I said. "The news photos in the paper are horrifying; I haven't wanted the children exposed to Vietnam tragedies on TV."

"But you need to watch Sesame Street! It's wonderful. All the kids love it. It's educational. Boris will feel left out if he can't talk about it and sing the songs with the others. Watch it with your children; do *not* turn on the news."

I consulted Noah. "As long as the set isn't placed in the living room," he said.

"The living room is for music and books and conversation," I replied, "and you won't see any of those awful frozen dinners on trays, either!"

I found Sesame Street delightful and watched it with the children every day. Its companion program, The Electric Company, with its whimsical interpretations of the alphabet, particularly interested Alexander. A trench-coated, fedora-wearing character named "Fargo North, Decoder" became a family favorite. I wished my brother had had such creative help with reading and writing.

We did not become television addicts. We did watch Walter Cronkite's nightly news report on CBS, and we saw replays of the moon landing. Later, in 1974, when the Watergate scandal broke, the set would be on for far too many hours.

As we moved into the seventies, I enjoyed seeing the boys develop their own special interests, even though there were some frightening moments. Alexander was fascinated by fireworks and gunpowder. The four sons of our next-door neighbor in East Hampton owned cap pistols or toy rifles. I hated the idea of guns as toys. I forbade gun ownership in our home; Noah backed me up. But the young warriors next door found a loft in their garage to serve as their fort and invited Alexander in.

I remembered playing Wild West games with Roland and our gang in Dachau; I concluded that children are not natural-born pacifists.

One night I checked the bathroom after the boys had finished their baths and gone to bed. Flecks of soot and charred pieces of paper clung to the wet walls of the tub. A faint smell of smoke lingered. I had to resist my impulse to wake the boys for questioning. Whatever they had been doing had not hurt them; I decided to wait and to enjoy a few hours of peace and quiet with Noah.

We both valued what we called "grownup time," when we listened to music or talked about books. Our favorite novel at the time was William Gaddis's *The Recognitions,* a complex story about art, forgery, capitalism, and artistic integrity. We wondered why the critics did not value this unique writer more highly.

"You guys were playing with fire in the bathroom last night," I said the next morning. "You know that's not allowed."

"It was an experiment, Mommy," Alexander answered. "I was trying to make Greek fire."

"The kind you can't put out with water. It didn't work," Boris added.

"Please ask your science teacher to do those kinds of experiments with you at school, where it's safe," I said, resolving to find hobbies that did not involve weapons of mass destruction.

We learned tie-dyeing and macramé. I bought a small loom and colorful wools, and a beadloom, on which we made headbands. We melted paraffin or beeswax or broken crayons to make candles, sometimes using wet sand as molds. I strung a necklace of small glass beads and limpet shells. Alexander pointed out that the tiny, round hole in the top of each conical shell had been drilled by a predatory snail that had eaten the mollusk's flesh.

Boris proved adept and endlessly patient at cat's cradle, learning the figures from a book. We sprouted mung beans in Mason jars. We created a terrarium in a small aquarium tank and sent away for Venus flytrap plants that would live in it.

In the art world, Happenings were being created by artists who had no tangible product to sell. Dance, music, and visual installations invited audiences to enter the artist's imaginative inner space and to contemplate the creative process as it unfolded.

We attended happenings in the city and in East Hampton. Alexander's favorite was an event in which a curtain made of large black trash bags that were tied in knots was suspended above a trough of water. As the artist set the bottom ends of the curtain's strands on fire, burning plastic fragments dropped into the water, drifting, and shifting shape as they cooled. In East Hampton, an evening happening staged in a meadow behind an art patron's home provided a tent with hundreds of large cushions for the audience to lounge on while listening to ethereal, minimalist music. Torches and fireflies lit the field outside the tent. The voracious swarm of mosquitoes I had expected as darkness fell did not harass us. It might have been the pot smoke that kept them at a distance. The best part of the event had been the cushions, Alexander commented afterwards; he and the other children had built enormous forts and intricate tunnels with them.

Every summer, in East Hampton, Alexander, who had become the family expert on marine science, would fill a large aquarium with sea water and collect hermit crabs and other small sea creatures.

"Boris, Mom, look -- their old shells are too small and they're crawling around looking for new homes," Alexander would announce. I no longer had my book about Dr. Kleinermacher, but I told the story to the children, and I bought a microscope so they could examine drops of water.

While Noah and I took pleasure in raising our family, I could never shake off the lurking anxiety about the unwinnable war in Vietnam that continued to claim young lives on both sides. When four unarmed student protestors were shot at Kent State University by soldiers in the Ohio National Guard, a fellow parent at the Earl Kelley School voiced outrage for all of us.

"Now they're shooting our children in our own country. It's unbearable," she cried.

The Kent State tragedy brought more civil unrest and attempts by the government to extricate America from the conflict, but the war would not end until April 1975.

By then, Alexander was thirteen years old, Boris was nine, and major changes had come about in our family.

CHAPTER 34

Changes

Ⓘn the early 1970s, several worrisome incidents appeared to show that Noah's health might be failing. But each incident could also have been explained in less ominous terms. It was difficult to interpret the signs.

One evening in 1973 Noah went to an Art Dealers' Association meeting. It was not a social event, so I stayed at home and went to bed early. I was a heavy sleeper; it was not until two o'clock in the morning that I woke, needing to use the toilet. Noah was not in bed with me. I found him on the bathroom floor, curled into a fetal position, snoring.

I touched his shoulder and said, "Wake up and come to bed, dear. What happened? Did you fall?"

Noah looked up, seeming dazed. "What happened? I don't know. Guess I passed out. What time is it?"

I offered to help him up, but Noah got to his feet and wobbled into the bedroom, slipped under the covers, and went to sleep. I could not bear to disturb him, so I lay down on the opposite side of the bed, close to the edge -- and stayed awake most of the rest of that night.

In the morning, Noah showed no signs of injury. As if nothing at all had happened, he showered and dressed, drank his coffee, and asked if the *New York Times* had been delivered yet.

"But what about last night? Did you feel sick? Was it the snacks they served? Too many martinis?" I insisted.

"It could have been the food. I didn't drink more than usual. The guys palavered on and on; I got tired and went home. I went to the bathroom. Then -- I don't know what then," Noah answered. "Anyway, it's all over. I'm fine. No harm done."

I let him go. Perhaps he had overindulged, I thought. But I was too concerned to simply forget his collapse in the bathroom. I called our family doctor. When she had listened to my description of the event, she said, "Tell Noah to come see me."

"It seems to be high blood pressure," Noah reported after his appointment.

"It can cause dizziness; that may be why I fainted. I've never fainted before in my life. I have pills for it now, and she recommends a low-salt diet."

"That's not hard to do," I answered. "I'll ask my mother about herbs to make the food tasty; she knows a lot about that."

Several weeks after Noah's night on the bathroom floor, his brother Joe, who kept the gallery's books, asked me which painting by a certain artist had been sold.

"There's a check to him for a thousand dollars, but no explanation of what it was for," Joe said. "Do you happen to know anything?"

"Sorry, I don't," I said. "As far as I know, nothing by that guy has sold."

A conversation between Noah, Joe, and me later revealed that the artist had asked Noah for an advance to buy paint and canvas.

"That's a lot of money for paint," Noah's brother remarked. But because Noah simply shrugged to indicate that the matter was trivial, Joe and I let the subject drop. It was possible, I thought, that Noah had simply forgotten to make a note of what the amount had covered.

A month later, another check to the same artist was entered in the register. This time, Joe gently suggested that he be consulted when large sums were to be disbursed. Noah looked a little skeptical, but he agreed. I was angry at the artist who was taking advantage of Noah's good nature. Later, I had a more frightening thought: What if it was not good nature but mental confusion that made Noah give in to this conman?

Every summer, Noah would spend an occasional week in the city to look after gallery business, leaving the children and me in East Hampton. I had finally learned to drive, so that I had the use of the family car while Noah used the Long Island Railroad. On Friday afternoons, the boys and I would meet the "daddy train" at the station. We greeted other families who had the same arrangement with their working fathers. The mothers exchanged small talk; the older children placed pennies on the rails of the track. The pennies, flattened by the train wheels, were picked up after the train had left the station. The game was officially forbidden because of its danger. But, somehow, every week a few more bits of shiny copper made their way into our children's pockets.

In the middle of one of these working weeks, my mother called me. She had stayed in the city to look after Ernst, who was recovering from a fall.

"I had an arrangement with Noah to come over for dinner last night. He didn't come and didn't come, so finally I called him at your apartment. He was there and I asked him if he forgot -- he said he started to walk over but he couldn't remember the address. He walked around, he said, and finally got back to Eighty-third Street. I can't understand it," my mother said.

"That's very strange," I agreed. "He doesn't visit you as often as I do, but he's been there often enough. He knows the address. I wonder if he's coming down with something and just didn't feel well. I'll call him right now."

Noah denied the episode. "I had no dinner date with your mother," he said. I did not know what to make of his answer. Surely, my mother had not invented the story she had told me. Why would she do that?

Noah and I were patients of the same doctor. When the family had moved back to Manhattan, I asked for an appointment and confided my disquiet about Noah's memory lapses. Dr. Porter asked whether there had been other fainting spells.

"No," I said. "Maybe he's just getting forgetful?"

Dr. Porter said she would order tests at New York Hospital. It might be that the hypertension medication needed adjustment, or perhaps the faint had been a mild heart attack or a mini stroke.

"Please call Noah and tell him about the tests," I said. "If I suggest it, he'll think I'm nagging."

"Your husband has sustained some cerebral atrophy -- that means loss of brain cells," the neurologist who had been consulted told me on the telephone. "I am telling you this because Noah may not. He may not want to upset you. Dr. Porter has informed him. He has had a series of small strokes -- these incidents are hardly noticeable, but some of his cognitive functions will have been impaired. He is a sixty-four-year-old man. You may want to encourage him to retire, or to take in a partner for his business. A less stressful life would be advisable."

I thanked the doctor, but I was sorry that I had answered the phone. I did not want to think of Noah as old, or ill, or *impaired* -- that was the most hideous thought of all. I wanted the tests and the neurologist to have been wrong.

As the doctor had predicted, Noah did not discuss his diagnosis with me. The only time he mentioned the tests he had undergone, he made light of them.

"I thought I had the big C -- cancer, you know," he said. "But I don't. So that's good."

Noah went to work at the gallery as usual. He had recently taken on a part-time employee, an old army buddy named Sonny. They had served together in the Panama Canal Zone; Noah trusted Sonny.

One of Noah's nephews, David, also came in occasionally to help organize and catalogue the inventory and to learn the art business.

I thought about these two helpers while I tried to absorb the neurologist's advice. After a week of walking around in a state of anguish, I had an idea. "A less stressful life," the doctor had advised. I knew where a less stressful life could be found -- in East Hampton!

In East Hampton there were clean ocean breezes, a comfortable house with a lawn and garden, a library and an art museum in walking distance, friendly neighbors, and compatible acquaintances. We knew the pediatrician and a doctor whom the whole family had visited for minor ailments or injuries.

As for schools, living in East Hampton would solve a major difficulty, especially for Alexander, who was now eleven years old. His reading was up to grade level, but he still required extra help with spelling.

The Earl Kelley School did not go beyond fifth grade. Mrs. Nelson had planned to add the higher grades as the school gained pupils, but this had not happened. Financial difficulties multiplied instead. Mrs. Nelson told me in confidence that her personal savings were exhausted. With Noah's consent, I gave her a check for several thousand dollars, as a loan. It was not enough; the school was about to close, bankrupt.

Noah said, "When you lend money, don't lend more than you are willing to lose. This is for the kids' education, so consider it a donation."

Alexander had already transferred to a private school on the West Side and I had found a place for Boris at another, on Ninety-sixth Street near Fifth Avenue. From a teacher at Boris's new school, I heard about a new, progressive private school in the Hamptons. It was located on a farm; classes were given in a converted barn; goats and chickens shared the campus. Wouldn't it be wonderful, I thought, if the boys could attend this school -- if Noah could sit in the garden or at the beach every day -- if I could recover some peace of mind?

I talked the matter over with my mother.

"Yes, by all means, go live in the country," Mother advised. "It will be good for all of you and easier on *you*. You're looking pale and nervous -- I've been worried about you for months."

When I brought up my idea with Noah, I encountered less resistance than I had feared from the city boy that he used to say he was.

Sonny can work full-time. He'll be good -- he likes to chat up the customers more than I do anyway," Noah said. "I'll keep making the decisions about the artists and when they should have a show. They'll just have to send me slides or bring their work out to East Hampton."

I said, "I'm so glad you'll consider it. The boys will be thrilled. But let's not say anything yet. We need time to talk it over with your brother Joe and with Sonny and David. It's a big decision. I know I'll be happy in East Hampton and I know it will be good for your health. If you start to miss Manhattan, we can come in and spend a night or two at a hotel."

"I want to drive down to the ocean every day," Noah said.

"Deal!" I said and kissed him.

It was the fall of 1973 when we made our decision. We agreed to let the boys finish their academic years, and to plan our move for the early summer of 1974.

In January 1954, Ernst died. Nearing ninety, he was almost blind; he had become increasingly frail and had passed away peacefully in his own bed.

"He wanted to be cremated. I'd like to bring his ashes to East Hampton and bury them in the garden. He loved to sit there, remember? It will make me feel he's still close to me," my mother said.

"Of course," I said. "He'll be close to all of us."

In May 1974, we hired Home Sweet Home Moving Company to transport our furniture from New York to Mill Hill Lane.

"What a nice name for the movers," my mother said. "I know that song!" And she sang it in German.

"This summer we'll go to the cottage the songwriter's relatives lived in," I said. "It's a museum now, on the Mulford Farm. Supposedly that little saltbox inspired the poet."

I could see that making the move had been a good choice for the family. Everyone's mood seemed to lift as we settled in quickly. Noah appeared livelier than he had been in the city. He visited Guild Hall, the local cultural center, and introduced himself to the curators of its art gallery. They already knew of him and invited him to help judge an upcoming exhibit.

Alexander and Boris asked for a trip to the beach to collect seawater and hermit crabs. I took the car, a used Chevrolet, to the dealer to have it inspected and made ready for use.

I had talked with the headmaster of the Hampton Day School during the winter, asking if there was room for my two sons. He had assured me that they would be welcome, if we decided to enroll them. Now that we were in East Hampton to stay, I made an appointment and took Alexander and Boris to visit the school in Bridgehampton, a village about eight miles to the west. I thought that this private school, with fewer than a hundred students in grades from kindergarten through eighth grade, would be more suitable for the boys than the East Hampton public schools that were much larger and might not provide the special help Alexander needed. Boris had no learning challenges, but I wanted a hospitable environment for both boys. I hoped the Hampton Day School would prove as fine as the teacher in New York had said it was.

At the farm that was the school's campus, we were greeted by a golden retriever and a couple of black-and-white-speckled, squawking Guinea fowl that sounded like rusty hinges. A tall, blond young man in shorts and a T-shirt approached and tried unsuccessfully to shoo them away.

"Hello," he said. "Henry. I teach shop and biology. Come in and meet Tony."

Tony was the headmaster, as I knew from my telephone conversations with him. I introduced the boys and myself as we all walked towards the main building.

I thought about taking the train to Munich, and about taking the entrance exam at the *Luisenschule*. I remembered my brother's terrible experience at his Chicago high school, and Alexander's two unhappy days at P.S. 6. This informal, friendly place was part of a very different world.

I was glad for my children; I knew they would learn and thrive here.

After a pleasant talk with the headmaster, I made a downpayment on the tuition and signed the papers to register the children. Tony thanked me, shook hands with us, and wished us a good day.

"See you in September. I hope to meet your dad when school starts. Meanwhile, enjoy your summer," he said.

"We will," we said.

And we did -- in our own individual ways and together. Alexander's interest in natural science and astronomy continued to grow. In 1974, the skies over the Hamptons were still dark enough for enjoyable skywatching. We bought a small telescope and subscribed to *Astronomy*. Boris enjoyed the activities at the day camp and became a frequent visitor to the children's room at the East Hampton Free Library.

My mother stayed with us during the month of June. For the rest of the summer, she had planned a trip to Europe to visit with relatives and friends she had left behind, and to realize a long-held wish to see Paris once again.

It was not her first trip back to Europe. In the 1960s, she had traveled to Germany and Norway on buying trips for Parkway Sweater Imports. This year's trip was to be for her own pleasure. Mother had made friends with a young German woman who was a flight attendant on Overseas National Airlines. With Rosemarie as her personal trip planner and ticket agent, Mother laid out an ambitious itinerary that included a stay in St. Moritz, Switzerland, visits to Stuttgart, Ettlingen, Munich, and Dachau; and Paris. Rosemarie arranged for a French colleague named Simone to meet Mother at the airport in Paris, and to act as her guide for that leg of the trip. From Paris, Mother would travel through Sarrebourg and Strasbourg back to Frankfurt, Germany, and home.

When my mother said, "Paris," her eyes sparkled, and she looked decades younger than her seventy-two years.

"There is only one Paris. I am so happy that I will see it once more. I know it is as beautiful now as it was then."

I was glad for my recently widowed mother. I was not worried about her setting off alone. She would soon have new friends wherever she went; with Rosemarie and Simone on hand to help on both sides of the ocean, I knew she would be safe. Mother promised Alexander and Boris many letters.

"Start a scrapbook," she said. "I will send you pictures of everything interesting I see, and I'll send you pressed flowers -- there are different kinds you don't have here."

In mid-July, Rosemarie came to East Hampton in her green Volkswagen beetle and drove Mother back to Manhattan, helped her pack, and then took her to the airport.

In East Hampton, Noah carried out his plan to visit the beach every day that it did not rain heavily. Most days, I went with him, enjoying long walks on the sand and collecting moon snails that lay on the sand like the detached breasts of small mermaids. At home, Noah read books and listened to classical music on a Zenith portable radio that also received shortwave broadcasts.

"The Russian fishing boats are talking to each other," he would report. The offshore limit for foreign vessels at the time was three miles; it was later raised to two hundred.

As we had done every summer in East Hampton, we attended the annual country fair given by the Ladies Village Improvement Society, and the Fourth of July fireworks display sponsored by the Volunteer Fire Department. Alexander wondered where he could find the materials to make gunpowder.

Alexander and Boris filled up a large scrapbook with drawings and maps of their grandmother's travels. As promised, she sent numerous letters and postcards, hotel restaurant menus, postage stamps from different countries, brochures advertising local festivals, and pressed leaves and flowers, including Alpine specialties like an edelweiss and a gentian flower.

To me, she wrote, "It is as if I am visiting all the stations of my life. I am happy it was granted to me. It does not happen to everyone."

There was no school bus for the Hampton Day School. When school started in September, I drove the boys to and from Bridgehampton. It was a good opportunity to meet the other parents and the teachers, who, like the staff at the Earl Kelley School, took a personal interest in each student.

The boys liked the school and had interesting stories to tell at home.

"Today we had sushi," Alexander mentioned.

"Fish?" I asked. "How come? I didn't know the school served lunch."

"Henry brought in a fish he'd caught, and we dissected it. Henry's rule is, 'don't dissect anything you're not willing to eat' -- with the exception of roadkill," Alexander answered.

Henry also taught archery, I learned, and Boris's home room teacher played the guitar and sang folk songs with the children. Arthur, the math and physics teacher, had studied astrophysics at the University of Cambridge. Several of these interesting young people were to become family friends with whom we stay in touch to this day.

After a few months, I offered to volunteer at the school for a few hours a week.

"Could you teach them typing?" the director asked.

"You mean touch-typing? Not looking at your fingers, I mean. I happen to be good at that. I think I know how to teach them," I said, thinking back to the AP newsroom in Chicago. It seemed eons ago.

I mail-ordered a chart of the typewriter keyboard and bought Dr. Scholl's molefoam tape that is used to ease sore toes. I cut up the foam and covered the keys of the typewriter the school made available and hung the chart on the wall. My course was open to all ages. I coached kindergarteners as well as older students in finding the letters *a,s,d,f,g* and *l,k,j,h,* by looking at the chart. Once the middle row had been memorized, we typed simple words that I dictated: *add, ask, kld, had, dad, dig, gas.* We repeated the process for the other rows, eventually typing short sentences.

"Touch-typing is a useful skill," I reminded my pupils. "I earned money with it when I was young."

Boris began to show an interest in learning to play the guitar. His teacher encouraged him and began to give him regular lessons. I had bought a guitar for Alexander while we lived in the city, and he had taken a few lessons. He loved music, as we all did, but playing an instrument was not a skill he wanted to pursue. Now Boris used the instrument; it soon became apparent that he had a talent for music.

In 1975, our second year of living year-round in East Hampton, I was invited to join the board of directors of the Hampton Day School, and Alexander became the first published writer in the family.

We subscribed to the *East Hampton Star*, an independent weekly newspaper that was founded in 1885 and has been owned and run by several generations of the same family ever since. The *Star* covers local and regional news, the arts, community events, and sports. The editorial section includes numerous letters to the editor, special-interest columns, and a once-weekly feature of fiction or memoirs written by authors who reside in the Hamptons. The whole family enjoyed these rich offerings. One particular favorite was a column about the flora and fauna of the East End. When an editorial note advised that its author was retiring, and that readers interested in replacing him should send in a sample column, Alexander decided to apply for the job.

"Would you type it for me if I write it out in longhand and read it to you?" Alexander asked. "You know what my spelling's like. But I know what to say."

I believed my thirteen-year-old naturalist. And I believed that poor spelling due to dyslexia should not keep him, or anyone, from creative expression.

"We do that," I said. "But when you dictate it, I'd like you to tell me when there's a period at the end of a sentence and when to start a new paragraph. The column will be *your* writing. I'm just the typist."

"Yes, I can do that" Alexander agreed. It will be called 'All Around Us.'"

We mailed the typewritten column, complete with a photograph Alexander had taken, to the *Star*. It appeared in the next issue.

On Friday, the day after the paper's publication, the *Star's* editor telephoned and asked for Alexander Goldowsky.

"He's not here right now," I answered. "May I give him a message?"

"Yes. Please ask him to come to the office. I'd like to meet him. I want him to do more of these columns. If he comes back soon, have him come in today, otherwise Monday," the editor said.

"Thank you. I'll let him know. He should be home soon."

"How did it go?" I asked Alexander when he came back from his meeting with Everett Rattray, the *Star's* editor.

"Fine," Alexander said. "He wants me to do a regular weekly column; and I'll get paid."

"Was he surprised at how young you are?"

"No -- I don't think so. He didn't mention anything like that. We just talked," Alexander said.

The new columnist's age did not leak out at once, but within a few weeks Alexander became a news item. Alden Whitman, a writer for the *New York Times,* came to East Hampton for an interview and wrote an article headlined "Age Is No Barrier." A reporter for *National Geographic* spent a day exploring Alexander's favorite haunts with him and using up multiple rolls of color film for her story, which would document notable achievements by young people. "All Around Us" became a regular feature of the *East Hampton Star*. It would run until 1979.

"All Around Us" was often illustrated with photographs Alexander had taken and had developed himself, using the darkroom at the Hampton Day School. We had also adapted our basement laundry room and had acquired an enlarger and other equipment. Alexander had learned the techniques in a photography course at the Baldwin School, the last school he had attended in New York before our move to East Hampton. He had graduated from using a Kodak Instamatic to a sophisticated Pentax camera.

With this interest in photography came a venture into films and animation. We bought a Super8 movie camera. Alexander and Boris teamed up to produce original short films that ranged from simple documentaries -- the family riding bicycles through the quiet streets of East Hampton -- to animated shorts in which small clay figures of animals "moved" their limbs frame by frame. The young producers even ventured into time-lapse photography, for which Alexander built an ingenious contraption that rivaled the inventions of Rube Goldberg.

Alexander became an environmental activist and raised the family consciousness in the process. He went to meetings of the East Hampton Town Board and spoke about the need for energy conservation, solar power, and responsible land use. Helped by his teacher Henry, he researched and organized an effort to bring wind power to the Hampton Day School, using a windmill donated by a local farmer whose children attended the school.

I became interested in organic gardening. I read about beneficial insects and ordered a box of ladybugs to use as natural pest controllers in place of pesticides. When the box arrived, I put it into the refrigerator for storage until I could find time to release the critters. The next morning, a colorful sprinkling of bugs was foraging for food among the lettuce and onions in the fridge.

"Hey, you're supposed to be dormant!" I yelled at them. And then I spent the next hour in the hilarious task of herding ladybugs out of the kitchen and into the yard.

With organic gardening came an interest in healthful foods. I read *Diet for a Small Planet,* by Frances Moore Lappé. It was the first book to describe the wastefulness of meat production, and its global impact on food scarcity. These were subjects I had never thought about, but they concerned Alexander deeply. I started to cook dishes made with soybeans and grains and reduced the amount of meat in our daily menus. I planted more herbs in the garden. The boys and I learned to bake bread, using whole grain flour. Because it was not readily available in the supermarket, I ordered it from Walnut Acres, a farm in Pennsylvania. I learned to make yogurt. Boris used our homegrown zucchini to bake bread that was so delicious that a neighbor put in an order for several loaves and paid Boris for them.

My mother said, "The vegetarians in Germany knew all about this in the twenties; now it's big news here?"

In 1976, my mother told me that she expected a visitor from Germany. "Someone from long ago. You won't believe who that can be."

"I can't wait to hear. Is it somebody I know?" I asked.

"No, but he met you as a baby."

I begged for the story.

"When I was in Germany two summers ago, I tried to find the judge who almost locked me up in 1937," my mother explained. "You know the Germans are fanatical record-keepers. Would you believe I found him? His name is Dr. Zorn. He lives in Munich; he's alone; his wife is dead. I called him up because he did a good deed for us and I wanted to thank him. We had a long talk. I told him if he ever wanted to visit New York he could stay with me. I think it's my turn to do something nice for him."

"The judge -- the judge who told you to get married -- the one who said he would've married you himself if he could?" I asked.

"Yes, he's coming to New York. We've been writing to each other. At first, he wasn't sure he wanted to make such a big trip, but now he's decided. I'm alone in the apartment now. I'll give him the bedroom and I'll sleep in the living room on the pull-out couch."

I said, "That's so exciting! When he's here, be sure to let me know. I'll take the train to the city and come to say hello. Imagine -- I was a baby and now I'm nearly forty."

Summer came. My mother remained in Manhattan because the judge was to arrive in July. In the middle of the month, my mother called to say her visitor was with her.

"Tell me when I can meet him," I urged. Mother said she would let me know.

Two more weeks passed; I heard nothing. I wondered if the two had eloped to consummate a romance that had been hinted at forty years ago. Finally, I could not stand the suspense and called my mother.

"How's it going? How is your friend? Doesn't he want to see what's become of me?" I asked.

"He's gone. What an *Arschloch!*" Mother said in a juicy Bavarian accent.

"What? What did he do? It must have been something really bad if he's an asshole."

"Oh, he criticized everything -- New York is the dirtiest city he ever saw -- why don't people scrub their sidewalks? What are all those black people doing on the street? he wants to know. Why isn't the government sending them back to the jungle--"?

"Oh, no! What about me? Why didn't you invite me?"

"Ha!" Mother said. "I told him you were married, and your husband's name is Noah and you have two children. He said, 'So she's a Jew brat after all and she married one and brought more Jews into the world.'" I kicked him out. He was a Nazi then and he's a Nazi now."

I was not surprised when my mother, shortly after this disaster, said yes to one of the bevy of gentlemen who had been paying court to her ever since Ernst had died.

"His name is Karl, like my brother. He's retired and he volunteers at the senior center where I help out too. He was a baker and confectioner. It's funny, you know. My mother is sitting up there in heaven, laughing her head off. I'm finally going to marry a baker, like she always wanted me to, and I always refused," my mother said as we both burst into laughter.

I wondered where my mother found the courage. She was seventy-four years old; Karl would be her fourth husband.

"Why not?" she said when I brought up the subject some weeks later. "He's good company; he likes to play the piano for the old people at the nursing home; we sing all the nice German songs together. He has a pension and a car."

While my mother looked forward to a new marriage and a honeymoon trip to Germany, I worried about my husband.

Noah was so forgetful that I became afraid to leave him alone in the house. One day the children and I came home from the school and found the kitchen very hot and filled with a strange smell. When I looked at the stove, I saw the teakettle on the front burner, which glowed red-hot. All the water had boiled away, and the kettle was sizzling as if it were ready to burst into flame.

I rushed to turn off the stove and to yank open the kitchen windows. Then I looked for Noah. He was asleep in his reclining chair in the living room. I stroked his hand to wake him gently.

"Did you want to make tea?" I asked when he opened his eyes.

"Tea? No. I don't like tea for breakfast," he said.

"It's four thirty in the afternoon now," I said. "It isn't breakfast time. The burner on the stove was on, turned up high. Please be careful next time. Turn the stove off when your water boils, okay?"

Noah looked at me with barely focused eyes, as if he were still asleep and dreaming. "Isn't it time for breakfast?"

There were better days, when Noah took an active part in family activities. He enjoyed going to a nearby nature trail where a little stream widened into a pond. Mallard ducks and an occasional swan congregated there and greeted visitors with inquisitive squawks. Another favorite excursion was to visit the fishing docks in Montauk and to stop for a lunch of lobster rolls or steamer clams.

Noah's brother Joe called often to talk about the gallery business; he usually asked me to join the call on the telephone extension. When we had first moved to East Hampton, Noah had continued to work with Sonny and David on planning future shows. Month by month, he had lost interest in meeting new talent and had advised Sonny to show works the gallery already owned.

"Put together things from the collection. There's plenty in the storage room," he said.

I was grateful that Joe gave us regular updates on the gallery's finances. Sales were satisfactory, he said, adding that selling off inventory might bring in clients who were more interested in established artists than in the latest hot trend.

In 1977, my mother and Karl were married in the Lutheran church in Yorkville. Karl, who had been living in a suburb with his niece, moved into Mother's apartment. Before flying to Germany on a trip to Freiburg, Karl's hometown that he had left as a teenager, they drove to East Hampton for a visit.

Karl told us he was one year older than Mother. He was as physically fit and lively as she was. They made a striking couple, with their clear blue eyes and trim figures. My mother had taken to wearing a dark-blonde wig to cover her baby fine white hair that she claimed was impossible to style. As usual, she looked twenty years younger than her age.

"I am a lucky man," Karl said more than once. "I am married to the most beautiful woman in the world."

My mother and Noah had always been comfortable with each other. He listened to the stories she liked to tell about her early life and never stopped her when she switched to German as the tale became exciting or complicated. Noah would smile and nod. I never knew whether the Yiddish his family had spoken at home helped him understand her or whether he was politely dozing.

Karl's outgoing personality and undemanding friendliness made him pleasant company during the weeklong visit. I made sure that a tour of the local beaches and lunch at Noah's favorite beachside lobster shack were included in our activities.

In private, Mother said, "Noah has changed. He hardly says a word anymore; sometimes he looks like he's not really listening either. And he doesn't walk right -- have you noticed?"

"It's true," I said. "He shuffles, and sometimes he seems to forget to move forward; he just stops. I wonder if it's his eyesight. I should ask the doctor and find out if he needs new glasses."

"Do that, *Kind.* Noah walks like an old man -- he's much too young to do that!"

I did not tell my mother about my other concerns about Noah. I did not describe the car accident when he had missed the turn at the bottom of our street and had struck a tree on the opposite side of the road. He had offered to go to the fish market for me and had been coming home from that errand. Fortunately, he had been driving very slowly and had not been injured. The front fender and a headlight had been damaged. After the repair, I had taken over the driving, without any discussion or objection from Noah. In fact, he seemed to have barely registered the incident. When I had asked him whether another car had been involved or whether a squirrel had run across the road and had startled him, he had responded in the negative. And then he had never again mentioned the car, or the fish market, or the tree. That worried me more than the accident itself.

In the past, Noah had managed his own medical appointments; more recently, I had arranged his visits to the doctor or the dentist. Taking my mother's advice, I went with Noah to see our family physician.

"The unsteady gait could be related to the blood pressure medication. Have you been feeling dizzy, Noah?" the doctor asked.

"Dizzy? Don't remember," Noah answered. I added, "He hasn't said anything like that to me."

The doctor wrote a prescription for Noah's hypertension pills. "And stay on the low-sodium diet; the pressure is still higher than I like to see," he said.

A new pair of glasses did not change Noah's halting walk, nor his apathy. I could see him struggling to finish a sentence he had started; he wore his wristwatch but often asked me what time it was. He asked for the *New York Times* every morning and spent most of the day in his reclining chair, holding sections of the paper. I was not sure what, if anything, he was absorbing.

When the boys came to talk with him about an article in the *Star* or to show him a *New Yorker* cartoon they liked, his attention refocused for brief periods. When we drove to Montauk to walk along the shore by the lighthouse, I could see that Noah enjoyed the slow, strolling pace that felt natural on the rocky, pebbly beach.

I thought about our move to East Hampton. The years since 1974 had brought many changes to the family, most of them beneficial. Now, in 1977, watching the deterioration that was taking place in my brilliant husband was like seeing someone being swallowed by quicksand. And I could not rescue him!

My reason foretold that more inevitable changes were still to come. My emotions wanted to deny this and said that whatever love can do to save a person would be done.

CHAPTER 35

Endings and Beginnings

" "Bury me in there, with my friends," Noah had said to me some years ago when we had visited an artist who lived near the cemetery in which Jackson Pollock's grave was marked by a large boulder with a small bronze plaque.

At the time I had laughed and said, "All right -- in fifty years or so."

By the beginning of 1978, Noah's health had deteriorated to the point where I found it difficult to care for him, even though my mother and Karl came to help me as often as they could. Noah's increasing confusion and his inability to communicate made it impossible to know how much he understood about his situation. Noah had fallen almost silent. Sometimes he would try to answer a question with more than a monosyllable, but he could not find enough words to complete a sentence. He would look at the clock but could not say what time it was. When I told him, I could see that the information did not mean anything to him.

During the night, Noah was restless, frequently getting up to go to the bathroom. Sometimes he would use the toilet; other times I would find him simply standing there, staring blankly at the wall.

I was exhausted from lack of sleep and worn down by fear that Noah would wander outside the house while I was asleep. This had not happened, but the possibility kept me awake. Our family doctor, a kindly man who liked and admired Noah, made a housecall to check on both of us.

"You can't go on like this," he said to me. "I don't want to see you break down. You can't help your husband if you're incapacitated yourself. Noah needs professional care. I will sign the papers to get him admitted to the nursing home. I want you to agree. Now, before I leave your house."

"I want to do what's best for Noah," I said. "And I'm so tired. If you think the nursing home is what he needs, I have to agree."

"It's an easy walk over to Huntting Lane. They're very good there; I know the staff. You'll help him more if you stay well and strong," the doctor assured me.

Noah agreed to move to the rest home once I had promised to visit every day and to take him for a drive in the car. Fortunately, a bed was available at the facility and Noah was able to move in shortly after our conference with the doctor, during the first week of January.

"Your husband is doing well. He likes your visits and he looks forward to mealtimes and his glass of wine at dinner. Our patients like routine," the nursing home director told me.

"Could I take him home to have lunch with me sometimes?" I asked.

"Certainly," the director answered. "He's quiet. I don't think he'd cause any problems."

For the rest of January and February, I visited Noah every day and once a week I brought him back to Mill Hill Lane to have lunch. Sometimes a friend would join us, and we would go out for pizza. I felt relieved and grateful that Noah seemed content and that some calm had returned to my life.

In the first week of March, Noah called me at home and said, "I had a heart attack this morning."

"What? Have you seen the doctor? Have they called him?" I asked.

"I didn't tell them," Noah said, sounding calm and more lucid than he had in months.

"But why? We need the doctor. I'm calling him right now. Please stay in bed, will you, dear?"

When Noah had been put into the intensive care unit at Southampton Hospital, and tests had confirmed that a cardiac event had indeed occurred, I asked Noah again why he had not wanted medical help that morning.

He shrugged. "I thought it was time. I was ready."

I was allowed to stay at Noah's bedside for the rest of the day. The nurse told me I could come back in the morning and stay for as much of the day as I wanted.

"Oh, and bring his newspaper," she said. "He asked for it as soon as he got here."

I spent another day sitting with Noah. When I arrived, I told him that it was very cold outside and that the boys sent their love. Noah smiled and nodded, but then said nothing more. At home, I told the children that he had looked comfortable, as if he were simply spending a lazy day in bed, perusing the *New York Times* through his new glasses.

The telephone woke me before dawn the next morning.

"I'm sorry to tell you that your husband died of a massive myocardial infarction," our doctor said. "He had no pain. He was sitting up in bed, reading the *New York Times*. I'm very sorry. You don't have to do anything right now; don't come to the hospital. Tell your children first. Then you can call me later."

On March 8, 1978, Noah Goldowsky was laid to rest in Green River Cemetery.

The day of the funeral was cold and windy. I stood at the graveside, clutching the boys' hands; I could not stop shivering. We did not belong to a temple. A rabbi I had met with briefly the day before conducted the burial service. My mother and Karl, Noah's brother Joe, and Sonny had come from New York. Two local friends joined us. Noah's father had moved to Israel the year before; I felt relief that he had been spared this moment. Joe had advised against telling Morris immediately; he wanted time for us to break the news to him as gently as we could.

Kindly neighbors brought food and comforting words to our home after the funeral, and my mother and Karl stayed with us for several days.

Aaron Siskind called and said, "I'm thinking of you, sweetie. He shouldn't have died so young. What was he? Only sixty-nine, you say? I'm so sorry for you."

The following week, Alexander and Boris returned to school. I met with lawyers and financial advisers and talked with David and Sonny about closing the gallery.

"Keep busy. It's important to get on with things; life will go back to normal eventually," friends advised. I thanked them without believing their words. I knew that our lives would go on, but "normal" had lost its meaning.

Noah and I had made our wills shortly after we were married, and we had updated them conscientiously. I knew that all the financial arrangements were in order, with Joe as Noah's appointed executor. My task was to sort out Noah's personal papers.

I found a document from the United States Army. It stated that Sergeant Nathan Gale had been honorably discharged. I recalled Noah's tale of going to court to restore the name his father had given him, and the close relationship between Noah and his father. I remembered how excited Noah had been about the birth of our sons, and how much he had loved them.

In an unlabeled manila folder tucked into the back of a file drawer, I found a dozen sheets of paper with Noah's name and a poem typed on each. He had never mentioned writing poetry. Now, as I read, I heard Noah's thoughtful, unsentimental voice accepting his own mortality.

"When I am dead my bones will grow / into sturdy trunks of trees," one poem began.

I had decided that a boulder would mark Noah's grave in the lovely natural landscape of the rustic little cemetery. The poem made me feel that I had understood my husband's wish to lie there, at peace.

Words have the power to heal, I thought. I had translated poems by Heinrich Heine, whose work Noah and I admired, but I had never written a poem of my own.

In fact, I had not done any creative writing in years. A small fire began to burn in my consciousness.

I closed the boxes I had been working on and pushed aside stacks of files on my desk to clear a space. I set up my portable Smith-Corona typewriter and started to write.

I wrote the outline of a short story. A woman stands by the open grave of her husband. Wet soil is being shoveled onto the top of the coffin. The new widow shivers and feels that the rest of her life will be as bleak as this winter day. She glances up briefly and sees a forsythia bush growing near the cemetery's fence. It is too early in the season for flowers, but one tiny branch has managed to open a row of yellow blossoms.

Within a few months of Noah's death, I learned that our trust in Sonny had been misplaced. Sonny was a thief. Paintings were missing from the inventory. When David asked about them, Sonny gave vague answers about clients who had taken them home for approval or other dealers who had borrowed them for exhibits. David's calls to our regular clients never turned up any such loans.

One afternoon I opened the door to what I thought was the mailman's knock. A stranger handed me a bulky package covered in blue paper.

"I have just given you a subpoena," he said and ran for his car that was idling in the driveway.

I read through the papers, hardly believing my eyes. The estate of Noah Goldowsky was being sued for three hundred thousand dollars by an art dealer with whom Noah had partnered to buy works by an American artist whose works had historical significance. The suit alleged that Noah had sold the paintings without paying the other dealer her share.

"This is totally false and impossible," I explained to my attorney when I had gotten over the first shock. "The paintings aren't sold-- they're sitting in the warehouse storage room! David can swear to that. And Noah was an honest dealer -- the entire New York art world will tell you so."

"The principal witness seems to be somebody named Sonny. Who's that?" Tom, the lawyer, asked after he had investigated the claim further.

For a long moment, I could not say Sonny's last name. The betrayal hurt my throat, all the way down into my chest and gut.

It would take months to defend the suit. The final settlement would come only after my attorney invoked the dead man's statute. This rule forbids a witness who has an interest in the outcome of the case to testify against an accused person who is deceased. It was clear to the judge that the dealer who had brought the suit had no eyewitness knowledge of the alleged wrongdoing; her information came only from Sonny. Neither of the accusers would be permitted to give testimony in a trial. Noah Goldowsky was dead. The judge ordered the parties to settle.

While the case was being argued and depositions were made, David had supervised the closing of the gallery space and the removal of the artworks to our storage room in a warehouse on upper Madison Avenue. David had also agreed to show works to interested buyers and to take a commission on future sales. Joe thought that this was a better plan than putting the entire lot into an auction.

"That would be like a fire sale," he said. "Take time."

I felt blessed by these compassionate family members.

David thought that Sonny was bitter because he believed Noah had not valued his work enough, or perhaps Sonny had felt underpaid. I did not think that had been the case. But if Sonny had a grievance, it seemed to me that he, as Noah's buddy, might have talked frankly with his friend years ago instead of taking his anger out on me now.

Alexander turned sixteen on March 20, 1978. He had finished the eighth grade at Hampton Day School, which to our sorrow, did not have a high school. Alexander was now attending the East Hampton public high school. Because he still needed special assistance with spelling, he had received permission to take his English classes at the Hampton Day School. The high school principal had somewhat reluctantly agreed to this part-time arrangement with the Hampton

Day School teachers, stipulating that it was to last through Alexander's freshman year only.

I was teaching Alexander to drive so that he could make the daily commute between schools by himself once he earned his learner's permit. We soon abandoned saying, "turn right" or "turn left," because these instructions were a recipe for possible accidents. I too can become confused about directions, though to a lesser degree than Alexander. Once we learned to use the terms "driver's side" and "passenger side," all went well.

We missed Noah. I encouraged trips to the library and the art museum, concerts, and lectures to distract us. Alexander introduced the family to Euell Gibbons's book, *Stalking the Wild Asparagus,* and treated us to experimental dishes like Japanese knotweed pie. It was surprisingly good.

On a Sunday afternoon in April, the three of us attended a concert at Guild Hall's charming John Drew Theater, whose small, acoustically excellent auditorium lends itself to chamber music performances. A young, highly accomplished cellist was the featured soloist. I sat between the boys and let the music calm me.

When I glanced at my sons while we applauded after each cello selection, I saw that Boris's big brown eyes seemed to have grown larger. He had been sitting very still in his seat, but I could sense his excitement. When the soloist had received the audience's enthusiastic ovation and had performed an encore, we walked out of the theater. I took a deep breath. Suddenly, I realized that it was spring -- the season of renewal.

"Do you think I could learn to play the cello?" Boris asked as we were walking home.

The question did not surprise me. I had felt his heightened attention throughout the concert. "I'm sure you could," I said. "It's different from the guitar; you could play it in an orchestra, or solo. You'll need lessons and a lot of practice. If you're serious we'll look into it. Let's ask at school about how to find cello lessons -- and you'll need an instrument too."

The following week, at the recommendation of Boris's teacher, I made an appointment with Dr. Robert Shaughnessy, a musicologist and instructor who lived in Southampton.

Dr. Shaugnessy, a tall, grey-haired man wearing horn-rimmed glasses, met us at the door of his Victorian home.

"Come in, come into the studio," he said as he led us into a front room. A grand piano and a harpsichord took up almost half of the space; bookcases and cabinets holding sheet music lined the walls. Music stands and chairs stood near the piano.

"So, you're the young man who's interested in the cello, and you're taking guitar now," Dr. Shaughnessy said to Boris. "Let's sit down and talk. Cello is an instrument I teach, among others. Every one of my children plays an instrument. I taught all seven of them!"

"You've got a whole orchestra," I said, laughing. This teacher's affable manner was putting both Boris and me at ease as I explained our family situation, our recent loss, and Boris's newfound interest in the cello.

"How can we get an instrument for Boris?" I asked. "Do you sell them or rent them out?"

"No," Dr. Shaughnessy said. "If you wanted to take up the recorder, I could perhaps help you. I have a few extra instruments because I'm interested in early music and I play in an ensemble with other aficionados. I myself play the viol or the viola da gamba. I don't have a cello to sell. But I know where you might ask."

"Oh, good! I would appreciate that," I said.

"Well now," Dr. Shaughnessy began, eyes twinkling. "There's a gentleman in Southampton, a rather eccentric gentleman -- he does a lot of different things including musical instruments. Norman Pickering is his name. He makes violins and does repairs on other instruments too. He may have a cello. I'll write his phone number down for you. Give him a call. Actually, he lives right in the village, not far from here."

"Thank you. That's so kind of you," I said. "If he can help us, may we call you back and arrange for lessons?"

"Surely. I will be happy to have the young man as my pupil," Dr. Shaughnessy said. "Good luck."

"What did he mean by 'eccentric,' I wonder?" I asked Boris as we got into our car. "We'll call Mr. Pickering from home. It's obviously not a store we can walk into. But we're making progress. It's exciting, isn't it?"

Boris agreed, but he couldn't guess why the gentleman might be eccentric.

Two days later, Boris and I drove to Southampton again, this time to keep the appointment I had made with Norman Pickering. The two-storey house with white shingles and narrow black shutters was surrounded by a thick privet hedge. A short walkway led to a small porch. We climbed the three wooden steps to the front door and rang the bell. Inside, a dog barked -- and kept barking for several minutes. Then the dog fell silent and the door opened. A man in a tan shopcoat and a large brown poodle looked at us.

"Hello, I'm Barbara Goldowsky and this is Boris. We were referred by Dr. Shaughnessy," I said.

"Norman Pickering," the man said, reaching out to shake hands. "Come in. I was working down in the shop; sometimes it takes me a while to get to this door. Good thing I have Rachel here; she's my doorbell," he added, patting the dog's woolly head, and smiling. The smile was for the dog. I wondered if I had mistaken the time of our appointment.

"Are we late? You said to come at--" I started.

"No, no, you're on time. In fact, you were two minutes early," Norman Pickering said. "I checked. I'm fussy about time." This time his smile was for me, as was an approving look from light blue eyes framed by horn-rimmed glasses like the ones Dr. Shaughnessy wore.

We walked into a room that had four large windows facing the street. Below the windows stood a long, narrow couch upholstered in beige corduroy. Three violins sat propped against the cushions like small visitors waiting politely for tea to be served. Floor-to-ceiling bookshelves took up most of the wall opposite the couch. A round table, an upholstered armchair, and several folding chairs made up the rest of the furnishings; there was no piano.

"Have a seat," Norman Pickering said, picking up two of the violins to make room on the sofa. "I hear from Bob Shaughnessy that you're interested in cello lessons and an instrument. Is that correct?"

"Yes, that's right. Boris goes to the Hampton Day School and has been taking guitar lessons with his teacher there. But now he's become very interested in learning to play the cello," I explained. "Dr. Shaughnessy said you might have an instrument we could buy."

"As it happens, I do have one; I don't always because I work mostly on violins and violas, but this cello came in all smashed up and I had to put it back together. I'll go get it and show it to you," Norman said as he went out through a doorway into an inner room.

He came back holding a honey-colored cello by the neck. With his free hand, he turned one of the folding chairs to face the middle of the room.

"Sit here, Boris, and hold this -- like this, between your legs -- left hand up here-- and -- just a second, I'll get you a bow."

Boris followed the directions he was being given. He looked a bit apprehensive but also curious. Norman handed him a bow and adjusted Boris's fingers to hold it in the right position.

Norman made a bowing motion and said, "Now make a sound."

Boris looked up and said, "I never held a cello before."

"That's all right; just use the bow and make a sound."

Boris drew the bow across the strings. I expected a squawk, but the tone was smooth and even.

"That's good. Your left hand makes the notes, like you do on the guitar; you bow with the right hand."

Boris smiled and tried a few more notes while Norman turned to me and said, "He'll do fine."

"Really? Thank you. I'm so happy to hear that," I said.

"I don't give cello lessons. Sign up with Bob Shaughnessy -- he's a good all-around musician; half the town goes to him."

"Yes, Dr. Shaughnessy already said he would take Boris as a student. As soon as we can get him an instrument. Can we talk about buying this one?" I asked.

"Did you say this instrument was broken?" Boris spoke up. "I don't see any cracks or marks anywhere."

"That's because I spent a couple of months restoring it. It was in pieces; literally a basket case when it came in. It was in a car accident. The driver wasn't badly hurt, fortunately," Norman said. "The cello originally belonged to a nephew of Thomas Edison and the man who owned it after that is a friend of mine. He was ready to sell it when they had the accident. He thought it was a total loss; when I told him I'd repair it, he told me to keep it for the price of the repair."

"You would never know," I said. "It looks perfect to me, and it sounds good."

"Sometimes instruments sound better after they've had a break or two," Norman answered. "That's a long story that has to do with the acoustics of wood and current research with spectrum analysis and so forth."

"I'm sure we'd like to hear more, even though science is not my strong subject," I said. "Have you been a musician all your life or are you in science?"

"Both. I learned to play the violin when I was seven, but my father wanted me to become an engineer. My father and my grandfather were engineers. When I was growing up, you did as your father told you. I went to engineering school, but after that I went to Juilliard…"

For the next twenty minutes, Norman talked about his dual careers, relating anecdotes about his life as an orchestra musician (he had played the French horn), as an engineer interested in the acoustics of bowed instruments, and as an inventor. He asked a few questions about the Hampton Day School and inquired if I had other children and whether they were interested in music. I told him about Alexander and his passion for natural science, but I kept my answers short, intrigued by the multitude of experiences this gentleman had lived through. It seemed like several lifetimes' worth. Norman Pickering had white hair and his fair-skinned face showed some wrinkles -- but he walked with a springy step and displayed the energy and enthusiasm of a teenager. He was not *that* old, surely?

Boris sat on his folding chair, holding the cello upright between his legs. He was quiet and thoughtful as he always was. He had never been a talkative child. I wondered what he was thinking.

A slender, dark-haired woman holding a laundry basket came through the doorway and walked past us without a word or a smile. She gave me an appraising look. Norman did not stop talking to greet or introduce her; she left the room by the door near the front hall. That's Mrs. Pickering, I thought. Maybe she needs her husband's attention. Is she annoyed that we're sitting here, taking up his time?

I took advantage of the next pause in Norman's story to say, "I'm afraid we are keeping you, fascinating as it is. Could we talk about the next step with the cello? The price, and how soon we can take it home? I know we want to buy it."

"Oh, yes -- the cello," Norman said, as if he had suddenly recollected why we were in his music room. "It's a good instrument. I think you'll be happy with it. And if anything needs attention in the future, I'm here. Just call me and I'll see to it."

I had no idea what a cello should cost, so that when Norman named a price, and a price for the bow, I said yes immediately. I thought about the selling price of the paintings in the gallery and about the Persian rug Noah had bought. The cost of a musical instrument for Boris compared very favorably.

"I need to set up the instrument and put new strings on it and so forth," Norman said. "I'll call you in a few days when it's ready. Leave me your phone number, would you please?"

"Thanks again, Mr. Pickering," I said. "I'll come and pick it up. And thank you for everything. It was nice meeting you."

"I'll call you soon, Mrs. Goldowsky. Goodbye, Boris."

"What a lot of stories," I said to Boris in the car. "A gentleman of many talents, just like Dr. Shaughnessy said. And of course, he's married; the interesting men are always married. Oh, well -- I'm not looking."

"Thanks for buying the cello," Boris said.

Several days later, I received a call from Norman Pickering.

"Your cello is ready," he said. "I want to deliver it to you. Where in East Hampton do you live?"

"Thank you for calling -- but you don't need to bring it. It's easy for me to drive to Southampton and pick it up. You don't need to take extra trouble," I said.

"No, no trouble at all. I prefer to bring it. What is the address and a convenient day and time?"

"Any day -- tomorrow if you like. Could you make it in the late afternoon? I pick Boris up at school and we get home about four thirty. We live at 98 Mill Hill Lane; do you know the street?"

"Near Town Pond, Guild Hall, and the Maidstone Inn. I will see you tomorrow at five," Norman said.

And he will be here precisely at five, I thought, as I thanked Norman and said goodbye. He's fussy about time.

My prediction proved correct. I was in the kitchen, looking out at the driveway, when a low-slung white sports car pulled in. I glanced at the wall clock, which I believed kept good time. It was four fifty-nine p.m.

Norman Pickering got out of his car, opened the trunk, and lifted out a cello-shaped cloth bag.

By the time he had closed the trunk, I had opened the side door of the house and stood aside to let him in.

"Welcome to East Hampton," I said. "Please come in. We call this the family entrance because it's next to the driveway. There *is* a front door, but I've learned that nobody ever uses it."

We walked into the living room. Boris came forward to say hello, and three other young people put aside books and drawing pads and got up from the couch or the floor.

Norman turned to me. "You have *four* children?" he asked in an undertone.

I laughed. "No, just two. You know Boris, and this is Alexander, my older son. We have houseguests. Valerie and Geoffrey are friends from New York. They were all at school together when we lived in Manhattan. Valerie and Geoffrey are spending a few weeks with us while their parents find an apartment in the city. They've been in Europe for a while."

"Hello, Mr. Pickering," the four young people said as Norman nodded a greeting and I moved to make room on the couch for the cello to be unpacked. Muschi, our grey tabby, was curled against the cushions; I reached out to nudge her aside.

"No, no; don't disturb her. That's her place," Norman said. "There's plenty of space."

I remembered the poodle in Southampton. I noticed that when Norman spoke to or about animals, his voice was warm and soft. We crowded around to admire the instrument. "You will need a case for this; I can order one for you. The bag is not safe enough in the car," Norman said.

I said, "Thank you again for all your help. Boris and all of us are very excited about the lessons. It was really good of you to bring the cello. Would you like to stay for dinner?"

"No, thank you, Mrs. Goldowsky. I will give you a call about the case. Good luck; good night."

"He's very formal," Alexander observed.

"Of course, he couldn't stay for dinner," I said. "He's expected at home; there's a Mrs. Pickering in Southampton. I forgot."

Boris started cello lessons with Dr. Shaughnessy in the first week of May. He remembered the exact date because it struck him as very special: 5/6/78.

About a week later, Norman Pickering called and asked me out to dinner.

"Would you be willing to meet me at Bobby Van's -- just you, I mean, on Friday evening?" he asked.

"That would be very nice. I'd be happy to meet you there. Thank you," I said, trying hard not to let my surprise show. A date? Just the two of us? I could understand his not inviting my crowd of kids, but what about the dark-haired woman with the laundry basket?

"Thank *you*," Norman said. "Could you meet me at five thirty? You do know Bobby Van's? It's in Bridgehampton -- I will look forward to seeing you. That's Friday, at five thirty."

"Yes. Friday. I'm looking forward to it. See you then."

I wrote the date and time on my notepad by the telephone and fell into a kitchen chair, convulsed with giggles. Bobby Van's was a restaurant and piano bar, named for its owner. It was a popular meeting place -- and sometimes a pickup spot -- for summer people and locals alike. You would have had to be a cloistered nun not to know about it. It was not the kind of place where a married man known in the community would normally wish to be seen with a woman who was not his wife. It was a puzzlement. I started thinking about what to wear.

My blue-flowered chiffon dress with its modest round neckline was formal enough for dinner; the ruffle at the hem gave it just a touch of the frivolity appropriate for a date at Bobby Van's. I parked my car on the street a few spaces away from the restaurant entrance and waited until my watch said five twenty-five. I wanted to make my entrance as close to five thirty as possible without being actually early and seeming too eager, and I was not going to be late by even one minute. When I strolled through the door of Bobby Van's I expected to see Norman sitting at the bar. He was not. I walked towards the back of the room to see if he might be sitting in a booth.

He was not. I took a stool at the bar, near the front door, expecting to see my date come rushing towards me. No one came rushing.

"May I get you something?" the bartender asked.

"No, thank you. I'm waiting for someone," I said. Norman made a rash decision and now he's sorry he asked me, I thought. I stood up and looked around the room once more. There were very few patrons at this early hour. Norman was not among them. I decided to leave in three minutes if he did not come through the front door or out of the men's room. Someone so fussy about time would have been waiting at the bar if he had intended to keep the appointment he had so carefully spelled out for me on the telephone. I was not about to waste more time on this no-show.

I was one step away from the front door when I heard a shout behind me.

"Wait, wait -- don't leave! He's here -- this way, this way!" The bartender was clutching my sleeve. "The gentleman is in the dining room, around the corner; he's waiting for you. He asked for a special table in the alcove. I'm so sorry; here, please come with me!"

I turned. It had not occurred to me to look into the dining area's alcove and no one had suggested it. Now, escorted by the apologetic bartender, I walked up to the room's only patron, who sat at a table that was beautifully set with candles and wine glasses and linen napkins in graceful folds.

Norman Pickering, dressed in a suit with a vest, a white shirt, and a navy-blue tie, rose from his chair and said, "Thank God! Thank God -- I thought you had changed your mind. I thought you weren't coming! I even thought you might be one of those women who are always late -- but I didn't want to think that."

I said, "Hello. I'm glad to see you. I thought *you* had changed your mind. I was at the bar; nobody told me you were here. I'm sorry -- but you know, I wasn't late. I know how you feel about time."

The bartender had retreated, and a waiter bustled up to take our order.

Norman took off his glasses and wiped them with a very clean, white handkerchief. He wiped his brow.

"I hope you have time -- do you have time to listen? We have so much to talk about. But first, you need to hear some things about me. May I call you Barbara?"

"Yes, Norman," I said and reached for his hand. It was large and strong; it gave my hand a firm squeeze. I felt relieved and happy that our relationship had not ended before it had had a chance to begin.

"I have time. The kids are all very responsible; they won't burn the house down," I said as the waiter brought drinks -- a martini with a lemon twist for Norman, a glass of wine for me.

"My life is very complicated," Norman said.

CHAPTER 36

Chamber Music

"My life is very complicated," Norman said on our first date. In the idiom current at the time, that was the understatement of the year.

At our table for two at Bobby Van's, we were sipping our drinks and looking over our menus.

"May I recommend the mussels? Do you like mussels?" Norman asked.

"Yes, I do like mussels and scallops too. Not raw oysters, though," I answered.

"Good, let's have the mussels and then perhaps the swordfish?"

"That sounds delicious," I agreed as Norman signaled the waiter.

"I've always preferred seafood to steak," Norman said. "But that shouldn't surprise you because I'm a native Long Islander. I was born in Canarsie. Do you know Brooklyn?"

"I lived in Manhattan for years -- but Brooklyn, I'm afraid, was a foreign country," I said. "No, wait a minute -- we did go to the botanical gardens once."

"Canarsie is a neighborhood in Brooklyn. It's changed for the worse over the years, but when I was growing up it was a nice little village. There was the Dutch Reformed Church around the corner from my grandmother's house, and there was an Italian neighborhood and a Jewish neighborhood. I wonder if my grandmother's house is still there--"

The waiter placed bowls of mussels and a basket of crusty bread on the table.

"Oh, my goodness -- this is the appetizer? It's enough for two dinners," I said.

Norman laughed. "We'll see. Let's take our time. You did say that you don't have to rush home? There's so much I want to tell you. I want you to know about me."

"No rush at all," I said. "These mussels are scrumptious! So, you were born in Canarsie. And then?"

Norman spoke of his mother who had played the piano and who had recognized her son's musical talent while the father did not allow the boy to play the violin at home, insisting instead on studies in math and science that would lead to an engineering career.

"I didn't go to Juilliard until after I'd graduated from college with a degree in electrical engineering," Norman related, and went on to tell me about his life as a musician with the Indianapolis Symphony Orchestra and later in New York, as a freelancer.

I listened -- and managed to eat not only my portion of mussels, but two large hunks of the warm bread that was irresistible when dunked into garlicky broth.

I learned that there had been an early marriage and a divorce and that now Norman was married -- I had guessed correctly -- to the dark-haired woman I had seen at his house. Her name was Juta; she was Estonian.

"Estonian? Is she an immigrant?" I asked.

"Yes. She was able to get out after the war and come to the U.S. I brought her father and mother over after we were married," Norman said. "But now we're getting divorced -- it's a long story; complicated."

"Yes. I can see that," I said.

There were children from both marriages, Norman said. He gave their ages. The older ones were close to my age, the younger ones about ten years older than Alexander.

I was about to interrupt in order to ask how the children felt about the divorce, when Norman went on to say, "I have a woman friend in Vermont; she's hoping I'll move to Bennington and marry her. She's about ten years younger than I am."

The mental arithmetic became too much of a struggle. I summoned all my *savoir faire* to say, "Since we're talking about life stories, I should tell you that my birthday is in November; I'll be forty-two. How old are you, Norman?"

"Uh, I am fifty-nine."

So, there were nearly twenty years between us. I knew what my mother would say.

As we prepared to leave, Norman said, "I hope you will let me see you again. I want to know you better. Now that you've come into my life, please don't walk out of it."

Bright yellow *Caution* signs flared in my mind: *Married! Not divorced! Grown children! Girlfriend!!*

I expected to hear myself make an excuse -- mentioning a nonexistent boyfriend, perhaps. But I said, "It's too soon to talk about the rest of my life. My husband died only two months ago. We can talk, though; we can walk on the beach or get together for dinner, if you like."

"If you can bear with me, I'll be happy," Norman said.

I answered, "Please don't make it sound like a burden. I enjoy your company."

As the spring of 1978 turned into summer and the school year ended, I was happy to have a busy household. Alexander and Boris had been friends with Valerie and Geoffrey since the early days of the Earl Kelley School. Now the four kept one another entertained without requiring much supervision from me. They helped with shopping, cooking, and gardening and could be trusted to go to the beach by themselves.

Alexander and Boris had become accomplished swimmers and Alexander had taken the junior lifeguard training that was offered by the town recreation department. I knew that if anyone needed rescuing, Alexander would be far more capable of doing that than I was. Nevertheless, I asked them to swim within the area of the beach that was protected by lifeguards.

On Saturdays, I took Boris to Southampton for his cello lessons. He was making good progress and was diligent about practicing at home.

Norman and I saw each other frequently. We enjoyed dinners at his favorite restaurants. Norman was friendly with the proprietors and they never hurried us as we sat talking. I told Norman about my mother and my brother and about our life in Germany and in Chicago. I talked about Noah and the art business and about Noah's last illness. Norman told me the tragic story of his and Juta's youngest son who had died in an automobile accident in 1976.

"He was seventeen," Norman said. "The kid who was driving was under the influence of drugs; he wasn't hurt; they took his license away for three months -- a slap on the wrist."

I thought about the young man, so near Alexander's age, and wondered whether it was painful for Norman to see my son full of life and vigor.

My mother and Karl were traveling in Europe, visiting relatives, and taking the waters at spas they remembered from their youth. Before leaving, they had asked me to help them find a small house that they could afford in East Hampton. I called several real estate agencies and was taken to view possible properties. I liked this type of window shopping. One of the salesmen, a handsome, athletic man who looked to be in his thirties, asked me out. I accepted, thinking about the advice I was constantly getting from friends and neighbors to enjoy my new, single life. The young man and I spent some pleasant evenings together, but we soon found that we had different priorities. He was a runner, ambitiously training for the New York Marathon. This involved rigorous attention to diet and exercise schedules. I did not want to go jogging with him. I preferred sitting on a lawn chair and sipping a glass of wine with delicious, locally grown strawberries floating in it.

We stopped dating but remained friends. He eventually found a secluded cottage that looked like an illustration for a German fairy tale. Later that year, it would become my mother and Karl's summer home.

Occasionally, Norman could be persuaded to have dinner with me and the children at home in East Hampton, but he never seemed completely at ease with what he called "your commune." He was most relaxed when our cat consented to sit next to him or on his lap. In conversation, I found that he was at his best when talking about his inventions -- notably the Pickering phonograph stylus that had revolutionized the world of high-fidelity sound. It was the invention that combined his engineering skill with his musical sensitivity -- a tale of two lives.

Norman invited me to musical evenings at the home of a Hampton Day School teacher, a classically trained pianist, and the pianist's wife, a book designer and artist. Norman and Joe would play duets for violin and piano, or sometimes viola and piano, working through pieces they wanted to polish. There would be stops and starts as they decided on the optimal tempo or the most expressive phrasing. They expressed opinions -- sometimes strong ones -- but in the end, their collaboration would result in a smooth, seamless performance.

I loved the interplay of musical voices and I loved seeing Norman's face when he played. His expression was both intensely concentrated and lost -- as if his feelings were roaming in another time and place while his fingers found the notes on the strings in the here and now. When Norman looked at me, I saw admiration accompanied by questions: *Will we ever be together? Do you want me?*

I wanted to say yes to both, but the multitude of problems he still faced intimidated me. Divorce proceedings were moving much too slowly, Norman told me.

"It was supposed to be no-fault and amicable, but now the lawyers have got hold of the situation and they're dragging it out to make more money for themselves," he said.

I did not know what Norman's sons, who were in their twenties and living independently, thought of me. Norman was evasive when I asked. I surmised that to them, I was the merry widow who was luring their father away from their mother, even though I had played no role in their estrangement.

And then there was the woman friend in Vermont! I knew that Norman would be seeing her in August, during his annual visit to Bennington College, where he coached chamber music groups at a summer festival. I could not begin to imagine how, or even if, this relationship would be resolved. Mr. Pickering's life was complicated indeed. I decided not to speak about any of these issues until Norman brought them up.

I found that this resolve gave me peace and time to remember Noah and recall how much he had loved his sons. They were growing into handsome, tall young men. How sad it was that he would not see them as adults!

School was not in session, but the boys and I were friendly with several of the Hampton Day School teachers. Alexander had finished his freshman year at East Hampton High School. I was not at all certain that continuing there would be good for him, given his ongoing struggle with dyslexia. There was no private high school in the area that might have been an alternative; boarding school was not an option we were willing to consider. I consulted the school's director and Henry the biology teacher, and Sam, the English teacher. All agreed to do their best for Alexander, whose special gifts they recognized. We brainstormed separately and together.

In August, Norman called from Bennington. "They want to establish a special department, so I can teach music and do my acoustical research," he said.

"Who's 'they'?" I asked.

"The committee -- I mean some of the trustees of the chamber music conference and the board members of the college. The idea is I would live in Bennington full-time."

"I am not a committee and I don't have a chairmanship to bribe you with," I said. "I'm one person who lives in East Hampton. Do you *want* to move to Bennington?"

"No! They're very insistent. I don't know how to tell her -- sorry -- them."

"I know it's a big decision. I also know you and I have deep feelings for each other. Think carefully," I said.

I thought I had conducted myself well throughout this call. I had kept my voice steady and my tone calm. But now I sat down and cried in sheer exasperation and fury. Later, I wrote a love poem to Norman. It was very sentimental. I tore it up and threw it away.

As summer drew to a close, a possible solution for the dilemma of Alexander's schooling emerged at last out of my ongoing discussions with the Hampton Day School staff. An idea was floated about approaching Southampton College. This was the smallest campus of Long Island University and was nationally known for its excellent marine science program and its research station on the shore of Shinnecock Bay. The college also had a thriving liberal arts program. The small campus on the Montauk Highway was two miles west of Southampton Village.

Although Alexander was only sixteen, he looked like a perfect fit for the college's marine science studies.

"Why don't we apply for early admission?" I asked. "Researching and writing *All Around Us* should count as independent study."

Alexander agreed. "Let's try it," he said.

As soon as I could get an appointment, Alexander and I went to the admissions office for an interview. The counselor asked Alexander about his previous schooling and asked how long we had lived in the Hamptons. He was aware of the newspaper column. He showed us brochures with course descriptions and gave us application forms to fill out. I was impressed by his friendly, forthcoming manner as he chatted with Alexander.

"Send me the transcripts and letters of recommendation from your HDS teachers, and the high school transcript, of course," he said. "You'll be one of the youngest freshmen -- I don't think we've ever had a sixteen-year-old. Stand up for a minute, would you?"

Alexander got up from his chair, smiling. I wondered what the request meant.

"Good. You're tall enough. You'll be fine. You'll hear from us soon. Goodbye for now."

In the parking lot, I hugged Alexander. "That sounds like you're in! But why do you have to be tall?"

"I guess so nobody will notice I'm young," Alexander said.

The letter of acceptance arrived within a week. I called my mother, who was back in the city, to tell her that her grandson was a college student.

Norman returned from Bennington and telephoned from Southampton.

"I am never going away from you again," he said. "I could hardly wait to get away from them. I want to be here, and with you for the rest of my life." He paused and then asked, "If you'll have me? Will you?"

I said yes, as I had known I would if he asked. My anger was gone, but I could not resist one small dig. "My committee says yes also."

Norman told me that he was now alone in the house in Southampton. The home he and Juta had lived in together in Sag Harbor had been sold, and Juta had bought a house of her own, with a large garden. "She loves that; she's a master gardener," Norman said.

"So, will you invite me to visit you in Southampton now? Or do you want this to be just a Platonic relationship?" I asked.

There was a short silence and then I heard a voice choked with laughter say, "My dear! You are a most unusual woman!"

When school started in September, Valerie and Geoffrey rejoined their parents in New York, Boris went back to the Hampton Day School, and Alexander entered Southampton College as a marine science major. I had replaced our used car with a Volvo station wagon. It was the first new automobile I had ever owned, and it became the school bus. On occasion, Boris would get a ride with a fellow student and Alexander, who had qualified for a learner's permit, would take the Volvo.

In the middle of the day, when I was home alone, my house was very quiet. The cat dozed on the sofa. I wrote more poems; this time I kept them and showed them to Norman. He was not yet divorced.

"It's complicated," he said.

"I know," I said, "your life is."

The fall and winter months gave us time to spend with each other and for Norman to become better acquainted with my sons. He talked with Alexander about solar energy and nuclear power, and with Boris about music. His life as an orchestra musician and his pioneering career in audio technology provided fascinating anecdotes. Occasionally, Norman would bring his violin when he came to visit us. While I cooked dinner, he would walk from the living room to the kitchen, playing Hungarian dances.

"It's your own strolling violinist, just like at a restaurant," he would quip. "Goulash music!"

The boys and I were invited to the evenings when Norman played duets with Joe, the pianist. Joe's wife, Vicky, and Alexander, both unrepentant punsters, often threatened the seriousness of the proceedings with hilarious banter.

During the holiday season, we attended concerts by the Choral Society of the Hamptons, with Norman playing violin or viola in the festival orchestra. Life was pleasant. It seemed almost normal.

In the spring of 1979, I told my mother that Norman and I planned to marry.

"You want to marry another old man?" Mother asked. "You'll have to bury him too, in a few years!"

"I'll take whatever time we have together -- years, or even months -- whatever," I said.

"He is a good, steady man. He wants to be a good father to the boys, and he loves you. Everybody can *see*," my mother conceded.

On September 11, 1979, Norman and I got into his white Lancia sports car and drove from Southampton to Westhampton Beach, where a justice of the peace was to marry us. Halfway to our destination, Norman pulled into a service station to fill up the tank.

"Where you are going, all dressed up?" the attendant joked, taking in Norman's three-piece suit, starched white shirt, and tie.

"We're on our way to get married, as a matter of fact," Norman answered.

The attendant craned his neck for a closer look at Norman's white hair.

"Are you sure you know what you're doing?" he asked. "Well, I guess at your age, you *should!*"

CHAPTER 37

A Child from Dachau

Before the wedding, the boys and I, and Muschi, the cat, had moved into Norman's home in Southampton in the summer of 1979.

"She's a member of the family," Norman had said about Muschi. "And particularly welcome now that my poor old dog is gone. There's something wonderful about animals; they are so honest."

Every personal relationship in the Hamptons is accompanied by a real estate transaction or two. I had rented out our house on Mill Hill Lane in East Hampton for the winter months; I intended to list it for sale the following summer when the market would be more lively. I had brought my Persian rug and essential pieces of furniture like bureaus, desks, and bookcases to Southampton.

Norman's house was built by a family named Culver in 1795; the street it stands on is called Culver Hill on some maps and Culver Street on others. The two-storey house, with a basement and an attic, had been expanded many times over the years; in 1980, we would enlarge it again. When I asked Norman how many rooms there were, he said, "Thirteen -- I think. There are alcoves and porches and nooks and crannies that may or may not qualify as rooms. The place was a rooming house when I bought it. I rebuilt it mostly by myself."

Norman used the ground floor as his music studio and office; the kitchen, sitting room, and bedrooms were upstairs. In the large basement was his workshop, fully equipped with machines and tools for wood and metalwork. Violin making was a whole new world to me, with specialized tools -- small planes and chisels, knives, scrapers, files, sanding blocks, clamps, gluepots, varnish brushes, and gadgets I could not name. Who knew that a violin has seventy parts? It was wonderful to watch Norman explain and demonstrate the venerable craft of lutherie -- to see his large hands manipulate tiny gouges and needle-thin files. We began to understand the complexity of the work that had gone into restoring the cello that had first brought us to Culver Hill.

"Isn't it nice we're all here together -- Norman, you, me, Alexander, the cello -- all of us?" Boris said.

In addition to maintaining his musical instrument business, Norman was the technical director of a laboratory in Southampton Hospital for the development of high-resolution ultrasonic imaging. A team of doctors was working on ways ophthalmologists could use ultrasound as a noninvasive method to scan patients' eyes. Norman designed the technology for this new concept, combining his knowledge of acoustics with his engineering expertise.

When I visited the laboratory, I saw violins lying on examination tables, with a spectrum analyzer charting their frequencies. Norman, clad in a white lab coat, looked like the distinguished medical specialist who had been called in to opine on their condition.

"Cats have nine lives; I seem to have nine careers going at once," Norman would say when people marveled at his multifaceted professional life.

Alexander had successfully completed the 1978 - 1979 academic year at Southampton College, but instead of returning there, he had enrolled in the Audubon Expedition Institute, an educational program focused on environmental science. The Expedition Institute had no physical building and no fixed location. It was a school for high school and college-age students who would travel with their instructors around the country by bus, pitching their tents at campgrounds in states all across the nation, helping out on Amish farms, and visiting Indian reservations to learn their history firsthand from Native American elders.

Alexander thought it was exactly the right course of study for him. Many of my fellow parents, as progressive as they were, were aghast.

"You're letting him go? Rattling around the country in a school bus, like a bunch of hippies?"

"They have teachers and classwork; college credit will be given," I answered. Alexander had chosen his life's work when he had brought the first hermit crab home in a bucket of seawater. I trusted my son to follow his path, no matter how unconventional. Norman agreed with me. He too had embraced a passion -- music in his case -- and had followed his dream.

Shortly after our September eleventh wedding, it was time to say goodbye to Alexander, while Boris began his final year at Hampton Day School. He would graduate in June 1980.

With a husband who was busy at the hospital or in his workshop from dawn to dusk, and only one child --a very self-sufficient thirteen-year-old -- living at home, I had time for myself. It was a luxury I had not enjoyed for many years. An added bonus -- the ice cream on the cake, so to speak -- was that Norman loved to cook!

Norman's intense involvement with music had breathed new life into my love of words. I set up a desk for my typewriter in one of the small first-floor rooms we used mostly for storage, notified the family that that was my office, and sat down to write poems. I thought of them as songs.

I went to the local bookstore and bought chapbooks by local authors; I attended poetry readings organized by the library. They were friendly affairs, with audiences that consisted mostly of fellow writers. Soon I was invited to join a poetry workshop that met weekly at the Southampton Library.

Like my colleagues, I looked through *Writers' Market* to find publishing opportunities. I sent out poems accompanied by self-addressed, stamped envelopes, keeping a list of what I had submitted.

"You should talk with Judy," Norman said after reading some of my poems. "She's associated with the literary magazine in Laurinburg."

I had met Norman's sons, Rick and Rolf, who lived in Sag Harbor, but I had not yet met Judy, Norman's daughter from his first marriage. I knew that she lived in North Carolina. She had sent us a friendly letter after our marriage, and we had spoken on the phone once or twice. I knew that Judy was the only one of Norman's children who was a musician. She played the piano and the organ and sang in her church choir.

"I didn't know that. Is she a writer?" I asked.

"No, she's an editor. I think it's called *St. Andrews Review*. It's published by the college there," Norman explained.

"It would be great to get a professional opinion," I said.

"Go ahead," Norman said. "She's a very nice person. She's nicer than I am."

With this encouragement, I sent a clutch of poems to Judy, who liked them and encouraged me to submit them to *St. Andrews Review*.

I remembered from *Chicago Review* days that answers from literary journals took time. I tried not to stray to the mailbox on the front porch as often as I would have liked and kept on writing.

St. Andrews Review was published twice yearly. I was delighted when five of my poems were accepted for publication in the spring and summer issue of 1980. Even more exciting was the invitation to send more.

Alexander called at random intervals -- whenever the Expedition happened to halt near a town or village with a payphone.

"Hi! I'm in Flagstaff," he would say.

"How are you, dear? What is Flagstaff?"

"A town in Arizona. I was bitten by a scorpion the other night. It really hurt. I'm fine. Don't worry. Bye, I'm out of coins."

"He sounds so happy," I said when Boris and Norman asked about the call.

Boris would be graduating from the Hampton Day School in June 1980. It was time to think about his high school education. He excelled in all of his subjects and wanted to continue his music lessons. I thought he needed and deserved a school that would both challenge his intellectual abilities and nurture his special talents. Norman and I agreed that Southampton High School was not the ideal choice. I asked Boris's teachers and other parents for advice.

"We're looking into a boarding school in Connecticut," the mother of another graduating student told me. "We think it'll suit our daughter; it may be good for Boris as well. Why don't you go visit?"

Private education was expensive, as I already knew. I blessed Noah's generosity and foresight once again. He had left life insurance and trust funds for the boys' education; his will had given me the house in East Hampton, the art business, and the investment portfolios he had carefully built with his brother Joe's advice. I remembered that Noah had started these funds when the boys had been very young. It made me happy that I was financially independent of Norman; Noah had provided for me and for his children. Had he somehow foreseen that he would not be alive when Alexander and Boris would be attending universities?

Norman, Boris, and I visited the Loomis Chaffee School in Windsor, Connecticut, in the spring of 1980. I had feared that boarding school would mean uniforms, school ties, and mandatory choir singing. The teacher who welcomed us wore sneakers and neon-pink athletic shorts; he introduced himself by his first name. I relaxed and began to admire the picturesque campus with its brick buildings topped by white cupolas, the well-kept grassy quadrangles, and the spacious sports fields we toured.

Loomis Chaffee had a large teacher-to-student ratio and an outstanding reputation for academic excellence. Its graduates, we were told, were accepted by Harvard and Yale, and other Ivy League universities. Music lessons could be arranged with instructors from the Hartt School of Music at the nearby University of Hartford. The three of us left Windsor with favorable impressions and application forms. We talked with Boris.

"It's only a hundred and twenty-some miles from Southampton," I said. "It won't be hard for us to visit and to drive you back and forth for vacations. It'll be easier to find you than Alexander. Who knows what pueblo he's exploring!"

We talked with Boris and with the Hampton Day School faculty. All were in favor of Loomis Chaffee. We completed the application procedures and Boris was accepted. During the summer after his Hampton Day School graduation, Norman gave Boris math and algebra textbooks. Boris worked his way through them so successfully that he was placed in an advanced math class when he entered Loomis Chaffee.

Alexander came home for the summer vacation and introduced us to a young woman he had met on the Expedition. Her parents owned a summer home in Southampton. The two spent most of their time together, but I enjoyed many afternoons on the beach with the three young people. Norman did not join us; he did not like sun or sand on his skin; he did not like to swim. He loved boats -- any craft from a rowboat to a yacht -- and said that he could swim well enough to save his life.

"I prefer being *on* the water to being in it," he declared as he headed for his cool basement. I sometimes called it "the mad scientist's lair," and Norman laughed with me.

In September of 1980, when Alexander had begun his second year with the Audubon Expedition and we had taken Boris to Connecticut to start his first year at Loomis Chaffee, the house on Culver Hill was quiet, except for the sound of Norman practicing his violin or giving an occasional lesson. I did not feel depressed by the empty nest. I was happy for my children, who were embarked on exciting voyages of learning and growing up. I was engrossed in poems and stories.

My first published poems, in *St. Andrews Review,* spoke about love and loss, and about natural beauty. I noted the perfect circle inscribed in the sand by a blade of beach grass that is bent down by the wind and the song of a bird that captures a whole summer's exuberance. In 1981, *St. Andrews* and several other journals would accept more of my work for publication.

Echoes of war found their way into poems that would be published by *Midstream* magazine in 1982. In "The Refugee's Garden," a woman plants seeds for flowers she will not see in bloom, as war forces her from her home.

"Remembering 1945" came out of a moment on a Southampton beach. My friend Ewa, a Polish immigrant, had joined my children and me on our blanket. We were chatting when we heard the sudden revving of an airplane engine. Ewa and I ducked our heads and flattened ourselves on the sand. We stayed down for only a second before we looked up at the small plane towing an advertising banner.

"Ewa," I said. "This is about a cream for jock itch! It's not 1945!"

"Right," she said. "Do you think we're going to have flashbacks all our lives?"

In 1982, Norman was elected president of the Violin Society of America, a group of violin makers, players, dealers, and scientists interested in the acoustics of stringed instruments. The society held annual meetings, with competitions for makers taking place every two years, and it published a journal of its proceedings. The officers were volunteers who lived in different cities. This loose-knit structure caused problems for the organization. When Norman took office, at the 1982 convention in Salt Lake City, Utah, the society's treasury was woefully low on funds, membership dues were in arrears because members were not reminded to renew, and the journal's publication had been delayed due to lack of funds.

When we returned to Southampton, Norman pointed to the collection of shoeboxes and narrow file drawers full of index cards we had carried home in our luggage, and he said, "The membership list! Have you ever seen such a mess? I need your help to straighten this out. It has to be put on the computer. Will you help?"

My heart went out to him; he looked as baffled as I had felt when I had first heard the word *hullabaloo.*

"I've been a secretary before, but I don't know how to work a computer," I said.

"Oh, that's easy. I'll show you. You'll have a program; it's called DBase. All you have to do is enter the data into fields," Norman said, not reassuring me at all.

It was painstaking, boring, and infuriating work to transcribe the handwritten or badly typed names and addresses on hundreds of index cards. It took many months, during which I often damned the Violence Society, as I called it, to hell and back. On the other hand, I found the society's members to be a very interesting group of people. From Norman and others, I had picked up historical facts as well as speculative lore about the art and practice of violin making. I drew on this material to write a short story, "The False Messiah," about the controversy surrounding the authenticity of a legendary violin made by Antonio Stradivari. It became the first piece of fiction ever published by the *Journal of the Violin Society of America.*

When word-processing programs became available, I was familiar enough with the computer to learn the new technology without fear. The ability to type text and to insert, delete, or change words and sentences as I went along was enormously liberating. In time, I learned how to create and store files, and how to print out pages of text. I wrote more than ever. I threw away my box of carbon paper.

The boys were growing up. Alexander had spent two years with the Audubon Expedition Institute. The Institute was not a degree program, so its students finished their studies and their required courses at Lesley College in Cambridge, Massachusetts. Alexander graduated from Lesley in May 1982, and he remained in the Boston area for further study and work.

At Loomis, Boris made friends with whom he would stay in contact for decades. At home, during the summer vacation, he helped Norman refine the computer program that tracked the Violin Society's membership.

The following summer, Boris and Sean, his best friend at Loomis, wanted to tour Europe on their own. Sean's father was a journalist who was based in London at the time. The boys were only sixteen but knowing that a safe haven was available to them, should they run into difficulties while traveling on the Continent, we let them go.

"Hi, Mom. It's Boris," I heard when I picked up the telephone one summer day. "I'm in Innsbruck. We're fine; we're having a great time; Sean's fine too -- oops, I have to go. I'm out of schillings. Bye!"

By 1983, I had written enough poems for a small book. I had joined the National Writers Club based in Aurora, Colorado. The club made it possible for aspiring writers to self-publish their work at an affordable price, guiding authors through the process of obtaining copyright, an International Standard Book Number, and a Library of Congress number. The author was responsible for typesetting, proofreading, and cover design. I took advantage of their tools to publish *Ferry to Nirvana,* a collection of thirty-nine poems written between 1979 and 1982. Producing the paperback was a family affair. I typed all of the content. A photograph taken by Alexander off the coast of Washington State became the cover; Norman took the author's picture. I dedicated the book to Norman.

I was an author with a published book! I became my own marketing department and took my creation to Canio's, a literary bookstore in Sag Harbor, and to Bookhampton in Southampton. Both establishments sell the work of local writers and offer readings by the authors. The proprietors accepted a number of copies for sale, with forty percent of the proceeds going to the author. I sent review copies to the *Southampton Press* and to the *East Hampton Star.*

The publication of *Ferry to Nirvana* brought me a modicum of name recognition. I began to find it easier to place work in different venues. In 1984, short stories and essays were published by *The Hamptons* and *Byline* magazines, several previously published poems were selected for anthologies, and two essays -- one in February and one in May -- appeared in the *New York Times's* Long Island section. When I saw my byline in *The New York Times,* I recalled standing on the observation platform of the *Chicago Tribune* and vowing that someday I would enter the magic world of the printed word. I sent copies of the articles to my mother. I knew she would share my elation.

Boris passed a milestone of his own in 1984 when he graduated from the Loomis Chaffee School. With Norman's enthusiastic encouragement, he had applied to MIT -- and had been accepted, making his parents very proud.

My mother and Karl had moved into a retirement community in Mount Vernon, New York. While packing for the move from their Manhattan apartment, my mother had stumbled over a packing box, fallen, and broken her left hip. She was still recovering from the accident when I relayed the news that her second grandson would be entering a world-renowned university near Boston.

"That is extra-wonderful news," she said to me on the phone. "I am so happy to see you settled in a good marriage -- and the children being so smart. This news is so good it takes all the pain in my hip away."

Early in 1985, Judy invited me to participate in a Writers Forum that would be held at St. Andrews Presbyterian College in Laurinburg on March 14. I was to read with Ronald Bayes, the founding editor of *St. Andrews Review.*

Judy was now living in Winston-Salem. I traveled there and stayed with her and her daughter, Sarah, for a few days. Judy drove us to Laurinburg -- more than a hundred miles -- on the night of the event. I was nervous. I had participated in group readings and open mic nights in Southampton, but I had never presented more than one or two selections at a time. Here, I was one of two featured poets; I had prepared material to fill approximately half an hour.

"You'll be just fine," Judy said. "They are all very friendly and they like your work -- they've published it."

When we arrived, the cordial welcome I received from the editor and other *Review* staffers instantly erased my jitters. I thoroughly enjoyed the presentations and the friendly socializing that followed.

Back in Winston-Salem, Judy took me on a tour of the city's bookstores and literary coffee shops, craft stores and art galleries, and the historic area of Old Salem. I returned home exhilarated, grateful, and filled with ambition to keep on working at my writing.

April 1985 marked the fortieth anniversary of V-E Day and the liberation of the concentration camp at Dachau. The newspapers reported that President Reagan would not be touring the site of the Dachau camp because he felt that the present generation of Germans should not be made to feel guilty for being "a part of that."

The president's announcement made me think back to 1945, when I had been a nine-year-old living in the town of Dachau. I thought about the American soldiers I had seen driving towards the concentration camp and about the weeks and months following the camp's liberation. I thought about Stefan and Casimir, the Polish survivors of the camp who had come to live with us, and who had become guides from the inferno. I thought about what I had seen at the site of the concentration camp, and about the still incomprehensible magnitude of the crimes that had happened there. I remembered the American visitor who had come to see us a year after the war's end, introducing himself as the milkman from Chicago.

I thought about all I had seen and felt -- because I was there -- and then I sat down and began to write...

"President Reagan announced in April that he would not tour the site of the site of the Dachau Concentration Camp this spring ... Chancellor Helmut Kohl of West Germany plans to mark the 40th anniversary of V-E Day by appearing at a cemetery in Bitburg that includes the graves of Nazi soldiers, and the president has said that he will join him in an act of reconciliation...I was born in the town of Dachau...I remember a summer day in 1946..."

I wrote the story of that astonishing afternoon when the man who delivered milk to my aunt's house in Chicago had come to visit us in Dachau. I recounted how suspicion of the stranger had turned to delight as the milkman, the American-born son of German immigrants, explained that he had brought his own car to tour his parents' homeland and that my aunt had begged him to bring her greetings to us personally. I described the milkman's good nature as he gave rides in his glamorous Cadillac to my brother and me and all the neighborhood children who had come out to gawk.

This American visitor had told us that he wanted to visit the former concentration camp and to pay his respects to the dead prisoners.

As I wrote my essay, I thought about how much of the past remains with us forever. By recounting events I remembered, I did not want to make the present generation of Germans feel guilty; they bore no guilt for their grandparents' deeds. At the same time, I believed that what had happened in Dachau should be acknowledged.

And at the end, I wrote about the way the past lives in the present:

"Since arriving in the United States in 1950, I have met a number of Americans who took part in the liberation of Dachau and other places of such horrors. Their sons and daughters -- and mine -- have toured the colorful mountains and rebuilt cities of Germany and Austria and have come back with lists of new friends whom they write to and invite to our homes. No matter how remote 1945 may seem, we are all part of that history. Its memories connect us."

I submitted the essay to the *Southampton Press,* whose "Viewpoints" column featured op-eds contributed by readers. When I received a phone call from the editor, I was happy and grateful to hear that my article had been accepted and would appear in the next issue.

It was published on April 25, 1985, titled "A Child from Dachau."

A number of friends and some strangers called to compliment me. Most of these readers did not know that I was an immigrant and expressed surprise that English was my second language.

Two weeks after the essay was published, the *Press* features editor telephoned to tell me that the paper had received favorable comments on my contribution.

"Would you like to try your hand at writing more articles for us?" the editor asked.

"They would be for the arts section, on a freelance basis. The articles will have your byline, and there is a payment for each piece. Are you interested?"

I tried to breathe calmly. I hoped that my voice wouldn't squeak as I answered.

"Yes. Yes, I would like that very much," I said. "Thank you. I'm really happy that you called. Just let me know when you have an assignment for me."

We went on to discuss the sort of articles I would be working on. As we talked about deadlines and word counts, I realized that this editor was treating me like a professional.

Had I just become a real journalist? I thought of all the years that had passed between my studies at Wright Junior College and my short stint in the Associated Press newsroom and now.

I was almost forty-nine years old. Many dreams had come true for the child from Dachau. I had earned a university degree and I had raised two children who valued education as much as my mother and I did. I had written poems and stories in my adopted language, and my work had found readers who appreciated it.

At this very moment, I was in conversation with the *Southampton Press* editor about a venture in the profession I had dreamed of entering since I had been a teenage immigrant.

I took a breath and said, "Thank you again for the opportunity. I really look forward to working for the *Press.*"

To myself, I said, "Dreams do come true. You are one lucky immigrant!"

About the Author

Barbara Goldowsky has written fiction, poems, and nonfiction articles that have been published by regional and national journals and newspapers. Born in Germany, Barbara came to the United States in 1950 with her mother and her younger brother. The family settled in Chicago, Illinois, where Barbara attended public schools and junior college, majoring in English and journalism.

Awarded a scholarship designated for a "deserving foreign-born student," she studied at the University of Chicago, majoring in political science, and receiving a Bachelor of Arts degree in June 1958. At the University of Chicago, fascinated by American literature and creative writing, she joined the staff of the literary magazine, the Chicago Review, just as American literature was being transformed by the Beat poets and writers. After years devoted to marriage and child-raising, Barbara's writing career began in the early 1980s when she was living in the Hamptons.

In 1985, she became a freelance contributor to the Southampton Press, writing articles about the arts, and reviews of books, music, theater. She produced and hosted radio programs that featured interviews with writers and poets for the radio station of Long Island University's Southampton Campus - now StonyBrook Southampton.

In 1989 Barbara helped to found Pianofest in the Hamptons and remained associated with the festival, serving first as general manager and then as publicity and publications manager. In 2016, Barbara moved to her present home in Lasell Village, in Newton, Massachusetts. She considers herself a fortunate immigrant because she was able to realize her twin dreams of attaining a world-class education and of becoming a writer in her adopted language.

About TBR Books

A Program of The Center for the Advancement of
Languages, Education, and Communities (CALEC)

 **TBR Books**

TBR Books is a program of the Center for the Advancement of Languages, Education, and Communities. We publish researchers and practitioners who seek to engage diverse communities on topics related to education, languages, cultural history, and social initiatives. We translate our books in a variety of languages to further expand our impact. Become a member of TBR Books and receive complimentary access to all our books.

Our Books in English

Rainbows, Masks, and Ice Cream By Deana Sobel Lederman

Can We Agree to Disagree? By Agathe Laurent and Sabine Landolt

Salsa Dancing in Gym Shoes: Developing Cultural Competence to Foster Latino Student Success by Tammy Oberg de la Garza and Alyson Leah Lavigne

Mamma in her Village by Maristella de Panniza Lorch

The Other Shore by Maristella de Panniza Lorch

The Clarks of Willsborough Point: A Journey through Childhood by Darcey Hale

Beyond Gibraltar by Maristella de Panniza Lorch

The Gift of Languages: Paradigm Shift in U.S. Foreign Language Education by Fabrice Jaumont and Kathleen Stein-Smith

Two Centuries of French Education in New York: The Role of Schools in Cultural Diplomacy by Jane Flatau Ross

The Clarks of Willsborough Point: The Long Trek North by Darcey Hale

The Bilingual Revolution: The Future of Education is in Two Languages by Fabrice Jaumont

Our Books in Translation

Rainbows, Masks, and Ice Cream By Deana Sobel Lederman is available in 7 languages.

Can We Agree to Disagree? By Agathe Laurent and Sabine Landolt is available in 2 languages.

The Bilingual Revolution by Fabrice Jaumont is available in 11 languages.

The Gift of Languages by Fabrice Jaumont and Kathleen Stein-Smith is available in 3 languages.

Our books are available on our website and on all major online bookstores as paperback and e-book. Some of our books have been translated in Arabic, Chinese, English, French, German, Hebrew, Italian, Japanese, Polish, Russian, Spanish. For a listing of all books published by TBR Books, information on our series, or for our submission guidelines for authors, visit our website at

http://www.tbr-books.org

About CALEC

The Center for the Advancement of Languages, Education, and Communities is a nonprofit organization with a focus on multilingualism, cross-cultural understanding, and the dissemination of ideas. Our mission is to transform lives by helping linguistic communities create innovative programs, and by supporting parents and educators through research, publications, mentoring, and connections.

We have served multiple communities through our flagship programs which include:

- TBR Books, our publishing arm; which publishes research, essays, and case studies with a focus on innovative ideas for education, languages, and cultural development;

- Our online platform provides information, coaching, support to multilingual families seeking to create dual-language programs in schools;

- NewYorkinFrench.net, an online platform which provides collaborative tools to support New York's Francophone community and the diversity of people who speak French.

We also support parents and educators interested in advancing languages, education, and communities. We participate in events and conferences that promote multilingualism and cultural development. We provide consulting for school leaders and educators who implement multilingual programs in their school. For more information and ways, you can support our mission, visit

http://www.calec.org

Lightning Source UK Ltd.
Milton Keynes UK
UKHW021906160820
368342UK00003B/3